Learning the Internet

■ Microsoft® Internet Explorer
■ Netscape Navigator™ ■ Search the World Wide Web
■ E-Mail ■ FTP (File Transfer Protocol)

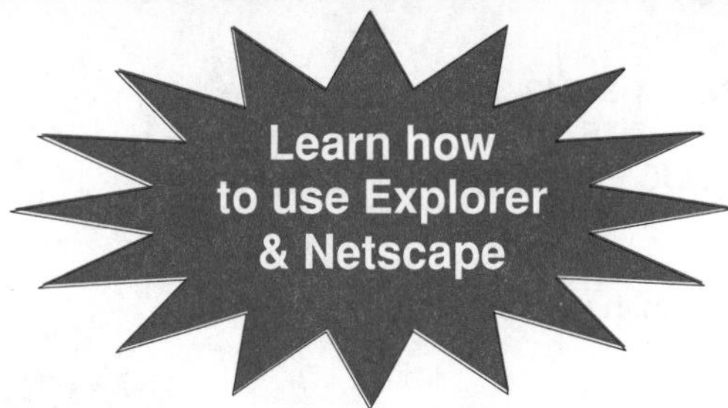

L. Joyce Arnston
Kathy Berkemeyer
Kenn Halliwell
Thomas Neuburger

Acknowledgments

Special thanks to:

Jennifer, Paul, Don, Marni, Shu, Peter, John, Leslie, and all the team at DDC.
Tom and Kenn for their excellent and fast work.
Margaret Brown and Ali Ware for creative input and constructive feedback.
Jeff Kenny at WebStyles for setting up the DDC Web site.
Additional kudos to Marni and Jennifer for the hours spent ensuring synchrony between the exercises and the Internet Simulation CD-ROM.

This book is dedicated to:

Jack Berkemeyer, for his love, patience, support, and sense of humor. *Kathy*
Linda, for her patience and tolerance during the writing of this book. *Kenn*
Alida, my river of gold. *Thomas*

Project Manager	Technical Editors	English Editors	DDC Web Site Development	Layout and Design
Jennifer Frew	Marni Ayers	Marni Ayers	Don Mayo	Shu Y. Chen
	Ayanna Gaines	Jennifer Frew	WebStyles	Paul Wray
	Don Mayo	Aegina Berg		Hollywood P Co.
				Maria Kardesheva

Published by DDC Publishing, Inc.
 For information, address DDC Publishing, Inc., 275 Madison Avenue, 12th Floor, New York, New York 10016
Internet address: ***http://www.ddcpub.com***

ISBN: 1-56243-345-8
Cat No. Z-15
First DDC Publishing, Inc. Printing:
10 9 8 7 6 5 4 3 2 1

Printed in the United States of America.

Contents

Lesson 4: File Transfer Protocol (FTP)

Lesson 5: Electronic Mail (E-mail)

Introduction

This Book is Designed for You . . .

if you are just beginning to use the Internet and would like to begin exploring the World Wide Web. Instead of just telling you about the Internet and the World Wide Web, though, this book offers easy-to-follow exercises that actually show you how the Internet works.

You will learn how to:

- Use Netscape Navigator and Microsoft Internet Explorer, two of the most popular World Wide Web browsers available today.
- Enter addresses to get to World Wide Web sites all over the world.
- Organize and save addresses of sites you want to access again.
- Navigate the World Wide Web using hyperlinks.
- Use a variety of search software programs that enable you to find information on a wide range of topics, products, etc.
- Download files and programs from FTP (File Transfer Protocols) sites.
- Compose and send e-mail.
- Understand Internet terms.

This book assumes that you have some general knowledge and experience with computers, and that you already know how to perform the following tasks:

- Use a mouse (double-click, etc.).
- Make your way around Microsoft Windows 3.1 and/or Windows 95 (copy, paste, print, etc.).
- Install and run programs.

If you are completely new to computers as well as the Internet, you may want to go through DDC's **Learning Microsoft Windows 95** or **Learning Microsoft Windows 3.1** before you go through the exercises in this book.

Be sure that you have established a connection to the Internet before going through the exercises in this book. How to get connected to the Internet is not covered in this book.

How to Use this Book

Introduction

Before you start Lesson 1, read the brief introduction. It will give you some basic concepts and terminology that will make navigating the World Wide Web easier.

Lessons 1-5

The exercises in each lesson contain two parts:

Notes

Explain and illustrate Internet concepts and tools being introduced.

The right column on each page frequently contains hints, notes, and cautions.

 cautions and warnings

 shortcut procedures for using an Internet feature

 hints and additional notes on an Internet feature and on how to make using the Internet easier and more interesting

Exercise Directions

Explain and illustrate how to complete the exercise. Many exercises will make use of the DDC Publishing Web site *(see page v)*, a unique feature that assures that the notes and lessons in this book remain constant – despite possible changes to actual Web sites. Details on how to order the Learning the Internet CD ROM, which offers an offline simulation of the DDC Publishing Web Site, are available at the end of this introduction.

Lesson Summary Exercises

Additional exercises following many of the lessons that allow you to use several of the features presented in that lesson.

Appendices

Netiquette. A set of behavioral guidelines to follow on the Internet.

Viruses. What are they and how to avoid them.

Internet History. An introduction to how the Internet evolved and how it works.

Glossary. A list of Internet Terms.

Learning the Internet Simulation CD-ROM

The **Learning the Internet Simulation CD-ROM** is designed to be used in conjunction with our Learning the Internet book. It simulates actual Internet sites so that you are not required to log onto the Internet in order to learn. That means no modems, no connection time or fees, no wandering to other Internet sites.

The exercises on the CD-ROM are designed to follow the exercises in the book in sequential step-by-step order. For example, if you start an exercise and skip a step or click the wrong object or item, the program will not proceed to the next step or you will receive an error message. *Note: should you receive an error message, simply click the BACK button on your browser toolbar to return to the exercise.*

The status bar at the bottom of your screen will inform you as to the step, exercise, and lesson you are currently working on. To manually move to a proceeding or preceding step, click the forward or backwards arrows in the bottom right corner of the screen. To move to another exercise, click MENU in the bottom left corner of the screen, click once on the desired lesson, and then click once on the desired exercise.

To install the program, place the CD in your CD-ROM drive and follow the listed steps below:

1. **To Install from Windows 95 or NT 4.0:** Click START on the Desktop, Click Run and then type:
   (CD-ROM drive letter) :\SETUP.EXE.
2. **To Install from Windows 3.1 or NT 3.51:** Go to File Manager in MAIN, click File, click Run and then type:
   (CD-ROM drive letter) :\SETUP.EXE.
3. Click NEXT at the Setup Wizard screen.
4. At the next screen, click NEXT to create an Innovus directory for storing program files. Then click YES to confirm the directory choice.
5. At the next screen, allow the default folder to be named Innovus Multimedia, and click Next.
6. At the next screen, choose one of the following options based on your individual system needs:

   Note: A **Typical** installation is standard for an individual installation.

   - **TYPICAL:** installs a minimum number of files to the hard drive with the majority of files remaining on the CD-ROM. ***NOTE: With this installation, the CD must remain in the CD-ROM drive when operating the program.***
   - **COMPACT:** installs the fewest required files to the hard drive. This is the best option for portable computers and computers with little available hard disk space. ***NOTE: With this installation, the CD must remain in the CD-ROM when operating the program***
   - **CUSTOM:** installs only those files that you choose to the hard drive. This is generally only recommended for advanced users of Innovus Multimedia software.
7. Click NEXT to begin copying the necessary files to your system.
8. Click OK at the Set Up status Window and then click YES to restart Windows.

   Note: *To run the program directly from your hard drive -- so that it is not necessary for the CD to remain in the CD-ROM drive during operation – you must do a **Custom** install (see above). Choose Select All to each prompt that follows, and at the netsim Template window, select the **Heavy** component install. This option requires a large amount of free disk space (see below).*

To launch the program in Windows 95 click the Start button on the desktop, select Programs, Innovus Multimedia, and then the *netsim* file. For the Windows 3.1, select the Innovus Multimedia icon, then select *netsim*.

System Requirements

Software	Windows 95, Windows 3.1 (or higher), or Windows NT 3.51 (or higher)
Hardware	80486DX or higher, 8 MB RAM, 256 Color Monitor, and CD-ROM Drive
Disk Space	30MB available hard disk space for a Typical installation, or 125MB for a Custom (heavy) installation

DDC Publishing World Wide Web Site

http://www.ddcpub.com

Before you start Learning the Internet, you should be aware of a phenomenon that is occurring every minute of every day: The Great Internet Metamorphosis. With its complex network of sites, connections and people, the Internet is constantly changing, constantly reinventing itself.

As a result, there are no guarantees. For example, a Web site you visit today may not look the same or, for that matter, even exist tomorrow! Obviously this can be frustrating. Be patient and look on these changes positively.

World Wide Web site are constantly changing. To insure that steps in many exercises in this book will yield the results that are illustrated, simulations of sites will be used. These simulated sites can be found on the DDC Publishing Web site.

The DDC Web sites has several areas you can explore; however, the area that contains the material needed for this book is named ***Learn the Net***. When you go to this area of the DDC Web site, you will be able to complete many of the exercises in this book.

IMPORTANT: Before you start this book and when you start a new exercise or lesson, check the DDC Publishing Web site (***Http://www.ddcpub.com***) for updates, changes and corrections that will make using this book easier. Changes on the Web that affect exercises in this book will be posted on the DDC Publishing Web site. You can print out new directions and insert them directly into the text.

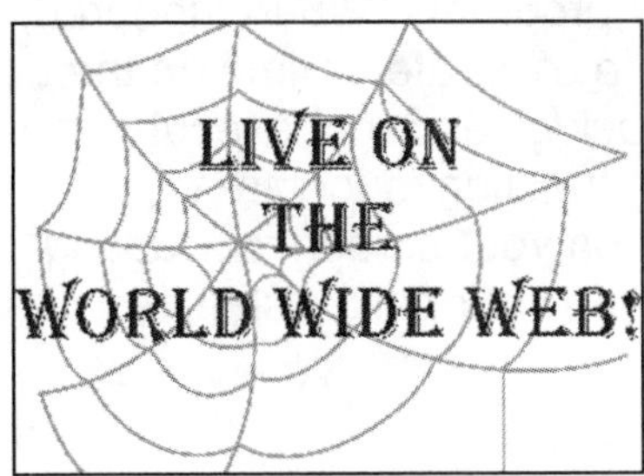

After you complete an exercise that uses a simulated site, you will be given the actual Internet address of the Web site illustrated in the exercise as well as additional "live" Web sites you may wish to explore.

To access the DDC Publishing Web Site

- Enter the following address for DDC Publishing on the Location (address) line of your browser and press Enter.

  http://www.ddcpub.com

  This will display the opening page of the DDC Publishing World Wide Web site.

- Click on the link to ***Learn the Net***.

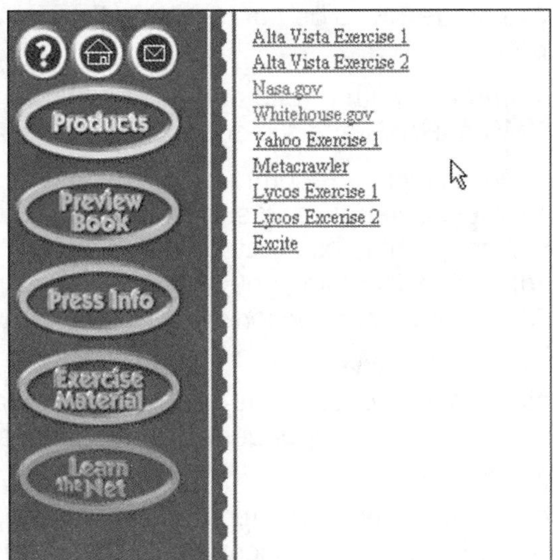

- Follow the instructions in the exercise.

Read This Before You Start This Book!

The following is essential information needed to begin understanding how the Internet works. In addition to providing a basic definition and history of the Internet, we are also including a list of certain concepts and terms. Though we have done our best to keep technical jargon to a minimum, there are certain words that will be referred to often throughout this book, as well as throughout your journeys on the Internet, so it is best to get an understanding of them from the start.

Must Haves

This book assumes that you already have a basic understanding of computers and that you have access to an Internet Service Provider. Please read over the list of "must haves" below to ensure that you are ready to be connected to the Internet.

- A computer (with a recommended minimum of 16 MB of RAM) and a modem port.
- A modem (with a recommended minimum speed of 14.4kbps, and suggested speed of 28.8kbps) that is connected to an analog phone line (assuming you are not using a direct Internet connection through a school, corporation, etc.).
- Established access to the Internet through an online service, independent Internet service provider, etc.
- Access to the browser applications: Netscape Navigator 3.0 and/or Microsoft Explorer 3.0 *(If you do not currently have these applications, contact your Internet Service Provider for instructions on how to download them.)*
- A great deal of patience. The Internet is a fun and exciting place. But getting connected can be frustrating at times. Expect to run into occasional glitches, to get disconnected from time to time, and to experience occasional difficulty in locating a certain Web site, sending e-mail, etc. The more up-to-date your equipment is, however, the less difficulty you will probably experience.

Cautions

ACCURACY: Be cautious not to believe everything on the Internet. Almost anyone can publish information on the Internet, and since there is no Internet editor or monitor, some information may be false. All information found on the World Wide Web should be checked for accuracy through additional reputable sources.

SECURITY: When sending information over the Internet, be prepared to let the world have access to it. Computer hackers can find ways to access anything that you send to anyone over the Internet, including e-mail. Be cautious when sending confidential information to anyone.

VIRUSES: These small, usually destructive computer programs hide inside of innocent-looking programs. Once a virus is executed, it attaches itself to other programs. When triggered, often by the occurrence of a date or time on the computer's internal clock/calendar, it executes a nuisance or damaging function, such as displaying a message on your screen, corrupting your files, or reformatting your hard disk (see *Appendix B*).

Basics

The Internet – What is it?

The Internet is a world-wide network that connects several thousands of businesses, schools, research foundations, individuals, and other networks. Anyone with access can log on, communicate via e-mail, and search for various types of information.

Internet History

The Internet began in 1969 as ARPAnet, a project developed by the US Department of Defense. Its initial purpose was to enable researchers and military personnel to communicate in the event of an emergency.

How to Access the Internet

Most people access the Internet by using a modem, communication software, and a standard phone line to dial in. Direct access is also available through most colleges and universities and through some large organizations and corporations.

If you plan to use a dial in connection to the Internet you will need to sign up with a public or private Internet Service Provider, or an online Service such as America Online, CompuServe, or Delphi. For a certain fee, such services generally provide you with a Web browser, an e-mail account, a pre-determined number of hours for Internet access time (or unlimited access at a higher fee), and various other features.

Common Uses of the Internet

- Communicate world-wide via e-mail.
- Use the World Wide Web to order products, read reviews, obtain stock quote information, make travel arrangements, do research for work or school projects, etc.
- FTP to a computer site to download or upload shareware items (software, fonts, games, etc.).
- Access a Search Engine to help you find Internet Sites on news articles that relate to a particular topic, subject, or product you need information about.

Internet Terms

The following is a list of basic terms that will help you start to understand the Internet. Please refer to the detailed glossary in the back of the book for those terms not covered below.

World Wide Web (WWW)
The WWW is a user-friendly system for finding information on the Internet through the use of hypertext and hypermedia linking.

Hyper links
On the Web, some words or graphics appear in a different **color**, are underlined, or **both**. This distinction indicates that the item is a link to another Web page or another Web site. Clicking your mouse on one of these links takes you to a new page with related information.

Home Page
All Web sites begin with a Home Page. A Home Page is like a table of contents. It usually outlines what a particular site has to offer and contains links that can connect you to other Web sites.

Network
Networks are groups of computers or other devices that are connected in such a way that they are able to share files and resources. The Internet is a global network of networks.

Browsers
Web browsers are graphic interface programs that provide simple techniques for viewing and searching the WWW. Browsers work in conjunction with the connection you establish to the Internet via your Internet service provider. The browser programs referred to in this book are Netscape Navigator and Microsoft Internet Explorer.

URL (Uniform Resource Locators)
A URL is a WWW address. It is a locator that enables the WWW system to search for linked sites.

E-Mail (Electronic Mail)

By far the most popular feature on the Internet, e-mail is a communication system for exchanging messages and attached files. E-mail can be sent to anyone in the world as long as both parties have access to the Internet and an Internet address to identify themselves.

Search Engines

Software programs that "surf" through the Internet for a given topic of information, catalog the results, and display descriptions of the suggested sites. Examples of search engines are Yahoo and AltaVista.

Internet Service Provider (ISP)

Companies that provide a dial-up connection to the Internet as well as other Internet services.

✓ *America Online, Prodigy, and CompuServe are online services that also provide access to the Internet.*

FTP (File Transfer Protocol)

File transfer Protocol is an Internet protocol that enables one computer to transfer files to another. An FTP site is a host computer that commonly contains executable application files, as well as documents, images, and multimedia files. An Internet Web browser will allow you to log into most FTP sites.

Many FTP sites are maintained by universities. Some are operated by companies that distribute their software (Netscape and Microsoft both maintain FTP sites). Not every software title is on the Internet, but three types are commonly available for download: freeware, shareware, and beta releases.

Viruses – Caution!

The Internet is a breeding ground for viruses (see *Appendix B*). Computer viruses are nasty little commands or programs hidden in executable program files. Some viruses won't cause any damage, but those that do can cause a loss of data and time.

Lesson 1: Netscape Navigator

Exercise 1

- About Netscape Navigator
- Start Netscape Navigator
- The Opening Screen/Home Page
- Online Help
- Netscape Tutorial
- Exit Netscape Navigator

Exercise 2

- The Toolbar
- Open World Wide Web Sites
- Stop a Load or Search
- Progress Bar
- Return to The Home Page

Exercise 3

- Shortcuts
- History
- Bookmarks
- Add and Delete Bookmarks
- Create Bookmarks from the History List
- Create, Delete, and Add to Folders
- Save Pages
- Print Pages

Exercise 4

- Organize Web Pages with Bookmarks
- Create Folders
- Use the Right Mouse Button to Create a Bookmark or Shortcut
- Edit Bookmarks
- Drag and Drop (Move) Bookmarks Among Folders

Exercise 5

- Directory Buttons

Exercise 6

- Capture Information from Web Pages
- Copy and Paste from Web Pages to Text Editors
- Download Files from Web Pages
- Save and Print Web Pages
- Mail Web Pages

Exercise 7

- Netscape Navigator – Summary Exercise

Exercise 1

◆ **About Netscape Navigator** ◆ **Start Netscape Navigator**
◆ **The Opening Screen/Home Page** ◆ **Online Help**
◆ **Netscape Tutorial** ◆ **Exit Netscape Navigator**

NOTES

- Internet browsers are software programs that provide the ability to navigate the Internet, locate data, and access sites worldwide.
- Using a World Wide Web browser, which is a straightforward graphical interface, you can move to sites around the world through thousands of interlinked text, graphic, audio, and video files.
- Though there are a number of browsers available (Spry, Mosaic, etc.) this book will focus on Netscape Navigator 3.0 and Microsoft Internet Explorer 3.0. Internet Explorer 3.0 will be explained in Lesson 2.
- The World Wide Web, as you read in the Introduction, links together vast amounts of information worldwide. Information stored on the Web is stored in an easy-to-use document format called Hypertext Markup Language (HTML).

About Netscape Navigator 3.0

- Netscape is a popular browser that allows you to navigate the World Wide Web and its many links or locations world wide. These locations are servers (computers with special software and high-capacity hard disks) on which vast amounts of information are stored. Netscape 3.0 has excellent programs such as File Transfer Protocol (FTP) and e-mail. File transfer protocol is a feature of the Internet used to send or receive files from remote computers. In addition, Netscape works with many search engines (special search software) which will allow you to search for topics of interest.

NOTE
Netscape Navigator 3.0 runs under 16 platforms including Windows 3.1, Windows for WorkGroups, Windows 95, or Windows NT, Macintosh, and Unix. This book will address Netscape running under Windows 3.1 and Windows 95.

Start Netscape Navigator 3.0

To start Netscape Navigator (Windows 95):

- Click Start button.
- Click Programs, Netscape Navigator 3.0, Netscape Navigator.

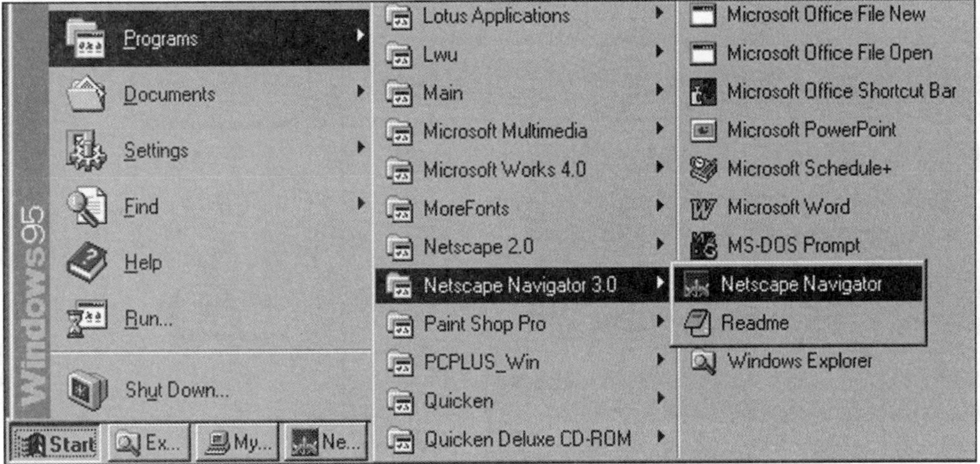

HINT

If you have a shortcut to Netscape Navigator

Netscape Navigator (2)

on your desktop, double-click it to start Netscape.

To start Netscape Navigator (Windows 3.1):

- Double-click on the Netscape Navigator icon from the Netscape Navigator 3.0 group window in Program Manager in Windows 3.1.

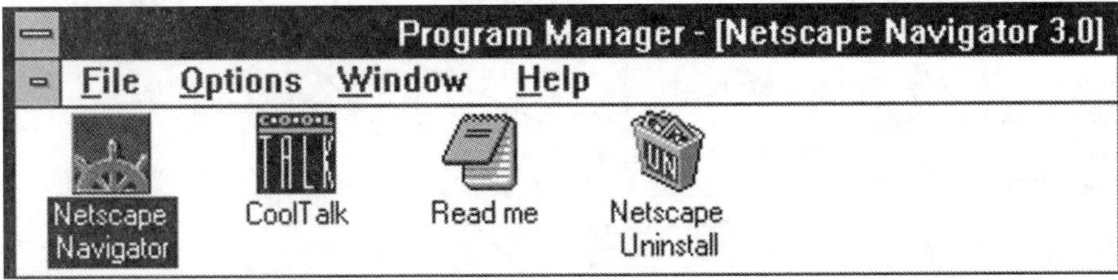

The Home Page

- The home page for Netscape Navigator 3.0 is the screen that displays when you have successfully connected to Netscape Navigator. The default home page upon installation of Netscape displays the Web site for Netscape Communications, Inc. You can change this default Web site to another Web site, if you wish. For example, you may prefer to display your company's Web site as your home page. Sometimes an Internet service provider will configure the software so that its home page will be the default upon connection with a browser such as Netscape.
- The term home page actually refers to the first page of any World Wide Web site. The first page is sometimes called the Start page. A Web site can have more than one page. This opening screen can be customized if you wish.

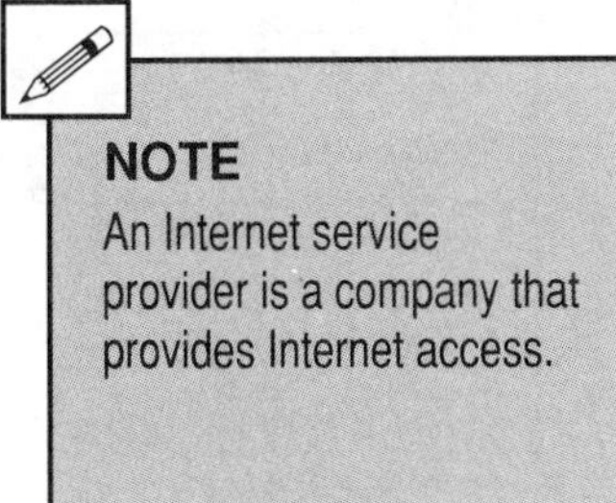

NOTE
An Internet service provider is a company that provides Internet access.

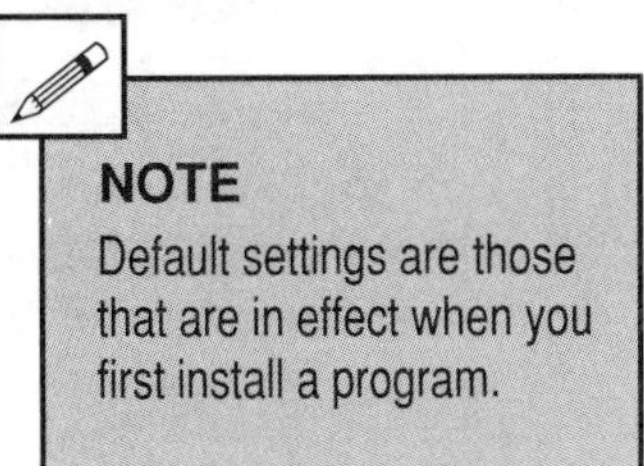

NOTE
Default settings are those that are in effect when you first install a program.

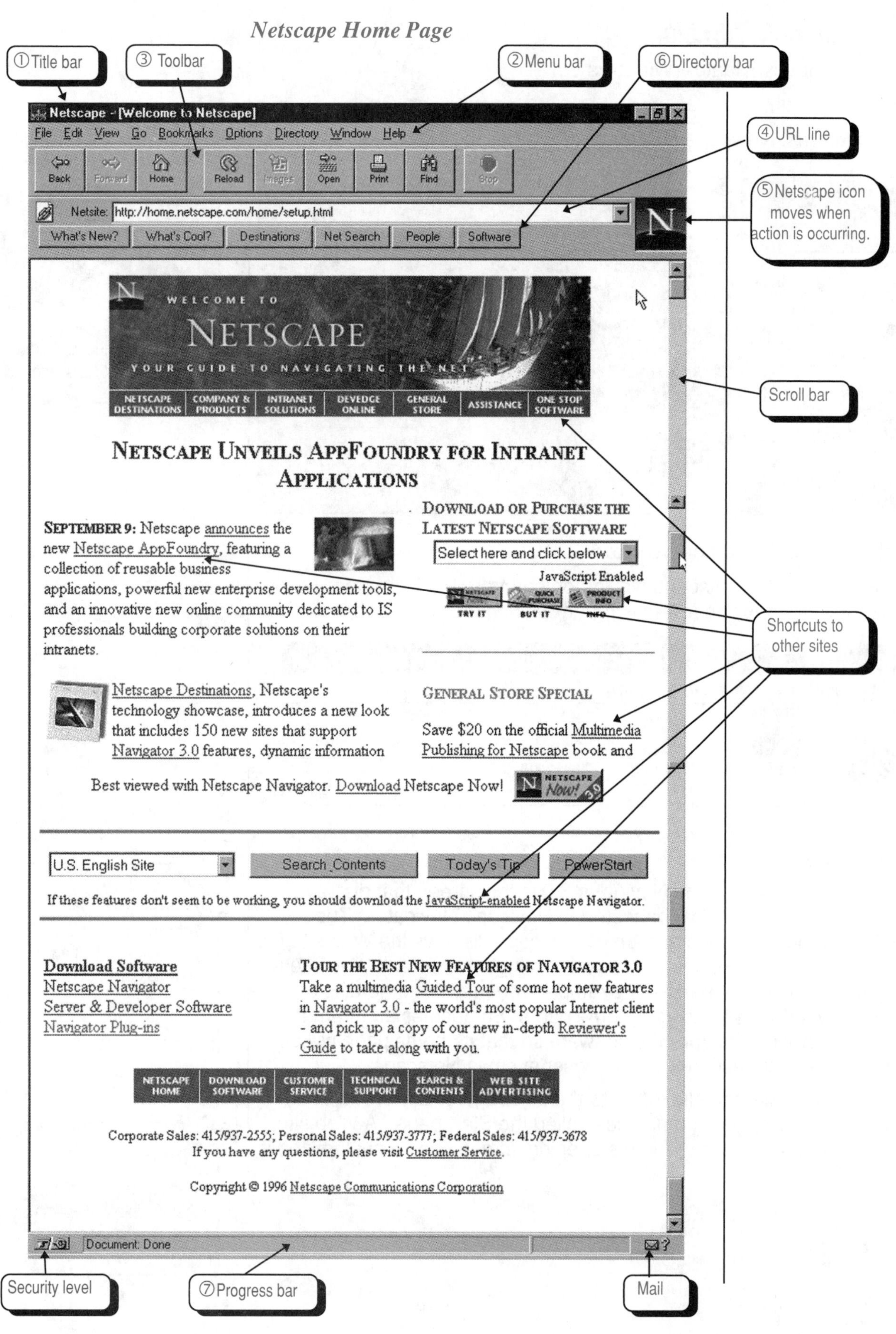
Netscape Home Page
①Title bar
③ Toolbar
②Menu bar
⑥Directory bar
④URL line
⑤Netscape icon moves when action is occurring.
Scroll bar
Shortcuts to other sites
Security level
⑦Progress bar
Mail
Netscape - [Welcome to Netscape]
File Edit View Go Bookmarks Options Directory Window Help
Back Forward Home Reload Images Open Print Find Stop
Netsite: http://home.netscape.com/home/setup.html
What's New? What's Cool? Destinations Net Search People Software
WELCOME TO NETSCAPE
YOUR GUIDE TO NAVIGATING THE NET
NETSCAPE UNVEILS APPFOUNDRY FOR INTRANET APPLICATIONS
SEPTEMBER 9: Netscape announces the new Netscape AppFoundry, featuring a collection of reusable business applications, powerful new enterprise development tools, and an innovative new online community dedicated to IS professionals building corporate solutions on their intranets.
DOWNLOAD OR PURCHASE THE LATEST NETSCAPE SOFTWARE
Select here and click below
JavaScript Enabled
TRY IT BUY IT INFO
Netscape Destinations, Netscape's technology showcase, introduces a new look that includes 150 new sites that support Navigator 3.0 features, dynamic information
GENERAL STORE SPECIAL
Save $20 on the official Multimedia Publishing for Netscape book and
Best viewed with Netscape Navigator. Download Netscape Now!
U.S. English Site
Search Contents
Today's Tip
PowerStart
If these features don't seem to be working, you should download the JavaScript-enabled Netscape Navigator.
Download Software
Netscape Navigator
Server & Developer Software
Navigator Plug-ins
TOUR THE BEST NEW FEATURES OF NAVIGATOR 3.0
Take a multimedia Guided Tour of some hot new features in Navigator 3.0 - the world's most popular Internet client - and pick up a copy of our new in-depth Reviewer's Guide to take along with you.
Corporate Sales: 415/937-2555; Personal Sales: 415/937-3777; Federal Sales: 415/937-3678
If you have any questions, please visit Customer Service.
Copyright © 1996 Netscape Communications Corporation
Document: Done

① Title bar Displays the name of the program (Netscape) and the current feature (Netscape Destinations). Note the three buttons on the far right of the title bar. Use these standard Windows features to minimize, maximize (restore), and close the window.

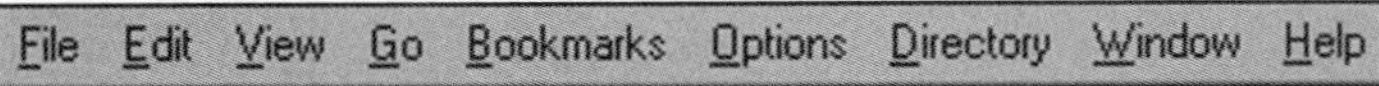

② Menu bar Displays menus currently available and provides commands to perform actions by categories of tasks in Netscape.

③Toolbar Displays Netscape's commonly-used features. Note that a name and an icon displays on each of the buttons. These frequently-used features are accessed quickly and easily by clicking on the button.

✓ *If the toolbar buttons are not visible, open the Options menu and click Show Toolbar.*

TIP
To gain more space on screen, you may want to hide the Toolbar, Location line, and Directory Buttons. Go to the Options menu and hide/show desired options.

④ Location Field Displays the electronic address of the current Web page. Provides the place to key the electronic address of the Web page you wish to access. This address is called a Uniform Resource Locator (URL). Note the icon resembling a chain at the far left of the location bar; this is available when running Netscape under Windows 95 to link to another location.

✓ *If the Location Field is not visible, open the Options menu and click Show Location.*

⑤ Netscape's status indicator Netscape's icon pulses when an action is being performed. Click on this icon to return immediately to Netscape's home page.

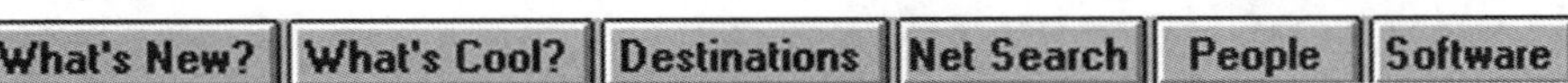

⑥ Directory bar Buttons on the Directory bar provide a quick and easy way to access other locations and Web pages.

✓ *If the Directory buttons are not visible, open the Options menu and click Show Directory Buttons.*

20K read (at 1.3K/sec)

⑦ **Progress bar** Shows the status of loading a page, the security level, and mail. The security level is shown as a key in the far-left corner, the status of the activity in the center, and access to Netscape mail is displayed in the far right corner. Mail has to be installed separately to work with Netscape.

NOTE

The key icon lets you verify the security of a document. For example, if you click on the key icon, you will see the message: "None of the files that you have requested are encrypted (scrambled). Unencrypted files can be observed by a third party while in transit." Security of files sent over the Internet is a continuing concern. Technology to secure information continues to develop. Check the Netscape Handbook for the levels of security available.

Online Help

- Netscape has a significant amount of online help.
- Help is available from the Help menu and from the Netscape home page.
- Help materials can be saved to disk or printed.
- To explore help features, click on Help on the Menu bar. Notice that you will see several types of help. For example, How to Get Support, Handbook, and Frequently Asked Questions are listed.

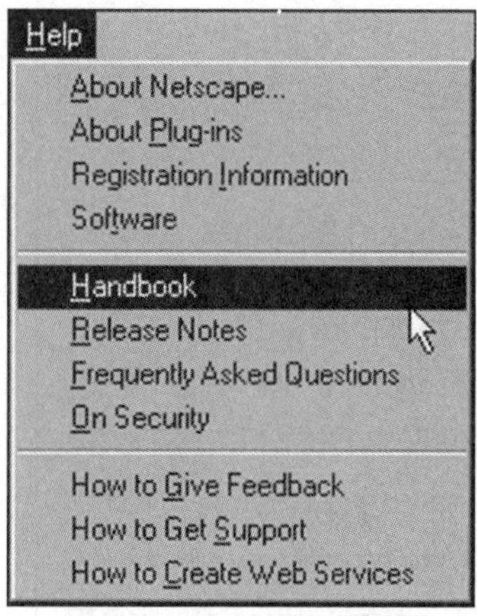

NOTE

If you click on a hypertext link, you will go to another source of information (text, graphics, sound, or video).

- The Handbook is Netscape's online help manual. It has hypertext links to other pages containing useful information. The Handbook is accessible from the Help menu.

Page title displays on title bar.

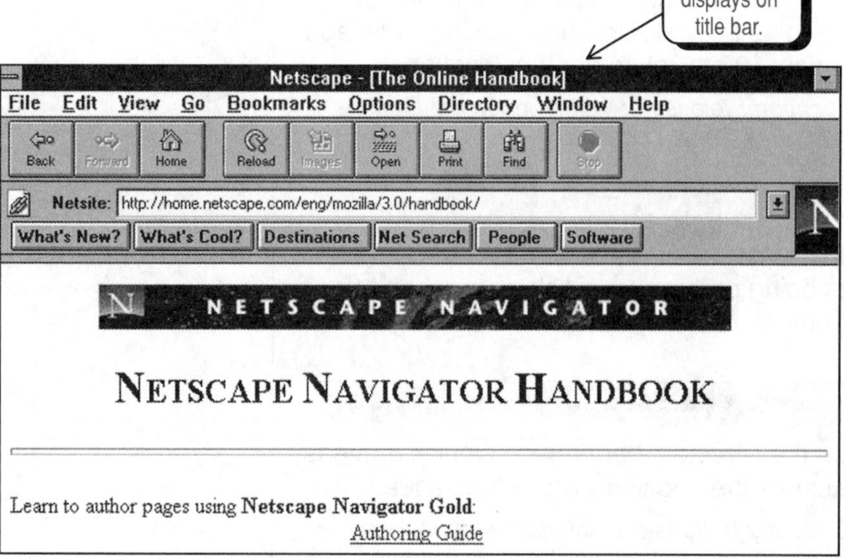

Netscape Tutorial

- The Netscape Navigator Handbook has a three-part tutorial that you may find helpful to browse. (You will explore it in Exercise 2.)
- The Tutorial has Netscape information as well as Internet basic concepts.

TUTORIAL

BEFORE YOU BEGIN
Basics to get you started with Netscape Navigator

HEARTWARMING INTRODUCTION
Elementary concepts of the Internet explained

LEARN NETSCAPE
Lessons instructing you on Netscape Navigator functionality

Hypertext Links

- More than anything else, the material on the Internet is made up of a lot of words. Some words appear in a different **color**, underlined, or **both**. Clicking your mouse on one of these links takes you to a new page with related information. After you have visited a link, the color of the link changes. This helps you remember which links you've visited.

CAUTION

When you exit Netscape, you do not necessarily exit from your Internet service provider. Be sure to check the disconnect procedure from your ISP so that you will not continue to be charged for time online. Some services do disconnect when a specific amount of time has passed with no activity.

Graphics and Images

- The Web has become more interesting because of increased use of graphics and illustrations. Some Web graphics are designed with hidden links. These images, called image maps, can also take you to different places on the Web. You know that you are pointing to a link (text or graphic) when the pointer changes to a hand. When that hand appears and you click on it, you should go to another location.

Exit Netscape Navigator

- Exiting Netscape Navigator and disconnecting from your service provider are two separate steps. You can actually disconnect from your service provider and still have Netscape Navigator open. There are times when you might want to keep Netscape open but disconnect from your service provider. It's important to remember that if you close Netscape Navigator (or any other browser), you must also disconnect (or hang up) from your service provider. If you don't disconnect, you'll continue incurring charges.

In this exercise, you will start Netscape Navigator 3.0, examine menus and other elements on your home page, and explore the help feature.

EXERCISE DIRECTIONS

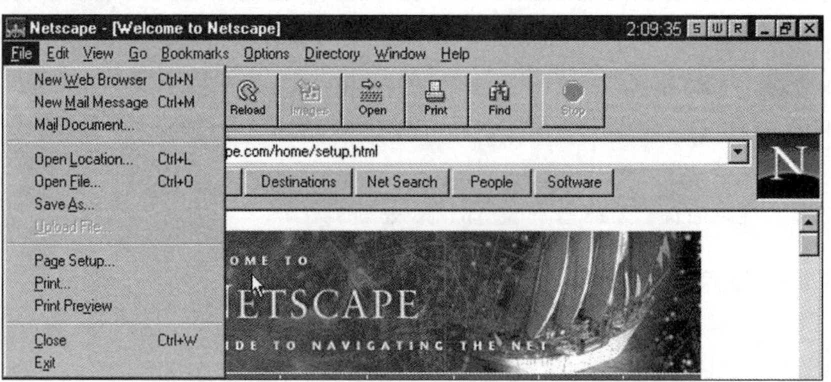

1. Connect to your Internet service provider and start Netscape Navigator.

   ✓ *These directions should work if you are using Netscape Navigator in Windows 3.1 or Windows 95.*
2. Use the scroll bar or scroll arrows to move up and down the current Web page.
3. Point to the File menu and click once to open it.
4. Notice the options available on the File menu.
5. Click on each of the menus and note the options available.
6. Press Esc to close any open menu.
7. Move your pointer over several objects on screen. Note that the pointer turns to a hand when it moves over certain locations. When the mouse pointer turns to a hand, it means that that item is a link to another part of the Web. You will explore links in other exercises in this book.
8. Click Go on the Menu bar. You will see options that are also available on the Toolbar, such as Back, Forward, Home, and Stop.
9. Click Directory on the Menu bar. You will see options that are also available on the Directory bar.

10. Click on the Help menu, click Handbook and do the following:
    - Move down the page using the vertical scroll bars on the right side of the screen to the Tutorial.
    - Click on **Learn Netscape** to access a short course on Netscape. The Handbook: Learn Netscape screen will display. Note that this line is in color and is underlined. This is your indication that this is a link to another location where you can get additional information, see another page, etc. 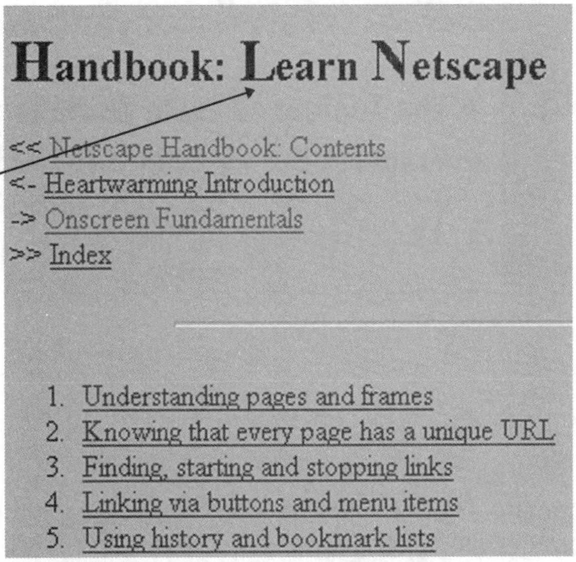
    - Click on **Onscreen Fundamentals** for details about the subjects listed. The Handbook: Onscreen Fundamentals screen displays. 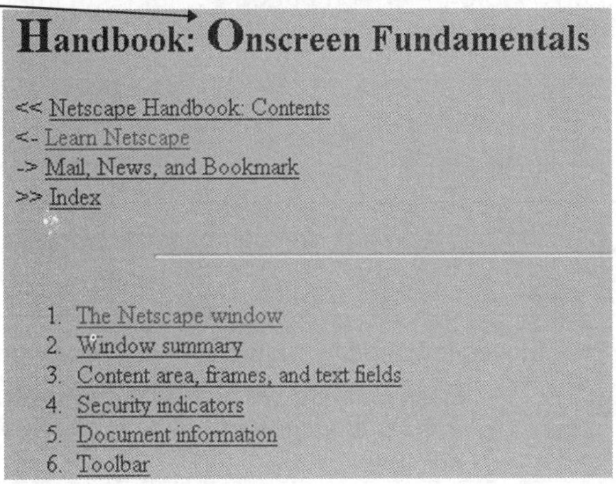
11. Continue on to the next exercise.

    OR

    Exit from Netscape and disconnect from your service provider.

Handbook: Learn Netscape

<< Netscape Handbook: Contents
<- Heartwarming Introduction
-> Onscreen Fundamentals
>> Index

1. Understanding pages and frames
2. Knowing that every page has a unique URL
3. Finding, starting and stopping links
4. Linking via buttons and menu items
5. Using history and bookmark lists

Handbook: Onscreen Fundamentals

<< Netscape Handbook: Contents
<- Learn Netscape
-> Mail, News, and Bookmark
>> Index

1. The Netscape window
2. Window summary
3. Content area, frames, and text fields
4. Security indicators
5. Document information
6. Toolbar

Exercise 2

◆ The Toolbar ◆ Open World Wide Web Sites ◆ Stop a Load or Search ◆ Progress Bar ◆ Return to the Home Page

NOTES

The Toolbar

- The Netscape Toolbar displays icons for Netscape's most commonly-used commands. Choosing any of these buttons will activate that task immediately. Note that each button contains an image and a word describing the function.

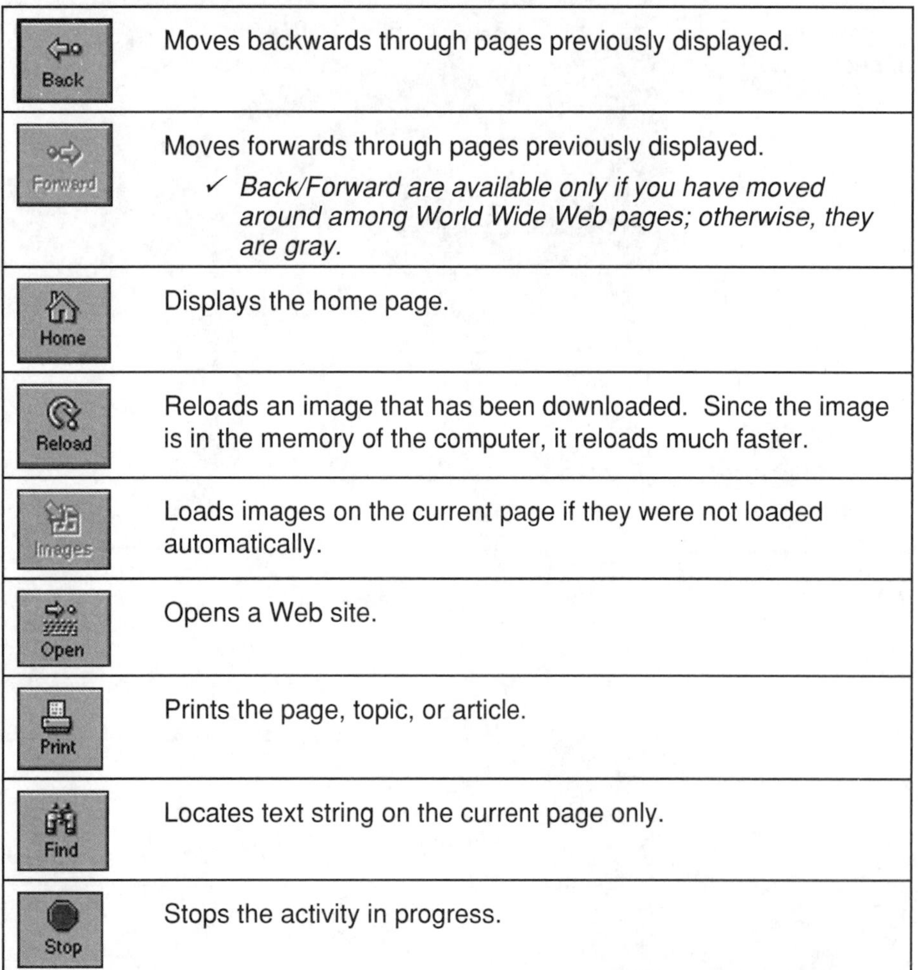

Back	Moves backwards through pages previously displayed.
Forward	Moves forwards through pages previously displayed. ✓ *Back/Forward are available only if you have moved around among World Wide Web pages; otherwise, they are gray.*
Home	Displays the home page.
Reload	Reloads an image that has been downloaded. Since the image is in the memory of the computer, it reloads much faster.
Images	Loads images on the current page if they were not loaded automatically.
Open	Opens a Web site.
Print	Prints the page, topic, or article.
Find	Locates text string on the current page only.
Stop	Stops the activity in progress.

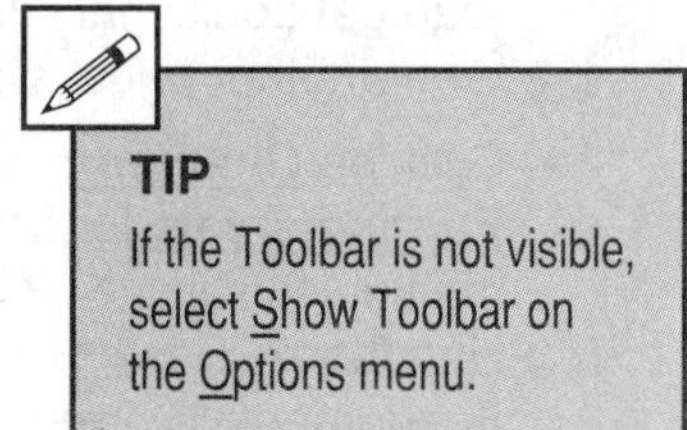

TIP
If the Toolbar is not visible, select Show Toolbar on the Options menu.

Open World Wide Web Sites

- As you learned in Exercise 1, a World Wide Web site is a location (server) which houses a great deal of information that can be accessed by anyone who has access to the Web. You can open a Web site in various ways:
  - Click Open [Open] on the Toolbar and enter the URL (for example, http://www.ddcpub.com) in the Open Location dialog box and click Open.

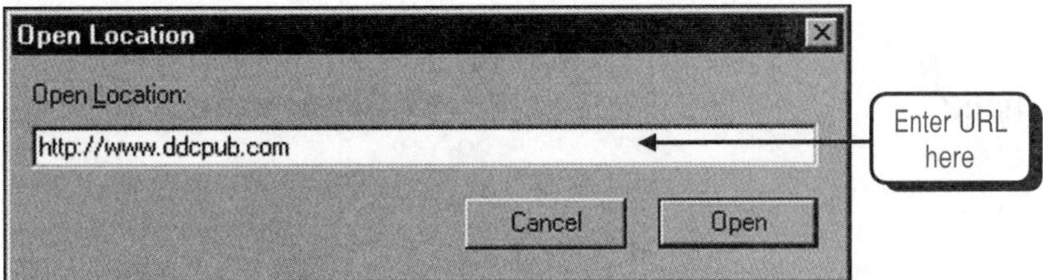

  - Click in the Location field on the Netscape home page, enter a new address and press Enter.

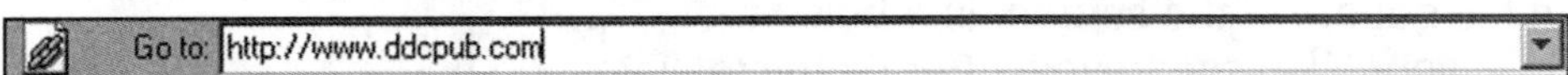

  - Select Open Location on the File menu, enter the URL in the Open Location box and click Open.

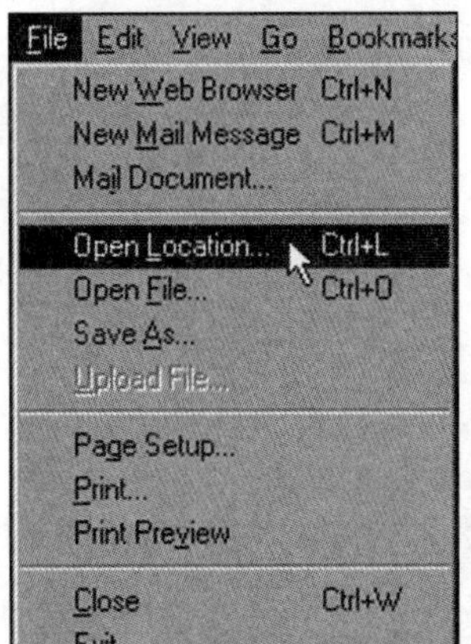

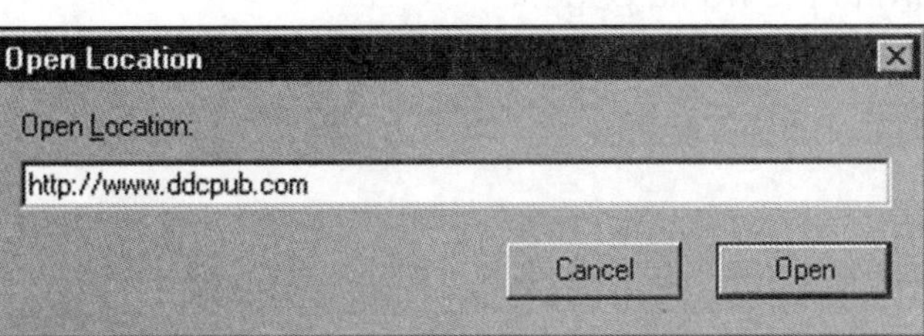

- URLs for Web sites always begin with **http://**. This is followed by the **domain** name of the computer at the Web site, for example, http://www.ddcpub.com. Domain names usually begin with www. The entire URL might read as:

  http://www.ddcpub.com

- There are seven types of Internet organizations for worldwide addressing purposes:

com	Commercial enterprise
edu	Educational institution
org	Non-commercial organization
mil	U. S. Military location
net	A network that has a gateway to the Internet
gov	Local, state, federal government location
int	International organization

NOTE
Remember that the URL is the electronic standardized form of an address of a Web site. URLs identify Web or home pages which are files stored on computers connected to the World Wide Web.

TIP
Don't be discouraged if the connection to the World Wide Web site is not made immediately. The site may be off-line temporarily. The site may also be very busy with others users trying to access it. Be sure the URL is typed accurately. Occasionally, it takes several tries to connect.

Stop a Load or Search

- Searching for information or loading a Web site can become time consuming, especially if the Web page has many graphic images. You may wish to stop a search or the loading of a large file after you have started it.
- There are at least two ways to stop a search or load:
  - Click the Stop icon on the right side of the Toolbar.

  OR

  - Click Stop Loading on the Go menu.

Progress Bar

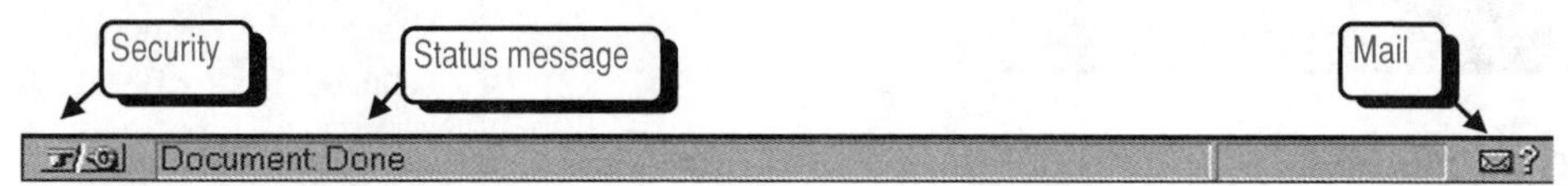

- The progress bar, located at the bottom of the screen, is a helpful indicator of what is occurring in your Web site travels. For example, if you are loading a Web site file, you will see the percentage of the task completed so far.
- The key icon in the far-left corner indicates the security level of the file in use (secure - key icon on blue, or insecure - broken doorkey on gray). In the lower–right corner is the icon for Netscape mail. You will work with mail later in this book.

NOTE
See the Netscape Handbook for more information about security levels.

Return to the Home Page

- There are four ways to return to the home page:
  - Click the Home icon on the Toolbar.

  OR

  - Click Home on the Go menu.

  OR

  - Click the Netscape icon to return to the Netscape home page.

  ✓ *Clicking this icon will take you to Netscape's home page.*

  OR

  - Click Back on the Toolbar to move back through the screens to the home page.

HINT
If you have explored many sites and would like to see the links that you followed, clicking Back is a good way to review your actions.

In this exercise, you will use the Toolbar, open a Web site, stop a search, and return to the Netscape home page.

NOTE: ***To ensure consistent results, this exercise uses simulated sites. Since Web sites are constantly changing or may no longer exist, these simulations are used to ensure that the actions you take in this exercise will give you the results illustrated. At the end of the exercise, you will find a list of Web sites that are "real" and that you are encouraged to explore. This actual exploration of the World Wide Web will give you the chance to practice the concepts learned in this exercise.***

EXERCISE DIRECTIONS

1. If you are continuing from the previous exercise, go to step 2.

   OR

   Connect to your service provider and start Netscape Navigator.
2. Click on the Location field on the Netscape home page.

   The text will become highlighted in blue.
3. On the Location line type the following and then press Enter:

   http://www.ddcpub.com/learn
4. Click the link to **Lesson 1: Netscape Navigator, Exercise 2 "White House"**.

   The White House opening page will appear.
5. Scroll down to the link for the **White House Help Desk** and click on it.

   The screen shown on the right appears.
6. Click on **Frequently Asked Questions**.

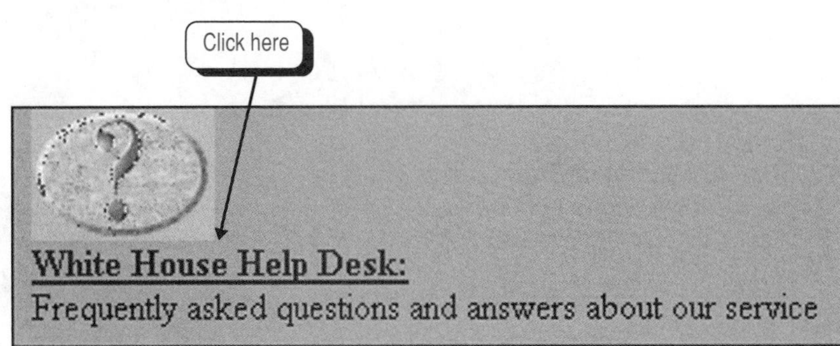

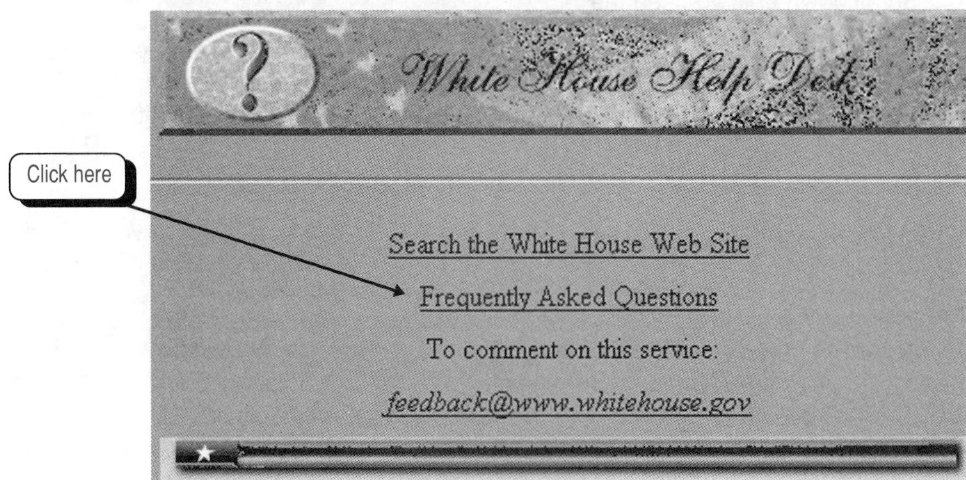

The screen shown on the right appears.

Frequently Asked Questions

What is *Welcome to the White House*?

Welcome to the White House is a key access point to government information that is available on the Internet, a network of computer networks used by people in over 150 countries. Using a service on the Internet called the World Wide Web (WWW), people all over the world can locate documents that not only contain text but also include graphics, photos, sound, and video.

7. Click on the Netscape icon to return to the Netscape home page.
8. Click Open [Open] on the Toolbar.
9. Type the URL to access the DDC Publishing home page (**http://www.ddcpub.com/learn**), then press Open.
10. Click the link to The Smithsonian Institution, **<u>Lesson 1: Netscape Navigator, Exercise 2 "Smithsonian"</u>**.

    The home page for the Smithsonian Institution appears.
11. Click the Museums/Organizations picture on the left side of the Smithsonian Home Page.

Click here

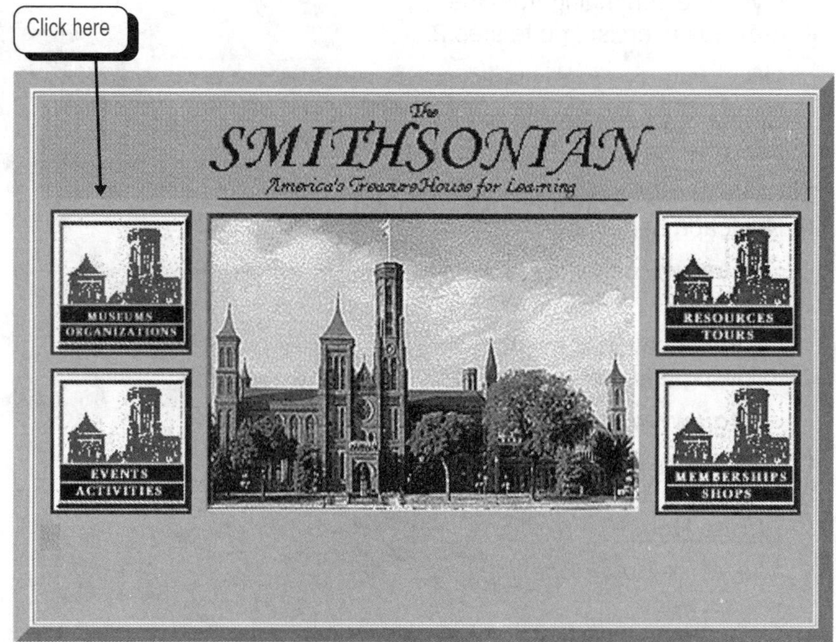

The Museums and Organization page shown on the right opens.

12. Locate the following link: **<u>An Overview of the Museums</u>**.
13. Click on the link.
14. Scroll down until you see the description of the National Museum of America History (as shown next to step 15.)

Click here

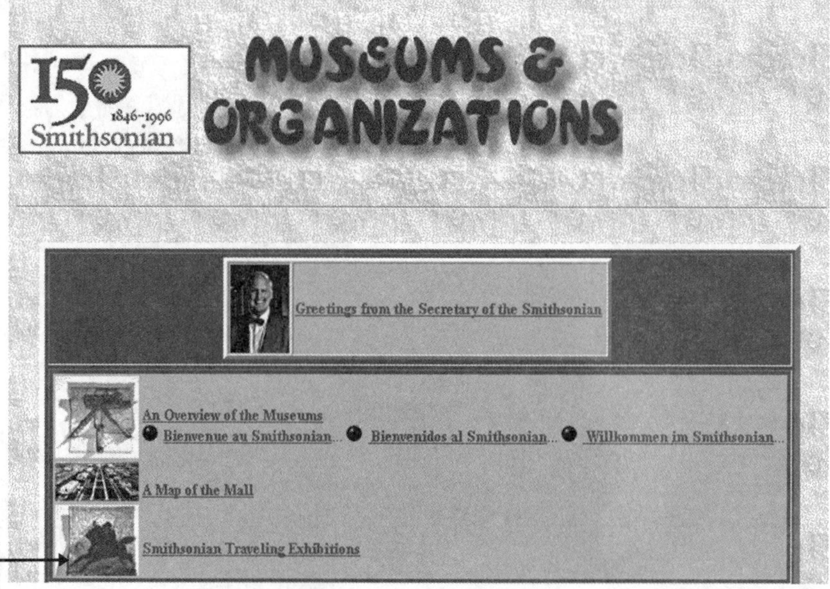

15. Click the link **the Foucault Pendulum**.
16. Click **Print** on the Toolbar to send this page to the printer.
    - ✓ *If you are using the Internet Simulation, printing will be demonstrated and simulated. The actual Print feature, however, will be disabled. You will not actually print any documents to your printer.*
17. Click **Home** on the Toolbar to return to the Netscape home page.
18. Continue on to the next exercise.

    OR

    Exit from Netscape and disconnect from your service provider.

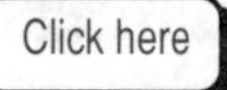

The National Museum of American History traces the American heritage through cultural, scientific, and technological exhibitions. Collections are displayed in settings that recapture and interpret the American experience from Colonial times to the present.

Highlights: Star-Spangled Banner; a selection of First Ladies' gowns, John Bull locomotive; Southern Railways "1401" engine; the Foucault Pendulum; Ben Franklin's printing press; Bell's original experimental telephones; Hands On History Room; Hands On Science Center.

Encyclopedia Smithsonian

Foucault Pendulum

Information or research assistance regarding pendulums is frequently requested from the Smithsonian Institution. The following information has been prepared by the National Museum of American History's Division of Physical Sciences in cooperation with the Visitor Information and Associates' Reception Center's Public Inquiry Mail and Telephone Information Service Unit to assist those interested in this topic.

The Foucault Pendulum is named for the French physicist Jean Foucault (pronounced "Foo-koh), who first used it in 1851 to demonstrate the rotation of the earth. It was the first satisfactory demonstration of the earth's rotation using laboratory apparatus rather than astronomical observations.

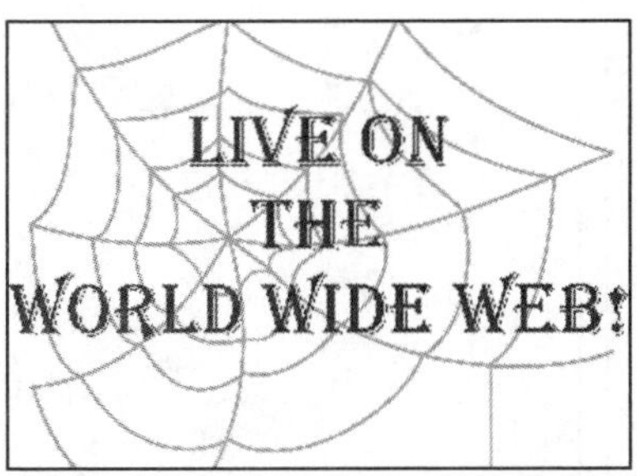

Netscape Navigator's Home Page
    http://www.netscape.com

The White House Home Page
    http://www.whitehouse.gov

The Smithsonian Instituition Home Page
    http://www.si.edu

L.A. Times Home Page
    http://www.latimes.com

The Nasa Home Page
    http://nasa.gov

DDC Publishing Home Page
    http://www.ddcpub.com

Exercise 3

◆ Shortcuts ◆ History ◆ Bookmarks ◆ Bookmarks Window
◆ Add and Delete Bookmarks
◆ Create Bookmarks from the History List
◆ Save Pages ◆ Print Pages

NOTES

Shortcuts

- Shortcuts are hyperlinks that let you move to other Web pages within a Web site, or to other Web sites altogether. Shortcuts are easily recognized because they are either underlined or appear in text of a **different color**. For example, on the following home page, **AOL Users!**, **Click here!**, **plug-ins**, and **sign up** are hyperlinks or shortcuts to different Web pages.

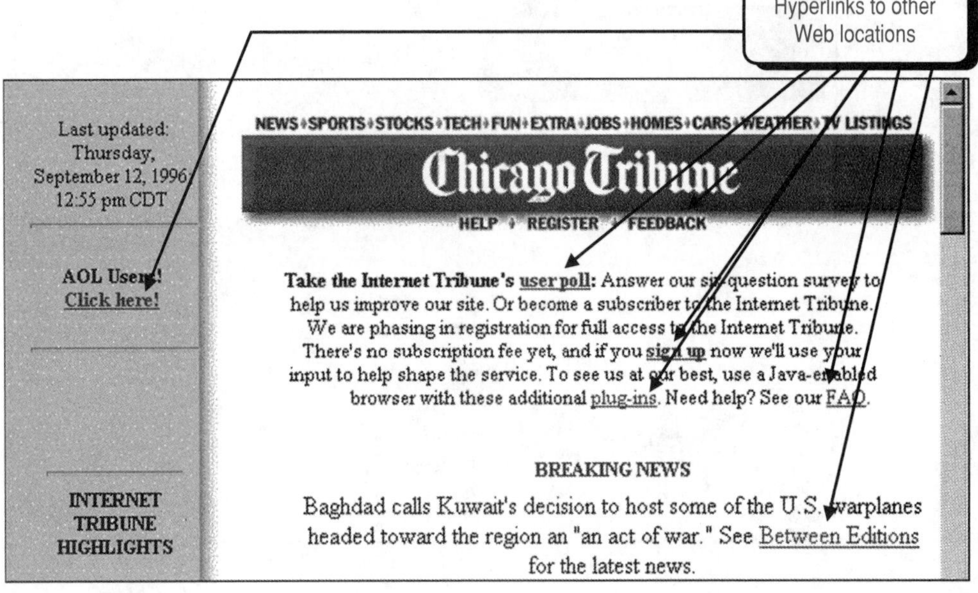

History

- While you are moving back and forth among Web sites, the computer is recording a **history** of the location of these sites in the memory of your computer. As long as you do not exit Netscape, the location of the sites remain in your computer's memory.

- To view history, click History on the Window menu.

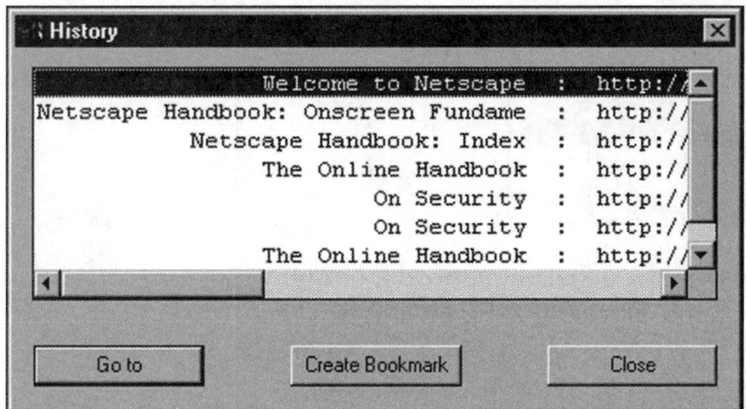

- You can use Back and Forward on the Toolbar to move from one page to another. However, this history of Web sites you have visited is temporary. When you end the Netscape session by exiting the program, you lose the record.

Bookmarks

- A **bookmark** is a placeholder with the title and the URL of a Web page. If you find a Web site that is of particular interest to you and that you may want to later revisit, create a bookmark to record its location electronically. Bookmarks maintain permanent records of Web sites so that you can return to them using Netscape.
- Bookmarks can be added and viewed from the Bookmarks menu.
- If you open a Web site and want to add it as a bookmark, click Add Bookmark on the Bookmarks menu (or press Ctrl + D). The new site will appear at the bottom of the Bookmarks menu.

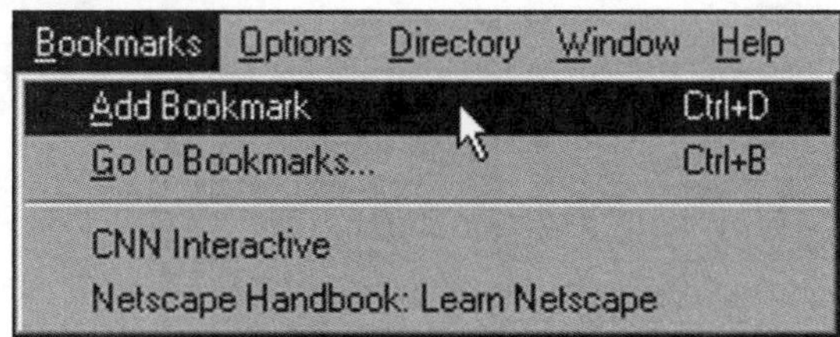

Bookmarks Window

- Bookmarks are stored in a separate bookmark.htm file. This file can be accessed by selecting Go to Bookmarks from the Bookmarks menu. The Bookmarks window appears when accessing the bookmark.htm file. All editing and organizing of bookmarks is done from within this window.

  ✓ *Bookmark.HTM files are automatically saved when you close the Bookmarks window. It is not recommended that you do a Save As to the file unless you wish to create more than one bookmark.htm file. This would only be necessary, for example, if you wanted to have only certain bookmarks appear under your Bookmarks menu, but would like to retain additional bookmarks in a separate bookmark file.*

HINT
You can create bookmarks from addresses in the History folder.

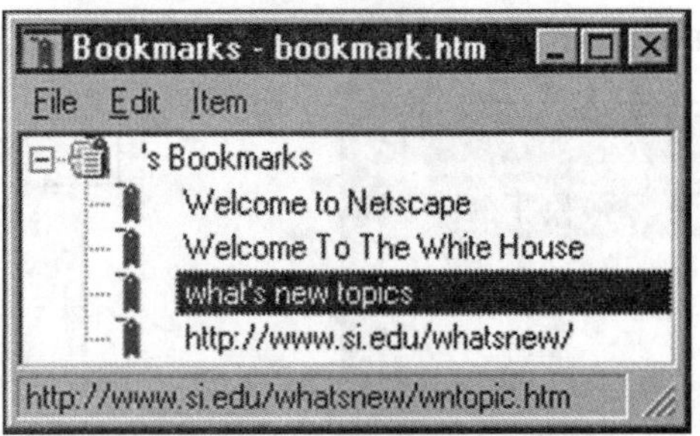

- If you are using Windows 95, you may see a question mark on a newly added bookmark. The question mark will disappear the first time you click on the new bookmark.

Delete Bookmarks

- Bookmarks may be deleted at anytime. For example, you may wish to delete a bookmark if a Web site no longer exists.
  To delete a bookmark do the following:
  - Click Bookmarks menu.
  - Click Go to Bookmarks.
  - Highlight the bookmark you want to delete.
  - Press the Delete key.

Create Bookmarks from the History List

- If you have a Web site in the History list that you would like to store permanently, do the following:
  - Open the Window menu and select History.

    The History window appears.

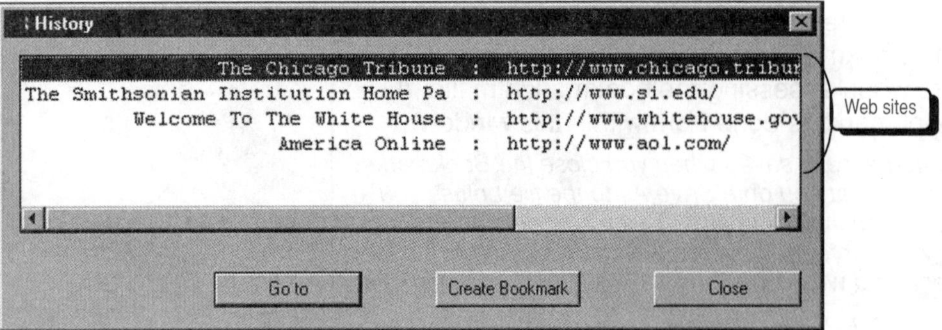

- Click the History item that you want to make a bookmark.
- Click the Create Bookmark button at the bottom of the dialog box. This will add the item to the Bookmark folder.
- Click the Close button to exit the History window.

Save Pages

- When you find a Web page that you particularly like and would like to review later, save it to the hard disk by clicking Save As on the File menu.
- When saving a Web page, you can use the current page name or create a new one.
- Saved Web pages can later be reloaded into Netscape by clicking File, Open File, and entering the name and location of the file.

Print Pages

- **To print a displayed Web page:**
  - Click the Print button on the Toolbar.

    OR
  - Click Print on the File menu.

    The Web page will be printed in the format shown in the Web page display.

In this exercise, you will add and delete Bookmarks and work within the Bookmarks window.

EXERCISE DIRECTIONS

1. If you are continuing from the previous exercise, go to step 2.

   OR

   Connect to your service provider and start Netscape Navigator.
2. Open the DDC Publishing home page.
   http://*www.ddcpub.com*
3. Click Bookmarks on the menu bar.
4. Click Add Bookmark.

   When you click on the Bookmark menu again, you should see a listing for DDC Publishing.
5. Repeat step 4 to add DDC Publishing a second time.

   When you click on the Bookmark menu again, you should see two listings for DDC Publishing.
6. To delete the second listing for DDC Publishing, select Go to Bookmarks on the Bookmark menu. *This will take you to the Bookmark window.*

   ✓ *Bookmarks are stored in a separate bookmark.htm file. This file is accessed by selecting Go to Bookmarks from the Bookmarks menu. The Bookmark window then appears. All editing and organizing of bookmarks is done from this location.*
7. Highlight the second occurrence of the DDC Publishing bookmark and press the Delete key.

   ✓ *Bookmark.HTM files are automatically saved when the Bookmark window is closed. It is not recommended that you do a Save As to the file unless you wish to create more than one bookmark.htm. file. This would only be necessary, for example, if you wanted to have certain bookmarks appear under your Bookmarks menu, but would like to retain additional bookmarks in a separate bookmark file.*
8. Continue onto the next exercise

   OR

   Exit from Netscape and disconnect from your service provider.

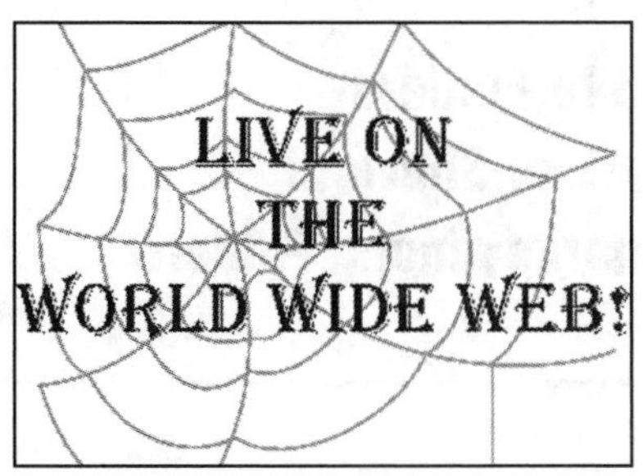

The Chicago Tribune Home Page
http://www.chicago.tribune.com

CNN Interactive
http://www.cnn.com

The Rocky Mountain News Home Page
http://www.denver-rmn.com

Annie's Homegrown Inc. Home Page – voted "coolest natural products site on the World Wide Web" by Eco-Network. Gives information on ordering their products (including their fabulous Macaroni and Cheese), recipes, and their Be Green magazine.
http://www.Annies.com

Maxis Home Page – computer game company. Has links to bulletin boards on the Web to discuss strategy or find teammates. You can also access tips and hints on their games, or get information on upcoming products. There is a link informing teachers how to use classroom-specific versions of their games (such as Sim City, Sim Farm, etc.). You can also find out about job opportunities and where to purchase their products.
http://www.maxis.com

Exercise 4

◆ Organize Bookmarks ◆ Create, Delete, and Add to Folders
◆ Use the Right Mouse Button to Create a Bookmark or Shortcut
◆ Edit Bookmarks ◆ Drag and Drop (Move) Bookmarks among Folders

NOTES

Organize Bookmarks

- Since remembering addresses of sites that you want to visit on the World Wide Web can be difficult, creating bookmarks to those sites is a convenient way to store the addresses. That list can grow long and cumbersome very quickly. The Bookmarks feature in Netscape lets you create folders to organize those addresses into logical categories.
- In Exercise 3, you learned how to add URLs to your Bookmarks list. In this exercise you'll learn how to categorize and organize that list.

Create Folders

- A folder, similar to a subdirectory that holds files, holds bookmarks by category. Creating folders is done as follows:
  - Click Go to Bookmarks on the Bookmarks menu to open the Bookmarks window.

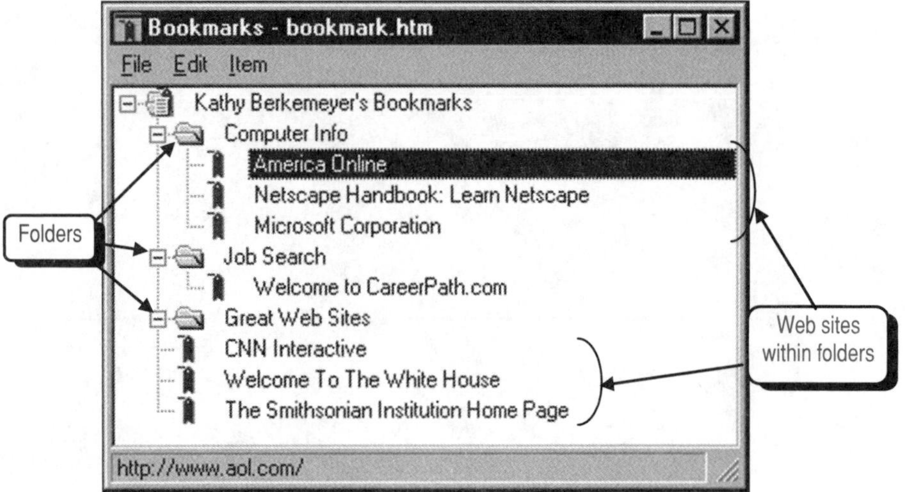

  - Click Item.
  - Select Insert Folder; the Bookmark Properties dialog box will display.

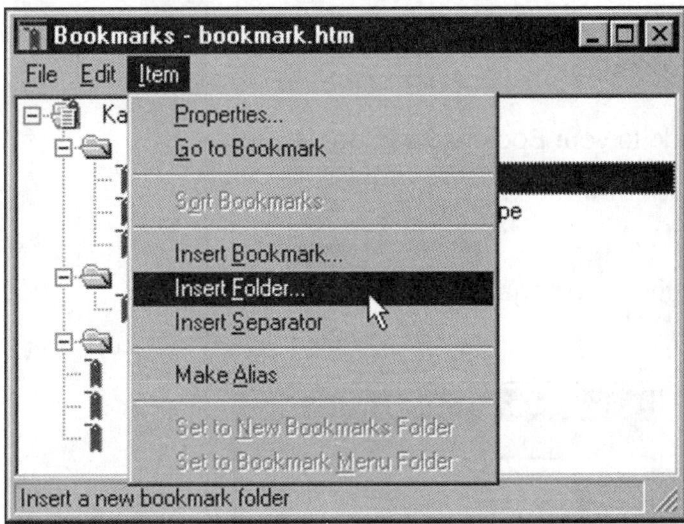

- Enter the name of the new folder in the Name field and click OK.

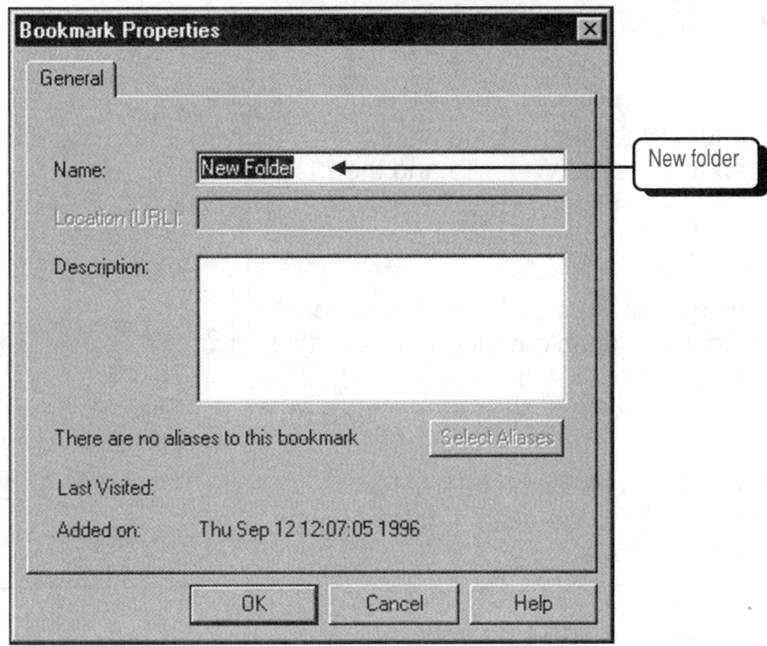

- To add a bookmark to a folder, click and drag the bookmark toward the folder. When the folder becomes highlighted, release the mouse button. The bookmark will now appear under the designated folder.

To Delete a Folder:

- From the Bookmarks window, highlight the folder.
- Press the Delete key.

HINT

You can use the Ctrl key to select multiple bookmarks and move them at once to a folder.

Use the Right Mouse Button to Create a Bookmark or Shortcut

Create a Bookmark

- Open a Web site that you want to add to your Bookmarks folder.
- Right-click the mouse anywhere on the Web page 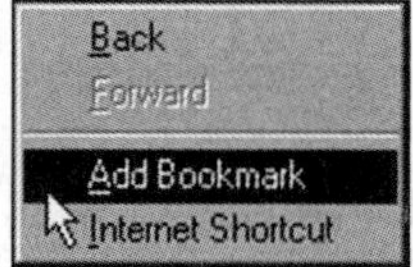.

- Click the Add Bookmark option.

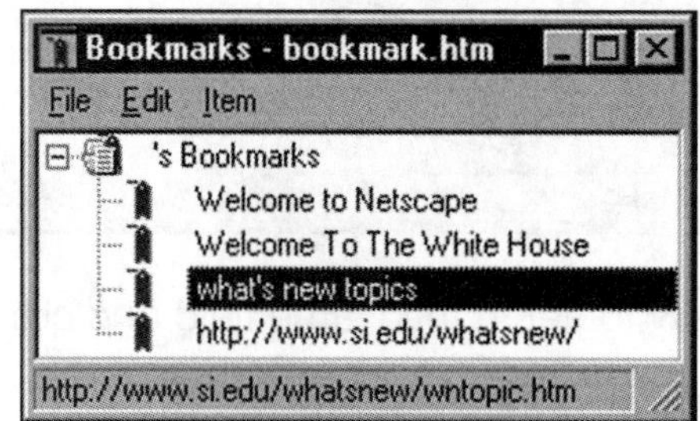

Create a Shortcut

- To create a shortcut (Windows 95) to a Web site that you want to access quickly and frequently, open the desired Web site and then:
  - *Right-click* on the Web site.
  - Click Internet Shortcut.

  A shortcut to the Web site will be placed on your desktop. When you are connected to your service provider and double-click on the shortcut, you will go directly to that Web site.

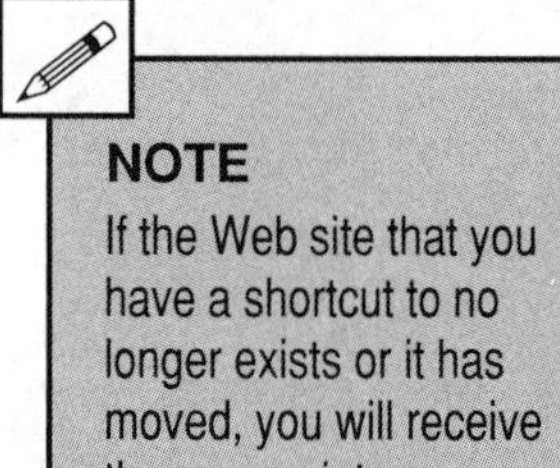

NOTE

If the Web site that you have a shortcut to no longer exists or it has moved, you will receive the appropriate message.

Edit Bookmarks

- A bookmark is likely to change with the dynamics of the Internet. Documents may be changed from one server to the next. If this happens, you will need to edit the Bookmark link as follows.
  - Select Go to Bookmarks.
    A list of your bookmarks displays in the Bookmarks window.

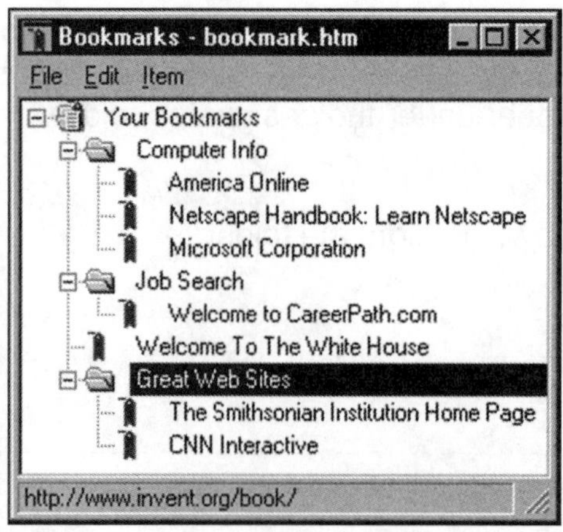

  - Select the specific bookmark to be edited.
  - Click Properties on the Item menu.

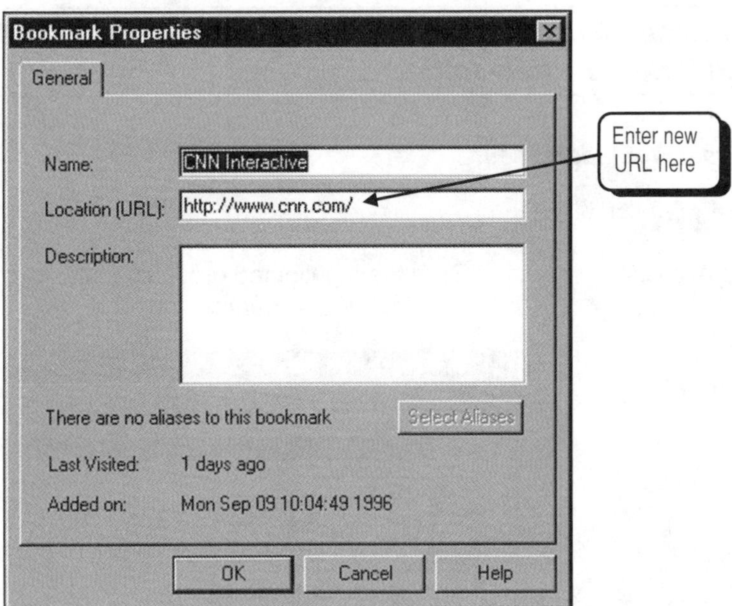

- In the Bookmark Properties dialog box that displays, change the URL in the Location box. Click OK.

Drag and Drop (Move) Bookmarks among Folders

- It is easy to move bookmarks among folders. Just click on the bookmark and while still holding the mouse button, drag it to the new folder and drop it on top of the name of the folder.

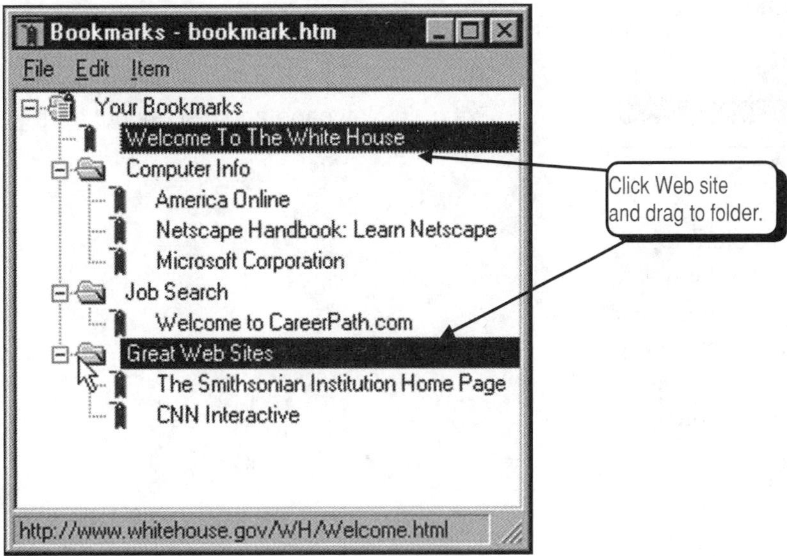

- When you move a folder, its contents move with it.

In this exercise, you will open Web sites, create new bookmarks and folders, and organize them by dragging bookmarks to a new folder.

NOTE: In this exercise you will use real Web addresses.

EXERCISE DIRECTIONS

1. If you are continuing from the previous exercise, go to step 2.

   OR

   Connect to your service provider and start Netscape Navigator.
2. Open the following Web sites:

   http://www.careerpath.com

   http://www.jobtrak.com

   http://www.monster.com

   http://www.jobseeker.com
3. Using the Back and Forward buttons on the toolbar, move to each site one at a time.
4. Click Go to Bookmarks from Bookmarks menu.
5. Click on the folder labeled **Your Bookmarks** and do the following:
   - Click Insert Folder from Item menu.
   - Type **Job Search** as the folder name.
   - Click OK.

6. Close the Bookmarks window.
7. Using the Back and Forward buttons, return to each Web site you've just visited and create a bookmark for each of the sites.
8. Return to the Bookmarks window by selecting **Go to Bookmarks** on the Bookmark menu.
9. Hold down the Ctrl key while you click on the following Web site bookmarks:
   - *Welcome to JOBTRAK*
   - *Welcome to CareerPath.com*
   - *The Monster Board-the #1 career site on the Web....*
   - *HE Weekly's Jobseeker's Web Page*
10. Release the Ctrl key.
11. Drag the highlighted group of Web sites to the new folder, *Job Search*.

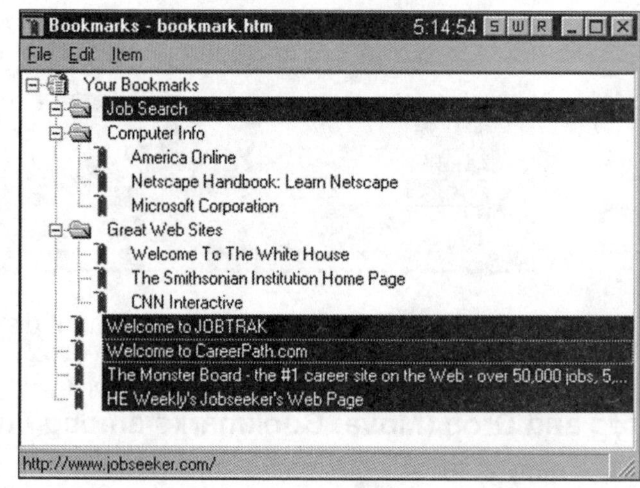

12. Delete jobtrak.com's (Welcome to JOBTRAK) bookmark.
13. Continue on to the next exercise.

    OR

    Exit from Netscape and disconnect from your service provider.

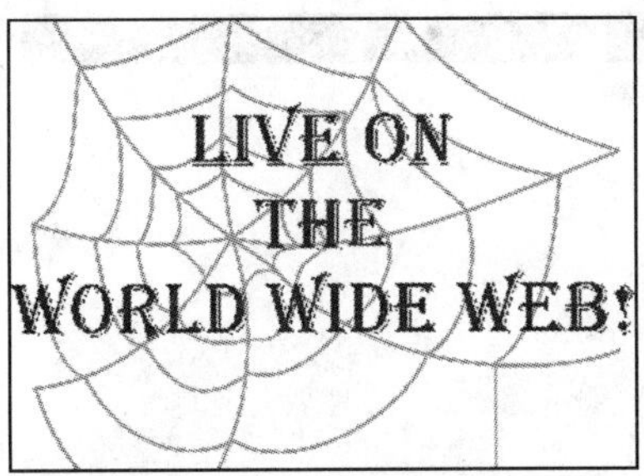

Career Path Home Page – Search newspaper want ads from 19 major cities.
http://www.careerpath.com/

JOBTRAK Home Page – Job listing service.
http://www.jobtrak.com/

The Monster Board Home Page – Job listing service.
http://www.monster.com/

Jobseeker Home Page – Employment opportunities available in hotels and restaurants in the San Francisco Bay Area.
http://www.jobseeker.com/

The ArtsNet Home Page – Career Services page provides information about opportunities in the arts and entertainment industries including jobs, internships, and resumes.
http://artsnet.heinz.cmu.edu/

Exercise 5

◆ **Directory Buttons**

NOTES

Directory Buttons

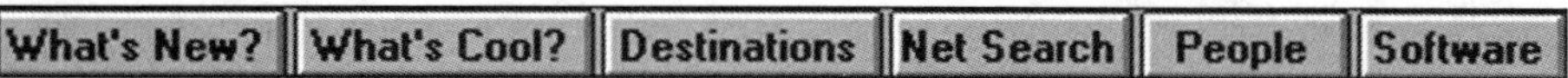

- Netscape has provided a shortcut to selected Internet resources such as Web sites and online white pages. You will find many interesting places and articles to browse.

What's New

- Displays latest sites on the Web with links to them.
- Discusses how the sites were selected.

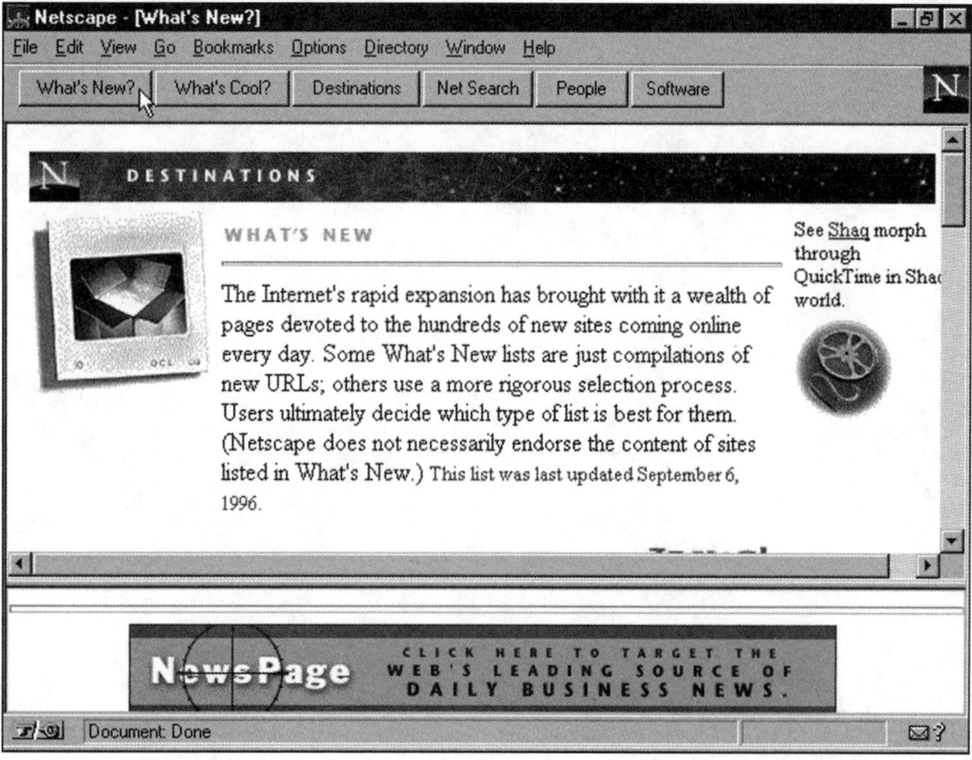

What's Cool **What's Cool?**

- Displays the "latest and greatest" Web sites according to popular opinion.
- Shows the latest topics of interest on the Web.

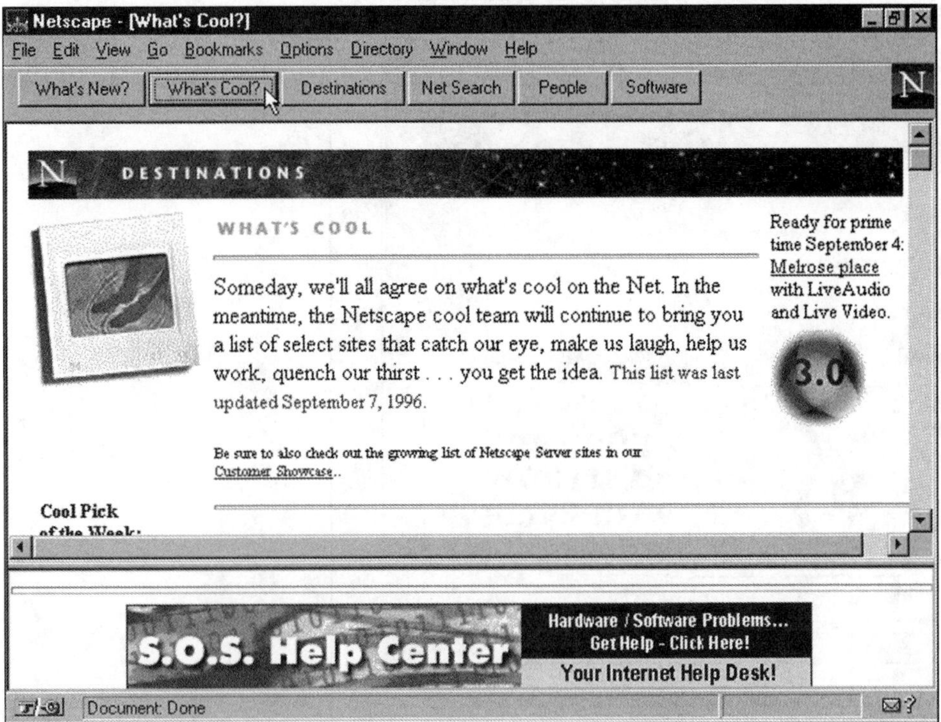

Destinations **Destinations**

- Displays places on the Web which utilize Netscape's latest technologies, such as live video and three-dimensional graphics.

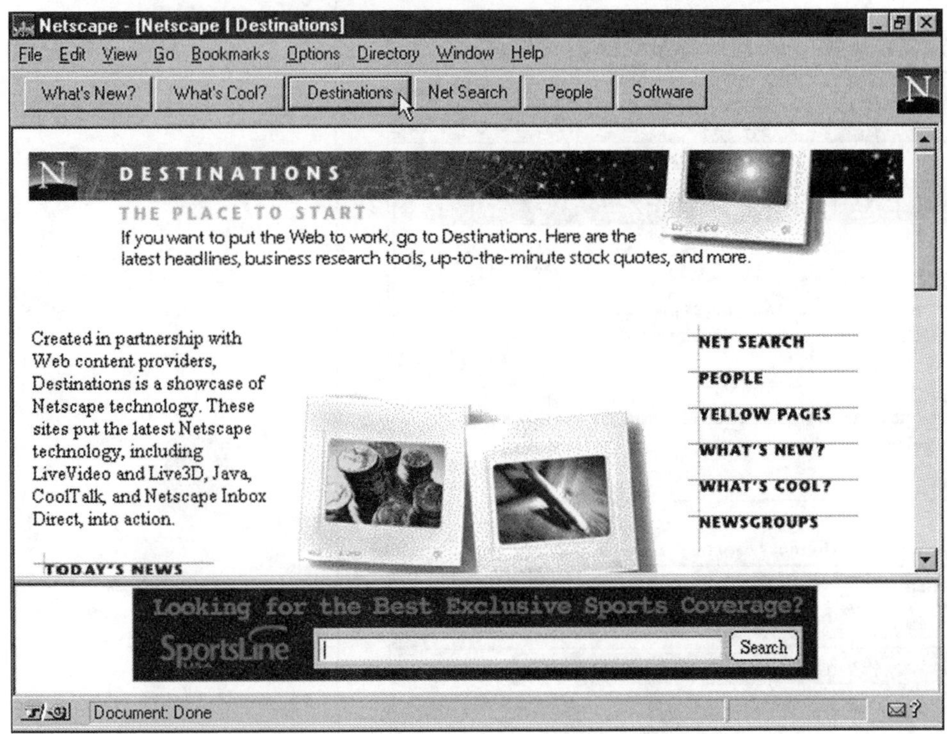

Net Search

- Displays Netscape's search technology, which allows you to choose among available search engines to search the Web.

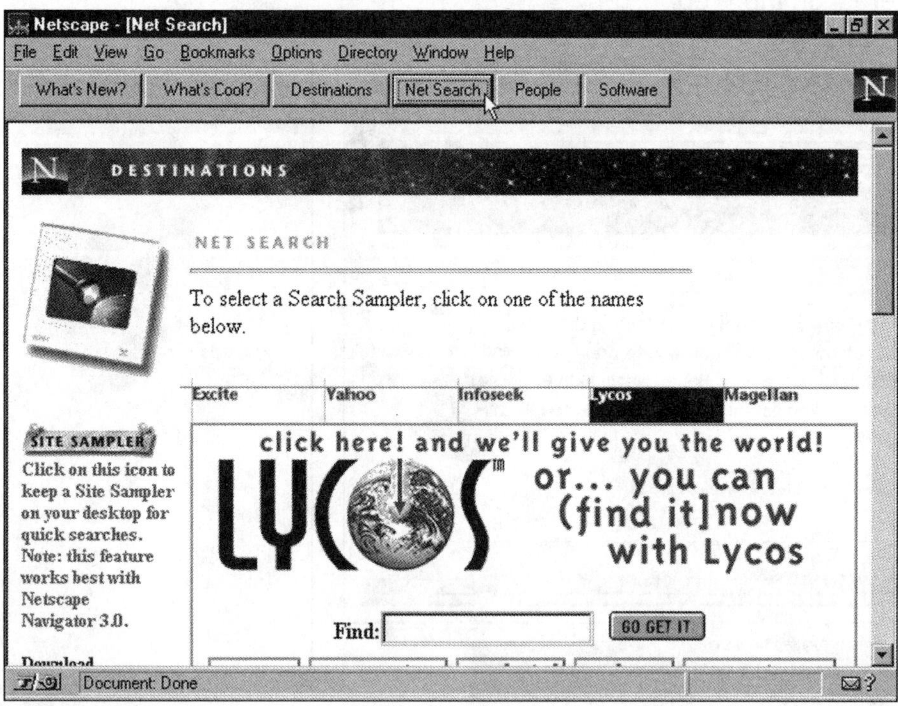

People

- Displays online white pages.
- Allows you to register your name in the Internet white pages.
- Provides several search directories for locating people across the country.

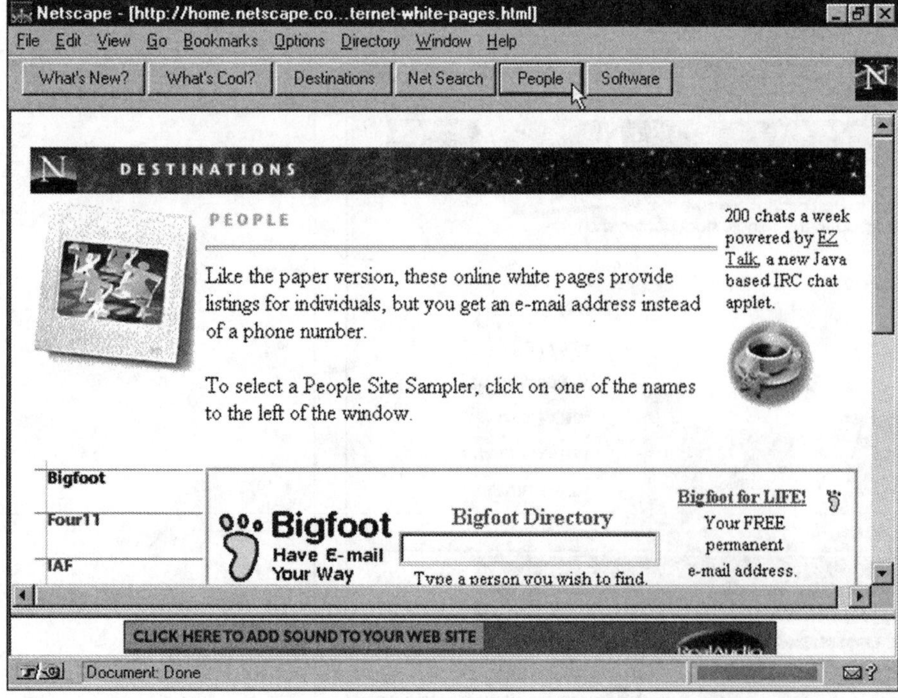

- Under the People directory, there are several directories, each sponsored by a different company or organization. You can think of these directories as separately sponsored Internet whitepages. They allow you to search for E-mail addresses, street addresses, and phone numbers. Most directories also offer you the opportunity to publish your own information. Different directories are featured at the opening People screen at different times. Scroll to select a directory from the list (Bigfoot, IAF, WhoWhere, etc.) and type your search information into the text field(s) provided. Or, type your information directly into the field(s) on the featured directory window of the opening People screen. Follow as prompted to complete your search.

Software Software

- Displays links to update and configure Netscape's latest version, plug-ins (add-on software for Netscape), and multimedia components.

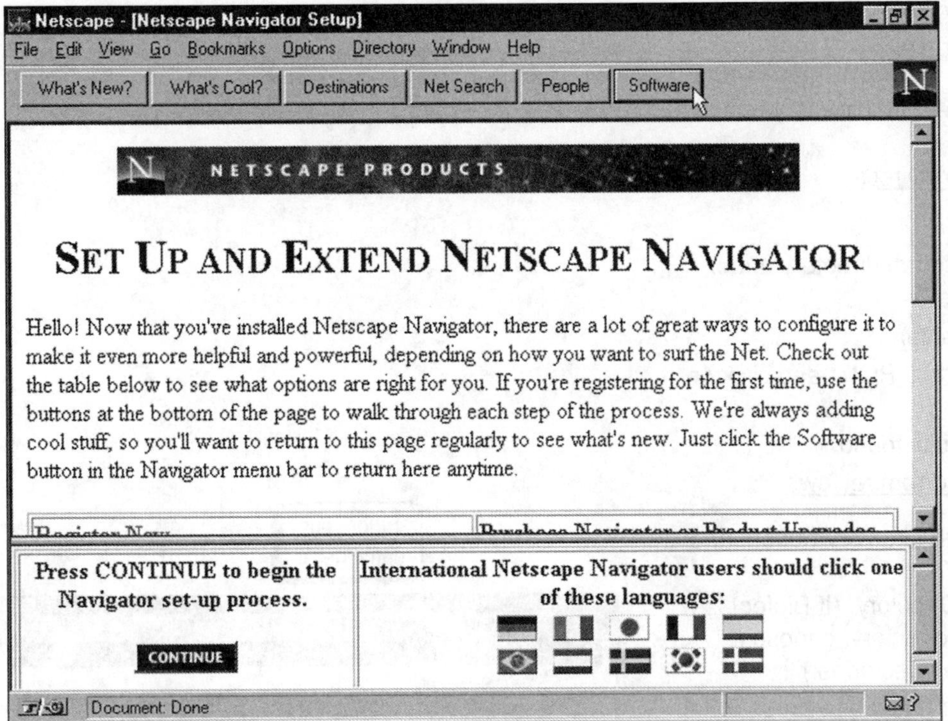

In this exercise, you will explore the Directory button options.

EXERCISE DIRECTIONS

1. If you are continuing from the previous exercise, go to step 2.

   OR

   Connect to your service provider and start Netscape Navigator.
2. Click on **What's New?**, the first directory button, and do the following:
   - Click on the link to 24 Hours in Cyberspace.
3. Click on **What's Cool?**, the second directory button, and do the following:
   - Click on the link The Firefly.
4. Click on **Destinations**, the third directory button, and do the following:
   - Click on the link to Inbox Direct.
   - Browse this selection.
5. Click on **Net Search**, the fourth directory button, and do the following:
   - Click on the link to Magellan.
   - In the Search box, key "CD ROM" and click on the Search button.
   - Note the number of results found.
   - Click on the link to Alt.cd-rom.reviews.
6. Click on **People**, the fifth directory button, and do the following:
   - Scroll down to Bigfoot Directory. (If Bigfoot is not the currently active directory, choose it from the list of available directories.)
   - In the text box, key your name and press Enter to see if you may already be included in the directory. Note whether or not a match was found.
7. Click Home on the Toolbar to return to your home page.
8. Continue on to the next exercise.

   OR

   Exit from Netscape and disconnect from your service provider.

Enter your name here.

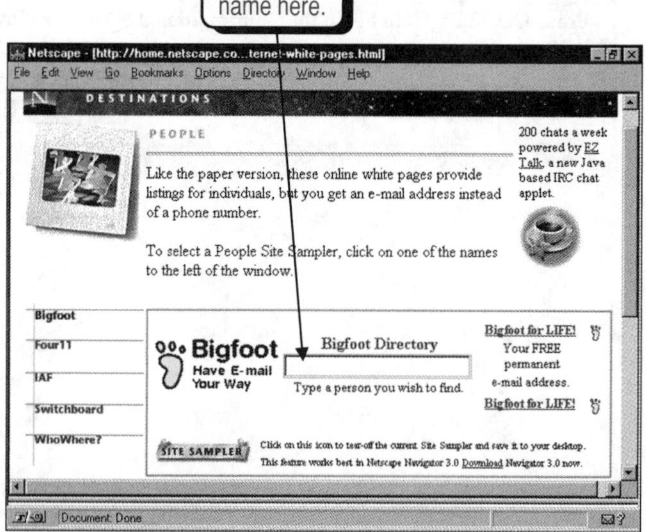

Netscape - [http://home.netscape.co...ternet-white-pages.html]
DESTINATIONS
PEOPLE
Like the paper version, these online white pages provide listings for individuals, but you get an e-mail address instead of a phone number.
To select a People Site Sampler, click on one of the names to the left of the window.
Bigfoot
Four11
IAF
Switchboard
WhoWhere?
Bigfoot Directory
Type a person you wish to find.
Document: Done

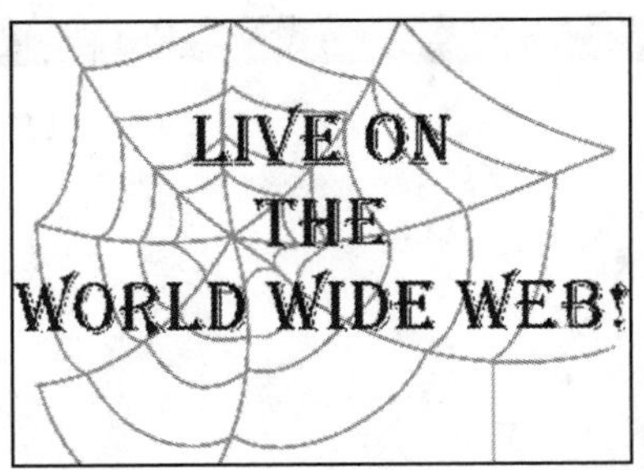

Lucas Arts Entertainment Company Home Page – Entryway to the world of Lucas Arts, creators of the *X-Wing* game. Find out about their latest products, get technical support on their current games, join the Rebel Recruitment Center, or read *The Adventurer*, their online magazine.
http://www.lucasarts.com

Justice Department Federal Bureau of Investigations Home Page
http://www.fbi.gov

United States Department of Justice Home Page
http://www.usdoj.gov

The Travel Channel Online Network –
http://www.travelchannel.com

Exercise 6	◆ Capture Information from Web Pages ◆ Copy and Paste from Web Pages to Text Editors ◆ Download Files from Web Pages ◆ Save and Print Web Pages ◆ Mail Web Pages

NOTES

Capture Information from Web Pages

- Capturing and using the information that you find is a major goal of most Web searches.
- Capturing data from the World Wide Web with Netscape Navigator can be done in several ways:
  - Copy and paste text to a text editor or word processor
  - Download files
  - Print a Web page
  - Save a Web page without images
  - Mail a Web page

  To Copy and Paste from Web Pages to Text Editors:

  - Highlight the desired text.

> **Welcome!**
>
> Thank you for visiting our WWW server. CAVIX is a bulletin board service (BBS) for **educators and their business partners**. If you have not done so before, please let us know where you are connecting from by filling out the "Check-In Form."
>
> Here are a few **examples of the information you can find on the CAVIX BBS.** To see more, telnet to cavix.org. If you do not have a CAVIX account, sign on as a new user. Be sure to read your e-mail and follow the instructions for registering. (You must have your web browser preferences set to load a telnet client.)

  - Click Copy on the Edit menu.
  - Open a text editor such as Notepad, WordPad, or a word processor, such as Microsoft Word.
  - Click on the page where you are going to place the text and click Paste from the Edit menu or press Ctrl + V, in the Windows application that you are using.

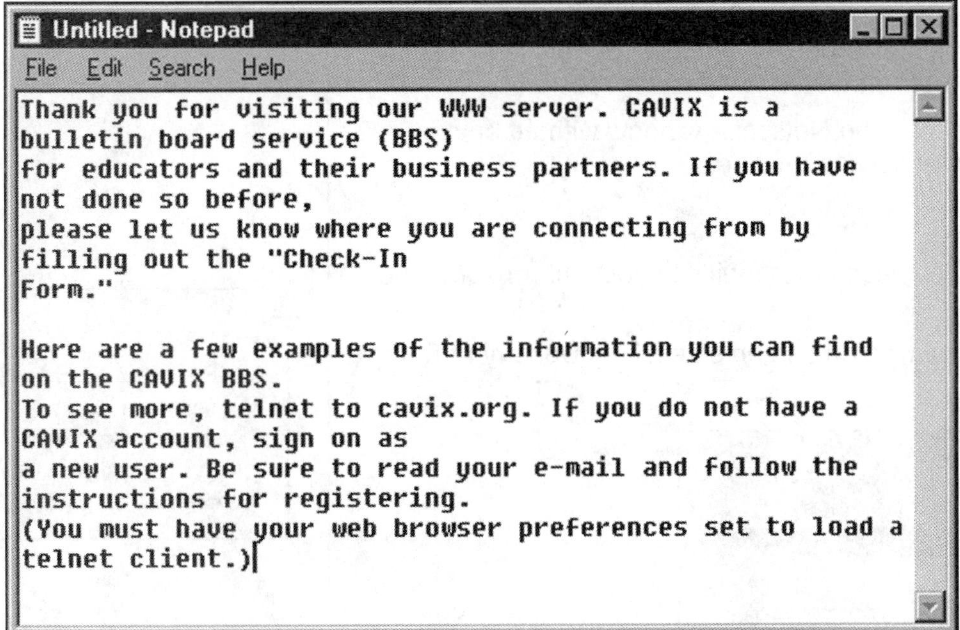

- Click File, Save As, then name and save the file.

To Download Files from Web Pages:

- Go to the Web site containing the files that you want to download.
- Follow the on screen prompts.

- When you have been successful in downloading a file, you may be asked if you want to open the file or save it to a disk. Saving the file to disk is usually a wise move. If the file is an executable program (installation files for a program), and you have to reinstall it for whatever reason, you'll still have the files from which you can install it.
- Downloading large files can take a long time, depending on the speed of your modem and computer. Downloading files using FTP (File Transfer Protocol) will be covered in Lesson 5.

To Print a Web Page:

- Open Web page that you want to print.
- Click Print [Print] on the Toolbar.

  OR

- Open the File menu, select Print, and click OK to send the page to the printer.

  The printed Web page should resemble the image of the Web page (including graphics). The quality of the printout depends on the quality of your printer.

To Save a Web Page without Images:

- Open the Web page that you want to save.
- Click Save As on the File menu.
- This will store the text part of the document.
- Disconnect from the ISP.

NOTE

Clicking a file or program downloads the item automatically to a designated file on your computer. Netscape then looks for a suitable helper application to launch the file. You can also download a file by right-clicking on the file and saving it to disk.

- Choose Open File from the File menu. Browse for the name of the file and click OK. (Do not be concerned when the error message displays telling you that you are not connected to a network socket.)
- The Web page will display in the Netscape window without being connected to your Internet service provider.

To Mail a Web Page:

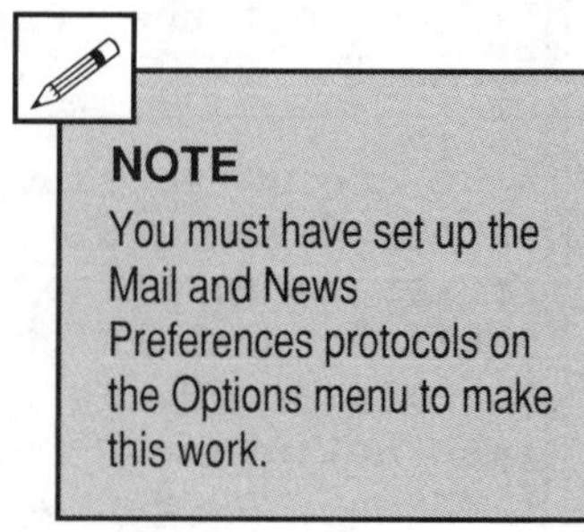

NOTE
You must have set up the Mail and News Preferences protocols on the Options menu to make this work.

- Another way to capture Web pages is to mail it to yourself (or someone else).
  - With the home page displayed on screen select Mail Document from the File menu.

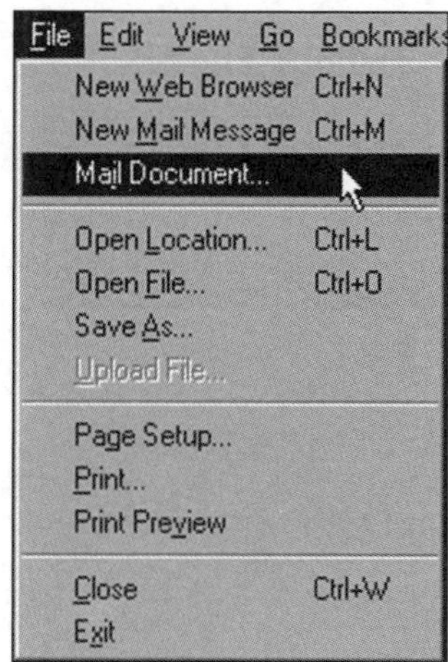

- Complete the Mail To: line with your own e-mail address.

  Note the Subject and Attachment lines are already filled in.

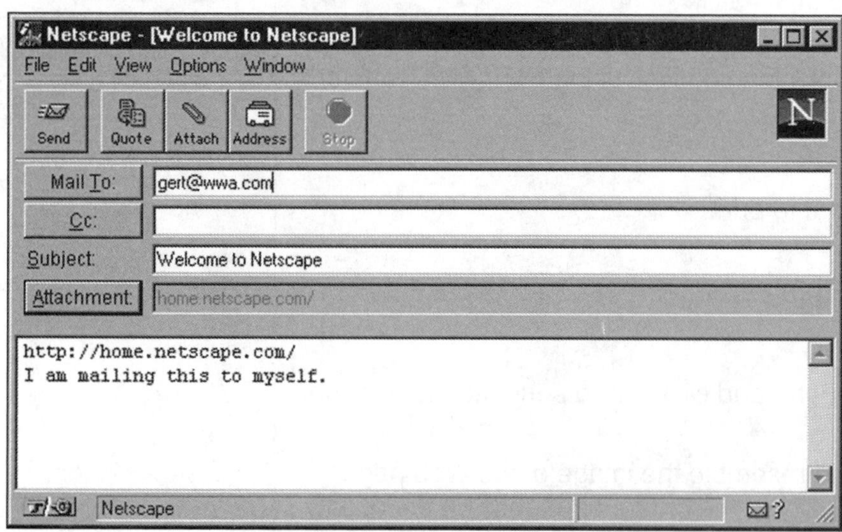

- The URL of the displayed home page displays in the bottom window. You can type text in this window.
- Click the Attach button [Attach] on the Toolbar.
- Click the radio button to convert the page to plain text [Convert to Plain Text] and click OK.

- Click the Send button on the Toolbar.

  The text portion of the home page will display with no HTML programming.
- Open your e-mail account and display the message.

In this exercise, you will copy and print text from a Web page and print a page.

NOTE: In this exercise you will use a real Web address.

EXERCISE DIRECTIONS

1. If you are continuing from the previous exercise, go to step 2.

   OR

   Connect to your service provider and start Netscape Navigator.
2. Connect to the ***careerpath.com*** home page by keying the following URL in the location box and pressing Enter:

   http://www.careerpath.com
3. Scroll down, highlight the first paragraph, and do the following:
   - Select Copy from the Edit menu.
   - Click the Minimize button in the top right corner of the screen to reduce Netscape to a desktop icon.
   - Open a Notepad document.
     ✓ *If you are using the Internet Simulation, select the Shortcut to Notepad.exe icon on the desktop .*
   - Select Paste from the Edit menu.
4. Select Print from the File menu to print the Notepad document.
5. Select the Netscape icon on the desktop to move back to the ***careerpath.com*** home page.
6. Click the Print button on the Toolbar. The Web page should print with all the graphics.
7. Save the **Web** page without images.
8. Exit your browser (by clicking the Close button in the top right corner of the screen) and disconnect from the Internet service provider.
9. Open the **Web** page you saved into Netscape. Do the graphics display?
10. Continue on to the next exercise.

    OR

    Exit from Netscape and disconnect from your service provider.

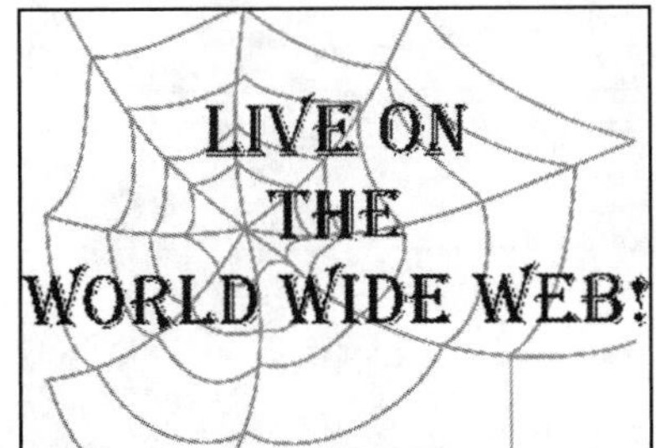

Career Path Home Page – Search newspaper want ads from 19 major cities.
http://www.careerpath.com/

Janus Funds Home Page – makes the investment process less intimidating and more personalized. Compares investing to downhill skiing.
http://janusFUNDS.com

Scudder Home Page – Accesses Scudder's resources on investments; gives information on all major markets on the planet.
http://funds.scudder.com

Maxis Home Page – computer game company. Has links to bulletin boards on the Web to discuss strategy or find teammates. You can also access tips and hints on their games, or get information on upcoming products. There is a link informing teachers how to use classroom-specific version of their games (such as *Sim City*, *Sim Farm*, etc.).
http://www.maxis.com

Exercise 7

◆ Netscape Navigator – Summary Exercise

In this exercise you will practice some of the skills you have learned in this lesson. In completing this exercise, you will acquire a booklet, Guide to the Internet.

EXERCISE DIRECTIONS

1. If you are continuing from the previous exercise, go to step 2.

   OR

   Connect to your service provider and start Netscape Navigator.
2. Enter the following URL (for the Electronic Frontier Foundation) in the Location field:

   http://www.eff.org

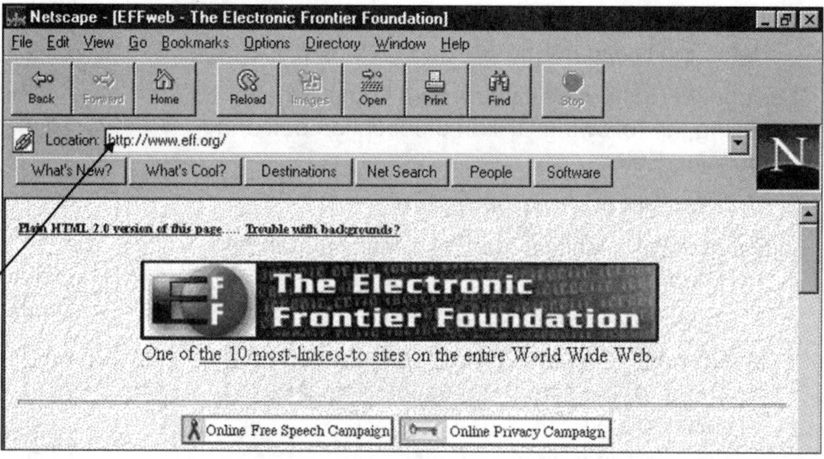

3. Scroll down the page to view the selections available on this page.
4. When you locate the **Net Guide** box under More Info, click on it.

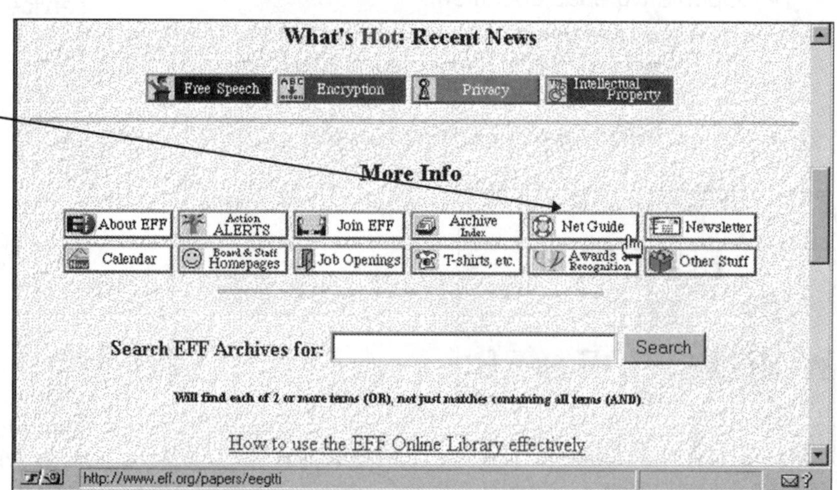

5. When EFF's (Extended) Guide to the Internet displays, scroll down to the link **Get <u>Your Own</u> Copy of the Guide (ASCII Text, English)**.

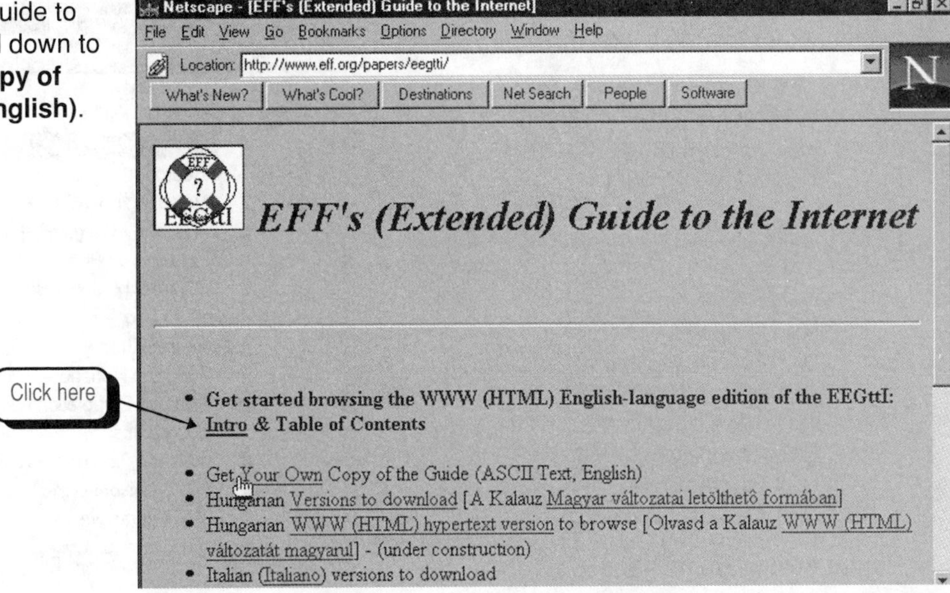

6. Download the file by clicking on the link **<u>Your Own</u>**.
7. Create a Bookmark to point to this page.

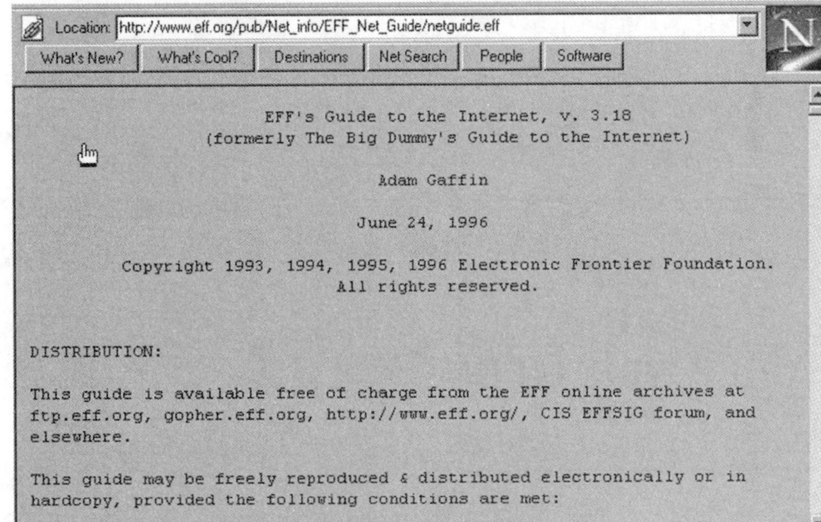

8. Create a folder, **Internet Information**.

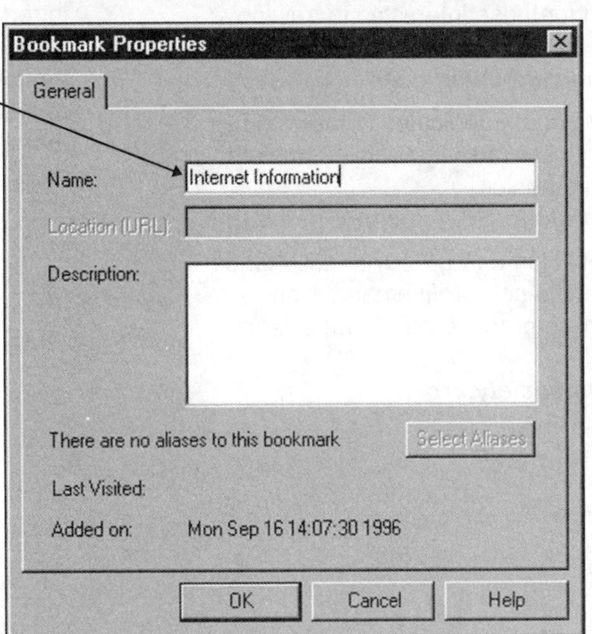

9. Place the new folder over the new bookmark for this Web site.
10. If you'd like to print the guide, click Print on the toolbar. In the Pages dialog box, select a range of pages that you would like to print.

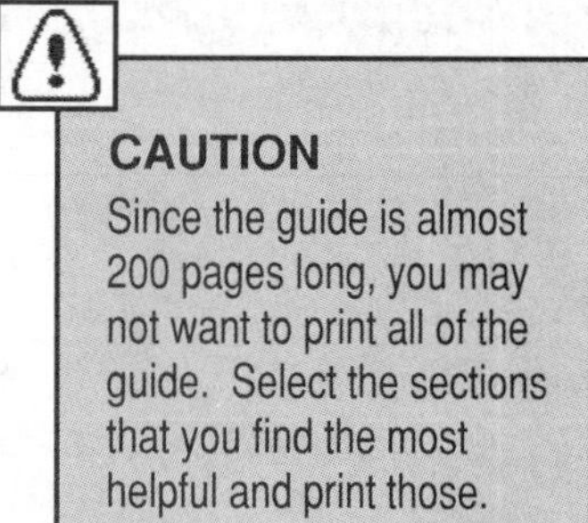

CAUTION
Since the guide is almost 200 pages long, you may not want to print all of the guide. Select the sections that you find the most helpful and print those.

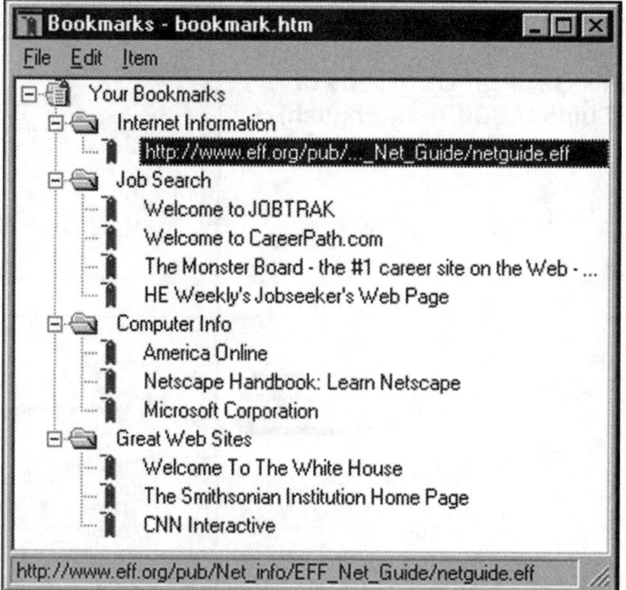

11. Return to your Home page.
12. Continue on to the next exercise.

    OR

    Exit from Netscape and disconnect from your service provider.

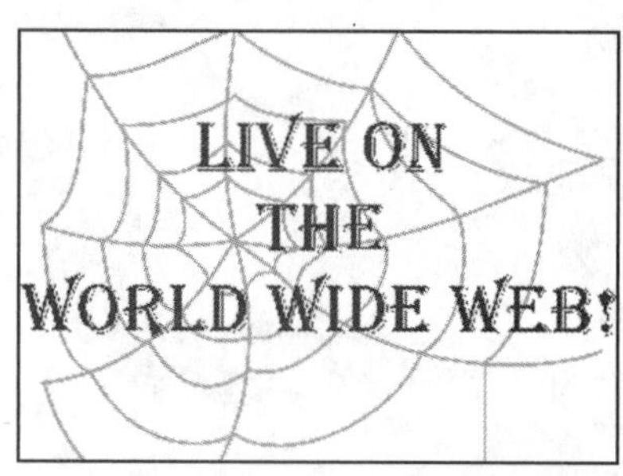

Rocky Mountain Snowboard Camp – registration and site information for those interested in training during the summer.
http://www.rockysnocamp.com

The Volcanic Home Page – dedicated to the world-wide study of volcanic activity using computers. Lots of volcano graphics.
http://www.aist.go.jp/GSJ/~jdehn/v-home.htm

The Dinosaur Society Home Page – Web site of the Dinosaur Society, a non-profit organization dedicated to giving grants for dinosaur science research.
http://www.dinosociety.org

Akiko on the Planet Smoo Home Page – an introduction to Akiko, a 4th–grader who has wondrous adventures in outer space. This beautifully drawn comic book, originally conceived to teach English to Japanese youngsters, is fun for all age groups.
http://www.insv.com/sirius/akiko.html

Lesson 2:
Microsoft Internet Explorer

Exercise 1

- Internet Explorer Screen
- Opening Screen (Home Page/Start Page)
- Toolbars
- Getting Help

Exercise 2

- Internet Explorer Toolbar
- Open World Wide Web Sites
- Back and Forward
- Stop a Search
- Return to Your Home Page

Exercise 3

- Open and Add to the Favorites Folder
- Open Web Sites from the Favorites Folder
- Organize Favorites Folders
- Create New Folders

Exercise 4

- Create a Shortcut to a Web Site on the Desktop
- Change Font Size and Appearance

Exercise 5

- History vs. Favorites
- Print/Copy/Save Web Pages

Exercise 6

- Change Your Start Page
- Customize Links

Exercise 7

- Internet Explorer – Summary Exercise

Exercise 1

◆ Internet Explorer Screen ◆ Opening Screen (Home Page/Start Page) ◆ Toolbars ◆ Getting Help

NOTES

About Microsoft® Internet Explorer

- When you connect to the World Wide Web using Internet Explorer, the first screen that displays is called a Home page. The term home page can be misleading since the first page of any World Wide Web site is called a home page. This first page is sometimes referred to as the Start page. You could think of the Home/Start page as the starting point of your trip on the Information Highway. Just as you can get on a highway using any number of on ramps, you can get on the Internet at different starting points.
- You can change (customize) the first page that you see when you connect to the Internet. You will learn how to change the opening page in Exercise 6.

  ✓ *The page that you see when you are connected may be different from the one illustrated below.*

Parts of Internet Explorer Screen

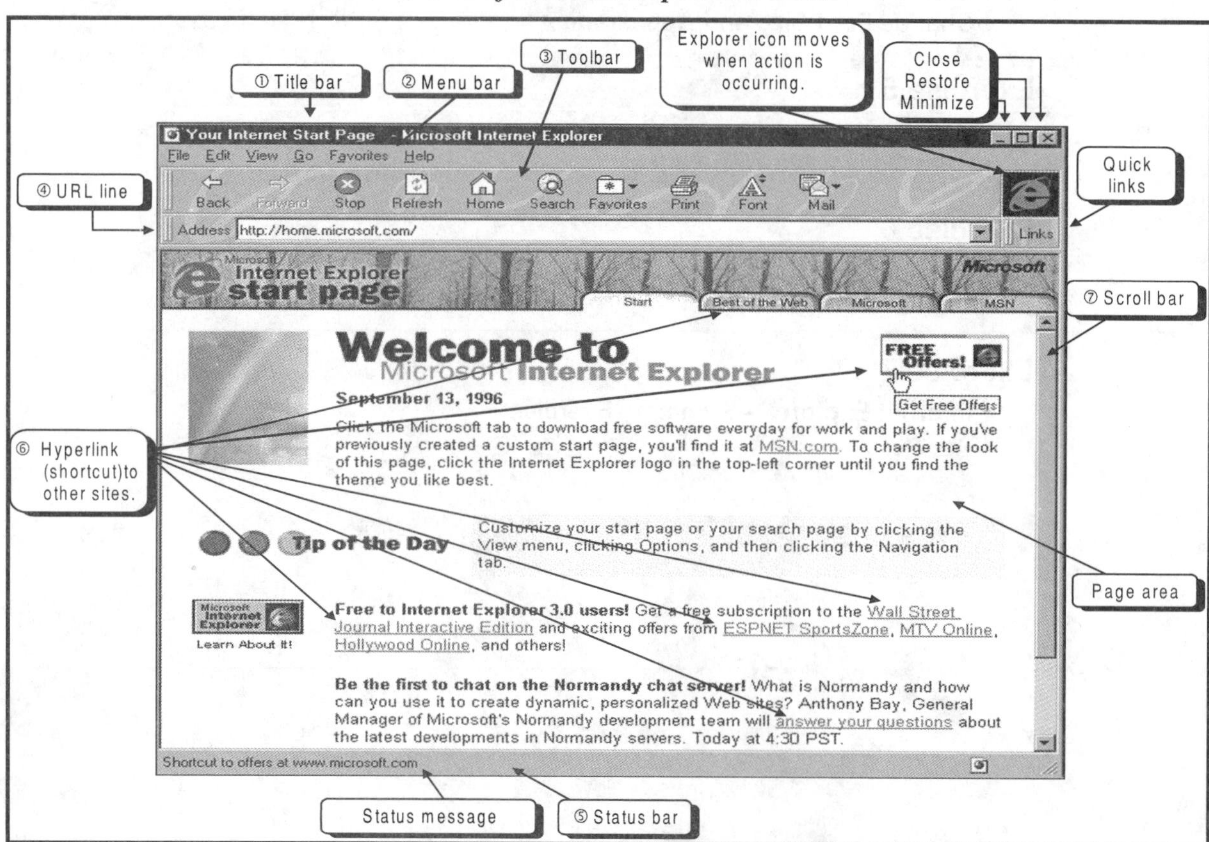

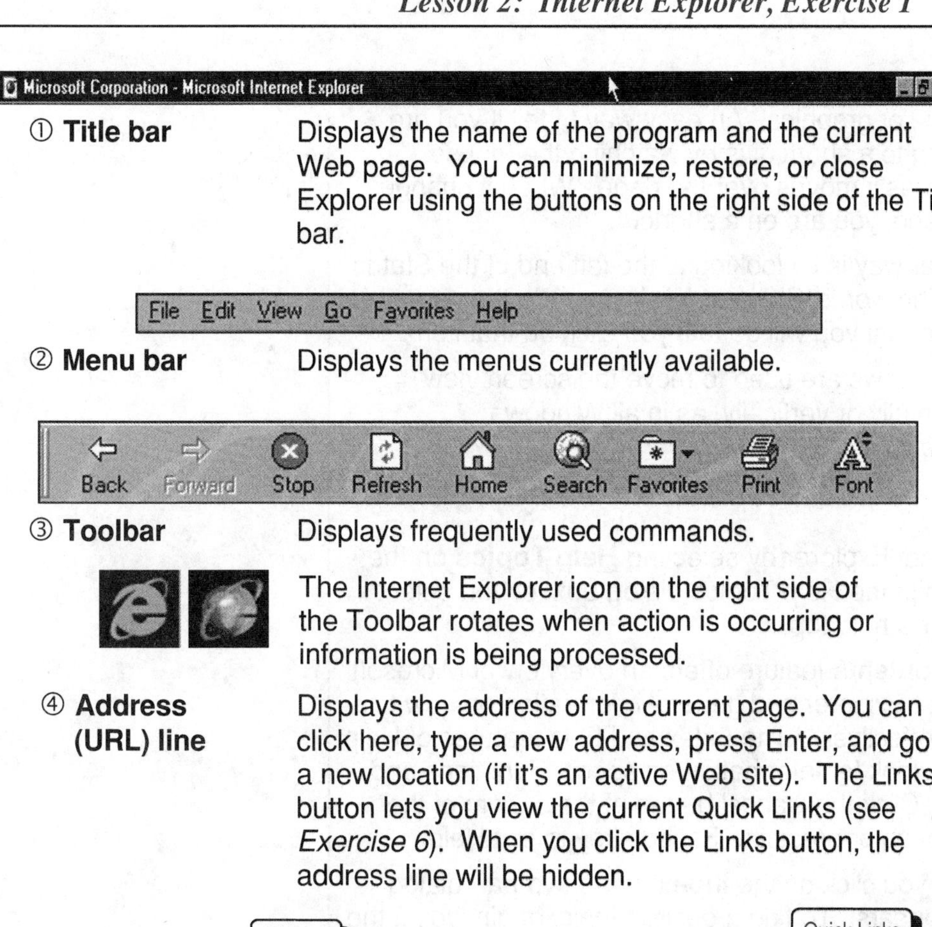

① **Title bar** — Displays the name of the program and the current Web page. You can minimize, restore, or close Explorer using the buttons on the right side of the Title bar.

② **Menu bar** — Displays the menus currently available.

③ **Toolbar** — Displays frequently used commands.

The Internet Explorer icon on the right side of the Toolbar rotates when action is occurring or information is being processed.

④ **Address (URL) line** — Displays the address of the current page. You can click here, type a new address, press Enter, and go to a new location (if it's an active Web site). The Links button lets you view the current Quick Links (see *Exercise 6*). When you click the Links button, the address line will be hidden.

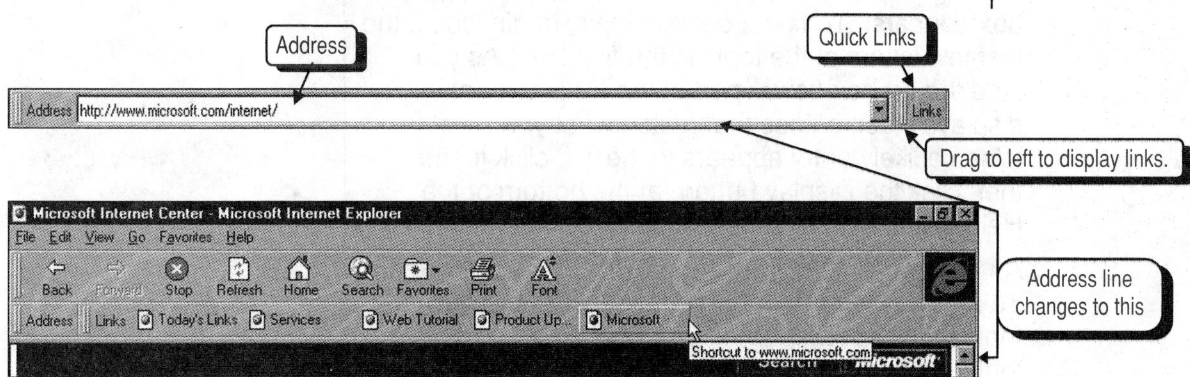

Just click on Links again to restore the address line. Note that the Links button has moved to the left side of the address bar. You can also drag the split bar, next to the Links button, to the left so that the Links and the Address line will both display. Dragging down displays both lines fully.

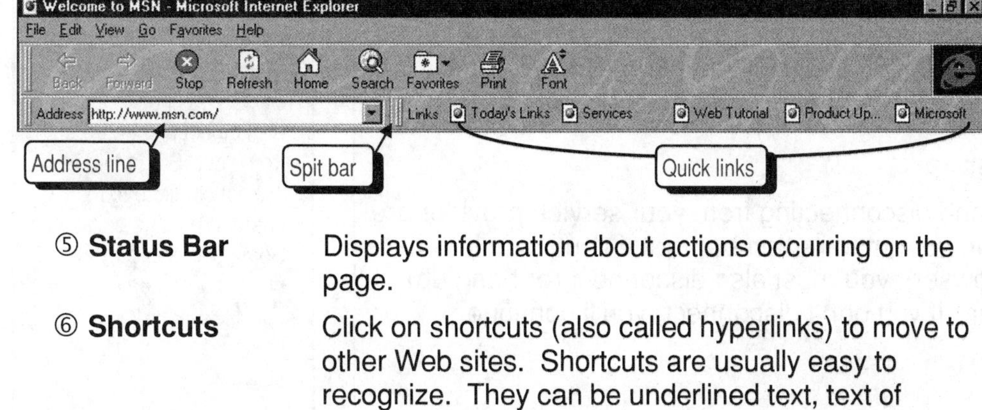

⑤ **Status Bar** — Displays information about actions occurring on the page.

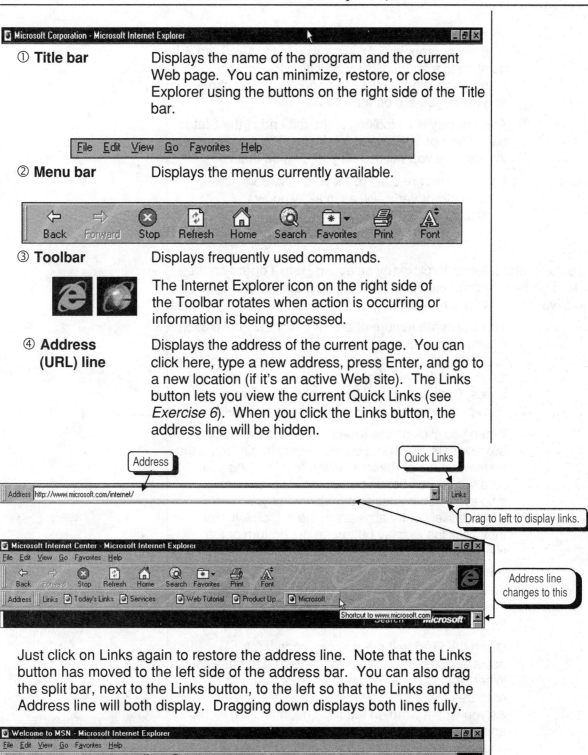

⑥ **Shortcuts** — Click on shortcuts (also called hyperlinks) to move to other Web sites. Shortcuts are usually easy to recognize. They can be underlined text, text of different colors, "buttons" of a various sizes and shapes, or graphics. An easy way to tell if you are pointing to a shortcut is by watching the mouse pointer as it moves over the page. When it changes to a hand, you are on a shortcut.

Another way is by looking at the left end of the Status bar. The words *Shortcut to* will precede the name of the site that you will go to if you click on that item.

⑦ **Scroll Bars** Scroll arrows are used to move the screen view horizontally or vertically, as in all Windows applications.

Getting Help

- You can get help with Internet Explorer by selecting **Help Topics** on the **Help** menu. The three tabs in the Help Topics dialog box let you select the way you want to look for a help topic.

Contents The **Contents** feature offers an overview of Microsoft Internet Explorer and general information on how to use it effectively. The Index and Find features of Help let you look for information on specific functions and topics. Click the Cancel button at the bottom of the Help page or press the Escape key to exit Help.

Index When you click on the **Index** tab, a two-part dialog box appears. To find a desired topic, begin typing the first few letters of the topic in the first line. As you type the list box (lower part of the Help screen) displays index entries that match what you type. When a likely entry appears in the list, click it and then click the Display button (at the bottom of the Help dialog box) or simply double-click the entry.

An additional dialog box appears with a list of topics. To display the full topic description, click the desired topic then click Display or simply double-click the topic.

Find Using the **Find** feature, you can search for occurrences of a word within the Help database itself. When you click the Find tab, Internet Explorer prepares a word list then displays a three-part screen. As you type a word on the first line, matching words appear in the second box and appropriate topics appear in the third. Click the topic and then the Display button or simply double-click the desired topic.

CAUTION

When you exit Internet Explorer, you do not necessarily exit from your Internet service provider. Be sure to check the disconnect procedure from your ISP so that you will not continue to be charged for time online. Some services do disconnect when a specific amount of time has passed with no activity.

Exiting Internet Explorer

- Exiting Internet Explorer and disconnecting from your service provider are two separate steps. It is important to remember that if you close Internet Explorer (or any other browser), you must also disconnect (or hang up) from your service provider. If you don't disconnect, you'll continue incurring charges.

In this exercise, you will examine an Internet Explorer page and access the Help feature.

EXERCISE DIRECTIONS

1. Start Internet Explorer and be sure you are connected to your service provider.
2. Use the scroll bar or scroll arrows to move up and down the current Web page.
3. Point to the File menu and click once to open it.
4. Notice the options available on the File menu.
5. Move the mouse pointer over the other menus and note the options on each menu.
6. Press Esc to close any open menu.
7. Look at the Title bar and make a note of the name of the current Web page.

   Microsoft Internet Explorer *will follow the name of the current page.*
8. Click the Minimize icon to reduce Explorer to a button on the task bar.

   You may notice that a modem symbol 12:40 PM *on the taskbar indicates that you are connected to the Internet. You may also have a dialog box on the desktop, indicating how you are connected to the Internet, for example:*

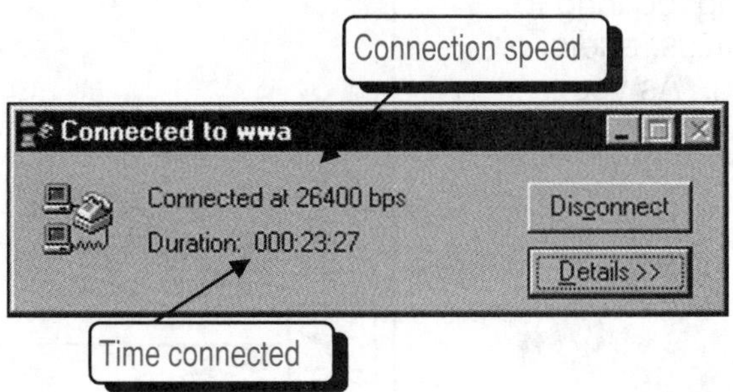

9. Locate the minimized Web page on the taskbar and click to restore it.
10. Click on the Help menu and do the following:
    - Click Help Topics.
    - Click Index tab.
    - Type *home*. (The highlight should move to the *home page*.
    - Click the Display button.
    - Click Changing your start page.
    - Click Display and note the steps that will let you change your start page.
    - Close the Help topic.
11. Click the Help menu again and select Web Tutorial.
12. Move your pointer over several elements on the page and notice the message that appears on the status line.
13. Point to the icon  next to **Introduction**.

14. Click Home on the Toolbar to return to your start page.
15. Continue on to the next exercise.

    OR

    Exit from Internet Explorer and disconnect from your service provider.

Exercise 2

◆ Internet Explorer Toolbar ◆ Open World Wide Web Sites ◆ Back and Forward ◆ Stop a Search ◆ Return to Your Home Page

NOTES

Internet Explorer Toolbar

- The **Internet Explorer Toolbar** displays frequently used commands. If the Toolbar is *not* visible when you start Explorer, open the View menu and select Toolbar.

Returns you to the previously viewed Web page.

Takes you to the next page.

✓ *These buttons are only available if you have moved back and forth on Web pages.*

Interrupts the opening of a page that is taking too long to display. Some pages are so filled with graphics, audio, or video clips that some delay can be expected. As you work with Web sites, you will develop a sense of when a search is taking too long.

Reloads the current page.

Returns you to your Home Page.

Takes you to Search programs that are available to you. This is where you can start looking for information that you don't have an address for. You will learn how to create effective searches as you go through the exercises in this book.

Lets you store and organize the Web sites that you want to visit again.

Takes you to the Print dialog box.

Increase or decrease the size of the font that displays on your screen.

TIP

You can change your Home (start) page. See Exercise 6.

TIP

You can also change the size of the font on screen by selecting Fonts on the View menu and choosing desired font size.

Open a World Wide Web Site

- There are a number of different ways to open World Wide Web sites:
  - Type the address in the address line and then press Enter.
  - Click Back/Forward to return to Web sites visited in the current session.
  - Select File, Open, enter the address, and click OK.

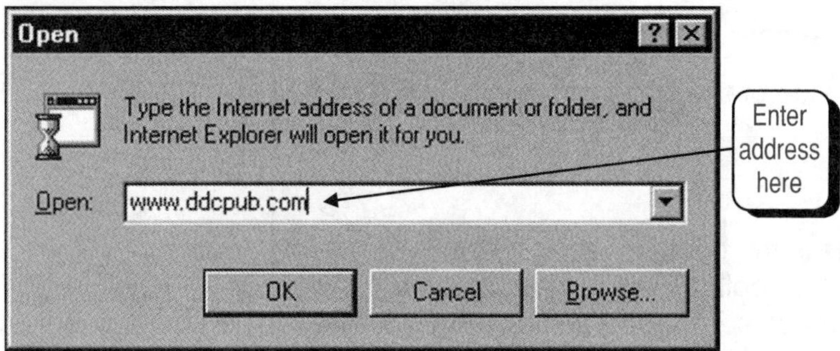

  - Use a Search engine (see Lesson 3, exercises 1-11) to locate a Web site and click the hyperlink (shortcut) to take you there.
  - Open your Favorites folder (or the Favorites menu) and select a site.

    ✓ *You must set up a list of your favorite sites. See Exercise 3.*

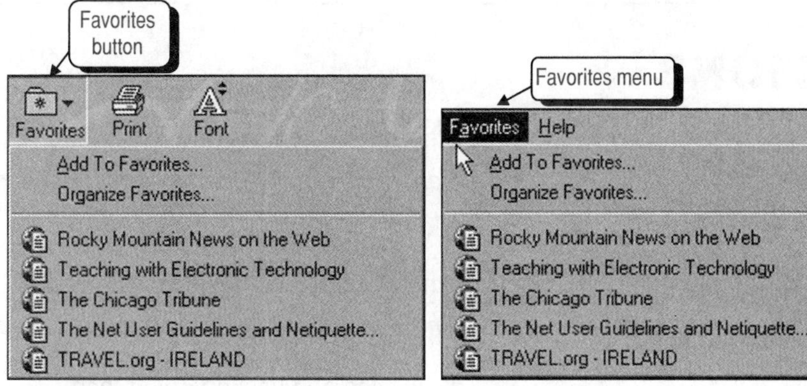

Back and Forward

- **Back** and **Forward** are quick ways to return to sites that you have visited in the current session. The Back and Forward buttons are dimmed when you first open Internet Explorer since you have not yet opened any Web sites during that session.

Stop a Search

- The length of time a page takes to open depends on the speed of your modem, the amount of graphics on the page you're opening, and the speed of your computer. As you gain more experience exploring Web sites, you will develop a sense of how long it takes for a page to open. If you want to interrupt the downloading of a page, click the **Stop** button [Stop]. Even if you stop a search, you may be able to still navigate the site if all the text has been downloaded.

To open a Web site, do one of the following

- Type the address in the address line and then press **Enter**.

  OR
- Click **Back/Forward** to return to Web sites visited in the current session.

  OR
- Select **File**, **Open**, enter the address, and click **OK**.

  OR
- Use a Search engine (see Lesson 3, exercises 1-11) to locate a Web site and click the hyperlink to take you there.

  OR
- Open your Favorites folder (or the Favorites menu) and select a site.

TIP

You can keep clicking the Back button until you return to your Home page. If you have visited several sites and want to return to Home quickly, click the Home button; otherwise, it will take you a long time to return to your Home page.

HINT

Watch the status bar as you're loading a new page. If you detect that the site doesn't exist, you can click Stop to halt the search

- You will receive a variety of messages and signals as a Page downloads on your computer.
  - The Status bar will tell you what is currently happening.

    Finding site: www.ddcpub.com

  - Images will start to "grow" on screen.
  - Placeholders for graphics will appear.
  - The status indicator on the right side of the status bar will indicate how much of the page is downloaded.

Return to your Home Page

- As you have learned, a Home page is the opening page of any Web site. When you click the Home icon on the Toolbar, you will return to your Home, or Start, page, the page that you see when you first start Internet Explorer. You can also return to your Home page by selecting Start Page on the Go menu.

In this exercise, you will use some of the navigational tools of Internet Explorer to open Web sites, interrupt searches, and get back to your Start Page.

EXERCISE DIRECTIONS

1. If you are already connected to your service provider and Internet Explorer is open, go to step 2.

   OR

   Connect to your service provider and start Internet Explorer.
2. Open the File menu and select Open.
3. On the Address line, type the following and press Enter:

   http://www.ddcpub.com/learn
4. Click the link to **Lesson 2: Internet Explorer, Exercise 2 "White House"**.

   The White House opening page appears.
5. Move your pointer over the page and note how it changes to a hand when it is over a hyperlink.
6. Find the link to **White House Help Desk** and click once on it.
7. Note the screen you are now on.

   Caution: Do not click on any links. Because this page is simulated, you will not go to another site.
8. Note that the Back button is now darkened.

   ✓ *The Forward button is probably dimmed at this point if you have not opened other Web sites and backed out of them.*
9. Scroll down and click the **Frequently Asked Questions** link.
   - Scroll down the page and find the link that says **link to all online resources**. Click once on the link.
   - Click the Back button twice and note the screen you are now on.
   - Click the Forward button once and note the page you are now on.

10. Click the Home icon on the Toolbar to return to your Start Page.

    ✓ *Note that the Back button is still available, but the Forward button is dimmed. If you click Back now, you will return to the Page you just left.*

11. Open the Go menu and note that you have a list of the last five pages you visited.
12. Click Welcome To The White House.
13. Now open the Go menu and click Start Page.

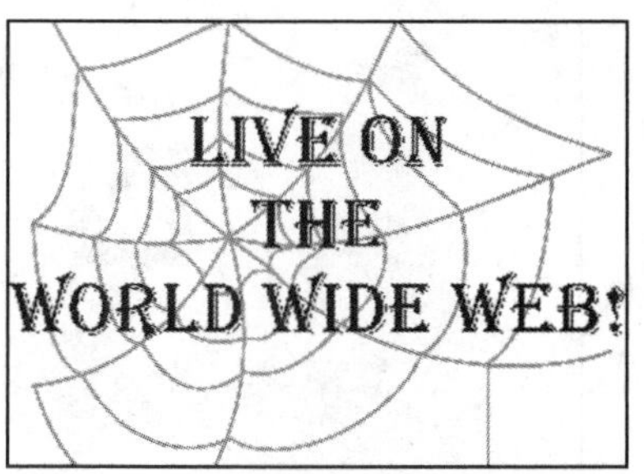

Internet Explorer Home Page
http://www.microsoft.com/ie

Microsoft Corporation Home Page
http://www.microsoft.com

The White House Home Page
http://www.whitehouse.gov

The Smithsonian Instituition Home Page
http://www.si.edu

14. Open the File menu, select Open, and do the following:
    - Type the following on the Address line and then press Enter.

      http://www.ddcpub.com/learn
    - Click the link to **Lesson 2: Internet Explorer, Exercise 2 "NASA"**.
    - Let the page start to load, but then click the Stop button before the page is fully downloaded.
    - Scroll down the page and note the symbol that indicates a graphic. You may see several of these on the page, depending on how quickly you clicked Stop.
15. Click the Home icon to return to your Start page.
16. Continue on to the next exercise.

    OR

    Exit from Internet Explorer and disconnect from your service provider.

Exercise 3

- ◆ Open and Add to the Favorites Folder
- ◆ Open Web Sites from the Favorites Folder
- ◆ Organize Favorites Folders
- ◆ Create New Folders

NOTES

Open and Add to the Favorites Folder

- As you spend more time exploring Web sites, you will find sites that you want to visit frequently. You can store the addresses of your favorite Web sites in Internet Explorer's Favorites folder.
- To add a site to the Favorites folder, first open the desired Web site.

  Then click the Favorites icon on the Toolbar and click Add To Favorites.

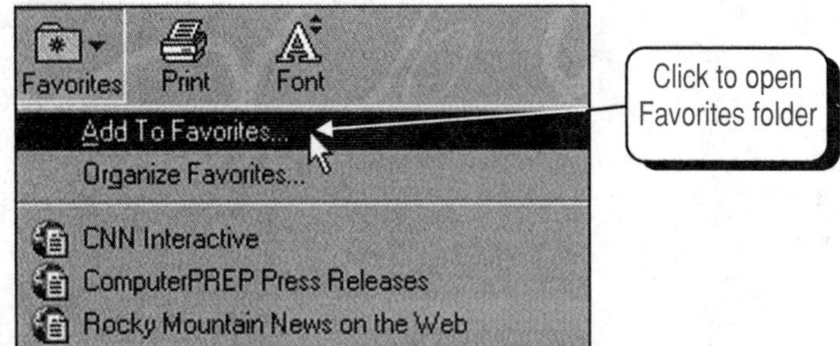

- The following dialog box appears when you open Add to Favorites.

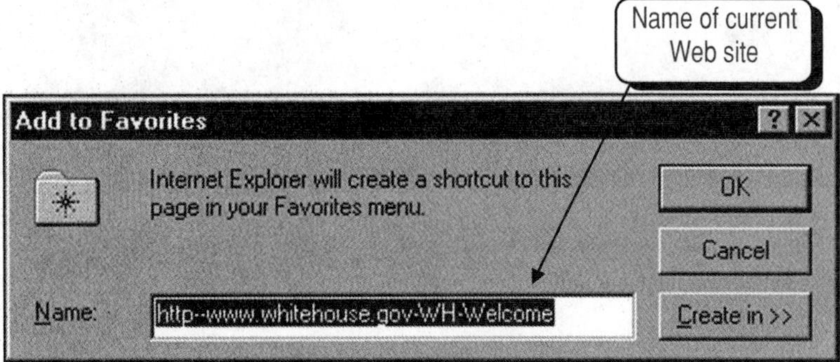

- The name of the Page you have opened appears in the Name box. Click OK to add the Web address to the Favorites folder.

  ✓ *You can also click Favorites on the menu bar and click Add To Favorites.*

Open Web Sites

- To open Web sites from the Favorites folder, Click favorites icon (or click Favorites menu) and select desired site.

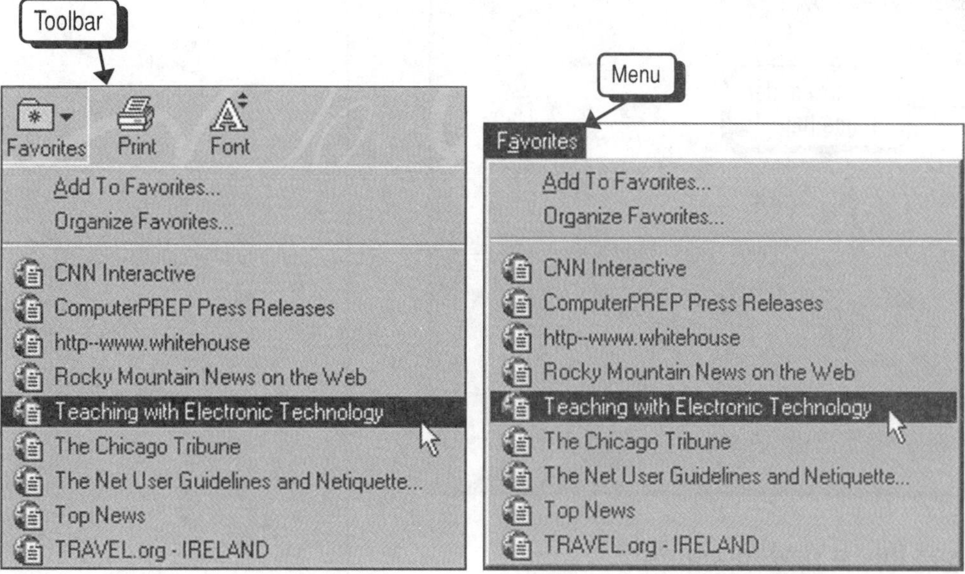

Organize Favorites Folder

- It won't take long for your Favorites folder to grow quite long. You will probably eliminate some of the addresses that you're no longer interested in, and the ones that you want to keep can be arranged to suit your needs. Just as you create folders for your word processing, spreadsheet, and other files, you can create folders for the Web addresses that you want to keep.

Create New Folders

- You can create new folders before or after you have saved addresses in your Favorites folder.

  To create new folders:

  - Click the Favorites icon and select Organize Favorites.
  - Click the Create New Folder button.

To create new folders

- Click the Favorites icon and select **Organize Favorites.**
- Click the **Create New Folder** button, type the name of the folder and press **Enter**.

- Type the name of the new folder and press Enter.

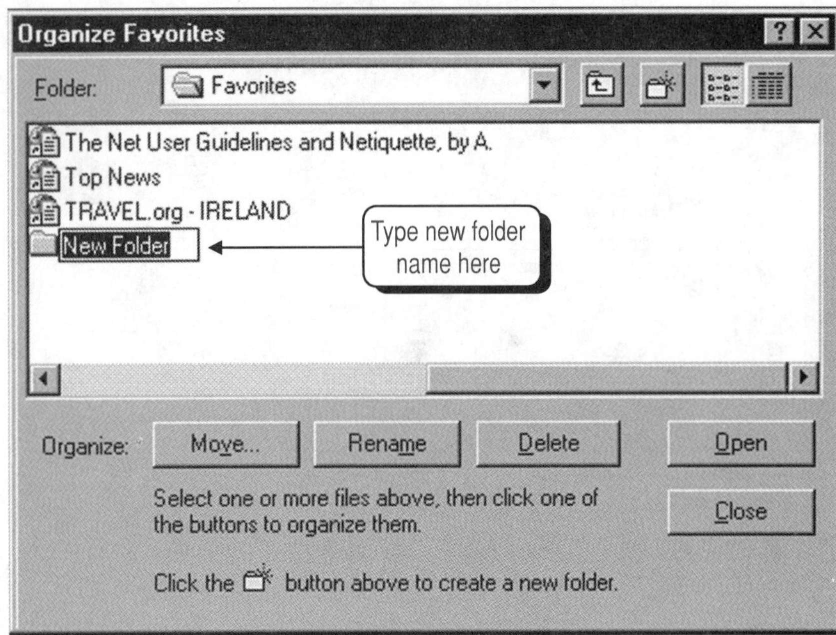

To move existing addresses into a new location:

- Open the Organize Favorites dialog box.
- Click once on the Web site to highlight it.
- Hold down the left mouse button and drag the highlighted Web site to the desired folder.

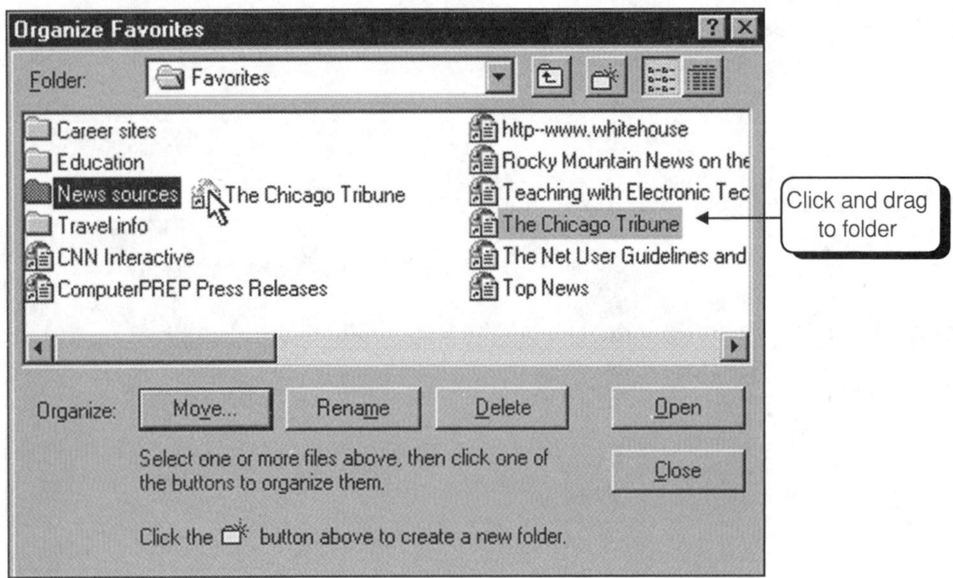

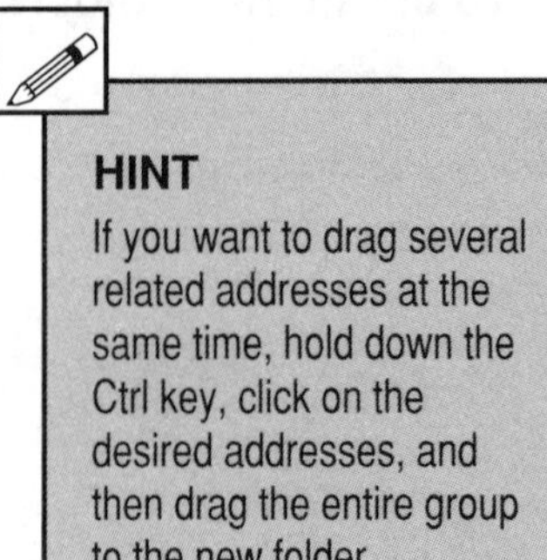

HINT

If you want to drag several related addresses at the same time, hold down the Ctrl key, click on the desired addresses, and then drag the entire group to the new folder.

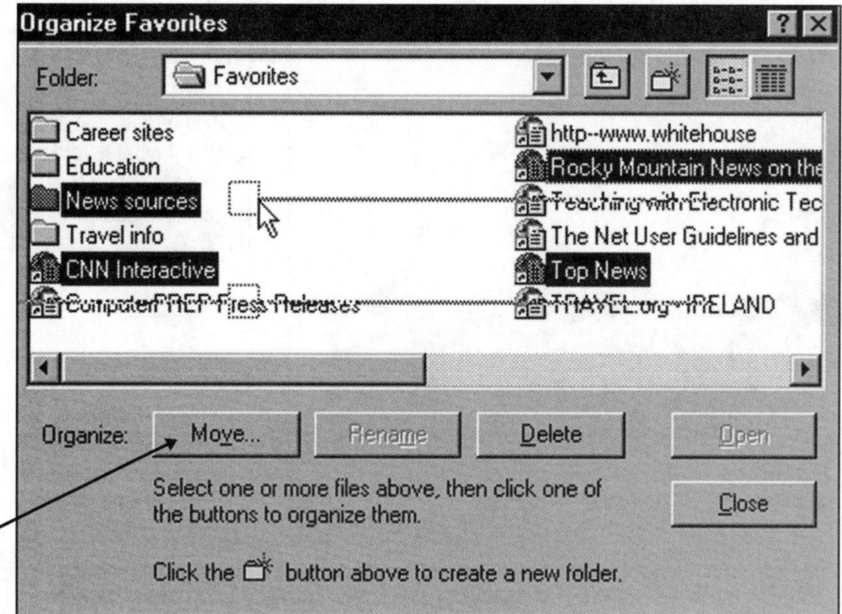

OR

- Open the Organize Favorites folder.
- Select desired address(es) to move.
- Click Move to open the Browse for Folder dialog box.
- Click desired location for the addresses that you want to move.
- Click OK.

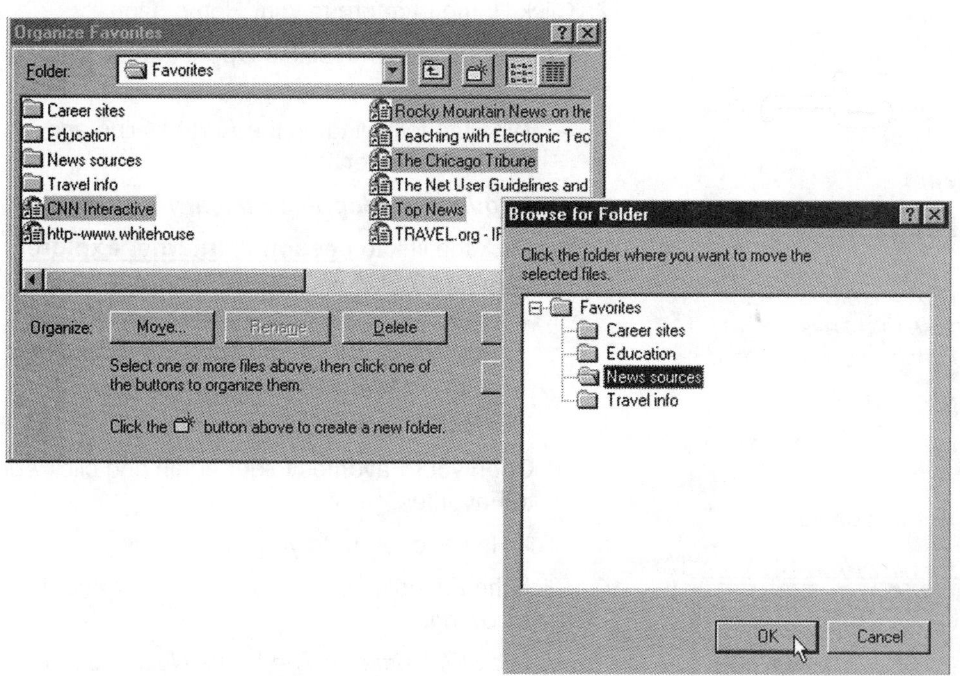

✓ *The address names will be grayed for a few moments as the move is completed.*

To move existing addresses into a new location

- Open the **Organize Favorites** dialog box.
- Click once on the Web site to highlight it.
- Drag it to the desired location.

OR

- Open the **Organize Favorites** folder.
- Select desired address(es) to move.
- Click **Move** button to open the **Browse for Folder** dialog box.
- Click desired folder for the addresses that you want to move.
- Click **OK**.

- When you open the Favorites menu, move the cursor to the new folder to display the addresses in their new location.

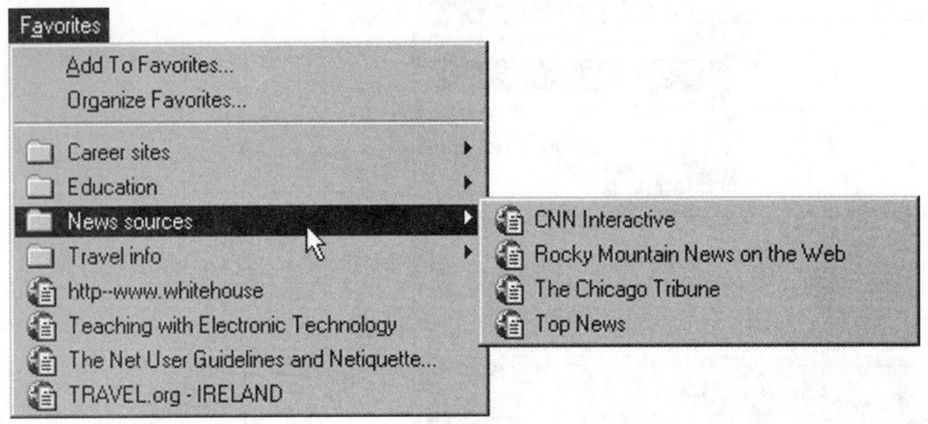

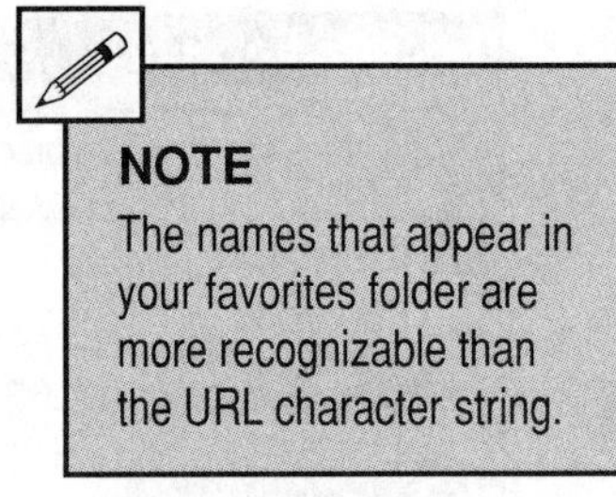

NOTE

The names that appear in your favorites folder are more recognizable than the URL character string.

In this exercise, you will add Web addresses to your Favorites folder, create new folders, and move and delete addresses.

EXERCISE DIRECTIONS

1. If you are continuing from the previous exercise, go to step 2.

   OR

   Connect to your service provider and start Internet Explorer.
2. Open the File menu and select Open.
3. On the Address line, type the following and press Enter:

   http://www.ddcpub.com/learn
4. Click the link to **Lesson 2: Internet Explorer, Exercise 2 "White House"**.

   ✓ *Even though you are in Exercise 3, select the link to the White House that says Exercise 2. It is the site where you should be.*

   The White House opening page appears.
5. Open Favorites on the menu and click Add to Favorites.

   You should see something like this on your screen:

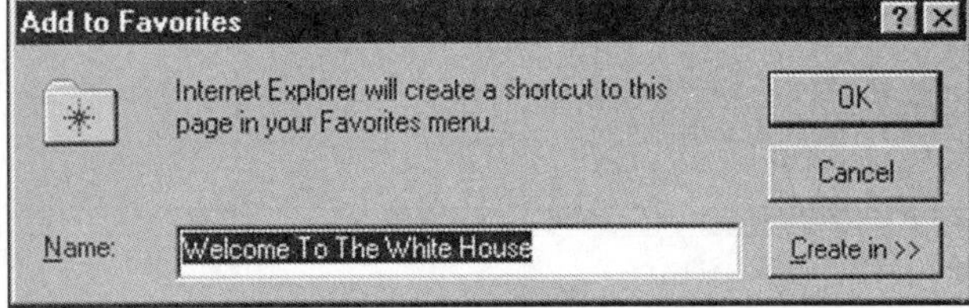

6. Click OK to add this site to your Favorites folder.

   ✓ *Note that the entry on the line is not the URL address you entered in the File, Open dialog box.*
7. Click Home to return to your Home page.
8. Open the File menu, select Open, and do the following:
   - Type the following on the Address line and then press Enter.

     http://www.ddcpub.com/learn
   - Click the link to **Lesson 2: Internet Explorer, Exercise 2 "NASA"**.

     ✓ *Even though you are in Exercise 3, select the link to NASA that says Exercise 2. It is the site where you should be.*

     The NASA opening page appears.
   - Open your Favorites folder again and click Add to Favorites.
9. Click Home to return to your Start Page.
10. Click the Favorites button on the toolbar and do the following:
    - Click *Welcome To The White House* to return to the first page of the White House Web site.
    - Scroll down the page and click on **The White House Help Desk**.
    - Open the Favorites on the menu and add The White House Help Desk page to your Favorites.

✓ *Note that you can add any page to the Favorites folder, not just the opening page.*

11. Click the Back button to return to your Start page.
12. Click the Favorites folder and click Organize Favorites. Do the following:
    - In the Organize Favorites dialog box, click the New Folder button.

    ✓ *If you accidentally click the icon that takes you up to a different site, click Close and start the procedure over.*

    - Name the new folder Education and press Enter.
    - Click the Close button.
    - Reopen the Favorites menu and note that the folder you just created is listed on the menu.
13. Select Organize Favorites and do the following:
    - Hold down the Ctrl key while you click on these addresses:
      The NASA Homepage
      Welcome To The White House
      The White House Help Desk
    - Release the Ctrl key, point to one of the highlighted addresses, click, and drag to the Education folder. Release the mouse when the Education folder is highlighted.
    - Click Close to close the Organize Favorites dialog box.
14. Click Favorites (menu or icon),point to the Education folder and do the following:
    - Click on NASA Homepage.
    - Click the Back button on the toolbar to return to the Start Page.
    - Click the Favorites button and select Organize Favorites.
    - Open the Education folder.
    - Click once on The White House Help Desk.
    - Press Delete and click Yes when asked if you want to send this address to the Recyle Bin.
    - Click the Close button.
15. Continue on to the next exercise.

    OR

    Exit from Internet Explorer and disconnect from your service provider.

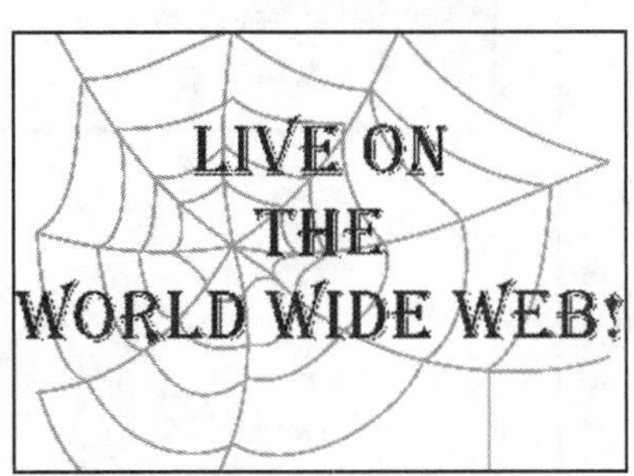

The White House Home Page
http://www.whitehouse.gov

The NASA Home Page
http://nasa.gov

The Vanguard Group Home Page
http://www.vanguard.com

Kemper Money Fund Home Page
http://www.kempercash.com

Seiko Epson Corporation Home Page – site for the Epson company.
http://www.epson.com

Exercise 4

◆ Create a Shortcut to a Web site on the Desktop
◆ Change Font Size and Appearance

NOTES

Create a Shortcut to a Web Site on the Desktop

- To create a shortcut to a Web site that you want to access quickly and frequently, open the desired Web site and then:
  - *Right-click* on the desired Web site.

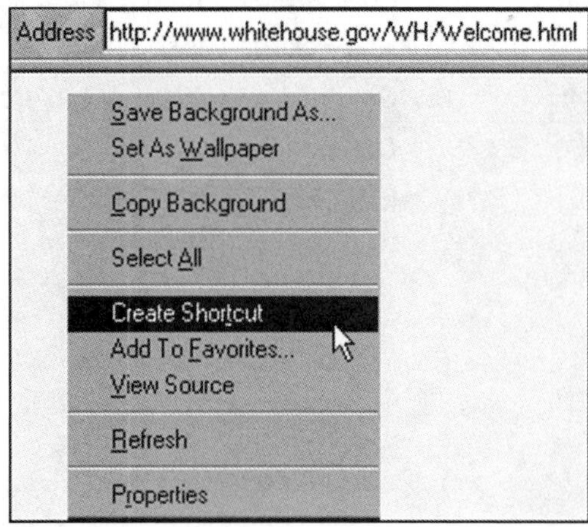

  - Click Create Shortcut.

    The following message shown in the illustration below appears.
  - Click OK to place a shortcut to the desired Web page on your desktop.

    OR
  - Open the Web site page that you want to create a shortcut for.
  - Open the File menu and select Create Shortcut

    The following message appears:

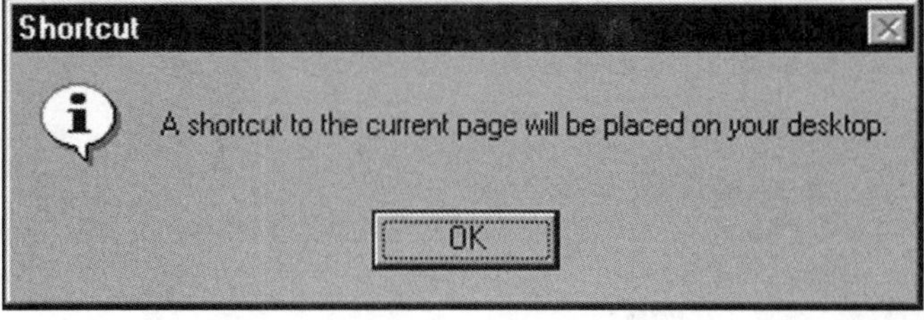

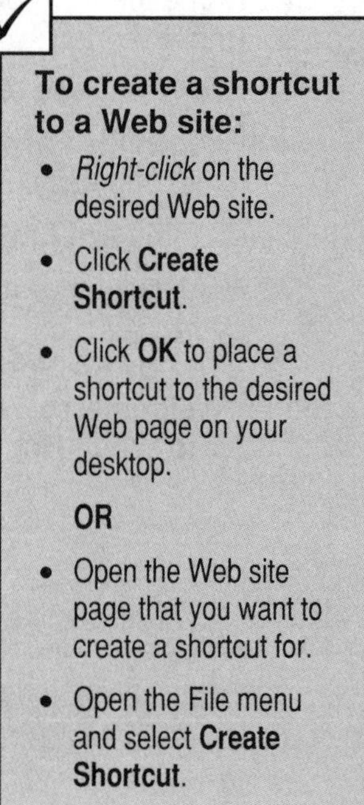

To create a shortcut to a Web site:

- *Right-click* on the desired Web site.
- Click **Create Shortcut**.
- Click **OK** to place a shortcut to the desired Web page on your desktop.

OR

- Open the Web site page that you want to create a shortcut for.
- Open the File menu and select **Create Shortcut**.

To open Web site from shortcut on your desktop:

✓ *Creating shortcuts on the desktop is a feature of Windows 95.*

- Connect to your service provider for the Internet.
- Double-click the shortcut to the desired Web site on your desktop. For example, double-clicking on the icon below, will bring you to the White House site.

Change Font Size and Appearance

Font Size

■ The font size on most Web pages can be increased or decreased by clicking on the Font icon Font. You can also adjust the font size of text on most Web pages by using the View, Fonts command on the menu bar.

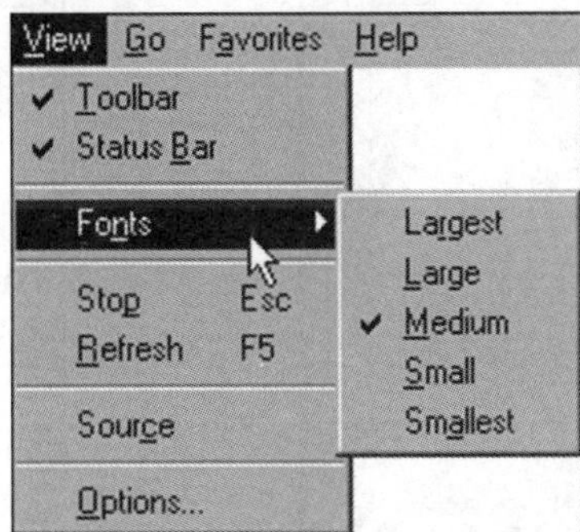

Below are examples of how the font size can be changed:

Smallest

White House Help Desk: Frequently asked questions and answers about our service

Small

White House Help Desk: Frequently asked questions and answers about our service

Medium

White House Help Desk: Frequently asked questions and answers about our service

Large

White House Help Desk: Frequently asked questions and answers about our service

Largest

White House Help Desk: Frequently asked questions and answers about our service

To open Web site from shortcut on your desktop:

- Connect to your service provider for the Internet.
- Double-click the shortcut (site icon) to the desired Web site on your desktop.

NOTE

If you are not connected to your Internet service provider, the page you created a shortcut for will probably appear, but you will not be able to move to another page.

NOTE

You will not be able change the size of text on every Web site.

Font Appearance

- You can also change the font of text on Web pages.

To change the font:

- Click View, Options, General.
- Select Font settings.
- Select desired font options.

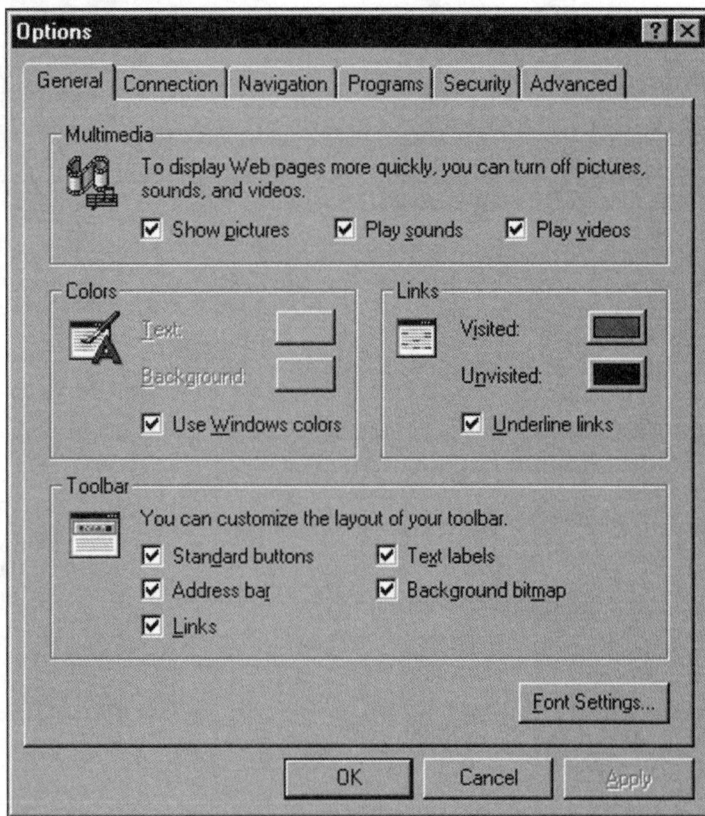

- To change the Proportional (or Fixed-width) font, click the drop-down arrow and select the desired font .

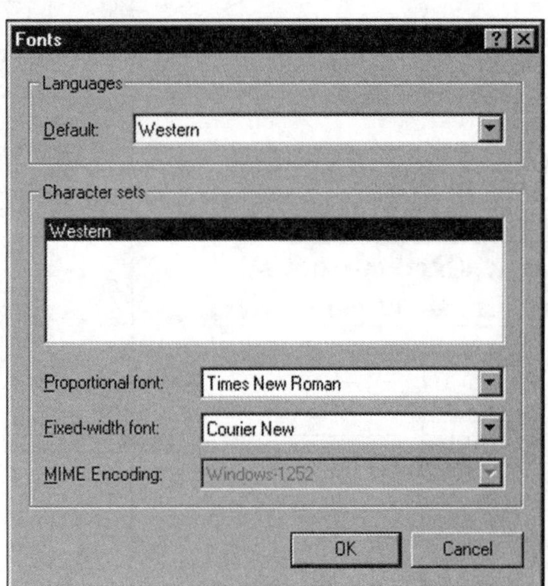

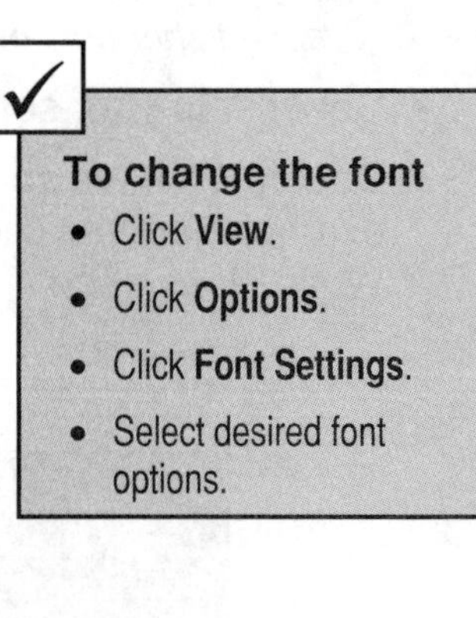

To change the font

- Click **View**.
- Click **Options**.
- Click **Font Settings**.
- Select desired font options.

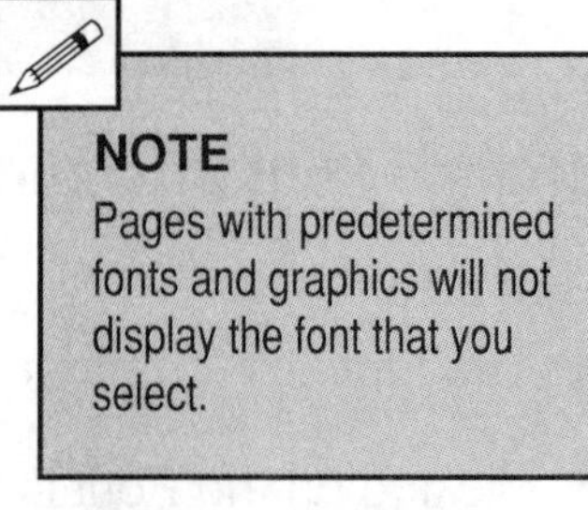

NOTE

Pages with predetermined fonts and graphics will not display the font that you select.

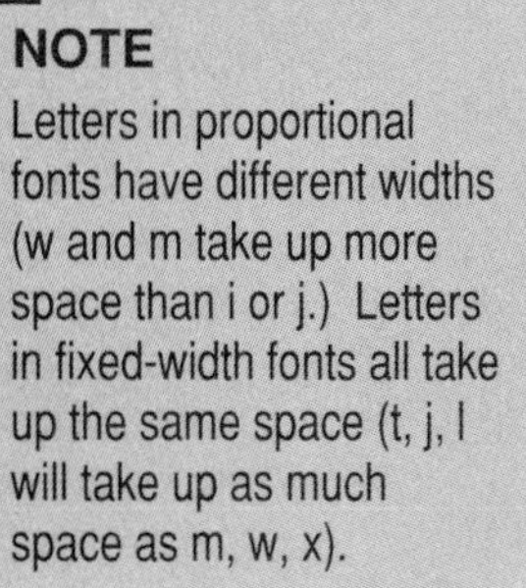

NOTE

Letters in proportional fonts have different widths (w and m take up more space than i or j.) Letters in fixed-width fonts all take up the same space (t, j, l will take up as much space as m, w, x).

Change Display Color(s)

- Internet Explorer uses Windows colors to display the color of the text and background on a page. You can change these colors in the View Options dialog box.

To change the color of the text and background:

- Click View, Options.

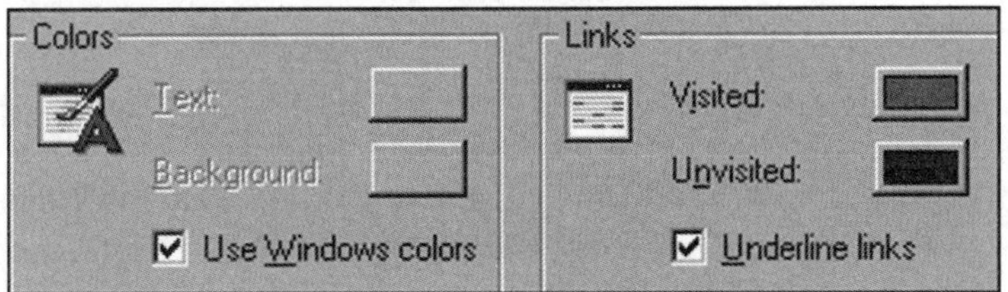

- If there is a checkmark in Use Windows colors, click to deselect it.
- Click Text or Background button.
- Select desired color combination, or click Define Custom Colors>> and create your own color.
- Click OK when desired color is selected.

To change the color of the Links:

- Click View, Options.
- If you do not want Hyperlinks to be underlined, click the checkmark in Underline links to deselect it.
- To change the color of visited or unvisited links, click the appropriate button and select desired color.

  ✓ *A **visited link** is one that you have opened during a session. If you return to the page where the link is displayed, the link will be a different color from the unvisited links. This is a good way to know which links you've already visited.*

To change the color of the text and background

- Click **View**, **Options**.
- If there is a checkmark in **Use Windows** colors, click to deselect it.
- Click **Text** or **Background** button.
- Select desired color combination, or click **Define Custom Colors>>** and create your own color.
- Click **OK** when desired color is selected.

To change the color of the Links

- Click **View, Options**.
- If you do not want Hyperlinks to be underlined, click the checkmark in **Underline links** to deselect it.
- To change the color of visited or unvisited links, click the appropriate button and select desired color.

In this exercise, you will create a shortcut to a Web site, change the font, font size, and color of text.

EXERCISE DIRECTIONS

1. If you are continuing from the previous exercise, go to step 2.

   OR

   Connect to your service provider and start Internet Explorer.

2. Open your Favorites folder and do the following:
   - Open the Education folder.
   - Click on Welcome to the White House.
   - Point to an area of the page that is *not* a hyperlink (the mouse pointer should look like this).

     ✓ *Remember that the mouse pointer will change to a hand if you are pointing to a hyperlink.*
   - Right-click to open the shortcut menu.

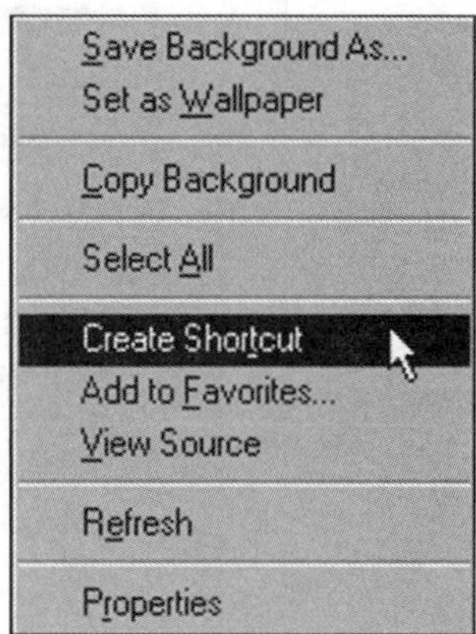

     ✓ *If you've pointed to a hyperlink on this page, you will see a different menu. Click Escape and try again.*
   - Click Create Shortcut.

     The following message should appear.

   - Click OK to place the shortcut on your desktop.

3. Exit Internet Explorer and disconnect from your service provider.

4. Note the shortcut to the White House Web site on your desktop.

5. Double-click on the White House shortcut on your desktop and do the following:
   - If a dialog box appears asking you to connect to your service provider, click Cancel.

     Important: Be sure that you are NOT connected to your service provider.

     The opening page of the White House Web site appears on screen.
   - Scroll down the page and click on the **White House Help Desk** hyperlink.

     Note the message that appears onscreen.

     The shortcut will display the page for which you have created a shortcut, but you will not be able to move any other page on the site. You are not really seeing "live" information.
   - Click OK and close the White House opening page. You should now be on the desktop.

6. Reconnect to your service provider, start Internet Explorer, and click the Minimize button in the upper right of the screen to minimize the screen.

7. Click on the shortcut to **Welcome to the White House**.

8. Scroll down the page and click on the **White House Help Desk** hyperlink. Since you are now connected to the Internet via your Service Provider, you will be able to move to the new page.
9. Click Back to return to the Start Page of the White House Web site and do the following.
   - Scroll down the page and look at the **White House Help Desk** link. Notice that this link has changed. This means that you have visited that site during this session.
   - Open the View menu and click Fonts.
   - Click Largest to see if you can change the font of the text on this page.
   - Click on the Font button [Font] twice and note how the size of the font changes.
   - Click Fonts on the View menu again and note that Medium is selected.
10. Continue on to the next exercise.

    OR

    Exit from Internet Explorer and disconnect from your service provider.

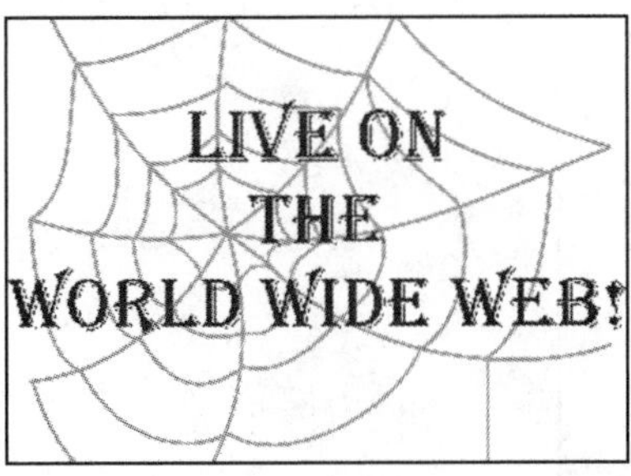

University of Illinois at Urbana/Champaign Home Page
  http://www.uiuc.edu

Department of Education Home Page
  http://www.ed.gov

Wall Street Journal Interactive Edition
  http://wsj.com

New York Stock Exchange Home Page – An educational tool for teachers, students, and investors interested in learning more about the stock market. This site also provides links to the NYSE's news, publishing, educational, research, and tourism services. Click links to access a market summary, an index of listed companies, or a glossary.
  http://www.nyse.com

Exercise 5

◆ History vs. Favorites ◆ Print/Copy/Save Web Pages

NOTES

History vs. Favorites

- In addition to the Favorites folder, where you store the addresses that you want to access easily, Internet Explorer keeps a record of the Web pages that you visit. The five most recent sites that you have visited during a current session appear at the bottom of the Go menu.

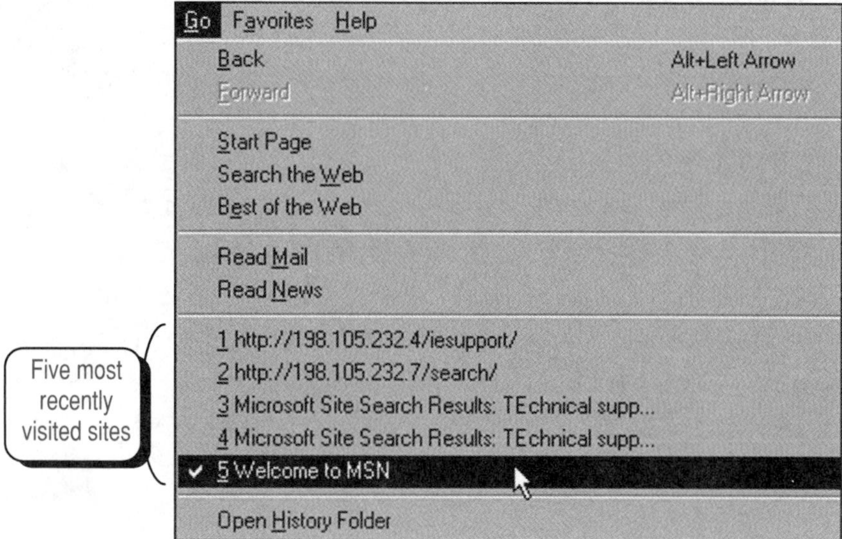

- You can open the Go menu and click any one of those five sites to return to it.
- When you exit Internet Explorer, the five sites that appear at the bottom of the Go menu are removed from the bottom of the list, but they are not deleted from the History Folder.
- The History folder keeps a record of all the sites that you have visited for a certain number of days. You can determine (up to 999) the number of days that Web sites are stored in your History folder.
- To select the number of days that you want to keep Web sites stored or to clear the history folder:
  - Click View, Options and then click the Navigation tab.

HINT
As you move from one site to another, you may find yourself asking, "How did I get here?" The history folder is an easy way to see the path you followed to arrive at the current location.

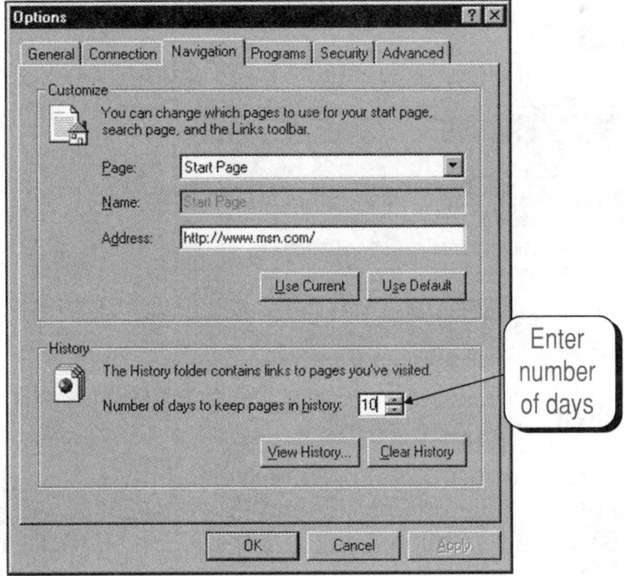

- Select or type in the Number of days to keep pages in history.
- Click View History to see the Web sites that are currently in your History folder.

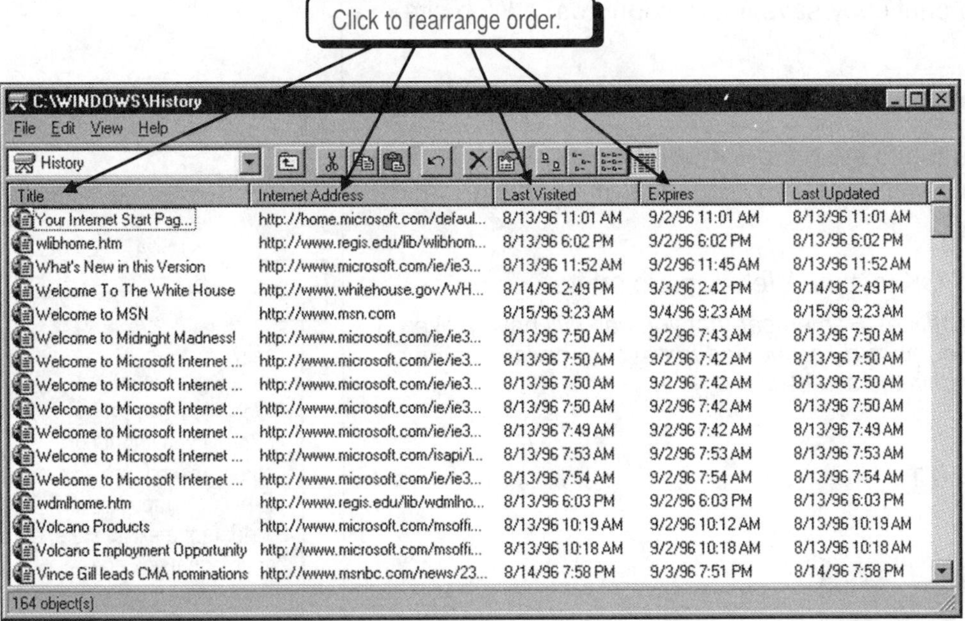

- You can click on any Web site and open it (if it still exists), see when you last visited it, when it was updated last, and when it is due to expire.
- To delete the contents of the History folder, click Clear History in the Navigation dialog box.
- You can rearrange the way the sites are displayed.
  - Click Title heading to arrange alphabetically. Click Title again and sites will appear in reverse alphabetical order.
  - Click Internet Address heading to view sites in alphabetical order. Click again to reverse the order.
  - Click on Last Visited heading to view sites according to date visited.

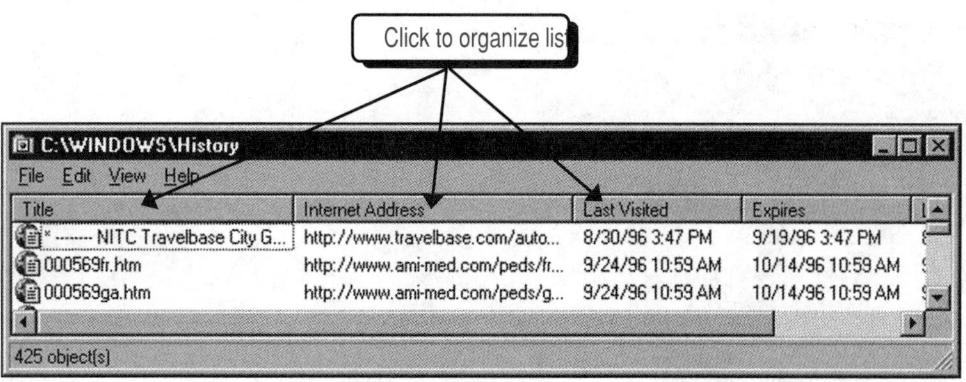

Print/Copy/Save Information from the World Wide Web

- One of the major reasons that you will probably use the World Wide Web is to acquire information that you want to use in a document, to send to another person, or to print out and keep as documentation if you use the material in a research project.
- For example, you may want to print out the map of a city that you are planning to visit; you may find an article that a colleague would find interesting; you might find a supporting source for a research project that you are working on.
- There are several ways to print/copy/save information from a Web site.

Print

- Click the Print [Print] button to send the current Web page to the printer. (Text and graphics will print if your printer can handle graphics.)

OR

- Click File, Print and click OK to send Web page to printer.

  ✓ *You can print online or offline. Remember that you can still have a Web site on screen even if you have disconnected from your service provider, but you cannot move within the site itself.*

Save

- Click File and select Send To.

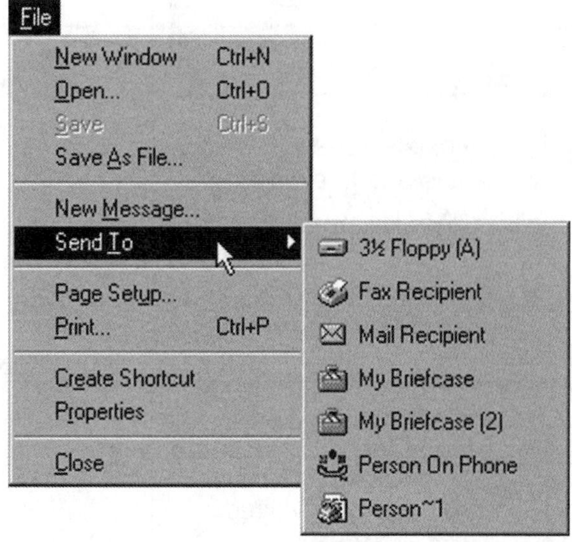

CAUTION

Be sure to check out the copyrights that apply to information you intend to use.

HINT

Keeping a record of a Web site that you reference in papers or other research projects is especially important to validate the existence of a source that you cite. Remember that the Web site you reference could disappear and you would have no way to document that your information came from an authentic location.

- Select desired option.

  OR

- Click File, Save As File, name the file you want to save, choose the desired location, and click Save.

  ✓ *The file that you save will contain only text; graphics will not be saved in this file.*

Copy

To copy text from a site to the clipboard:

- Open the Web site from which you want to copy text.
- Click Ctrl+A to select the text on the Web page.

  ✓ *This copies the text to the clipboard.*

- Open the location where you want to copy the text (for example, Microsoft Word, WordPerfect, etc.).
- Press Ctrl+V to copy the text to the new location.

  Placeholders will indicate where graphics appeared on the Web site.

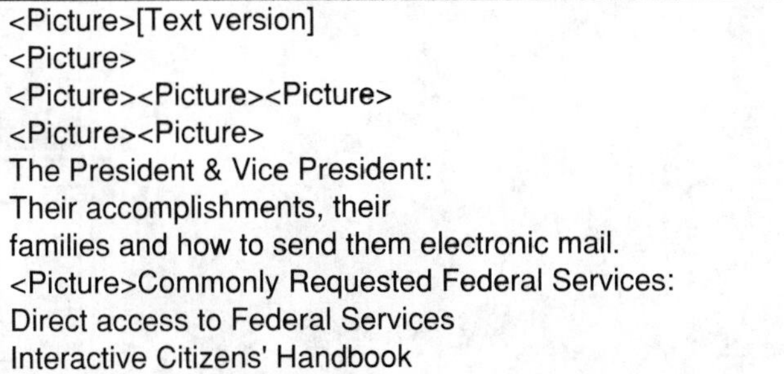

<Picture>[Text version]
<Picture>
<Picture><Picture><Picture>
<Picture><Picture>
The President & Vice President:
Their accomplishments, their
families and how to send them electronic mail.
<Picture>Commonly Requested Federal Services:
Direct access to Federal Services
Interactive Citizens' Handbook
Your guide to information about the Federal government

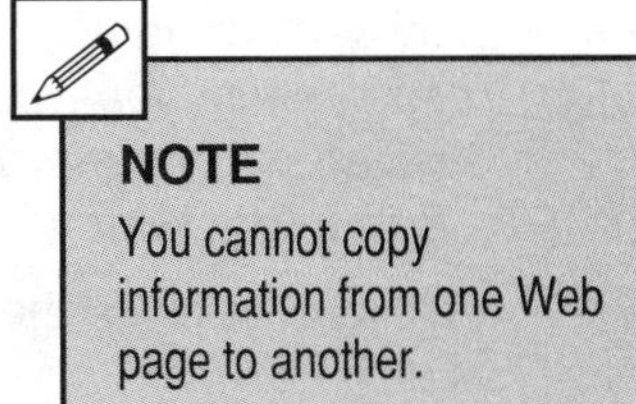

NOTE
You cannot copy information from one Web page to another.

In this exercise, you will print information from a Web site and clear your History Folder.

EXERCISE DIRECTIONS

1. If you are continuing from the previous exercise, go to step 2.

   OR

   Connect to your service provider and start Internet Explorer.
2. Click Open History Folder on the Go menu.
3. Click on the Last Visited heading to rearrange the sites by date visited.
4. Click again on the Last Visited heading and note that the dates are rearranged again.
5. Close the History Folder.

6. Click View, Options and the Navigation tab and do the following.

   ✓ *Note the number of days that sites are stored in the History folder.*

   - If desired, change the number of days that sites are stored in your History folder.
   - If desired click Clear History to empty the History folder.

     Important: *You may not want to empty the History folder. If you can't remember the address of a site that you would like to visit again, you may be able to find it in the History folder.*

   - Click OK to close the Navigation dialog box.

7. Go to the DDC Publishing Web site by typing the following URL in the Address line: ***http://www.ddcpub.com***

   - Click 

on the DDC home page.
   - Click on the link **Lesson 2: Internet Explorer, Exercise 5 "Smithsonian"**.
   - Click Print button to send the page directly to the printer.

     ✓ *Note that text and graphics (if your printer can handle graphics) print.*

We'd like to hear from you. Please take a minute to tell us about yourself and what you would like to see on our web site.

Have a "byte" of the Smithsonian's electronic birthday cake.

[Text Version]

If this server is busy, you may want to visit the Smithsonian mirror site in California.

Last updated by P. W. House (webmaster@si.edu) on 26 AUGUST 1996

Copyright © 1995 by Smithsonian Institution

8. With the **The Smithsonian Home** still open, Click File, Save As File and do the following:
   - Name the file ddctest. Leave the file type as html.
   - Click Save to save the file to your desktop.
   - Minimize Internet Explorer by clicking the Minimize button. You will still be connected to your service provider.
   - Double-click ddctest.html  on your desktop. Note that the page contains place holders for graphics.
   - Click the Print button on the toolbar to print the file.
   - Select Close from the File menu.
     - ✓ *This may also close Internet Explorer.*
9. If you are continuing on to the next exercise, start Internet Explorer (you should still be connected to your service provider).

   OR

   Disconnect from your service provider.

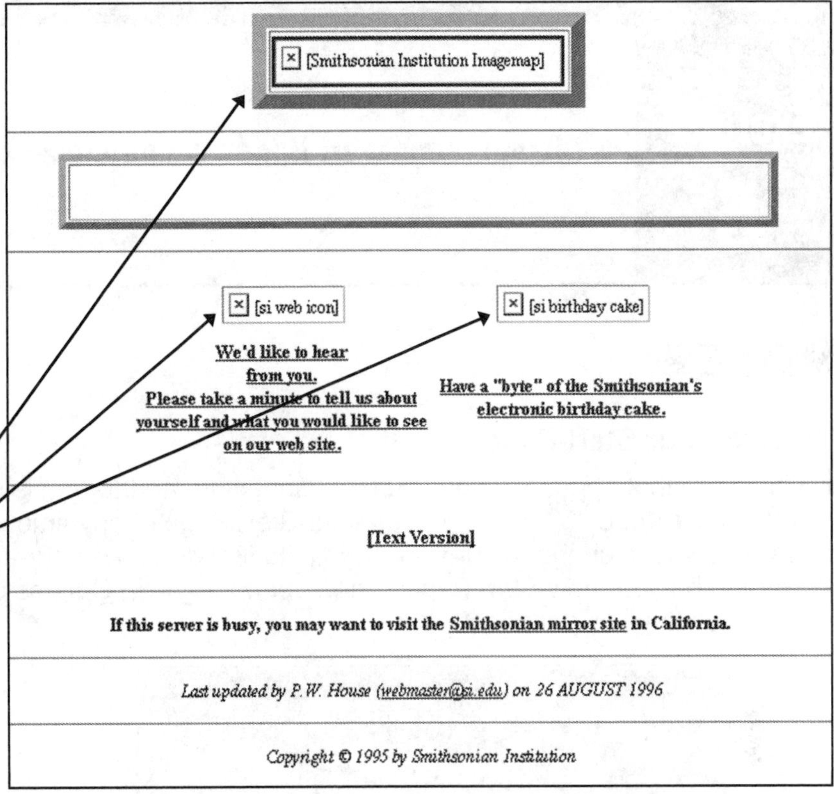

Morgan Stanley Home Page
http://www.ms.com

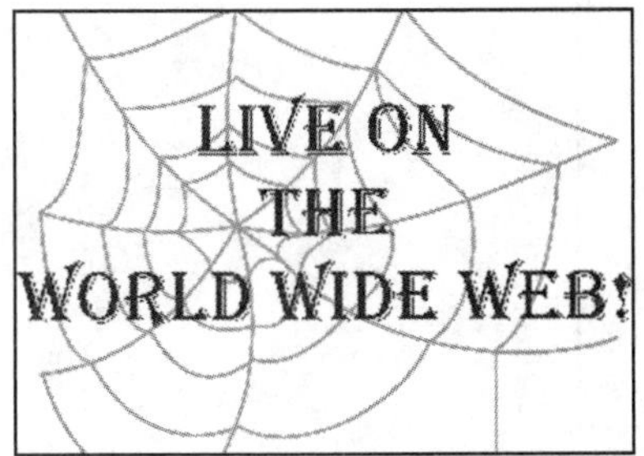

The Smithsonian Instituition Home Page
http://www.si.edu

MSNBC Home Page
http://www.msnbc.com

CNN Interactive
http://www.cnn.com

Exercise 6

◆ Change Your Start Page ◆ Customize Links

NOTES

Change Your Start Page

- The page that appears when you first connect to the Internet is called your **Start Page**. You can change your Start Page at any time. The easiest way to change your start page is to first go to the page that you want to be your new Start Page. Then open the View, Options dialog box and click the Navigation tab.

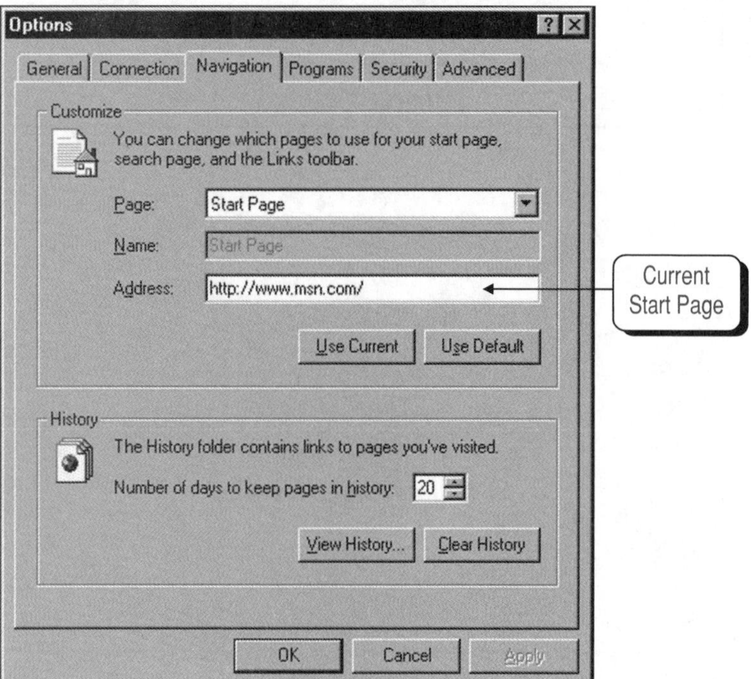

  - In the Page box, be sure that Start Page is selected.
  - In the Name box, Start Page is grayed because you cannot change the name of the Start Page.
  - The address of your current Start Page displays in the Address box.
  - Click Use Current to change the Start Page to the page you are currently on. The address of your new Start Page will now display in the Address line.
  - Click OK to close the dialog box.

    ✓ *The next time you connect to the Internet and start Internet Explorer, you will start at the new location.*

- You can change your Start Page as often as you would like. Select Use Default to restore the original Start Page.

Customize Links

Move Links Section

- The **Links** section of the Toolbar offers you another way to customize Internet Explorer and make it easier to access frequently used links quickly.

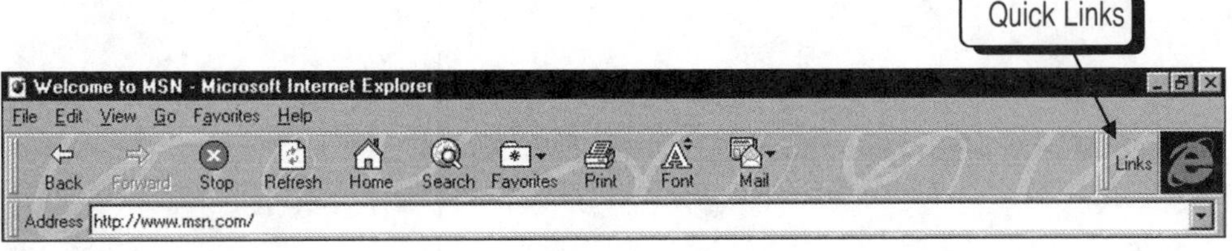

- You can move the Links section to display:
  - on the Toolbar

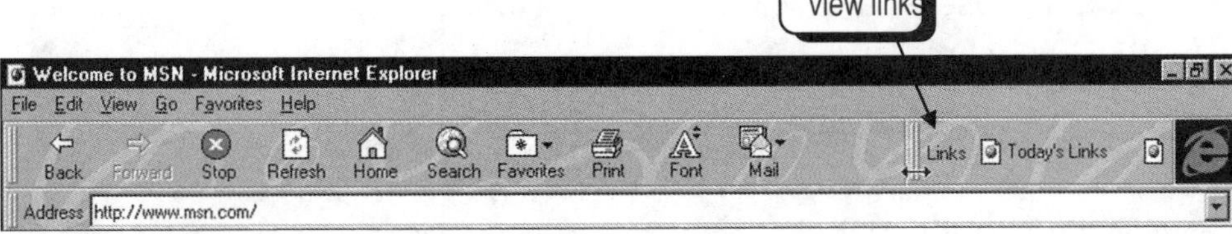

  - instead of the Toolbar

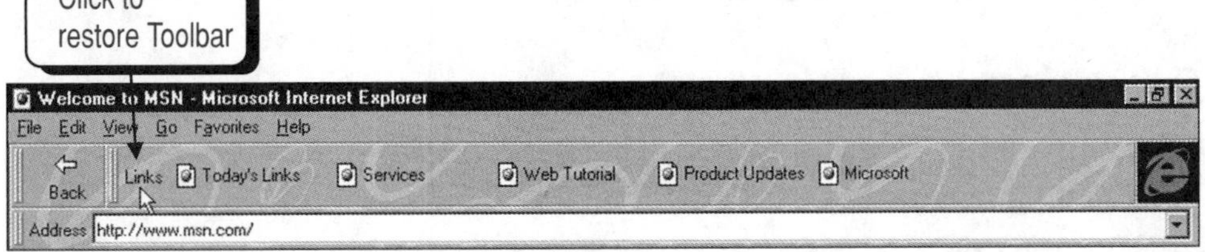

  - on the Address line

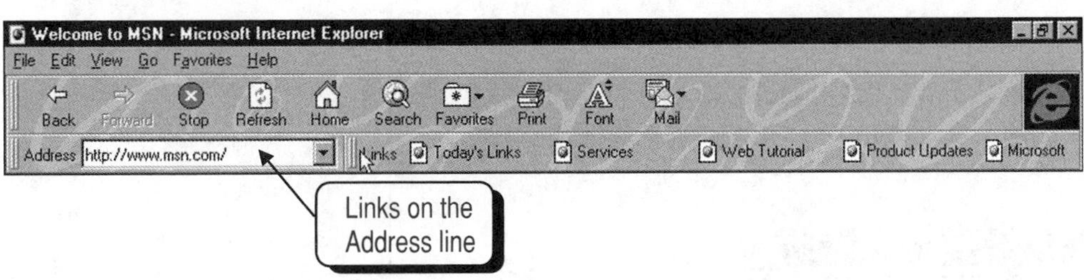

  - instead of the Address line

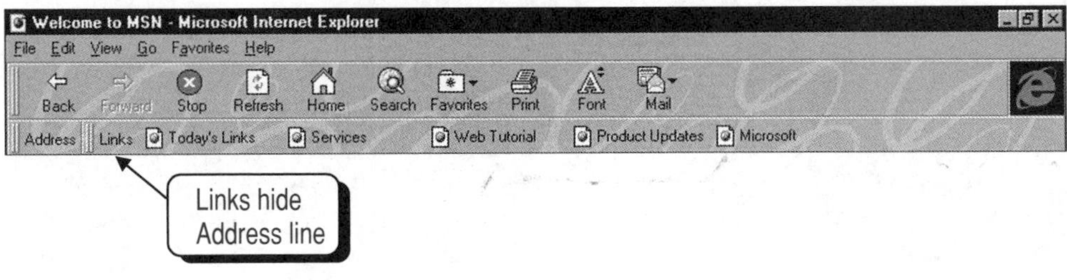

- below the Address line

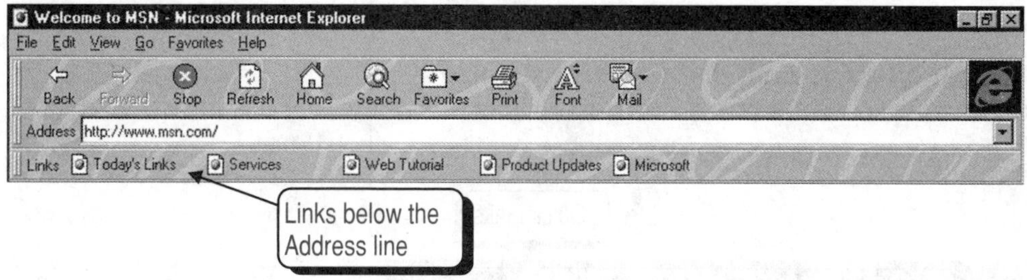

- The default links will take you to several Microsoft sites.

Customize Links

- You can customize five links in Internet Explorer.

  ✓ *You can also change the Search Link, but you cannot change the name. You will learn about using Searches in Lesson 3.*

- The easiest way to change a Quick Link:
  - First display the page that you want to use as a Quick Link.
  - Click View, Options and select the Navigation tab.
  - Click Page arrow and select Quick Link # to change. *Example: New York Times*
  - Enter a name for the Quick Link in the Name box.
  - Click Use Current to change the Link.

    ✓ *You can enter the address without being on the page that you want to be the Quick Link; however, many addresses are long and it is easy to enter an incorrect character.*

  - Click OK and move the Quick Links so you can view them.

  You will move to that page when you click on the Link.

  - You can revert to the default name of the Quick Link by selecting Use Default for the appropriate Quick Link in the Navigation dialog box.

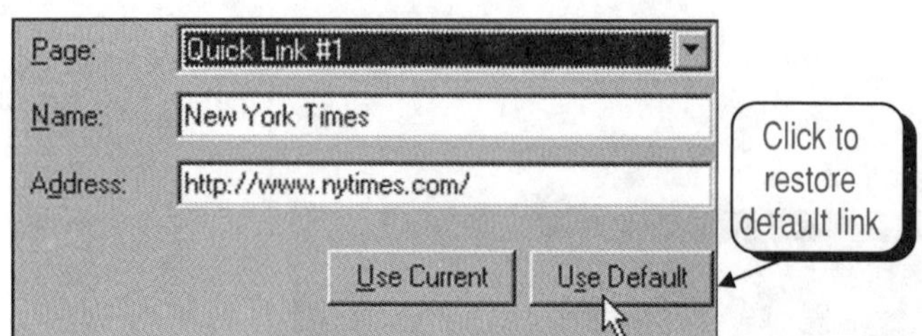

In this exercise, you will change your start page and customize two Quick Links.

EXERCISE DIRECTIONS

1. If you are continuing from the previous exercise, go to step 2.

   OR

   Connect to your service provider and start Internet Explorer.
2. Open the ddcpub Web site by typing the following URL on the address line:
   http://www.ddcpub.com
3. Click View, Options, and select the Navigation tab. Do the following:
   - Be sure the Start Page is displayed in the Page textbox.
   - Note the address that displays in the Address textbox.
   - Click Use Current to make the **ddcpub.com** as your Start Page.
   - Note that the address changes to the **ddcpub.com** Home page.
   - Click OK.
   - Click on the link to the White House Home page, **Lesson2: Internet Explorer, Exercise 2, "White House."**

     ✓ *Even though you are in Exercise 6, select the link to the White house that says Exercise 2. It is the site where you should be.*
   - Open the View, Options, Navigation dialog box.
   - Click the drop-down arrow next to the Page text box and click on Quick Link #1.
   - In the Name textbox, enter The White House.
   - Click the Use Current button.
   - Click OK.
4. Click the Home button to return to your new Start Page.
5. Click on the link to the White House Home page and do the following:
   - Click Home to return to your Start Page.
   - Drag the Links button to the left to view the Quick Links.
   - Click on the White House Quick Link.

   ✓ *If you are using the Internet Simulation, skip step 6. Go directly to step 7.*
6. Repeat step 5 to create and view a Quick Link to Web page of your choice.
7. Change the Start Page back to its Default setting by doing the following:
   - Click View, Options.
   - Select the Navigation tab.
   - Click the Use Default button.
8. While still in the Navigation tab of the Options window, change Quick Link #1 back to its original setting by doing the following:
   - Click the drop-down arrow next to the Page text box and click on Quick Link #1.
   - Check the Use Default button.
   - Click OK.
9. Continue on to the summary exercise.

   OR

   Exit from Internet Explorer and disconnect from your service provider.

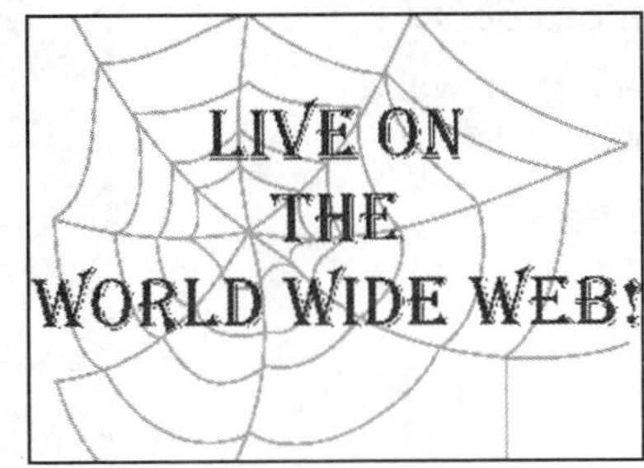

Australian World Direct – Australian Trade Commission (Austrade) Online – Austrade's home page allows you to search for Australian suppliers, products, or services, and provides information onupcoming trade events
http://www.austrade.gov.au

American Business Brokerage, Ltd. – Professional listing services worldwide. Allows visitors to advertise commercial and business property to be sold, search for properties and businesses on sale, and read about investment opportunities.
http://www.businessmls.com

SchwabNOW! – Schwab's page allows you to trade on the Web, read about international stock portfolios, and research other financial options.
http://www.schwab.com

Teaching with Electronic Technology – Information about conferences, publications, and general discussions of teaching with electronic technology.
http://www.wam.umd.edu/~mlhall/teaching.html

Exercise 7

◆Internet Explorer – Summary Exercise

In this exercise, you will practice some of the skills you have learned in this lesson.

EXERCISE DIRECTIONS

1. If you are continuing from the previous exercise, go to step 2.

   OR

   Connect to your service provider and start Internet Explorer.
2. Enter the following URL in the Address field:

   http://www.invent.org/book/
3. Scroll down the page to view the selections on this Web site.
4. Click on **The Inventors (alphabetical index)**.

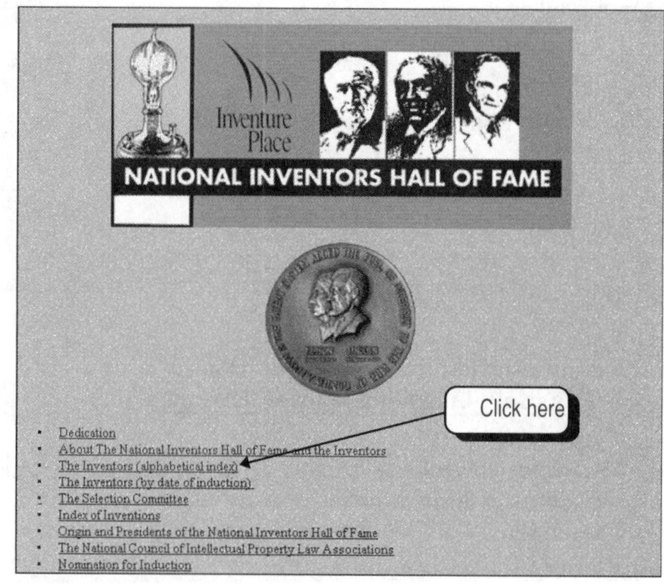

5. Scroll down and click on **Alexander Graham Bell**.

   ✓ *Note that there are links to other locations on the World Wide Web.*

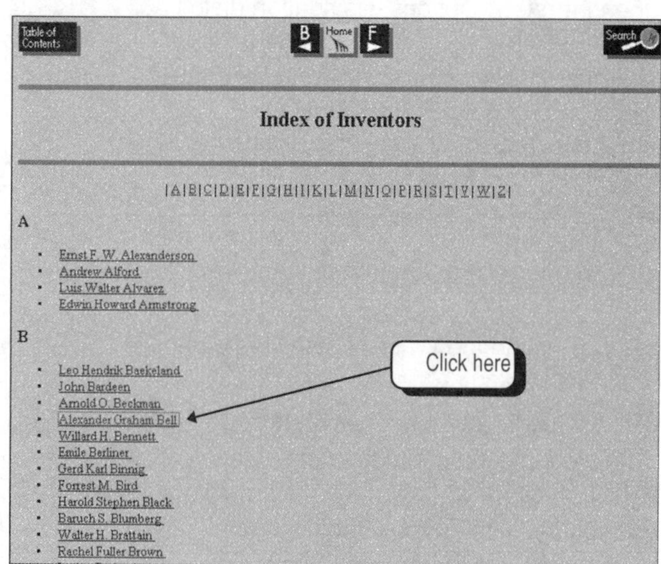

6. Click the Print button on the toolbar to send this page (shown at the right) to the printer.
7. Click on the link to **Edinburgh University**.

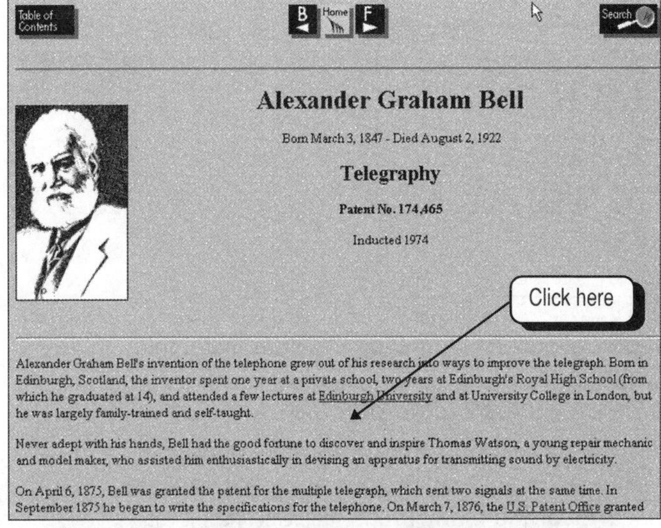

8. Explore some of the options available on the Edinburgh University Web site.
9. Click Back until you reach the first page of the National Inventors Hall of Fame.
10. Add this page to your Favorites folder.
11. Continue on to the next lesson.

    OR

    Exit from Internet Explorer and disconnect from your service provider.

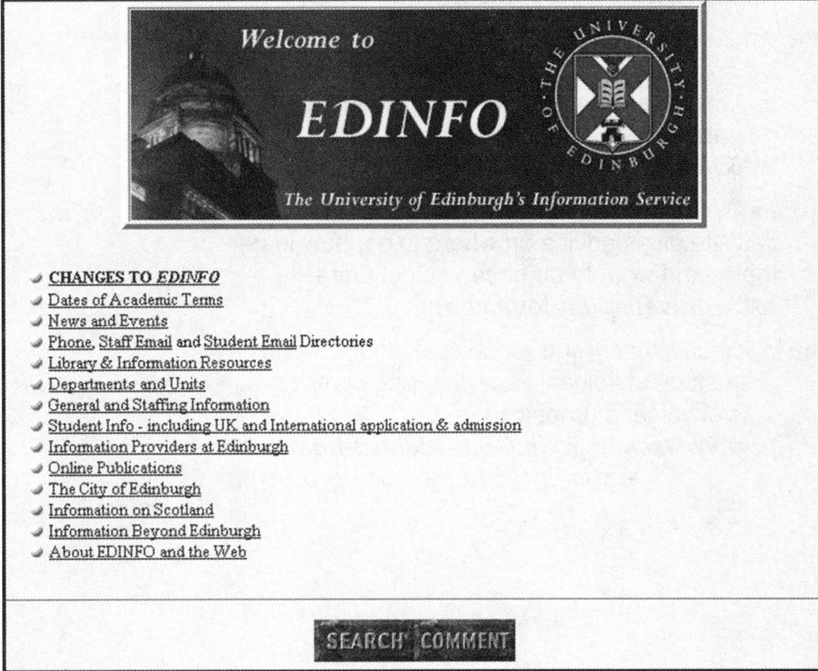

HINT

If you would like to download a guide to the Internet, do the following:

- Enter http://www.eff.org in the address line.
- Click on **Net Guide** under More Info.
- Click **Get Your Own Copy of the Guide (ASCII Text, English)**.
- Print the guide, if desired (150+ pages).

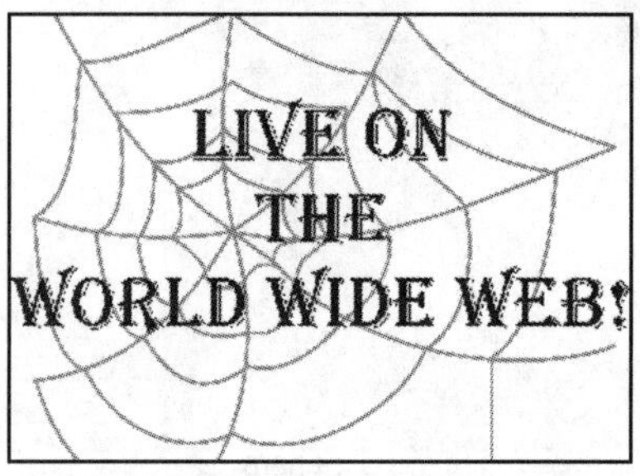

The Brownie Collection Home Page – Order incredible brownies.
http://www.surfspin.com/brownie

Aardvark Magic Company – from easy mental tricks you can perform in front of your computer, to feats of magic involving many props, this site has it all.
http://www.netpath.net/aardvark

The Dinosaur Society Home Page – Web site of the Dinosaur Society, a non-profit organization dedicated to giving grants for dinosaur science research.
http://www.dinosociety.org

Epicurious Travel Home Page – an online travel guide, this site gives advice on where to go, how to get there, and what to do once you get there.
http://travel.epicurious.com

The Volcanic Home Page – dedicated to the world-wide study of volcanic activity using computers. Lots of volcano graphics.
http://www.aist.go.jp/GSJ/~jdehn/v-home.htm

Lesson 3: Search Engines

Exercise 1
- Search Sites
- Search Engines
- Search Site Catalogs

Exercise 2
- Subject-and-Keyword Search Engines
- Multi-threaded Search Engines
- Types of Search Catalogs

Exercise 3
- Search Basics
- Search Results

Exercise 4
- Simple Searches
- Complex Searches

Exercise 5
- What is Lycos?
- Lycos Home Page Location
- Lycos Search Options
- Lycos Search Strings and Operators

Exercise 6
- What is Excite?
- Excite Home Page Location
- Excite Search Options
- Excite Search Strings and Operators

Exercise 7
- What is AltaVista?
- AltaVista Home Page Location
- AltaVista Search Options
- AltaVista Search Strings and Operators

Exercise 8
- What is Yahoo?
- Yahoo Home Page Location
- Yahoo Search Options
- Yahoo search strings

Exercise 9
- Common Errors when Searching Catalogs
- Common Errors when Following Links
- When to Stop an Attempt to Connect to a Site

Exercise 10
- Determine the Text String
- Access the Search Engine Sites
- Key the Search
- Examine the Search Results
- Use Different Search Engines

Exercise 11
- Search Engines – Summary Exercise

Exercise 1

◆ Search Sites ◆ Search Engines ◆ Search Site Catalogs

NOTES

Search Sites

- The Web is a vast source of information, but to use that information, you must be able to find it. The Web has many thousands of locations, containing hundreds of thousands of pages of information.
- To find the information that you want, you can connect to a site that contains a catalog of Web resources and search that catalog for the location of the information you want.
- There are many **search sites**, such as Yahoo, Lycos, and Magellan.

Search Engines

- A search site builds its catalog using a **search engine**. A search engine is a software program that goes out on the Web, seeking Web sites and cataloging them, usually by downloading their home pages.
  - Search engines are sometimes called **spiders** or **crawlers** because they crawl the Web.
  - Search engines constantly visit sites on the Web to create catalogs of Web pages and keep them up to date.
- Search engines save you time (time connected to a service provider and your own personal time) by seeking out Web sites and displaying descriptions that you can read before visiting them. You can then decide, based on these descriptions, which sites are likely to contain the information you want. This technique eliminates the need to surf (browse) many sites looking for what you want, which can take a long time (waiting to connect to the site, downloading the pages, scanning the information, etc.).

Search Site Catalogs

- Web sites that use search engines can build large catalogs of Web resources. You can search the descriptions of Web sites in these catalogs, instead of searching on the Web itself for the names of URLs that *might* contain the information you are looking for.
- A Web site with a search engine is a good place to start when you are looking for information on the Web. For example, if you are researching a subject for a school project, looking for a particular product or service, planning a business trip or a vacation, checking the weather, or checking local traffic conditions, start with a search site.

Note
URLs are not very descriptive. Some URLs, for example, contain only the name of a company. Some URLs are also long and contain odd characters. Mistyping is easy. A mistake in the URL will give you a "Does not exist" message. Check your typing and try again.

In this exercise, you will connect to a search engine Web site and do a simple catalog search.

EXERCISE DIRECTIONS

1. If you are already connected to your service provider and your browser is open, go to step 2.

   OR

   Connect to your service provider and open your browser.
2. On the Location line, type the following and then press Enter:

   http://www.ddcpub.com/learn
3. Click the link to ***Lesson 3: Search Engines, Exercise 1 "Yahoo"***.

   The Yahoo home page appears.

   ✓ *You will learn more about Yahoo, a very popular search site, in Exercise 8.*
4. In the search text box, type:

   IRS
5. Click the Search button next to the text box.

   ✓ *The search of the catalog may take a minute or more to complete.*

   When the search is finished, the browser displays the results of the search as shown on the next page.

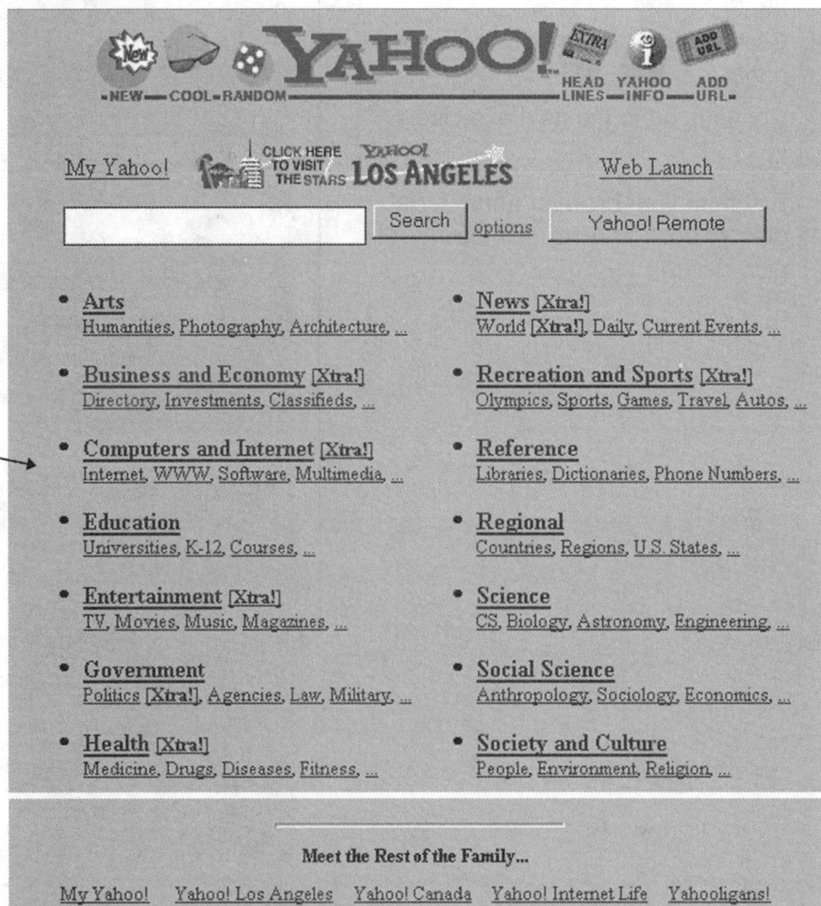

6. Read through a few of the matches to see what they say.
7. Click on ***1040.com*** to move to that Web site.
8. Click back to return to the previous page.
9. Click Home to return to your home page.
10. Continue on to the next exercise.

    OR

    Exit from your browser and disconnect from your service provider.

My Yahoo! - Yahoo! L.A. - Stock Quotes

NETSCAPE NAVIGATOR 3.0 NOW FINAL!
THE MOST POPULAR NAVIGATOR IS NOW LIVE

Found 67 matches containing **irs**. Displaying matches 21-40.

Yahoo Categories - **Yahoo Sites** - AltaVista Web Pages

Yahoo Sites

Business and Economy:Companies:Financial Services:Taxes

- PC-1099 Software - from Graves Data Systems, is Information Return Filing Software. It handles electronic and paper filing of **IRS** forms 1098, 1099, 5498, 1042-S, and W-2 forms.
- Prairie Specialties - Be prepared for an **IRS** tax audit on automobile, motel and other business travel expenses with The Mileage Manager record system.
- US Tax - a CPA firm specializing in **IRS** tax disputes.

Business and Economy:Companies:Financial Services:Taxes:Accounting

- Crawford, Pimentel & Company, Inc. - specializing in tax planning, consulting, tax audits,**IRS** examination, and payphones.
- Maese & Associates - provides consulting services regarding Internal Revenue Service (**IRS**) Collection Division Procedures against businesses and individuals (tax liens, levies and seizures).

****

Business and Economy:Products and Services:Business Opportunities

- Abuse the **IRS** Right Back!
- Share the Magic - offers a program to help individuals increase their income through an easy system of gifting, approved by the **IRS**.

Business and Economy:Taxes

- 1040.com - Federal & state tax information, forms, instructions and **IRS** publications. Electronic tax filing information.
- Analysis of **IRS** Guidelines for Independent Contractor and Employee Status
- Internal Revenue Service@
- National Association of Computerized Tax Processors - contains links to the **IRS** and state sites which have tax forms available for download.
- Nest Egg's **IRS** Tax Information Center - Nest Egg has added an **IRS** Download Center, including most forms and schedules suitable for a small business owner or personal investor in Acrobat format. Also includes links to Nest Egg''s tax-related articles.

Next 20 matches

Other Search Engines

Alta Vista - Open Text - WebCrawler - HotBot - Lycos - Infoseek - excite - DejaNews - More...

Copyright © 1994-96 Yahoo! All Rights Reserved.

Sponsored by: Drake

Welcome to the most comprehensive source of tax information and resources on the World Wide Web

If you're in need of tax information, whether it's forms, regulations, the latest federal or state rulings...if it has to do with taxes you'll find it here.

Taxing Subjects General information and frequently needed data, including late breaking news

Forms Download federal and state forms, instructions and regulations in PDF format

Tax Links Links to additional sources of federal and state tax information

CONTENTS UNDER CONSTRUCTION

Questions, comments, problems? Please send e-mail to info-1040@1040.com

This site maintained by Drake-Software.com

Copyright 1996

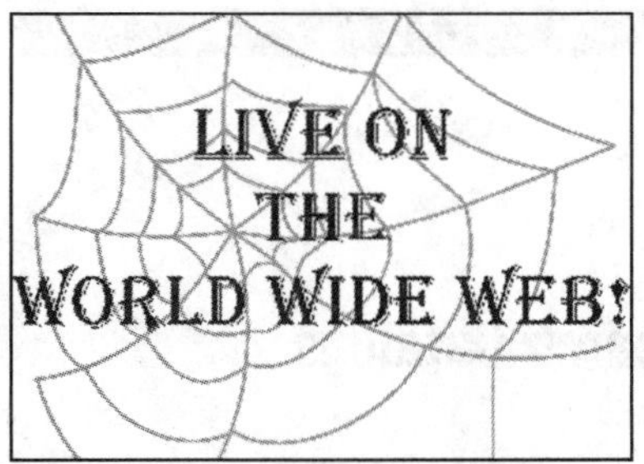

The Yahoo Home Page
http://www.yahoo.com

The Smithsonian Institution Home Page
http://www.si.edu

MSNBC Home Page
http://www.msnbc.com

CNN Interactive
http://www.cnn.com

Morgan Stanley Home Page
http://www.ms.com

Exercise 2

◆ Subject-and-Keyword Search Engines ◆ Multi-threaded Search Engines ◆ Types of Search Catalogs

NOTES

Subject-and-Keyword Search Engines

- Search engines are classified by the way they gather Web site information.
- A **subject-and-keyword search engine** searches the Web, gathers information, and builds a catalog of information about the sites it finds. You can then search this catalog for the information you want.
- These sites use software, called Web **robots**, which automatically search the Web for new sites and site information.
- Subject-and-keyword search sites include Lycos, AltaVista, and Excite.

Multi-threaded Search Engines

- The second type of search engine, called a **multi-threaded** search engine, searches other Web search sites and gathers the results of these searches for your use.
- Because they search the catalogs of other search sites, multi-threaded search sites do not maintain their own catalogs. These search sites provide more search options than subject-and-keyword search sites, and they typically return more specific information with further precision. However, multi-threaded search sites are much slower to return search results than subject-and-keyword search sites.
- Multithread search sites include SavvySearch and Internet Sleuth.

Types of Search Catalogs

- Web sites with search engines can also be classified by the way their catalogs are organized. There are two main catalog types – hierarchical catalogs and subject catalogs.

Hierarchical Catalogs

- A catalog may be organized in a **hierarchical**, or **meta tree**, structure.
- At a hierarchical search site, items in the catalog are organized into a few major categories, such as Art, Science, and Entertainment, which have sub-categories under them. To use a site like this, you click on categories and sub-categories, until you get into the area you want, and then start your search for keywords in site descriptions.

- A search site with a hierarchical structure looks like this:

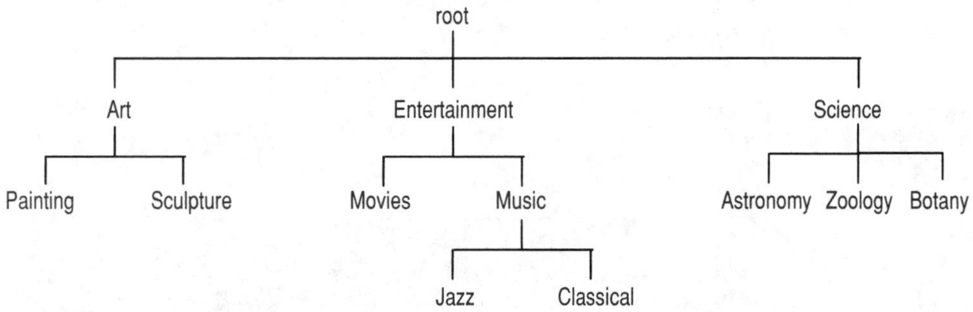

For example, sub-categories under Science may include Astronomy, Botany, and Zoology, while sub-categories under Art may include Painting and Sculpture. Each sub-category may have additional sub-categories under it. How detailed this structure is depends on the particular Web site.

- In a hierarchical search, you narrow a search of the catalog by beginning somewhere down the tree. For example, instead of searching the entire catalog starting at the root level for sites containing information about the planet Mars, you can begin at the Science, Astronomy level. Your search will go faster that way.

Subject Catalogs

- Another way to organize a search site catalog is by **subject**.
- In a catalog structured by subject, the Web sites gathered by the search engine are organized under many broad subject headings. The number and name of these headings depends on the particular Web site.

  For example, headings may include Astronomy, Botany, and Zoology (without a level above them named Science or any sub-categories below them). Web site information is placed under the heading. For example, a Web site for a zoo would be located under Zoology.
- The major difference between a hierarchically structured catalog and a subject-structured catalog is that you cannot narrow your search in a subject structured catalog by starting the search in a sub-category. You must use the search options in the text search to narrow your search (see Exercise 4, *Simple and Complex Searches*).

In this exercise, you will connect to a subject-and-keyword search site and a multi-threaded search engine site and do simple searches.

EXERCISE DIRECTIONS

To search using a *subject-and-keyword* search site:

1. If you are already connected to your service provider and your browser is open, go to step 2.

   OR

   Connect to your service provider and open your browser.
2. On the Location line, type the following and then press Enter.

   http://www.ddcpub.com/learn
3. Click the link to ***Lesson 3: Search Engines, Exercise 2 "Yahoo"***.

   The Yahoo home page appears.
4. Click on the ***Business and Economy*** link.

   The Business and Economy topic page (shown next to step 5) will appear.

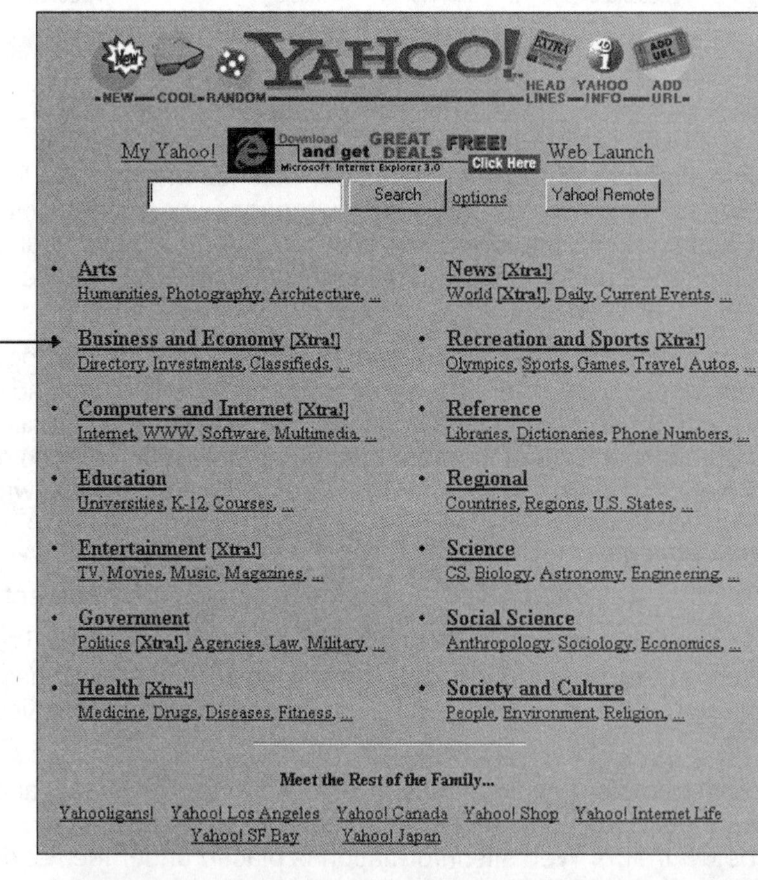

5. Click on the ***Business Directory*** link.

   The Business Directory topic page (shown next to step 6) will appear.

Click here

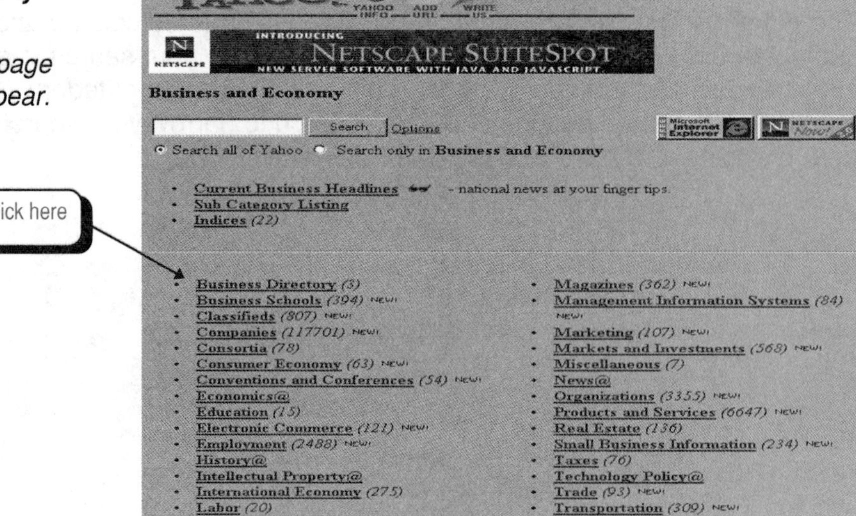

6. Click on the ***Companies@*** link.

   The Companies topic page (shown next to step 7) will appear.

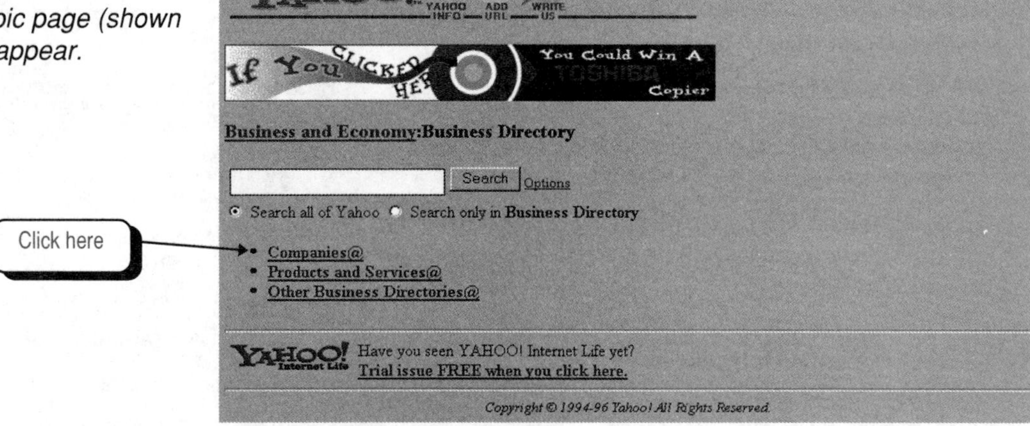

7. In the search text box at the top of the page, type:

   Microsoft

8. Click the Search Only In **Companies** button.
9. Click the Search button next to the search text box.

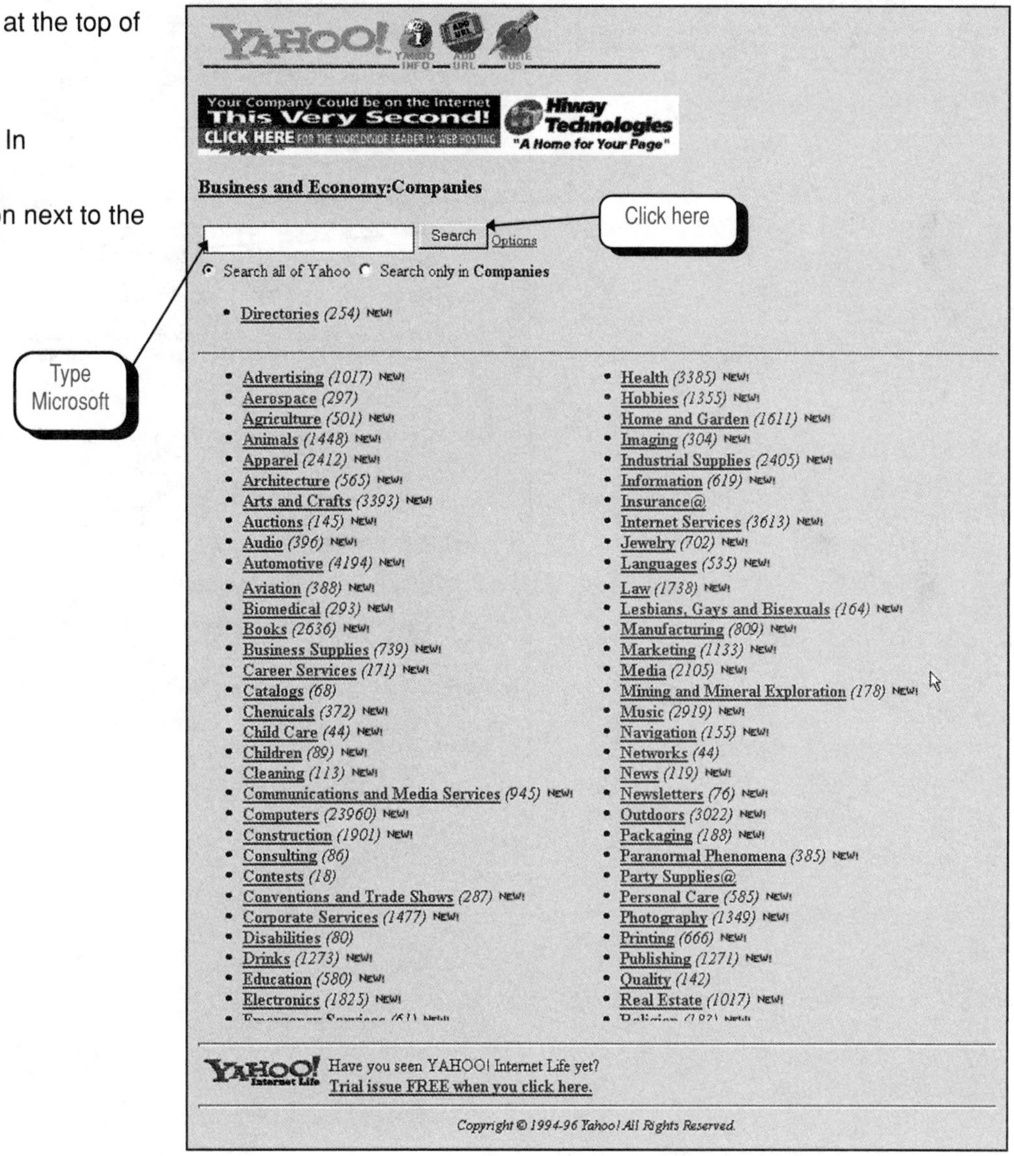

YAHOO!
YAHOO INFO
ADD URL
WRITE US
Your Company Could be on the Internet
This Very Second!
CLICK HERE FOR THE WORLDWIDE LEADER IN WEB HOSTING
Hiway Technologies
"A Home for Your Page"
Business and Economy:Companies
Search
Options
Click here
Type Microsoft
Search all of Yahoo
Search only in Companies

- Directories (254) NEW!

- Advertising (1017) NEW!
- Aerospace (297)
- Agriculture (501) NEW!
- Animals (1448) NEW!
- Apparel (2412) NEW!
- Architecture (565) NEW!
- Arts and Crafts (3393) NEW!
- Auctions (145) NEW!
- Audio (396) NEW!
- Automotive (4194) NEW!
- Aviation (388) NEW!
- Biomedical (293) NEW!
- Books (2636) NEW!
- Business Supplies (739) NEW!
- Career Services (171) NEW!
- Catalogs (68)
- Chemicals (372) NEW!
- Child Care (44) NEW!
- Children (89) NEW!
- Cleaning (113) NEW!
- Communications and Media Services (945) NEW!
- Computers (23960) NEW!
- Construction (1901) NEW!
- Consulting (86)
- Contests (18)
- Conventions and Trade Shows (287) NEW!
- Corporate Services (1477) NEW!
- Disabilities (80)
- Drinks (1273) NEW!
- Education (580) NEW!
- Electronics (1825) NEW!
- Health (3385) NEW!
- Hobbies (1355) NEW!
- Home and Garden (1611) NEW!
- Imaging (304) NEW!
- Industrial Supplies (2405) NEW!
- Information (619) NEW!
- Insurance@
- Internet Services (3613) NEW!
- Jewelry (702) NEW!
- Languages (535) NEW!
- Law (1738) NEW!
- Lesbians, Gays and Bisexuals (164) NEW!
- Manufacturing (809) NEW!
- Marketing (1133) NEW!
- Media (2105) NEW!
- Mining and Mineral Exploration (178) NEW!
- Music (2919) NEW!
- Navigation (155) NEW!
- Networks (44)
- News (119) NEW!
- Newsletters (76) NEW!
- Outdoors (3022) NEW!
- Packaging (188) NEW!
- Paranormal Phenomena (385) NEW!
- Party Supplies@
- Personal Care (585) NEW!
- Photography (1349) NEW!
- Printing (666) NEW!
- Publishing (1271) NEW!
- Quality (142)
- Real Estate (1017) NEW!

YAHOO! Internet Life
Have you seen YAHOO! Internet Life yet?
Trial issue FREE when you click here.
Copyright © 1994-96 Yahoo! All Rights Reserved.

When the search is finished, the browser displays the results of the search, as shown at the right.

At the top of the results page is a list of Yahoo Categories that contain the search text Microsoft. Notice the hierarchical structure.

At the bottom of the page is a list of Yahoo Sites that contain the search text Microsoft.

10. Scan the lists. When you are finished, continue with this exercise.

My Yahoo! - Yahoo! LA - Stock Quotes

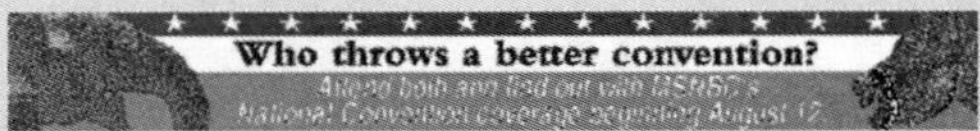

This search has been restricted to the category **Business and Economy:Companies**. For more matches try an unrestricted search across all categories.

Found 513 matches containing **microsoft**. Displaying matches 1-20.

Yahoo Categories - **Yahoo Sites** - AltaVista Web Pages

Yahoo Categories

Business and Economy:Companies:Computers:Software:**Microsoft** Corporation

Business and Economy:Companies:Computers:Software:**Microsoft** Corporation:Divisions:**Microsoft** Research

Business and Economy:Companies:Computers:Software:**Microsoft** Corporation:Products and Services:**Microsoft** BackOffice

Business and Economy:Companies:Computers:Software:**Microsoft** Corporation:Products and Services:**Microsoft** Home Products

Business and Economy:Companies:Computers:Software:**Microsoft** Corporation:Products and Services:**Microsoft** Internet Center

Business and Economy:Companies:Computers:Software:**Microsoft** Corporation:Products and Services:**Microsoft** Network

---

Yahoo Sites

Business and Economy:Companies:Advertising:High Technology

- AfterHours Communications Corp. - advertising agency and graphic design firm specializes in the technology company. Clients include: Aladdin Systems, K2, Cedars-Sinai, Adobe, and **Microsoft**.

Business and Economy:Companies:Arts and Crafts:Directories:Commercial Website Directories

- Artspeaks - promotes the arts by the Internet, Q2 television, **Microsoft** Network, Time Warner's Dreamshop and Holland Cruiseships.

Business and Economy:Companies:Automotive:Buyers' Services:Buyer's Guides

- CarPoint - by **Microsoft**.

Business and Economy:Companies:Automotive:Repairs and Service

- Hunter Engineering Company - A world leader in automotive service equipment, manufactures wheel alignment consoles running **Microsoft** Windows, wheel balancers, tire changers, lift racks, and brake testers.

Business and Economy:Companies:Books:Computer Books

- DataWorks Express Technical Books - We feature **Microsoft** Press Books at discount prices. Providing information on **Microsoft** products and certifications to the technical professional.

Business and Economy:Companies:Career Services:Training

To search using a *multi-threaded* search site:

11. On the Location line, type the following and press Enter:

    http://www.ddcpub.com/learn

12. Click the link to **Lesson 3: Search Engines, Exercise 2, "MetaCrawler"**.

    The Metacrawler home page (shown at right) appears.

    Hint: You can also use the Back button to return to the ddcpub.com/learn page and then click the link to Metacrawler.

13. In the search text box, type:

    Netscape

14. Click the Fast Search button below the search text box.

    When the search is finished, the browser displays the results of the search as shown on the right.

    The results page shows titles which are links to the Web site, the first few words of the document found, the full name of the URL for the site, and the search site where the results were found (for example, AltaVista).

15. Scan the results.
16. Continue on to the next exercise.

    OR

    Exit from your browser and disconnect from your service provider.

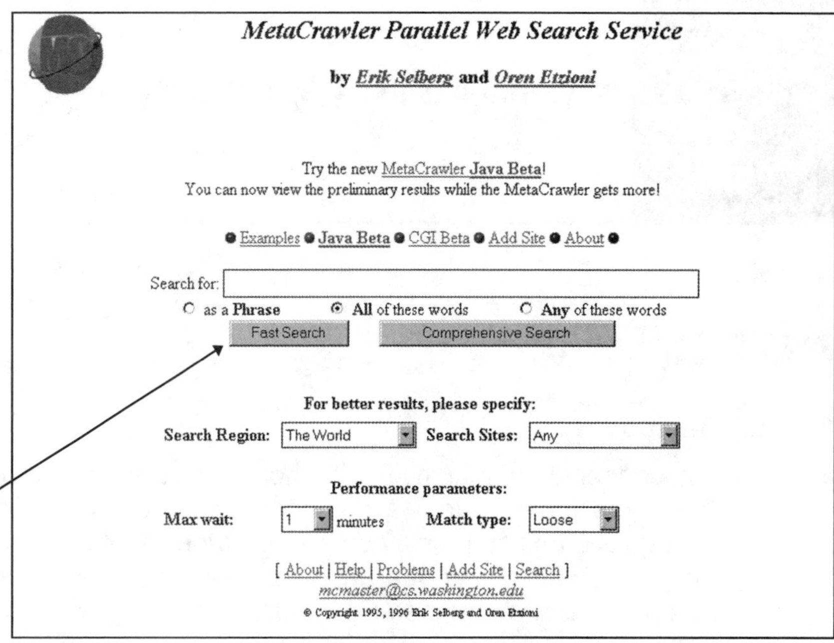

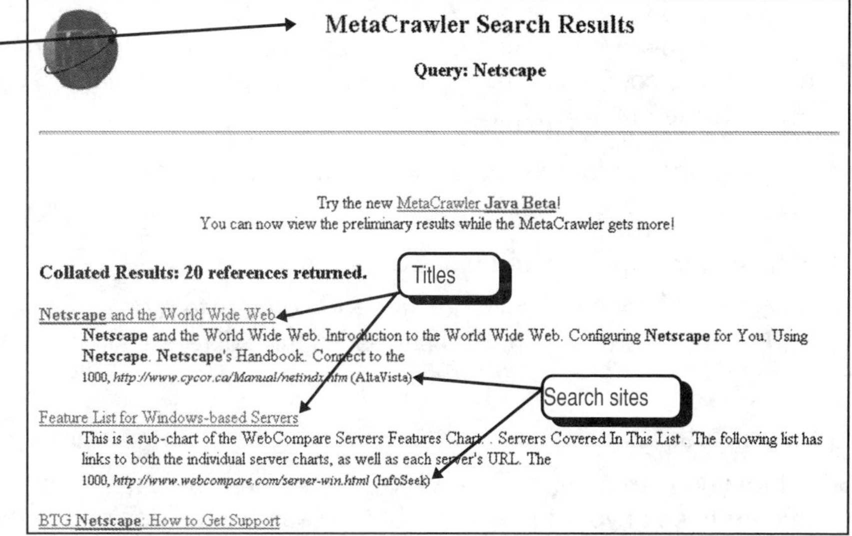

Yahoo! Home Page
http://www.yahoo.com

Metacrawler Home Page
http://www.metacrawler.com

Microsoft Corporation Home Page
http://www.microsoft.com

Netscape Navigator Home Page
http://www.netscape. com

IBM Home Page
http://www.ibm.com/

Lotus Development Corporation Home Page
http://www.lotus.com

Corel WordPerfect Home Page
http://www.wordperfect.com

Exercise 3

◆ Search Basics ◆ Search Results

NOTES

Search Basics

- When you connect to a search site, the home page has a text box for typing the words you want to use in your search. These words are called a **text string**. The text string may be a single word or phrase, or it may be a complex string which uses **operators** to modify the search (*see Exercise 4, Simple and Complex Searches, for more information on operators*).
- Once you have entered a text string, initiate the search by either pressing the Enter key or by clicking on the search button. This button may be named Search, Go Get It, Seek Now, or something similar.
- For the best search results:
  - Always check for misspelled words and typing errors.
  - Use descriptive words and phrases.
  - Use synonyms and variations of words.
- If you don't find what you're looking for, connect to a different search site and try the search again. Search results from different sites can vary greatly.

NOTE

Do not confuse the text search of the catalog with the search engine itself, though sometimes the term "search engine" is used interchangeably for both.

The search engine is a program that searches the Web for sites and (in most cases) creates a catalog of information on Web sites. The text search searches the catalog for occurrences of your text string or strings that are similar to your text string.

Search Results

- When you start a search, the Web site searches its catalog for occurrences of your text string. (Some search sites don't have their own catalog, so they search the catalogs of other search sites.) The results of the search, typically a list of Web sites whose descriptions have words that match the words you are searching for, are displayed in the window of your browser.

  ✓ *The information displayed on the results page will vary, depending on the search and display options selected and the search site you are using. The most likely matches for your text string appear first in the results list, followed by other likely matches on successive pages.*
- Each search site has its own criteria for rating the matches of a catalog search and setting the order in which they are displayed.
- The catalog usually searches for matches of the text string in the URLs of Web sites. It also searches for key words, phrases, and meta-tags (key words that are part of the Web page, but are not displayed in a browser) in the cataloged Web pages.

NOTE

There may be thousands of matches that contain the ASCII string you specified. The matches are displayed a page at a time. You can view the next page by clicking on the "next page" link provided by the site at the bottom of each search results page.

- You can scan the displayed results to see if a site contains the information you are searching for. Site names are clickable links. After visiting a site, you can return to the search site by clicking the Back button on your browser, and then choose a different site to visit or do another search.

In this exercise, you will connect to a search engine Web site and do a search.

EXERCISE DIRECTIONS

1. If you are already connected to your service provider and your browser is open, go to step 2.

   OR

   Connect to your service provider and open your browser.

   ✓ *The examples here will use Netscape Navigator.*

2. On the Location line, type the following and press Enter:

   http://www.ddcpub.com/learn

3. Click on the link **Lesson 3: Search Engines, Exercise 3 "Lycos"**.

   The Lycos search engine home page appears.

   ✓ *You will learn more about Lycos, a popular search site, in Exercise 5.*

4. In the search text box, type:

   Explorer

5. Click the Go Get It button next to the search text box.

   When the search is complete, the browser displays the results of the search.

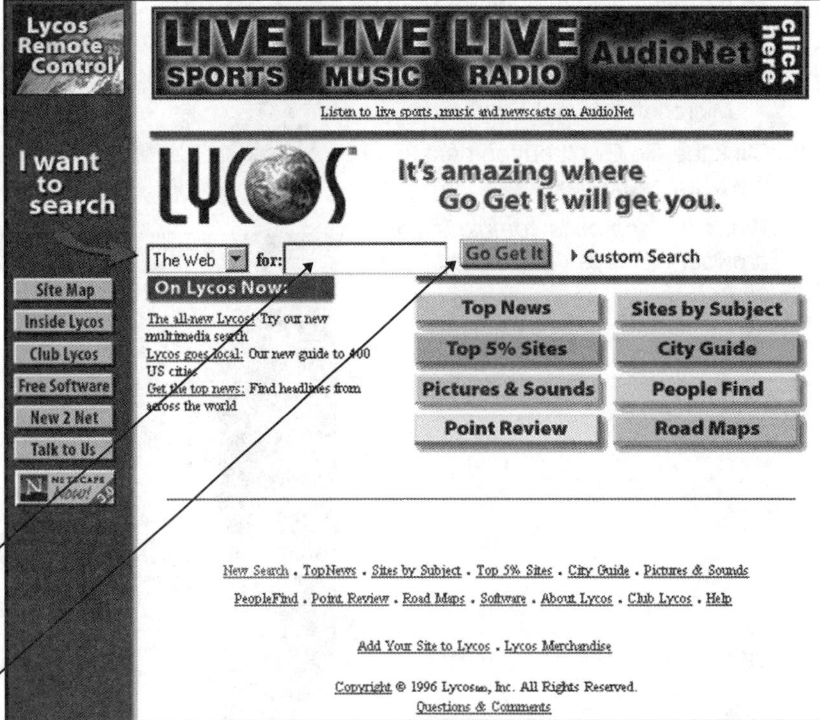

6. Review the results. Searching for *Explorer* matched Internet Explorer, IRIS Explorer, SGI Explorer, and many others.

   Notice the information presented on the results page. You are shown how many documents contain your search text. Each result has a title (a link to the site), a brief description of the site, the URL of the site, and the relevance to your search text.

7. To narrow the search, in the search text box at the bottom of the page, type:

   Microsoft Internet Explorer

8. Click the Go Get It button next to the search text box.

   When the search is complete, the browser displays the results of the search.

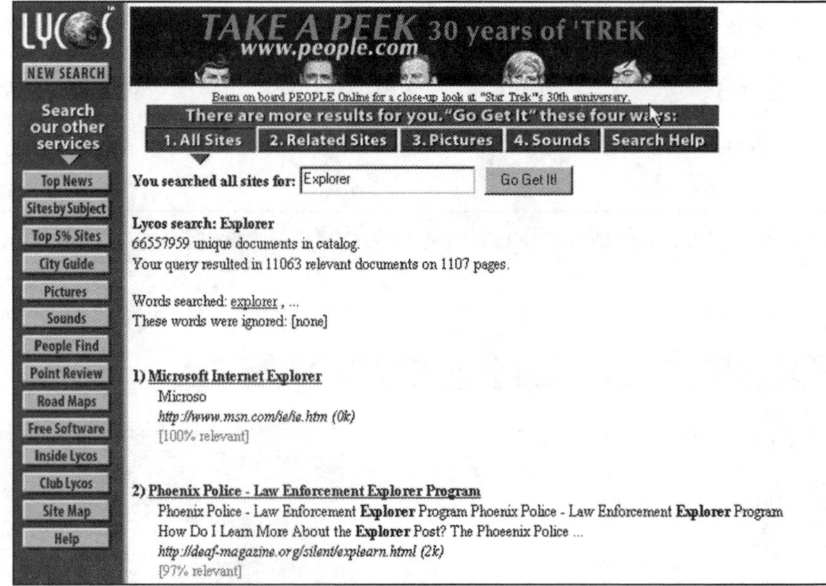

****

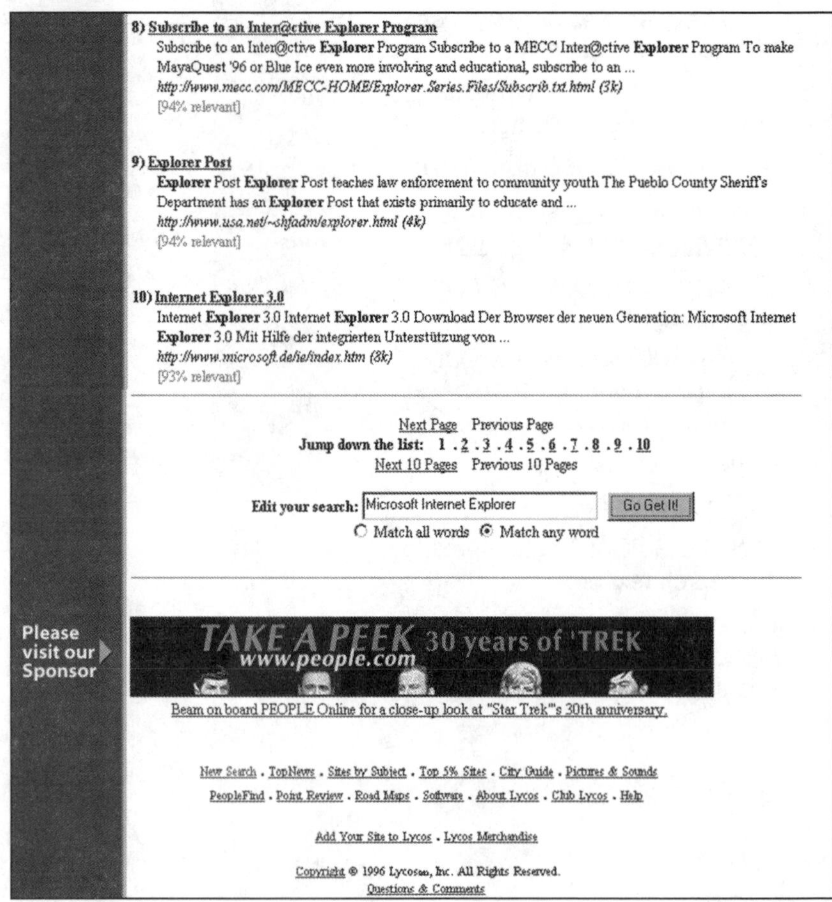

9. Review the results. They differ significantly from the previous results. Again, examine the information presented on the results page.
10. Return to your home page.
11. Continue on to the next exercise.

    OR

    Exit from your browser and disconnect from your service provider.

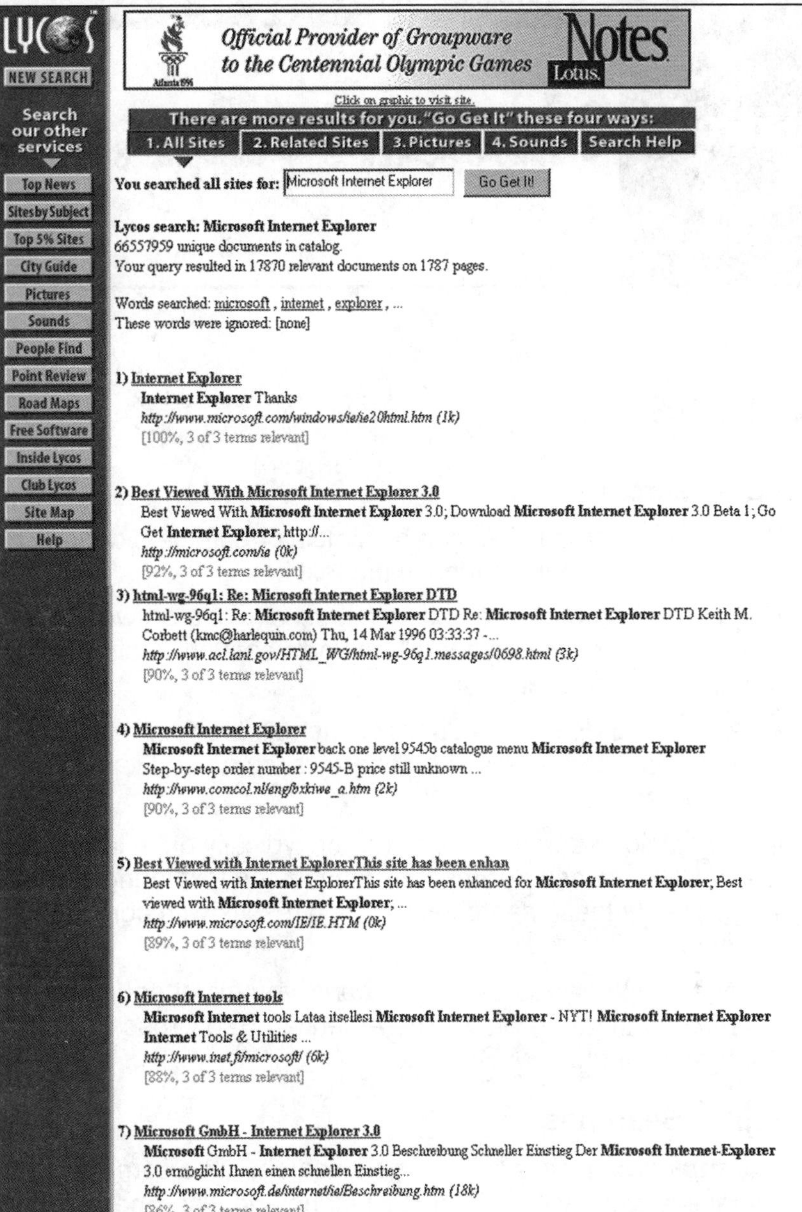

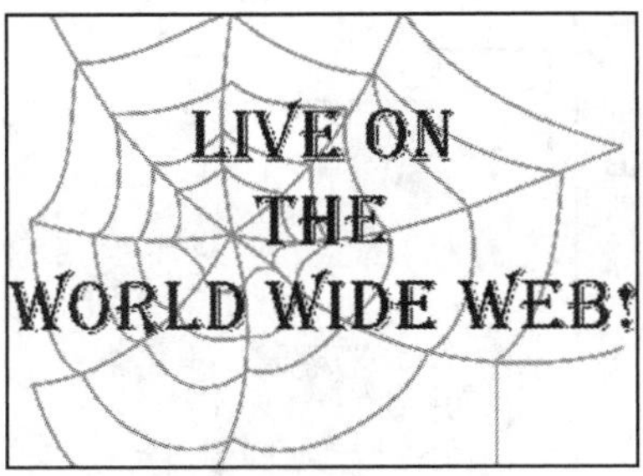

****

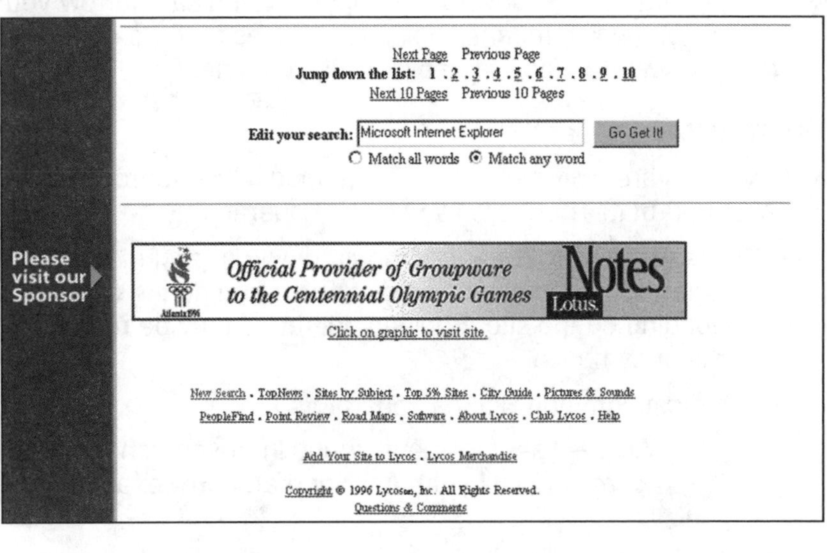

Lycos Home Page
    http://www.lycos.com

Microsoft Internet Explorer Home Page
    http://www.microsoft.com/ie/

SPRY, CompuServe Internet Division Home Page – Internet access, services and software for the home and business markets.
    http://www.spry.com/

CompuServe Home Page – Online service with access to Internet
    http://www.compuserve.com/

America Online Home Page – Online service with access to Internet
    http://www.aol.com/

Exercise 4

◆ Simple Searches ◆ Complex Searches

NOTES

Simple Searches

- Searches at search sites can be simple or complex, depending on how you design the search string in the text box.
- A **simple search** uses a text string, usually one or two key words, to search for matches in a search engine's catalog. A simple search is the broadest kind of search.
  - The key words may be specific, such as *browser* or *stock quotes* or *Macintosh*, or they may be general, such as *software* or *economy* or *computer*.
  - The catalog search will return a list, typically quite large, of Web pages and URLs whose descriptions contain the text string you want to find. Frequently these searches will yield results with completely unrelated items.
  - For example, if you search for *bank*, you might get matches for the Chase Manhattan *Bank*" The American Red Cross Blood *Bank*" and the left *bank* of the river Seine.

Complex Searches

- A **complex search** is like a simple search, but a complex search usually contains several words in the text string and also **operators** that modify the text string.
- Using operators and several descriptive words can narrow your search for information (which means finding fewer sites that are more relevant to what you want to find), thereby saving you time.

Operators

- Operators are words or symbols that modify the search string instead of being part of it. There are two types of operators:
  - **Boolean operators** specify required words, excluded words, and complex combinations of words to be found during a search. Depending on the site, Boolean operators may be represented by words or symbols.

    The most common Boolean operators are:

    AND—The documents found in the search must contain *all words* joined by the AND operator. For example, a search for

TIP

The syntax of the search string and a list of operators that can be used at a search site is usually available at the site. Look for a button or clickable link with a label like "Search Options," "Help," or "Information."

NOTE

There are search sites that do not support the use of operators in the search string. Some of these sites, however, do provide pop-up menus which provide the operator functions.

Microsoft AND *Internet* AND *Explorer* will find sites which contain all three words (*Microsoft, Internet*, and *Explorer*).

OR—The documents found in the search must contain *at least one of the words* joined by the OR operator. The documents may contain both, but this is not required. For example, a search for *Web* OR *Internet* will find sites which contain either the word *Web* or the word *Internet.*

NOT—The documents found in the search must not contain the word following the NOT operator. For example, a search for *orange NOT county* will find sites which contain the word orange but not the word *county*.

NEAR—The documents found in the search must contain the words joined by the NEAR operator within a specified number of words, typically ten. For example, *RAM NEAR* memory will find sites with the word *RAM* and the word *memory* within ten words of each other.

- The **grouping operators** join words and phrases together to be treated as a single unit or determine the order in which boolean operators are applied.

  The most common grouping operators are:

  Double quotes—The documents found in the search must contain the words inside double quotes exactly as entered. For example, a search for "*World Wide Web*" will find sites whose descriptions contain the phrase *World Wide Web*, not the individual words separated by other words or the same words uncapitalized.

  Parentheses—Words and operators can be grouped to refine searches using parentheses or to define the order in which boolean operators are applied. For example, a search for (*Internet OR Web*) AND *browser* will find sites whose descriptions contain the words *Internet* and *browser* or *Web* and *browser*. (Note that this is *not* the same search as *Internet* OR *Web AND browser*, which finds sites whose descriptions contain either the word *Internet* or both of the words *Web* and *browser.)*

In this exercise, you will connect to a search site and do a simple search and a complex search.

EXERCISE DIRECTIONS

1. If you are already connected to your service provider and your browser is open, go to step 2.

   OR

   Connect to your service provider and open your browser.
2. On the Location line, type the following and press Enter:

   http://www.ddcpub.com/learn
3. Click the link to **Lesson 3: Search Engines, Exercise 4 "AltaVista"**.

   The Alta Vista search page appears.
4. Do a simple search. In the search text box, type:

   stock prices
5. Click the Submit button.

   When the search is complete, the browser displays the results of the search.

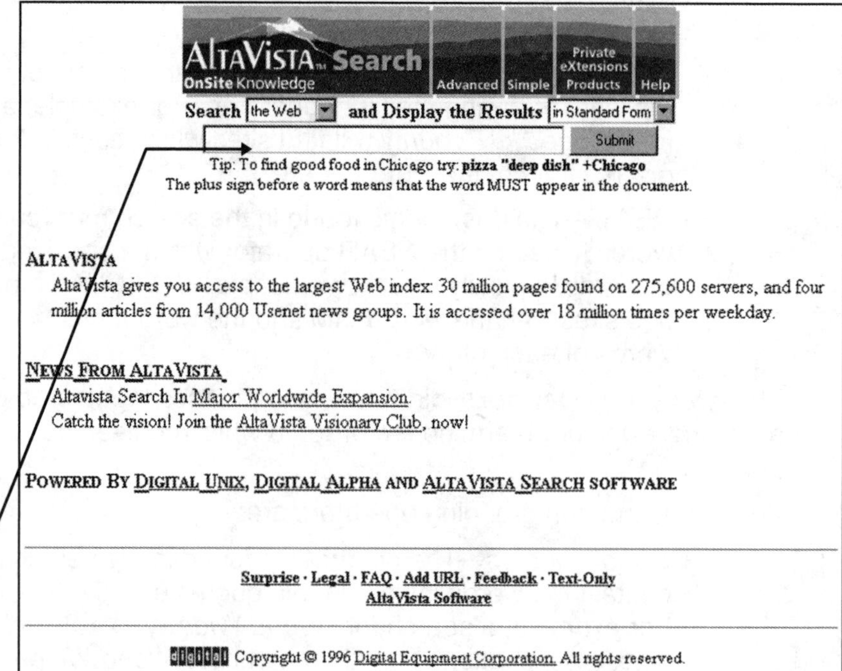

6. Read some of the matches.
7. Do another simple search. In the search text box, type:

   stock quotes
8. Click the Submit button.

   When the search is complete, the browser displays the results of the search.

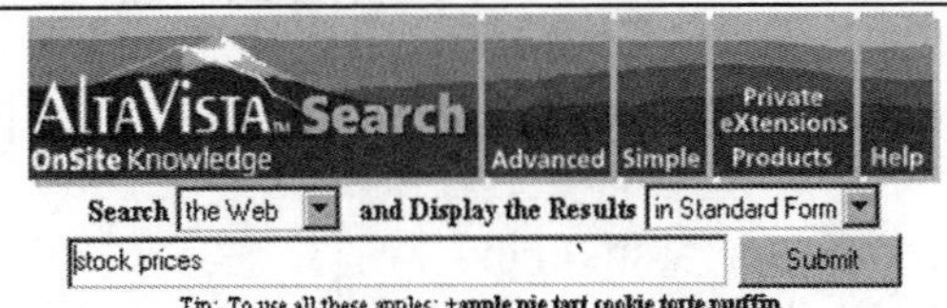

Search the Web **and Display the Results** in Standard Form

stock prices Submit

Tip: To use all these apples: **+apple pie tart cookie torte muffin**

Word count: prices:1055041; stock:1343119

Documents 1-10 of about 500000 matching the query, best matches first.

Selected Financial Data and Quarterly Stock Prices
Data Translation, Inc. and Subsidiaries 1995 Annual Report. Selected Financial Data. Fiscal Years Ended November 30, (in thousands, except per share data..
http://www.datx.com/annual95/selecfin.html - *size 9K - 6 May 96*

Forecasting stock market prices = Prediccion de las cotizaciones bursa- tiles
Template-Type: Document. Title: Forecasting stock market prices = Prediccion de las cotizaciones bursa- tiles. Keywords: Financial market. Author-Name:...
http://netec.mcc.ac.uk/~adnetec/BibEc/ceebbv.vale/ceebbv.93-2.afa.html - *size 607 bytes - 19 May 96*

Authorware Hypermail Archive: Re: MACROMEDIA STOCK PRICES?
Re: MACROMEDIA STOCK PRICES? Ron Fitch (Ronald.Fitch@UNI.EDU) Wed, 26 Jun 1996 16:14:44 -0600. Messages sorted by: [date][thread][subject][author].
http://pa.cc.kuleuven.ac.be/aw2html/current/0557.html - *size 3K - 27 Jun 96*

'No PKO for Countermeasures Against Stock Prices,' says Permanent Vice-Ministe
No PKO for Countermeasures Against Stock Prices,' says Permanent Vice-Minister of the Ministry of Finance. Mr. Kyosuke Shinozawa, permanent Vice-Minister..
http://www.smn.co.jp/business/0037bu03e.html - *size 738 bytes - 23 Oct 95*

Stock Prices
Stock Prices. This Week's Quotes. Last Week's Quotes. January Quotes. February Quotes. March Quotes. April Quotes. May Quotes. June Quotes. 1995 Quotes....
http://hackberry.chem.niu.edu:70/1/Stock%20Prices - *size 1K - 15 Jun 96*

NSE Stock Prices: O
Stock Prices: O. A B C D E F G H I J K L M N O P Q R S T U V W X Y Z. Prices As Of: Tue June 18, 1996. Company Name. Open. High. Low. Close. Prev Close....
http://www.nseindia.com/htdocs/market/O.htm - *size 11K - 19 Jun 96*

NSE Stock Prices: N
Stock Prices: N. A B C D E F G H I J K L M N O P Q R S T U V W X Y Z. Prices As Of: Tue June 18, 1996. Company Name. Open. High. Low. Close. Prev Close....
http://www.nseindia.com/htdocs/market/N.htm - *size 20K - 19 Jun 96*

NSE Stock Prices: M
Stock Prices: M. A B C D E F G H I J K L M N O P Q R S T U V W X Y Z. Prices As Of: Tue June 18, 1996. Company Name. Open. High. Low. Close. Prev Close....
http://www.nseindia.com/htdocs/market/M.htm - *size 35K - 19 Jun 96*

NSE Stock Prices: K
Stock Prices: K. A B C D E F G H I J K L M N O P Q R S T U V W X Y Z. Prices As Of: Tue June 18, 1996. Company Name. Open. High. Low. Close. Prev Close....
http://www.nseindia.com/htdocs/market/K.htm - *size 19K - 19 Jun 96*

NSE Stock Prices: J
Stock Prices: J. A B C D E F G H I J K L M N O P Q R S T U V W X Y Z. Prices As Of: Tue June 18, 1996. Company Name. Open. High. Low. Close. Prev Close....
http://www.nseindia.com/htdocs/market/J.htm - *size 15K - 19 Jun 96*

p. **1** 2 3 4 5 6 7 8 9 10 11 12 13 14 15 16 17 18 19 20 [Next]

Surprise · **Legal** · **FAQ** · **Add URL** · **Feedback** · **Text-Only**

---

digital Copyright © 1996 Digital Equipment Corporation. All rights reserved.

9. Review some of the matches.
10. Notice how these results differ from the results for “stock prices.”
11. Now do a complex search. In the search text box, type:

    stock AND (prices OR quotes)
12. Click the Submit button.
13. When the search is complete, the browser displays the results of the search.

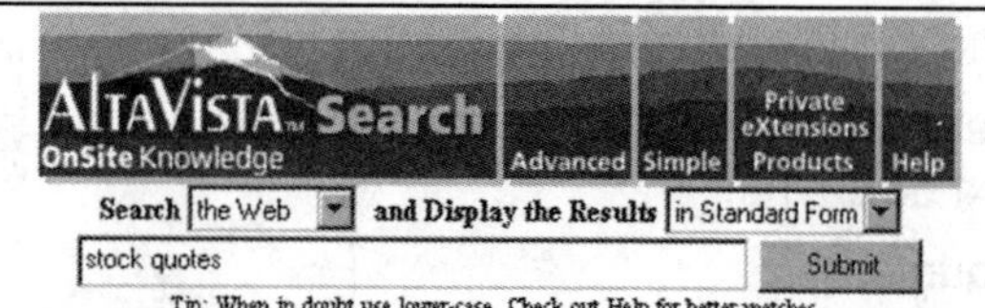

Search the Web and Display the Results in Standard Form

stock quotes Submit

Tip: When in doubt use lower-case. Check out Help for better matches.

Word count: quotes:323274; stock:1243118

Documents 1-10 of about 100000 matching the query, best matches first.

Quote.com Stock Quotes
Ticker Symbols for Futures. Description. Ticker symbols for commodity futures are formed by a combination of the underlying symbol followed by the month...
http://fast.quote.com/fq/intsu/futures_symbols.html - size 5K - 21 Jun 96

Charles Schwab - Stock Quotes
Quotes and Charts Help. Customer Support. Quote Definitions. Price Charts Legend. Quote Definitions. 52 Week High: The highest price at which a security...
http://schwab.quote.com/fq/schwab/schwab.help.html - size 6K - 21 Jun 96

Charles Schwab - Stock Quotes
Ticker Symbols for Street Bond Pricing. Description. Street Software provides several types of fixed-income pricing of government bonds, based on prices...
http://schwab.quote.com/fq/schwab/street_symbols.html - size 6K - 21 Jun 96

GNN Select Daily News: Stock Quotes
GNN Select : Daily News. Stock Quotes. Stock Quotes. Briefing: Concise Market Analysis. CNN Financial Network. DBC Online. Holt's Market Report. Money...

Charles Schwab - Stock Quotes
Ticker Symbols for Options. Description. Ticker symbols for options are formed one way for stock and index option, and another way for futures options....
http://schwab.quote.com/fq/schwab/option_symbols.html - size 6K - 21 Jun 96

Toronto Stock Quotes
Toronto Stock Quotes A Service provided by Telenium A B C D E F G H I J K L M N O P Q R S T U V W X Y Z...
http://www.telenium.ca/TSE/header.html - size 1K - 5 Jun 96

Lombard Stock Quotes
Personal Finance - Stock Quotes & Market Data. Click the review title below to go to the site, or use the arrows to flip through other reviews in this.
http://wc2.webcrawler.com/select/invest.94.html - size 2K - 21 Jun 96

Hooked Stock Quotes
Please direct problems or questions to staff@hooked.net, or call (415) 281-6550. Copyright © 1995, 1996 Hooked, Inc. and 1996 Quote.com, Inc.
http://fast.quote.com/fq/hooked/option_symbols.html - size 1005 bytes - 21 Jun 96

Stock Quotes for Windows 3.x
Overview: These programs allow you to receive stock quotes directly to your computer. They all are wonderful programs and have a lot of options. Well...
http://www.lancite.net/tucows/stock.html - size 4K - 21 Jun 96

Stock Quotes for Windows 95
Overview: These programs allow you to receive stock quotes directly to your computer. They all are wonderful programs and have a lot of options. Well...
http://jocker.reu.edu.uy/MIRRORS/TuCows/stock95.html - size 4K - 21 Jun 96

p. 1 2 3 4 5 6 7 8 9 10 11 12 13 14 15 16 17 18 19 20 [Next]

Surprise · Legal · FAQ · Add URL · Feedback · Text-Only

14. Review some of the matches.
15. Notice how these results differ from the two previous results.
16. Click on the link to to the **Russian Stock Agency Disclaimer**.
17. When you are finished, click the browser's Back button until you return to the AltaVista opening page.
18. Do another complex search. In the search text box, type:

    stock AND quotes AND NOT prices

19. Click the Submit button.

    When the search is complete, the browser displays the results of the search.

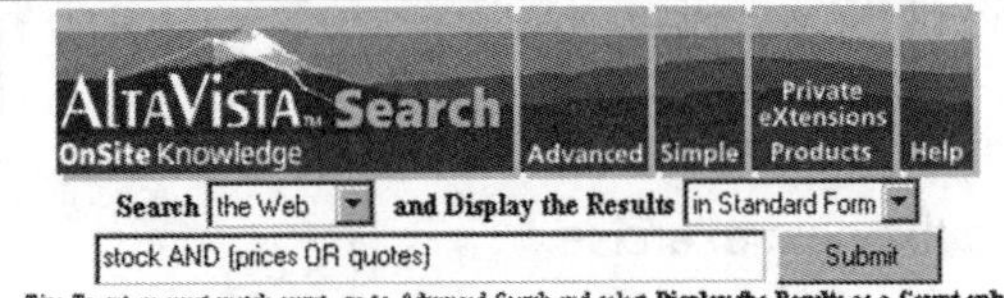

Search the Web **and Display the Results** in Standard Form

stock AND (prices OR quotes) Submit

Tip: To get an exact match count, go to Advanced Search and select **Display the Results as a Count only**

Word count: quotes:323274; prices:1088841; OR:1090286; stock:1343119; AND:2383754

Documents 1-10 of about 200000 matching the query, best matches first.

Prices and Quotes - Webpage Design and Editing
MCN Intl.,Inc. BASIC QUOTES on WebPage Design & Editing. Basic WebPage Construction - Contract Grundlegende WebSeiten Erstellung - Vertrag. Business...
http://www.domina.com/info/quote.html - *size 10K - 22 May 96*
http://www.mcnintl.com/info/quote.html - *size 10K - 21 May 96*

Eyes for U Quotes & Prices
Quotes via e-mail. We need to know the manufacturer and style number of the frame you are requesting price information on. Name: E-mail address:...
http://www.eyesforu.com/quote.html - *size 1K - 26 Apr 96*

Quotes & Earnings - Daily Unit Prices
Quotes & Earnings - Daily Unit Prices. First Canadian Mutual Funds - Assets and Unit Prices..............as at June 20, 1996. T-Bill Fund Total Unit..
http://www.fcfunds.bomil.ca/forms/fb1/fb1a.html - *size 8K - 21 Jun 96*

Quotes & Earnings - Daily Unit Prices
Quotes & Earnings - Daily Unit Prices. First Canadian Mutual Funds - Assets and Unit Prices..............as at June 19, 1996. T-Bill Fund Total Unit..
http://www.fcfunds.bomil.ca/fcfunds/forms/fb1/fb1a.html - *size 8K - 20 Jun 96*

Russian Stock Agency - Disclaimer
Disclaimer. Russian Stock Agency (Russkoe Fondovoe Agentstvo) is a company duly established and operating under the laws of the Russian Federation. All...
http://www.rfanet.com/disclaim/ - *size 2K - 16 Jun 96*

Stock/Portfolio Updater
Stock Quotes Updates prices of stocks, mutual funds and other securities traded in the United States and Canada. Twenty-minute delay from live trading...
http://www.suntimes.com/business/pcgt.html - *size 2K - 27 Jun 96*

****

- Disclaimer

Russian Stock Agency (Russkoe Fondovoe Agentstvo) is a company duly established and operating under the laws of the Russian Federation. All relationships with clients are conducted in accordance with the laws of the Russian Federation. It is the responsibility of the client to comply with the securities and other laws of his/her country of domicile.

This WWW site is for informational purposes only and is not intended as an offer or solicitation with respect to the purchase or sale of any security. All research materials found here are intended for the use of the general public and may be outdated and incomplete. Forecasts constitute our judgement as of the date of the report. Research materials are provided as is. Russian Stock Agency will not be liable for any losses caused directly or indirectly by the use of the information found on this WWW site.

Quotes and prices listed on our Bids and Offers Page may or may not reflect our current quotes and prices due to the high volatility of the Russian securities market.

The choice of country of this WWW site (USA) was based on technical and cost considerations only. No exclusive attraction of American investors is intended. We developed this site for the global community in accordance with Russian laws and international practices.

[Back to Russian Stock Agency Homepage]

Copyright (c) 1996 by Russian Stock Agency (Russkoe Fondovoe Agentstvo)
Last Update: June 15, 1996

20. Read some of the matches. Notice how these results differ from the three previous results.
21. Continue to the next exercise.

OR

Exit from your browser and disconnect from your service provider.

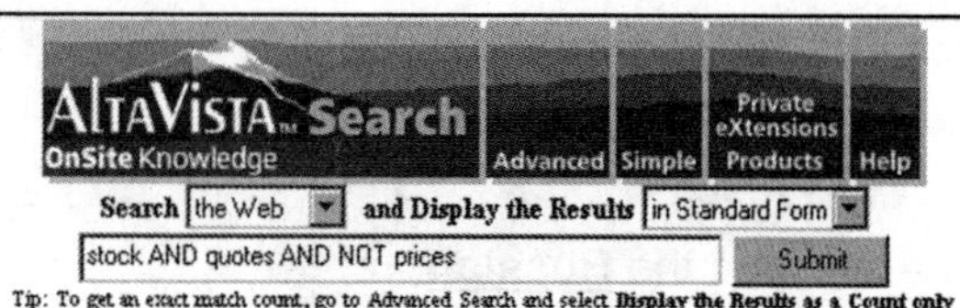

Search the Web **and Display the Results** in Standard Form

stock AND quotes AND NOT prices Submit

Tip: To get an exact match count, go to Advanced Search and select **Display the Results as a Count only**

Word count: quotes:323274; NOT:750872; prices:1088841; stock:1343119; AND:3283754

Documents 1-10 of about 500000 matching the query, best matches first.

Some NOT So Famous Quotes
Famous Quotes. Computers are useless. They can only give you answers. Pablo Picasso. I haven't failed, I've found 10,000 ways that don't work. Ben...
http://www.tri-c.cc.oh.us/CS270/znidarsi/znidarsi/web/pages/quotes.htm - size 2K - 16 Mar 96

No Title
PWCYOKOINST 4200.2 800 25 April 1996 PWC YOKOSUKA INSTRUCTION 4200.2 Subj: MANAGEMENT OF THE GOVERNMENT-WIDE COMMERCIAL PURCHASE CARD PROGRAM Ref: (a)...
http://199.208.5.19/instr/4200-2.txt - size 33K - 10 May 96

WPL - The WISE Programming Language
WPL - The WISE Programming Language (version 1.0) This file briefly describes the syntax and semantics of the WISE Programming Language (WPL - pronounced..
http://research.ivv.nasa.gov/projects/WISE/WPL.html - size 12K - 6 Nov 95

MancWatch Part I
MancWatch Part I. The Pilot Episode. ScouseWatch vs. MancWatch. Festive MancWatch. MancWatch Mortis. Mystic MancWatch. FA-Cup MancWatch. Euro MancWatch....
http://www.globalcafe.com.my/community/anfield/mwatch/mwatch1.htm - size 28K - 1 Jun 96

No Title
Quick Start: IBM FORTRAN. COMPILING AND RUNNING FORTRAN. Academic Computing presently offers FORTRAN 77, version 1.3, on the IBM 9000. This document will..
http://magic.hofstra.edu/~acchelp/quickstart/FORTRANqs.html - size 8K - 5 Jun 95

Search BENE or BIN21
Home Page | Information | Search | BIN21 | Projects | Resources | History. Search BENE or BIN21. BENE. BENE Directory. Index. Table of Contents (TOC)...
http://straylight.tamu.edu/bene/home/bene.search.html - size 3K - 5 Dec 95

LIS From The Workstation
LIS From The Workstation. Note: things we want you to type - commands, search strings, etc. - we enclose in single quotes (' '). Do NOT include the...
http://www.csw.cmu.edu/coursework/UT6.html - size 9K - 29 Feb 96

What did it all mean?
What did it all mean? OK, you've now learned to compile a program, but I still haven't said anything about what all that mysterious stuff meant. So what...
http://www.nmr.mgh.harvard.edu/C/explain_hello.shtml - size 5K - 16 Jun 96

INTOUCH® 4GL A Guide to the INTOUCH Language
INTOUCH. ® 4GL A Guide to the INTOUCH Language. Previous page... | Contents. VAL returns the floating-point value of a numeric string....
http://www.ttinet.com/doc/language_023.html - size 37K - 8 Feb 96

No Title
Table of Contents * Previous Chapter * Index. Advanced Package Writing. 11.1 There Be Dragons Here. □ The purpose of this section is to warn you to...
http://www-phys.llnl.gov/X_Div/htdocs/author/chap11.html - size 67K - 24 Jan 95

p. 1 2 3 4 5 6 7 8 9 10 11 12 13 14 15 16 17 18 19 20 [Next]

Surprise · **Legal** · **FAQ** · **Add URL** · **Feedback** · **Text-Only**

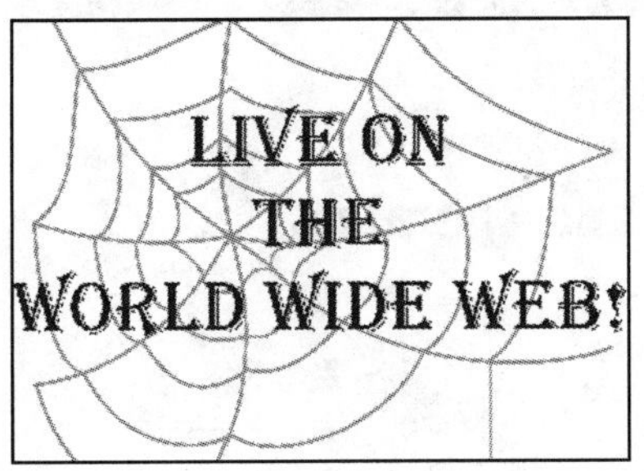

AltaVista HomePage
http://www.altavista.digital.com

Wall Street Journal Interactive Edition
http://www.wsj.com

New York Stock Exchange Home Page – An educational tool for teachers, students, and investors interested in learning more about the stock market. This site also provides links to the NYSE's news, publishing, educational, research, and tourism services. Click links to access a market summary, an index of listed companies, or a glossary.
http://www.nyse.com

Stock Smart Market News Home Page
http://www.stocksmart.com/newsmarket.html

UWMC WWW Server at University of Wisconsin Marathon Center – A University Web site containing information on News, News Sources, Weather, Stock Market, TV, Radio and Hot Topics.
http://mthwww.uwc.edu/wwwmahes/news.htm

Exercise 5

◆ What is Lycos? ◆ Lycos Home Page Location
◆ Lycos Search Options ◆ Lycos Search Strings and Operators

NOTES

What is Lycos?

- The Lycos Web search site, named after the Latin name of the wolf spider, claims to have mapped 90% of the Web. It is a free search service that sells advertisement space on its home page and search results pages.
- You can search the Lycos catalog of Web sites for document titles, headings, links, and key words. The first 50 words of each Web page that Lycos finds is displayed for you.

NOTE
Remember that search engines are called "spiders" because they crawl the Web.

Lycos Home Page Location

- To connect to the Lycos search site, type:

  http://www.lycos.com

  on the Location line of your browser and press Enter.

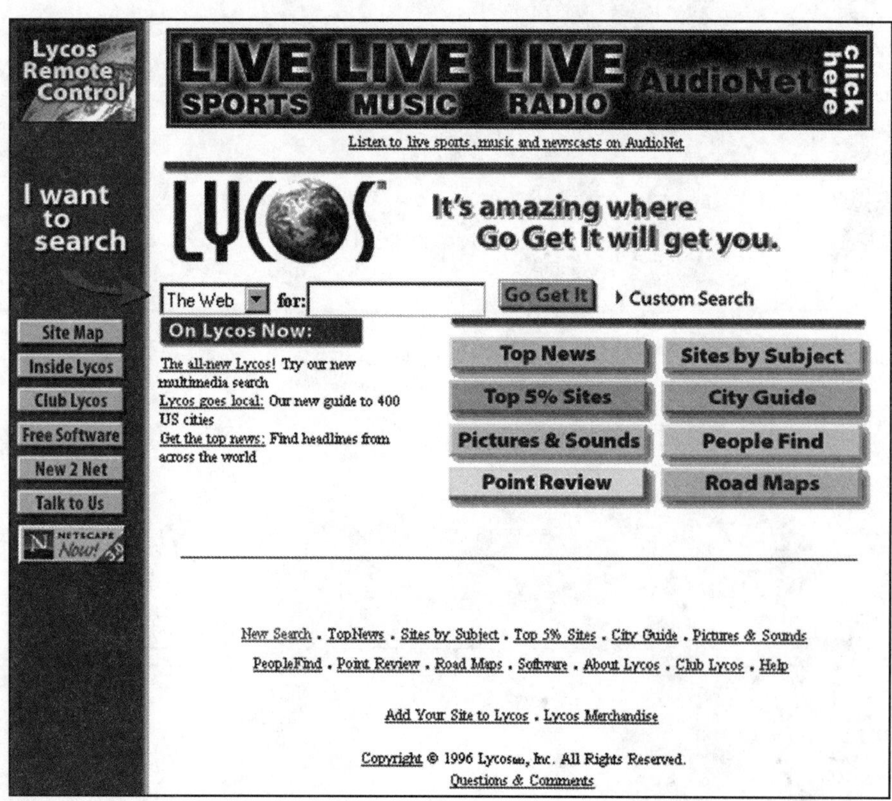

Lycos Search Options

- Lycos provides a simple search interface without search or display options on its home page. The text box, labeled **for:**, accepts text strings and operators (Lycos operators are explained on the following page), and a Go Get It button to start the catalog search.
- Lycos also provides an advanced search interface with search and display options, at the following URL:

  http://www.lycos.com/customsearch.html

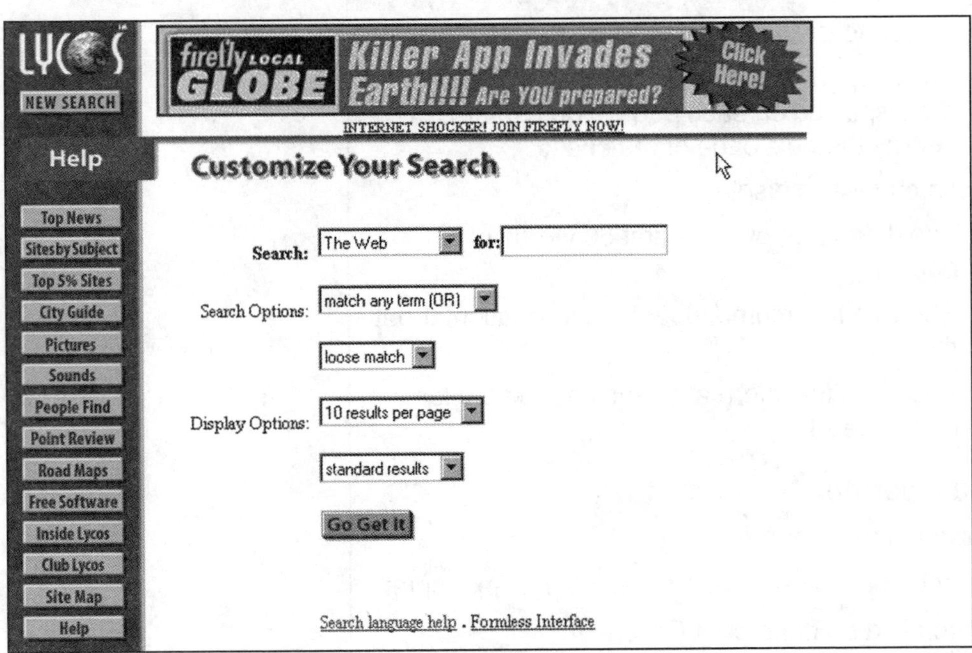

- Like the Lycos home page, the custom search page has a text box for entering text strings and operators (Lycos operators are explained on the following page), and a Go Get It button used to initiate the catalog search.
- There is a pull-down menu to select where to search. You can choose from the following: The Web, Sound, Pictures, or Sites by Subject.
- In addition, there are four pull-down menus you can use to customize your search.
- Two of the pull-down menus modify Search Options.

  In the first menu, you can choose to:

Match Any Term (OR) This is the default search. It finds a match if *any* term in the search string is found in a document, heading, or link. (This is the Boolean OR function.)

Match All Terms (AND) The search finds a match only if *every* term in the search string is found in a document, heading, or link. (This is the Boolean AND function.)

Match *n* Terms (2 - 7) These search options find a match if the specified number of terms from the search string are found in the document, heading, or link.

In the second menu, you can choose one of the following:

Loose Match (the default)	Fair Match, Good Match, Close Match, or Strong Match—these options set how many search results you see. For example, a loose match will find all sites with a faint relation to your search string, while a strong match will find only sites that pertain exactly to your search string.

- Two pull-down menus set Display Options.

  In the first menu, you can choose to display:

***n* Results Per Page (10 [default] - 40)**	These options set how many search matches are displayed on each page. You can also display the next page of matches.

In the second menu, you can choose to display:

Standard Results	The default. Shows the first 50 words of a document.
Summary Results	Shows a minimum amount of information about the site.
Detailed Results	Shows all the information the catalog contains about the site.

Lycos Search Strings and Operators

- Lycos recognizes the following search operators:
  - A period (.) limits the search to the exact string entered. For example:

    Type *account.* in the search text box and click Go Get It.

    This finds sites whose descriptions contain the word "account," but not the words "accountants" or "accounting."
  - A dollar sign ($) expands the search string. This is useful if you are not sure how to spell the key word you want to find. For example:

    Type *enter$* in the search text box and click Go Get It.

    This finds sites whose descriptions contain words like "enterprise" and "entertainment."
  - A minus sign (–) is used to narrow your search. (This is similar to the Boolean NOT function.) For example:

    Type *database – program* in the search text box, select the Match All Terms (AND) search option, and click Go Get It.
  - This finds sites whose descriptions contain the word "database," but not "program."
- Here are some things that you cannot search for in Lycos text strings:
  - Words shorter than three characters.
  - The minus sign (–), which is used as the NOT operator.
  - Words like "a," "an," or "the," which are always ignored in searches.

In this exercise you will perform searches at the Lycos search site using multiple key words and operators.

EXERCISE DIRECTIONS

1. If you are already connected to your service provider and your browser is open, go to step 2.

   OR

   Connect to your service provider and open your browser.

   ✓ *The examples here use Netscape Navigator.*

2. On the Location line, type the following and then press enter:

   http://www.ddcpub.com/learn

3. Click the link to **Lesson 3: Search Engines, Exercise 5 "Lycos"**.

   The Lycos advanced search page appears.

4. In the search text box, type:

   gold prices

5. Select the *Match All Terms (AND)* and *strong match* search options. Use the default Display Options (*10 results per page* and *standard results*).

6. Click the Go Get It button.

   This finds sites which contain the words gold and prices.

7. Read through a few of the matches to see what they say.

8. In the search text box, type:

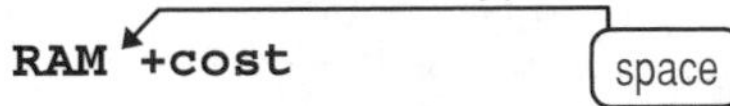

9. Click the Go Get It! button.

   This finds sites which contain the word cost and word RAM.

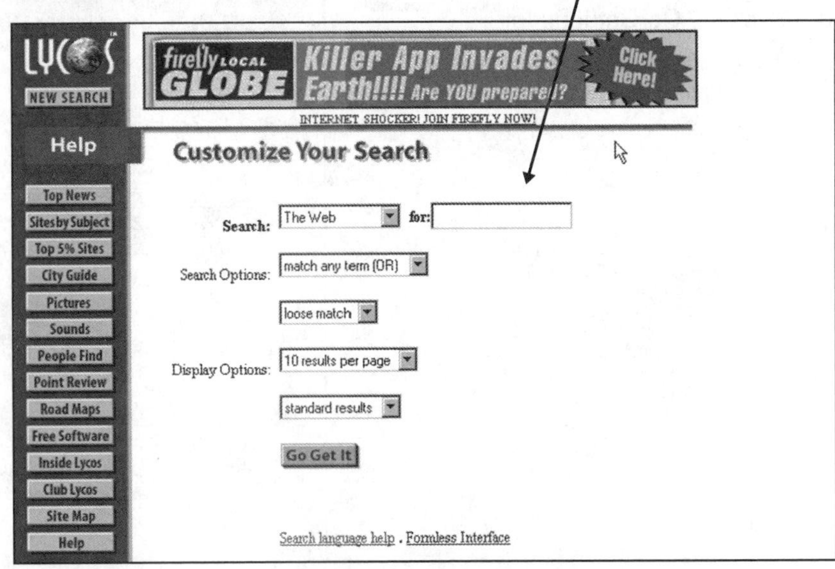

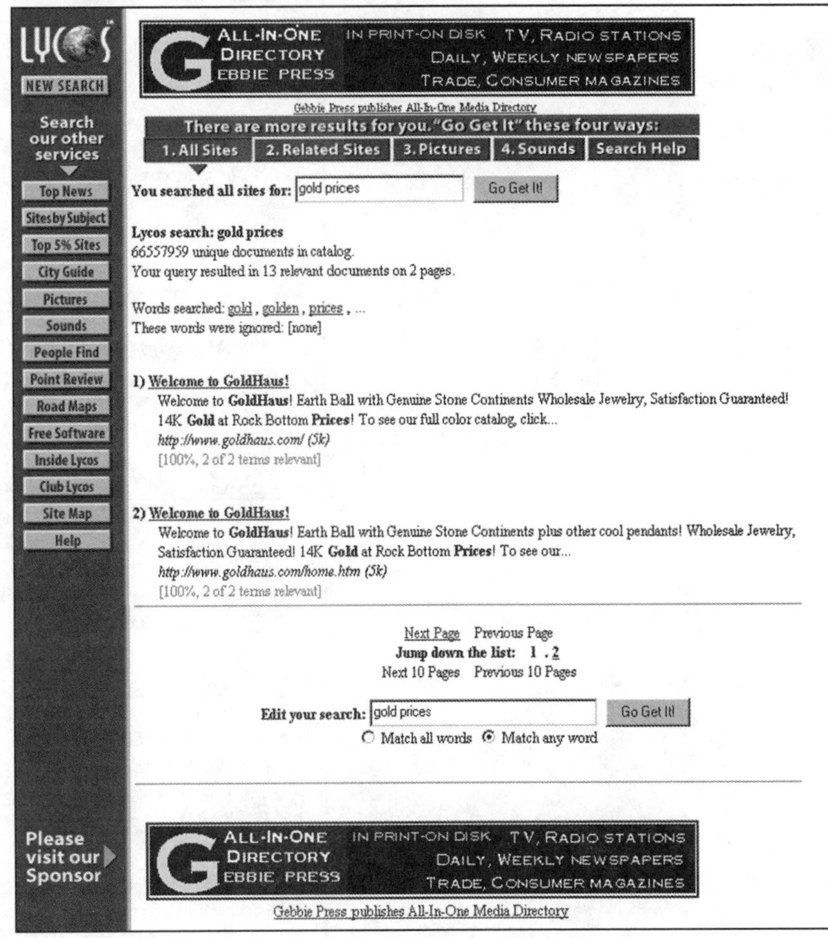

10. Read through a few of the matches to see what they say.
11. In the search text box at the bottom of the results page, type:

    `NCAA +football` (space)

12. Click the Go Get It button.

    This finds sites which contain the words NCAA and football.

CTS is your *SOURCE* for Memory at discount prices!!!

LINK TO LYCOS | INFORMATION | ADD A SITE | NEW2NET

Lycos search: RAM cost
59,945,140 unique URLs
Found 100,393 documents with the words ram (41,339), cost (34,857), costs (54,143), ...

1) **EMail Msg <9312290718.AA24776@csd4.csd.uwm.edu>**
EMail Msg <9312290718.AA24776@csd4.csd.uwm.edu> Re: Low **Cost Ram** and Flash CardsAnthony J Stieber <anthony@csd4.csd.uwm.edu> Mail folder: Zoomer-List Mailing List Archives, 1...
http://www.eit.com/mailinglists/zoomer/zoomer-list/zoomer-list-1993.messages/315.html (14k)
[100%, 2 of 2 terms relevant]

2) **Computers R US!!**
; rev="Made" Computers R US!! Buy Below Dealer **Cost**!!! Buy a 586 133mhz Cpu and Motherboard For only $250.00 Plus Shipping/Handling!!
http://www.bestmall.com./computer/ (3k)
[100%, 2 of 2 terms relevant]

3) **Cost Areas and Metrics**
Cost breakdowns Hardware **Costs**: - needs a mid-486, 8-12mb **RAM**, 200mb (minimum config / 1.5 yr life) - needs a Pentium, 16-24mb **RAM**, 500mb (3 yr life) -$1,000-$3,200 per system...
http://www.entex-is.com/WIN9503.HTM (2k)
[65%, 2 of 2 terms relevant]

4) **[SND] costillo.ram**
[SND] costillo.ram;
http://ww2.audionet.com/pub/lax/m/costillo.ram (0k)
[63%, 2 of 2 terms relevant]

5) **Construction of Low Cost Carbon Electrodes**
Construction of Low **Cost** Carbon Electrodes Construction of Low **Cost** Carbon Electrodes Adapted from original work by K.V. Sane, University of Delhi, India **Ram** S. Lamba and Ramón...
http://www.lce.org/equipment/phmeter/electrodes.html (2k)
[52%, 2 of 2 terms relevant]

6) **Construction of a Low Cost pH Meter**
Construction of a Low **Cost** pH Meter Construction of a Low **Cost** pH Meter **Ram** S. Lamba and Ramón De La Cuétara, Locally Produced Low **Cost** Equipment Project, UNESCO-IUPAC...
http://www.lce.org/equipment/phmeter/phmeter.html (25k)
[50%, 2 of 2 terms relevant]

7) **TruCost Catalog: Systems PDA**
TruCost Catalog: Systems PDA TruCost Enterprises. 1-800-892-9476 Order Now:. Systems- PDA [58 Matches.] Mfgr.: HEWLETT PACKARD TruCost Catalog# HPD633754 Model #F1060A#ABA: 200LX PALMTOP 1MB **RAM**...
http://www.trucost.com/xsy05.html (11k)
[50%, 2 of 2 terms relevant]

8) **Albert J leBlanc Computer Specials**
Albert J leBlanc Computer Specials Here are a few good items on sale (my **cost**) *These prices are dealer **cost** yourpay cost+freight+taxes I get a 10% consulting fee. order are payable on arrival...
http://www.newedge.net/albert/special.htm (3k)
[50%, 2 of 2 terms relevant]

13. Read through a few of the matches to see what they say.
14. Continue on to the next exercise.

    OR

    Exit from your browser and disconnect from your service provider.

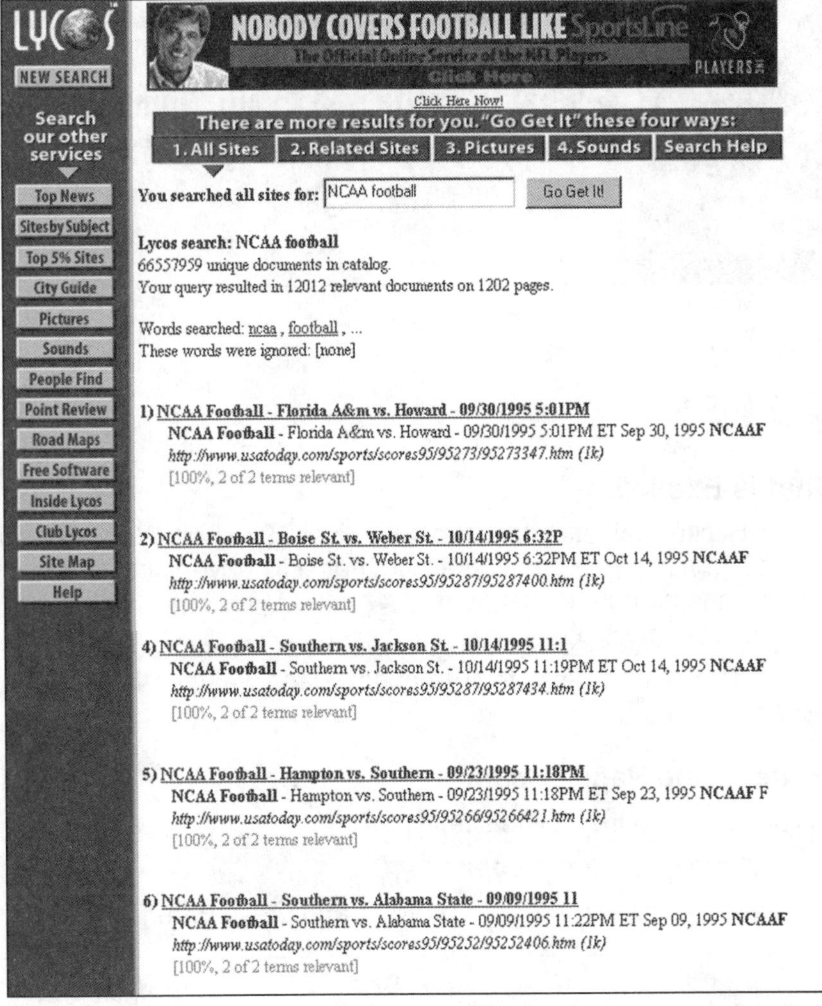

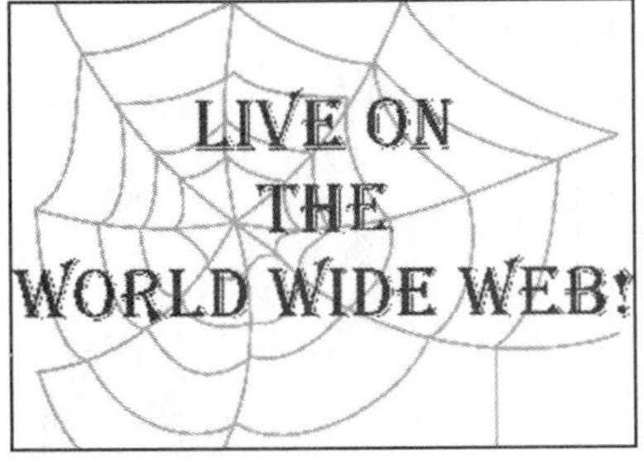

Lycos Home Page
http://www.lycos.com

Banking on the WWW – The Institute of Finance and Banking at the University of Göttingen, Germany has a depository of Web links relating to business and finance. The banking page has Web sites for banks worldwide as well as academic information relating to banks.
http://www.wiso.gwdg.de/ifbg/banking.html

Federal Reserve Bank of Philadelphia Home Page – Information on the Federal Reserve Bank of Philadelphia. Get more information on reserve banks and the U.S. monetary system.
http://www.libertynet.org/~fedresrv/fedpage.html

World Wide Web of Sports – Resource for sports information. Find sections devoted to a wide range of sports (basketball to sailing to cricket)
http://www.tns.lcs.mit.edu/cgi-bin/sports

Exercise 6

◆ What is Excite? ◆ Excite Home Page Location ◆ Excite Search Options ◆ Excite Search Strings and Operators

NOTES

What is Excite?

- The Excite Web site claims to have over 50 million Web pages in its catalog. It is a free search service that sells advertising space on its home page and search results pages.
- The Excite site also contains two weeks of **Usenet** articles and classified ads. The site has links to current news and weather that is updated every 30 minutes.

Excite Home Page Location

- To connect to the Excite site, type:

  http://www.excite.com

  on the Location line of your browser and press Enter.

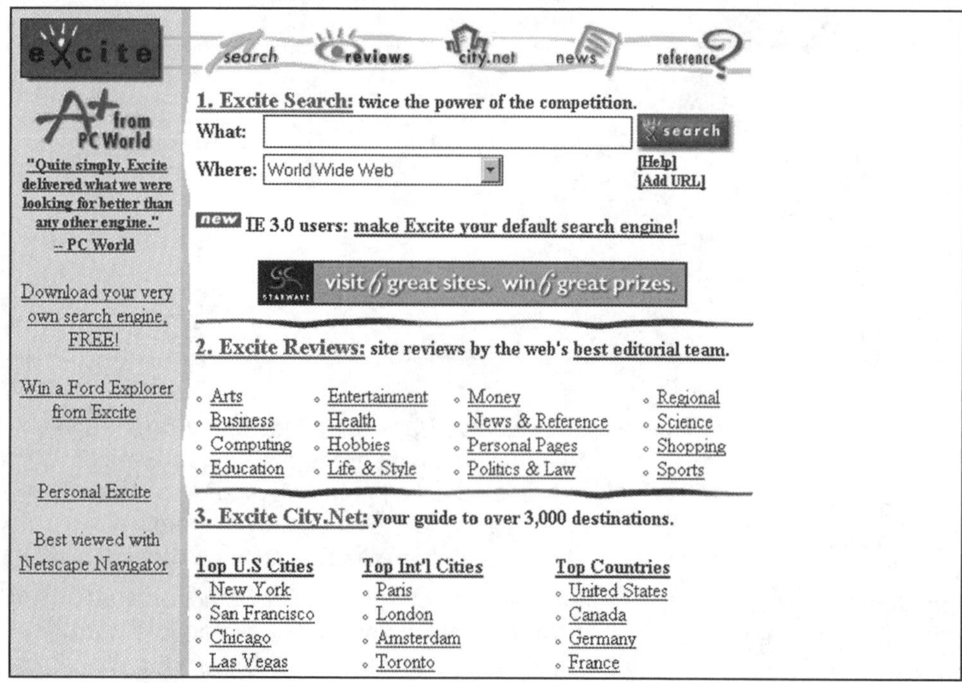

(continued)

TIP

To access Excite quickly, add its URL to your browser bookmarks.

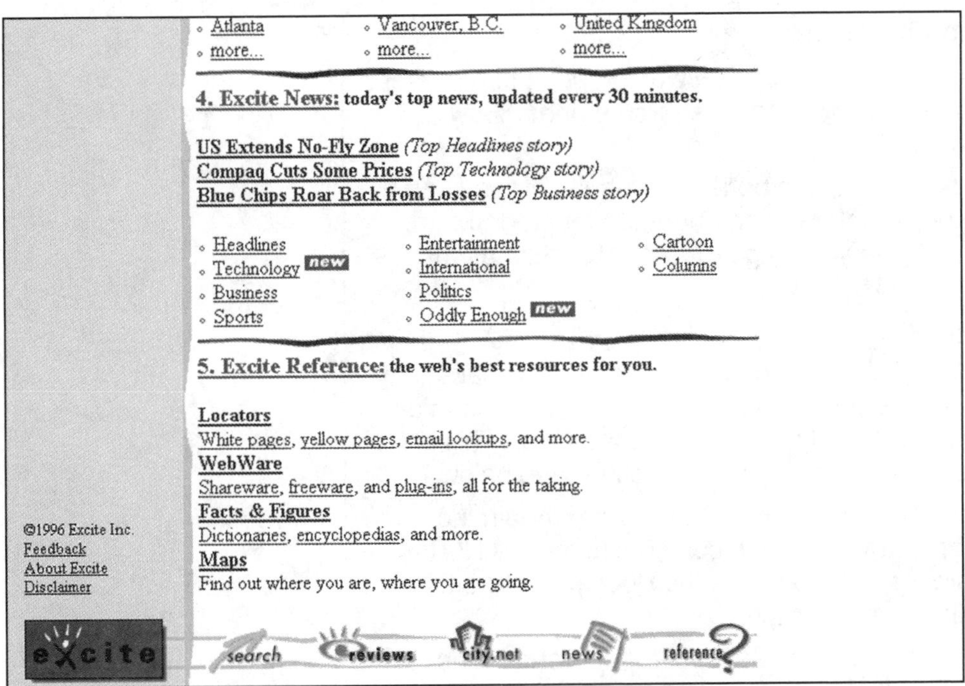

Excite Search Options

- Excite provides a search interface on its home page called Excite Search. There is a text box, labeled *What*, that accepts text strings and operators, and a Search button that starts the catalog search. (Excite operators are explained below.)
- A pull-down menu, labeled *Where*, selects the catalog to search. The choices are:
  - World Wide Web
  - Excite Web Site Reviews (over 60,000 sites reviewed by an editorial staff)
  - Usenet Newsgroups
  - Usenet Classifieds
- Search results are displayed 10 at a time in decreasing order of confidence rating. Each result consists of a title, a URL, and a brief summary of the page.
- The confidence rating is displayed on the left of the result. This shows how closely the result matches what you are searching for. A result rated close to 100% has a good chance of being what you want.
- To see the next 10 results of the search, click on Next Documents.
- To see which Web sites have the most pages relevant to your search, click on *Sort By Site*.
- If a result on your list is close to what you are looking for, click *More Like This* next to the title. This finds other Web pages related to the same topic.
- The Excite search interface appears at the top of each results page so you can easily start a new search.

TIP

For more information about search options and the Excite site, click on the Help link.

Excite Search Strings and Operators

- You can enter search text phrased the way you would speak to a person. For example, you could use the following as a search string: "How to vacation on five dollars a day."
- The more descriptive words you use, the better the results of the search. For example, if you're looking for information about life found on Mars, using the word "Mars" will not give you as good a list of results as the phrase "Life found on Mars."
- Excite recognizes the following search operators:

Plus sign (+) Placed immediately in front of a word (no space between the plus sign and the word) means that all documents found must contain that word. (This is similar to the Boolean AND function. See below.)

Minus sign (–) Placed immediately in front of a word (again, no space) means that all documents found will NOT contain that word. (This is the Boolean AND NOT function. See below.)

- Excite supports full Boolean operators and syntax for searches. The Boolean operators must be in ALL CAPS to be recognized as operators. The Excite Boolean operators are:

AND The documents found in the search must contain all words joined by the AND operator. For example:

Type *water AND skiing* in the search text box and click Search.

This finds sites whose descriptions include both *water* and *skiing*.

OR The documents found in the search must contain *at least one* of the words joined by the OR operator. For example:

Type *flowers OR plants* in the search text box and click Search.

This finds sites whose descriptions include either the word *flowers* or the word *plants*, or both.

AND NOT The documents found in the search must *not* contain the word following the AND NOT operator. For example:

Type *peanut AND NOT butter* in the search text box and click Search.

This finds sites whose descriptions include the word *peanut*, but not the word *butter*.

Parentheses ( ) Parentheses are used to group portions of the search string. For example:

Type *plants AND (tropical OR exotic)* in the search text box and click Search.

This finds sites whose descriptions include *plants* and *tropical* or the words *plants* and *exotic* or all three words.

In this exercise you will perform searches at the Excite search site using multiple key words and operators.

EXERCISE DIRECTIONS

1. If you are already connected to your service provider and your browser is open, continue to step 2.

   OR

   Connect to your service provider and open your browser.

   ✓ *The examples here use Netscape Navigator.*

2. On the Location line, type the following and then press Enter.

   http://www.ddcpub.com/learn

3. Click the link to **Lesson 3: Search Engines, Exercise 6, "Excite"**.

   The Excite search site home page appears.

4. In the search text box, type:

   Price of gold in the international market

5. Click the Search button.

   This finds sites whose descriptions contain the words price, gold, international, *and* market. *The more these words appear in a document, the higher the confidence rating.*

6. Read through a few of the matches to see what they say. Compare the results of this search to the results of the similar search you made in the previous exercise.

7. Click the browser's Back button to return to Excite's opening screen.

8. In the search text box, type:

   (RAM OR memory) AND cost

9. Click the Search button.

   *This finds sites whose descriptions contain the words **RAM** and **cost**, or the words **memory** and **cost**, or all three of the words.*

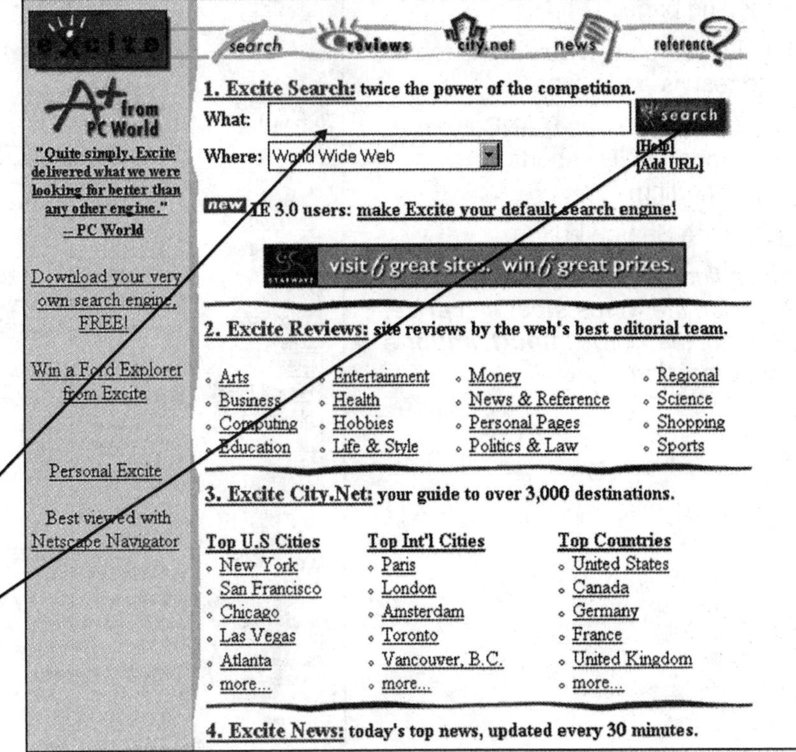

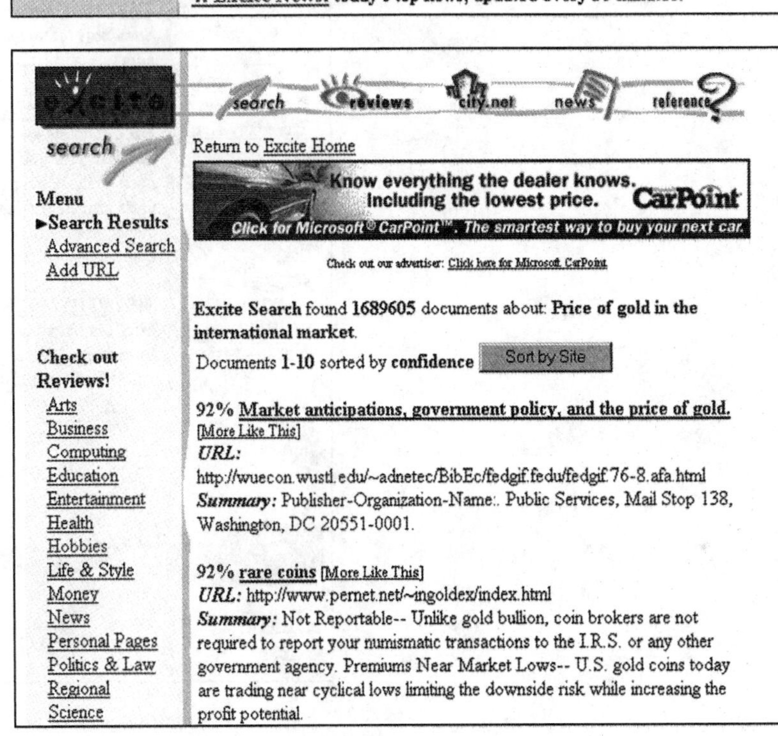

10. Read through a few of the matches to see what they say. Compare the result of this search to the result of the similar search you made in the previous exercise.
11. Click Back to return to Excite's opening page.
12. In the search text box at the top of the results page, type:

    (steel AND price) AND NOT (import AND imports AND importing)

13. Click the Search button.

    *This finds sites whose descriptions contain the words **steel** and **price**, but not the words **import**, **imports**, or **importing**.*

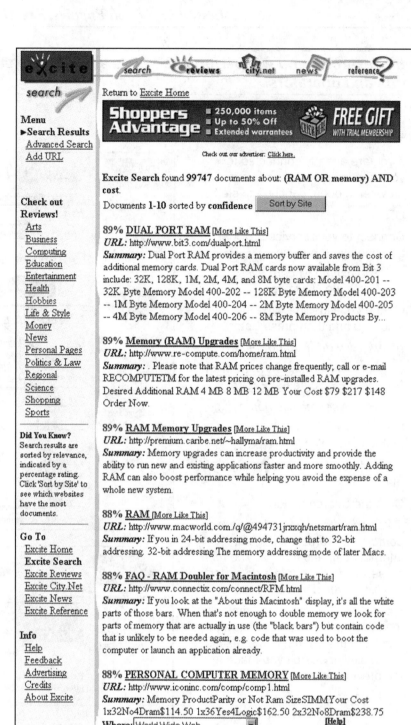

excite — search — reviews — city.net — news — reference

search

Return to Excite Home

Shoppers Advantage ■ 250,000 items ■ Up to 50% Off ■ Extended warrantees FREE GIFT WITH TRIAL MEMBERSHIP

Check out our advertiser: Click here.

Menu
- ►**Search Results**
- Advanced Search
- Add URL

Check out Reviews!
- Arts
- Business
- Computing
- Education
- Entertainment
- Health
- Hobbies
- Life & Style
- Money
- News
- Personal Pages
- Politics & Law
- Regional
- Science
- Shopping
- Sports

Did You Know? Search results are sorted by relevance, indicated by a percentage rating. Click 'Sort by Site' to see which websites have the most documents.

Go To
- Excite Home
- **Excite Search**
- Excite Reviews
- Excite City.Net
- Excite News
- Excite Reference

Info
- Help
- Feedback
- Advertising
- Credits
- About Excite

Excite Search found **99747** documents about: **(RAM OR memory) AND cost**.

Documents **1-10** sorted by **confidence** [Sort by Site]

89% **DUAL PORT RAM** [More Like This]
URL: http://www.bit3.com/dualport.html
Summary: Dual Port RAM provides a memory buffer and saves the cost of additional memory cards. Dual Port RAM cards now available from Bit 3 include: 32K, 128K, 1M, 2M, 4M, and 8M byte cards: Model 400-201 -- 32K Byte Memory Model 400-202 -- 128K Byte Memory Model 400-203 -- 1M Byte Memory Model 400-204 -- 2M Byte Memory Model 400-205 -- 4M Byte Memory Model 400-206 -- 8M Byte Memory Products By...

89% **Memory (RAM) Upgrades** [More Like This]
URL: http://www.re-compute.com/home/ram.html
Summary: . Please note that RAM prices change frequently; call or e-mail RECOMPUTETM for the latest pricing on pre-installed RAM upgrades. Desired Additional RAM 4 MB 8 MB 12 MB Your Cost $79 $217 $148 Order Now.

89% **RAM Memory Upgrades** [More Like This]
URL: http://premium.caribe.net/~hallyma/ram.html
Summary: Memory upgrades can increase productivity and provide the ability to run new and existing applications faster and more smoothly. Adding RAM can also boost performance while helping you avoid the expense of a whole new system.

88% **RAM** [More Like This]
URL: http://www.macworld.com./q/@494731jrxxqh/netsmart/ram.html
Summary: If you in 24-bit addressing mode, change that to 32-bit addressing. 32-bit addressing The memory addressing mode of later Macs.

88% **FAQ - RAM Doubler for Macintosh** [More Like This]
URL: http://www.connectix.com/connect/RFM.html
Summary: If you look at the "About this Macintosh" display, it's all the white parts of those bars. When that's not enough to double memory we look for parts of memory that are actually in use (the "black bars") but contain code that is unlikely to be needed again, e.g. code that was used to boot the computer or launch an application already.

88% **PERSONAL COMPUTER MEMORY** [More Like This]
URL: http://www.iconinc.com/comp/comp1.html
Summary: Memory ProductParity or Not Ram SizeSIMMYour Cost 1x32No4Dram$114.50 1x36Yes4Logic$162.50 2x32No8Dram$238.75

Where: World Wide Web **[Help]** **[Advanced Search]**

IE 3.0 users: one click here makes Excite your default search engine!

14. Read through a few of the matches to see what they say. Compare the result of this search to the result of the similar search you made in the previous exercise.
15. Continue on to the next exercise.

    OR

    Exit from your browser and disconnect from your service provider.

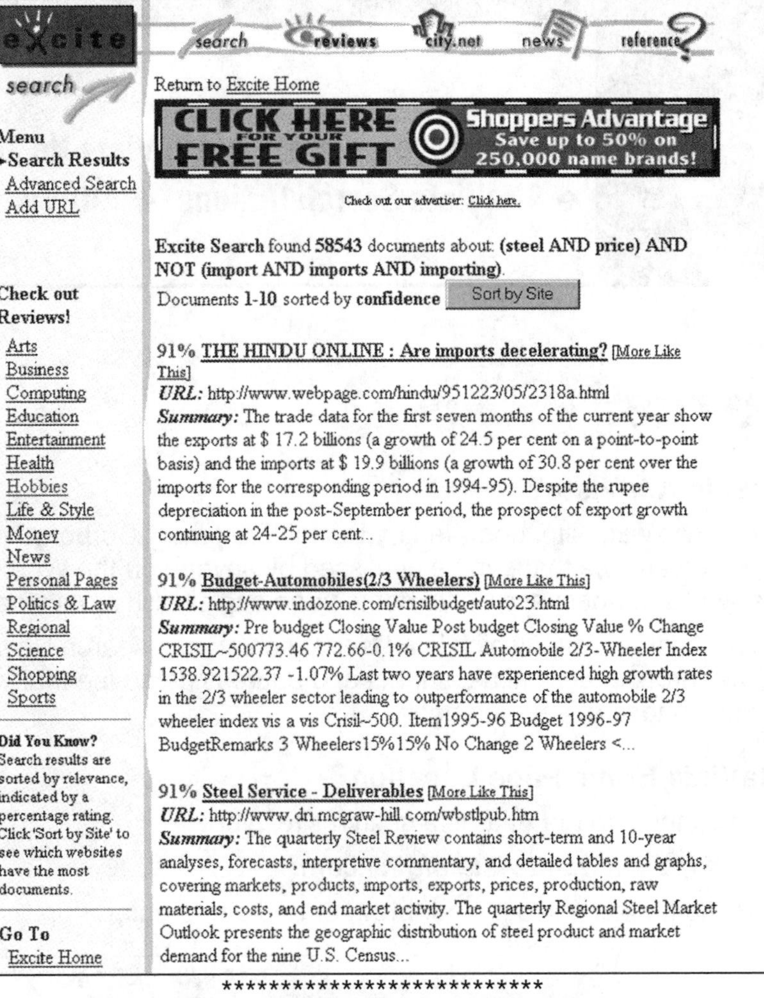

****

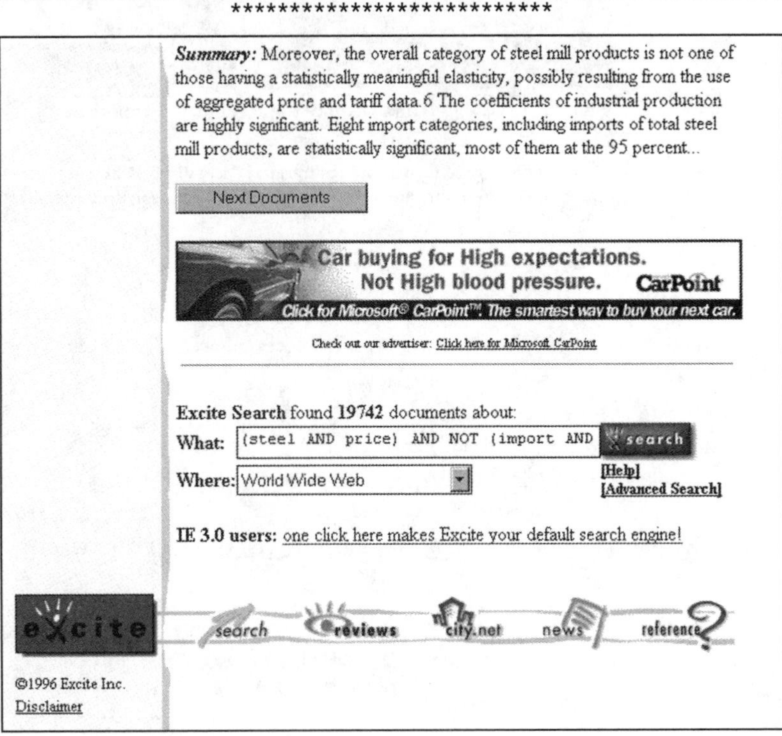

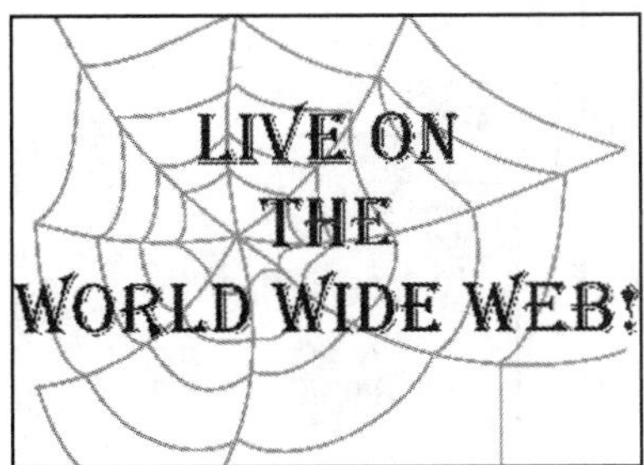

Excite Home Page
    http://www.excite.com

Colorado Resort Net Home Page – Online guide to various Colorado ski resorts. Contains links to a vacation planner, a discount desk (where you can get the latest discounts on local services), and an up-to-the-minute ski condition report.
    http://www.toski.com:80/CRNMAIN.HTM

The Globe Corner Bookstore - Product Catalog – General Travel Guides
    http://www.globecorner.com/p/i50.html

American Express Travel Guides
    http://www.globecorner.com/s/46.html

AAA source of travel guides Walkabout Travel Gear™ foreign travel books
    http://www.walkabouttravelgear.com/planet.htm

Exercise 7

◆ What is AltaVista? ◆ AltaVista Home Page Location ◆ AltaVista Search Options ◆ AltaVista Search Strings and Operators

NOTES

What is AltaVista?

- The AltaVista site, operated by Digital Equipment Corporation, is a free search service that can be accessed by anyone on the Web. It sells advertisement space on its home page and search results pages.
- The AltaVista site, which is a Usenet server, can search Usenet newsgroups, as well as a name and address database that works like the white pages of a phone book.

AltaVista Home Page Location

- To connect to the AltaVista search site, type:

  http://www.altavista.digital.com

  on the Location line of your browser and press Enter.

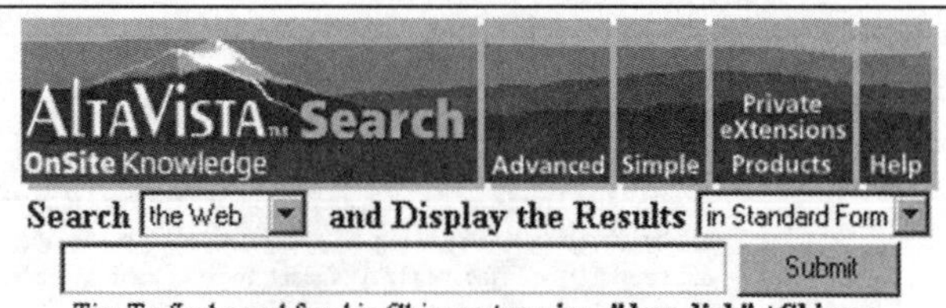

Search [the Web] **and Display the Results** [in Standard Form]

[Submit]

Tip: To find good food in Chicago try: **pizza "deep dish" +Chicago**
The plus sign before a word means that the word MUST appear in the document.

ALTAVISTA

AltaVista gives you access to the largest Web index: 30 million pages found on 275,600 servers, and four million articles from 14,000 Usenet news groups. It is accessed over 18 million times per weekday.

NEWS FROM ALTAVISTA

Altavista Search In Major Worldwide Expansion.

Catch the vision! Join the AltaVista Visionary Club, now!

POWERED BY DIGITAL UNIX, DIGITAL ALPHA AND ALTAVISTA SEARCH SOFTWARE

Surprise · Legal · FAQ · Add URL · Feedback · Text-Only
AltaVista Software

digital Copyright © 1996 Digital Equipment Corporation. All rights reserved.

TIP
To access AltaVista quickly, add its URLs to your browser bookmarks.

TIP
For more information about search options and the AltaVista site, click on the Tips link.

AltaVista Search Options

- The search interface has a text box that accepts text strings and operators (AltaVista operators are explained on the following page), and a Submit button to start the catalog search.
- Two pull-down menus help you customize your search. These menus can be found in the line that reads (by default) "Search the Web and display the results in Standard form."
- In the Search menu, you can choose to search either The Web (the default) or Usenet.
- In the Display menu, you can choose to display the results In Standard Form (the default), In Compact Form, or In Detailed Form.
- The search interface appears at the top of each results page.

AltaVista Search Strings and Operators

- AltaVista recognizes the following search operators:
- A plus sign (+) placed immediately in front of a word (no space between the plus sign and the word) means that all documents found must contain that word. (This is similar to the Boolean AND operator. See below.)
- A minus sign (–) placed immediately in front of a word (no space) means that all documents found will NOT contain that word. (This is the Boolean NOT operator. See below.)
- Quotation marks ("") can be placed around words or phrases that must appear next to each other in the results found. (This is similar to the Boolean NEAR operator. See following page.)
- An asterisk (*) expands the search string. This is useful if you are not sure how to spell the key word you want to find. You can use an asterisk in the middle of a word. For example:

  Type *col*r* in the search text box and click Search.

  This finds sites whose descriptions contain words like color, colour, collar, collector, etc.
- AltaVista supports full Boolean operators and syntax for searches. The Boolean operators can be in lowercase or in all capital letters to be recognized. You can also use symbols for the operators.

AND — The documents found in the search must contain all words joined by the AND operator. For example:

Type *Internet AND Explorer* in the search text box and click Search.

This finds sites whose descriptions contain the words *Internet* and *Explorer*.

OR — The documents found in the search must contain at least one of the words joined by the OR operator. The documents may contain both. For example:

Type *stocks OR bonds* in the search text box and click Search.

This finds sites whose descriptions contain the word *stock* or the word *bonds* or both words.

TIPS

- Use the ampersand symbol (&) for the AND operator.
- Use the vertical line symbol (|) for the OR operator.
- Use the exclamation point symbol (!) for the NOT operator.
- Use the tilde symbol (~) for the NEAR operator.

NOT The documents found in the search must not contain the word following the NOT operator. For example:

Type *iron NOT steel* in the search text box and click Search.

This finds sites whose descriptions contain the word *iron*, but not *steel*.

NEAR The documents found in the search must contain the words joined by the NEAR operator within ten words of each other. For example:

Type *Web NEAR browser* in the search text box and click Search.

This finds sites whose descriptions contain the words *Web* and *browser* within 10 words of each other.

Parentheses ( ) Parentheses are used to group portions of the search string. For example:

Type *(national AND bank) NOT river* in the search text box and click Search.

This finds sites whose descriptions contain the words *national* and *bank*, but not *river*.

In this exercise you will perform searches at the AltaVista search site using multiple key words and operators.

EXERCISE DIRECTIONS

1. If you are already connected to your service provider and your browser is open, continue to step 2.

   OR

   Connect to your service provider and open your browser.

   ✓ *The examples here uses Netscape Navigator.*
2. On the Location line, type the following and press Enter.

   http://www.ddcpub.com/learn
3. Click the link to **<u>Lesson 3: Search Engines, Exercise 7, "AltaVista"</u>**.

   The AltaVista search site home page appears.
4. In the Search text box, type:

   personal computer clones
5. Click the Submit button.

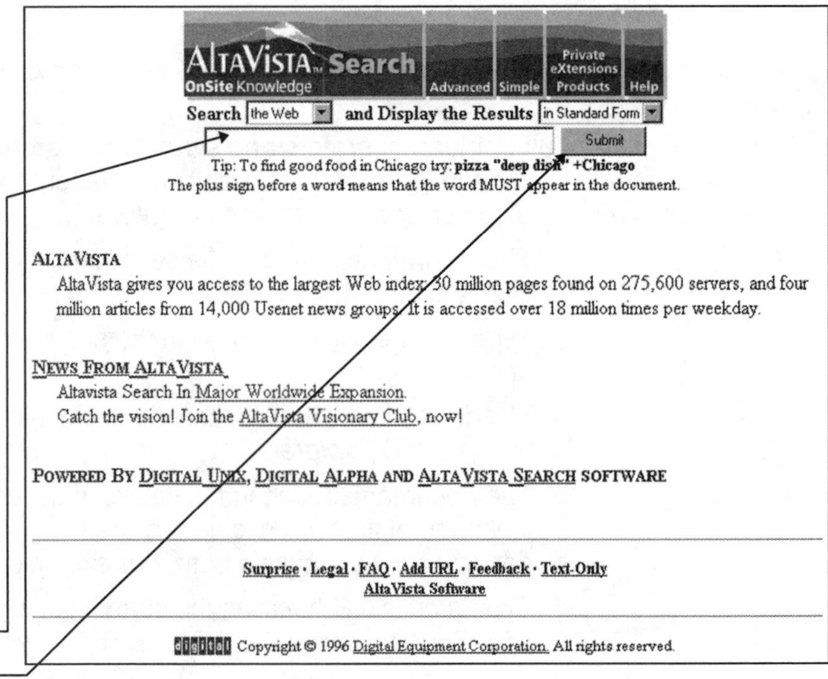

AltaVista Search
OnSite Knowledge
Advanced
Simple
Private eXtensions Products
Help
Search the Web and Display the Results in Standard Form
Submit
Tip: To find good food in Chicago try: pizza "deep dish" +Chicago
The plus sign before a word means that the word MUST appear in the document.
ALTAVISTA
AltaVista gives you access to the largest Web index: 30 million pages found on 275,600 servers, and four million articles from 14,000 Usenet news groups. It is accessed over 18 million times per weekday.
NEWS FROM ALTAVISTA
Altavista Search In Major Worldwide Expansion.
Catch the vision! Join the AltaVista Visionary Club, now!
POWERED BY DIGITAL UNIX, DIGITAL ALPHA AND ALTAVISTA SEARCH SOFTWARE
Surprise · Legal · FAQ · Add URL · Feedback · Text-Only
AltaVista Software
digital Copyright © 1996 Digital Equipment Corporation. All rights reserved.

This finds sites which contain the words personal, computer, or clones. The more these words appear in the site, the higher the site will be rated in the results.

6. Read through a few of the matches to see what they say.
7. In the search text box on the results page, type:

   (trade AND agreement) NOT Europe
8. Click the Submit button.

   This finds sites which contain the words trade and agreement, but not the word Europe.
9. Read through a few of the matches to see what they say.
10. In the search text box on the results page, type:

    (stainless AND steel) OR (iron AND metal) NOT (import OR foreign)
11. Click the Submit button.

    This finds sites which contain the words stainless and steel, or the words iron and metal, but not the words import or foreign.

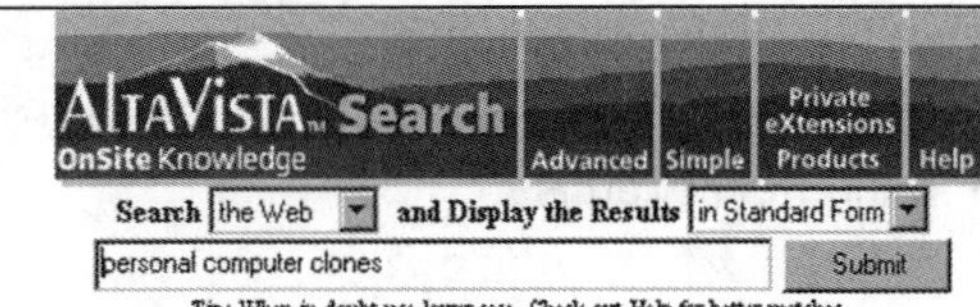

Search the Web **and Display the Results** in Standard Form

personal computer clones | Submit

Tip: When in doubt use lower-case. Check out Help for better matches.

Word count: clones:58388; personal:2819591
Ignored : computer: 7297474

Documents 1-10 of about 30000 matching the query, best matches first.

Summary Information
Module Title COMPUTER SALES Module Number ITE403 Module Purpose This module will enable the student to carry out effective computer sales tasks by...
http://www.cs.ntu.edu.au/staff/sitvetinfo/scitf/scitmodules/ite403.html - *size 33K - 25 May 95*

ICA Surf: IBM & Clones Page
ICA Surf: IBM & Clones. Your Gateway to IBM & Clones Links. Acorn Computer Group. Follow the links to find out more. Apple Computer. About Apple ! Axil...
http://www.compass.net/surfcom/com_0005.htm - *size 3K - 26 Jun 96*
http://www.icanect.net/surfcom/com_0005.htm - *size 3K - 1 Jun 96*

Is Apple Serious about Clones?--Special Report
Is Apple Serious about Clones?--Special Report. Some would-be clone makers say that Apple's efforts are only halfhearted. A Macworld investigation. by...
http://www.macworld.com/password/pages/august.95/Feature.1123.html - *size 31K - 27 Jun 96*

****

p. **1** 2 3 4 5 6 7 8 9 10 11 12 13 14 15 16 17 18 19 20 [Next]

Surprise · Legal · FAQ · Add URL · Feedback · Text-Only

digital Copyright © 1996 Digital Equipment Corporation. All rights reserved.

12. Read through a few of the matches to see what they say.
13. Continue on to the next exercise.

    OR

    Exit from your browser and disconnect from your service provider.

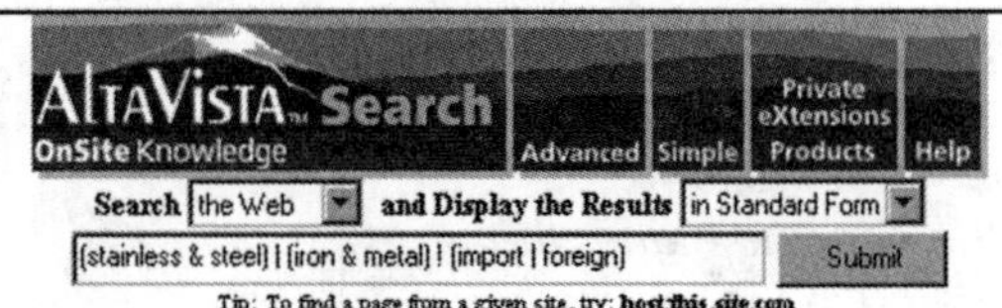

Search the Web **and Display the Results** in Standard Form

(stainless & steel) | (iron & metal) ! (import | foreign) Submit

Tip: To find a page from a given site, try: **host:this.site.com**

Word count: stainless:187628; iron:364328; import:377458; steel:562874; metal:718555; foreign:1257854

Documents 1-10 of about 200000 matching the query, best matches first.

1996 May/June IMEX Catalog
METALS/METAL SLUDGES. W1001182 - ALLOYS Wanted from Anywhere: Metals, alloy aircraft & alloy parts. Defective, scrap, & surplus. CONTACT: Rocky Frie,...
http://www.metrokc.gov/lhwmp/cesqg/wmetal.html - size 13K - 28 May 96

E.D.E.C. HOME PAGE
C.E.D.A.M. 1995. Texte Français. COMPARISON AND DESIGNATION OF METAL ALLOYS. We search for distributors for all countries. THE SOFTWARE PACKAGE. It is a...
http://www.pweb.com/edec/edec-a.htm - size 7K - 25 Apr 96

No Title
Bugs: 1. Does not work correctly for tell 2. Cannot handle references crossing files 3. Not all Loom keywords are handled Created: 4/28/95 ;; -*- Mode:...
http://abu.isi.edu:4000/pump_core.html - size 152K - 3 Apr 96

HUOSHAN CASTING COMPANY, CHINA
High quality, precision metal casting from 1 oz. to 2 tons. We also making high quality valves.
http://china-times.com/huoshan/huoshan.htm - size 2K - 12 Aug 96

No Title
Mode: LISP; Syntax: Common-Lisp; Package: ACC -*- ;; Main idea: ;; ========== ;; There are two concept space (domain, range) ;; domain space -- pump...
http://abu.isi.edu:4000/pump_core.loom - size 65K - 12 Feb 96

No Title
William J. Ray glasgow@mcimail.com Sat Jun 10 23:37:01 EDT 1995 I recently fell in love and found myself purchasing a 1990 Honda CB-1 (400). I have ridden.
http://www.motorcycle.com/mo/mobbs/tech2.html - size 64K - 15 Aug 95

Door & Hardware Considerations
Door & Hardware Considerations. Matching materials, products to facilities' rigorous demands. TODAY'S FACILITIES PRESENT many specification and...
http://www.facilitiesnet.com/guest/NS/NS3mf6g.html - size 10K - 15 May 96

Curriculum Vitae
Kathleen G. Holland. (Previously Kathleen G. Gallagher) Nationality: United States. Education: B.A. (Physics) Pomona College, 1990 M.S. (Geophysics)...
http://www.gps.caltech.edu/~kathleen/cv.html - size 5K - 12 Jun 96

Part II
PART II - Design. GENERAL BUILDING REQUIREMENTS. INTENTIONS. The following guidelines within this Section are meant to generally apply to all new...
http://www.ae.ucdavis.edu/Partii.htm - size 54K - 24 Jan 96

Swisstrade - Product information
BUSINESS OPPORTUNITIES WITH SWITZERLAND OPPORTUNITES D'AFFAIRES AVEC LA SUISSE GESCHÄFTSMÖGLICHKEITEN MIT DER SCHWEIZ. A29. Productinformation...
http://swisstrade.com/c0043-e.htm - size 3K - 21 May 96

p. 1 2 3 4 5 6 7 8 9 10 11 12 13 14 15 16 17 18 19 20 [Next]

Surprise · Legal · FAQ · Add URL · Feedback · Text-Only

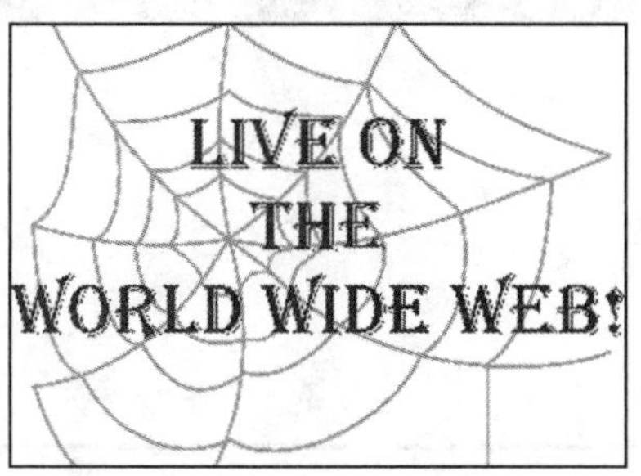

AltaVista HomePage
http://www.altavista.digital.com

INTERNATIONAL ACADEMY of Sciences, Education, Industry & Arts
http://www.akademy.com

Alaska Pipeline – Photo of TransAlaskan pipeline with links to Petroleum Institute
_http://www.api.org/photo_credits/pip-19.html_

Alaska Highway Gas Pipeline. Routing Alternatives. Whitehorse/Ibex Region. Rep
_http://www.utoronto.ca/env/lib_hold/db3/files/1098_TE.htm_

Museum of Science and Industry – 57th Street and Lake Shore Drive Chicago, Illinois 60637
http://www.nwu.edu/ev-chi/musgal/science/science.html

Exercise 8

◆ **What is Yahoo?** ◆ **Yahoo Home Page Location**
◆ **Yahoo Search Options** ◆ **Yahoo search strings**

NOTES

What Is Yahoo?

- The Yahoo Web site is a hierarchically organized catalog of links to World Wide Web sites. Yahoo is one of the first search sites established on the Web. It is a free service that sells advertisement space on its home page and search results pages.
- Though the Yahoo site uses Web robots to look for new announcements at various places, user site submissions comprise almost all of its entries. Because of this, the Yahoo catalog may not contain some recent Web sites.
- You can also search for Usenet newsgroups and e-mail addresses.

Yahoo Home Page Location

- To connect to the Yahoo site, type:

  http://www.yahoo.com

  on the Location line of your browser and press Enter.

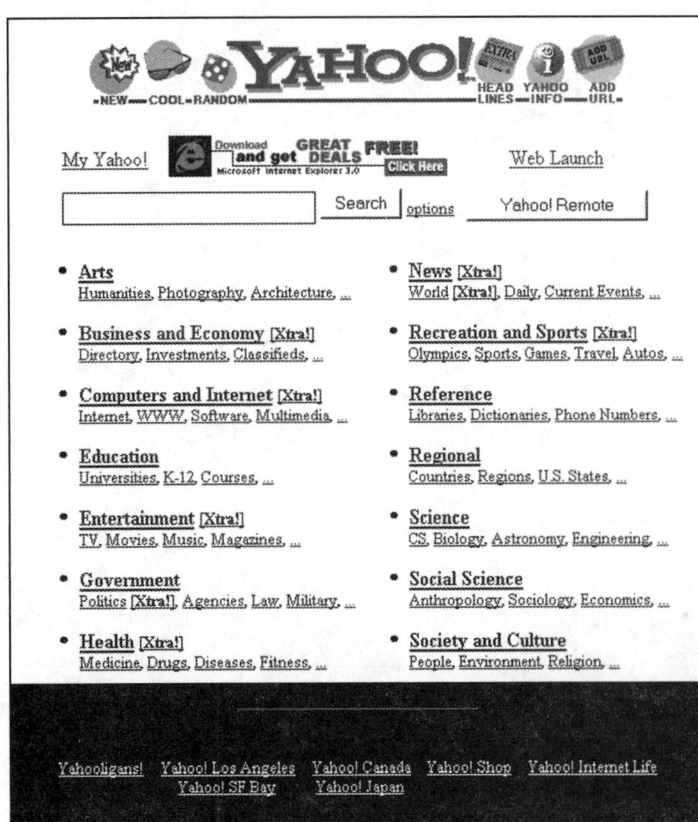

TIP
To access Yahoo quickly, add its URLs to your browser bookmarks (favorites).

- Yahoo has a simple search interface without search or display options on its home page.
- Yahoo also provides an advanced search interface with search and display options. To access the advanced search interface, click the Options button on the home page, or type:

  http://www.yahoo.com/search.html

  on the Location line of your browser and press Enter.

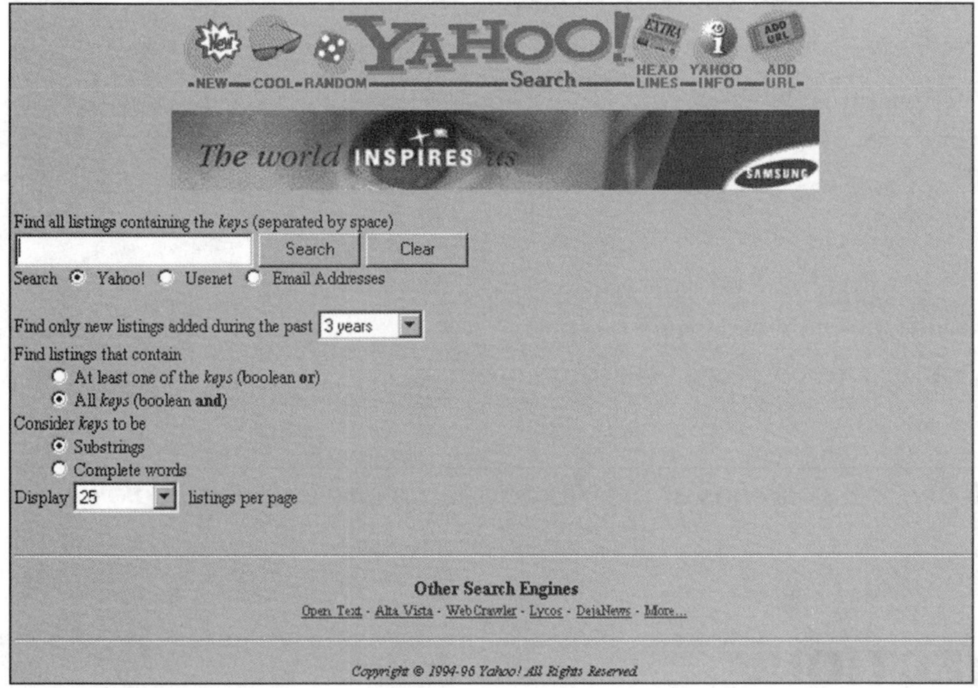

Yahoo Search Options

- Yahoo provides a search interface on its home page. There is a text box that accepts text strings and a Search button that starts the catalog search.
- Like the Yahoo home page, the advanced search page has a text box, labeled *Find All Listings Containing The Keys (Separated By Space)*, for entering text strings and a Search button used to start the catalog search.
- In addition, there are five search and display options you can use to customize your search.

  In the first option line, you can choose to:

  - Search Yahoo (Web site listings–the default)
  - Search Usenet (newsgroups)
  - Search E-mail Addresses

  In the second option line, you can choose from a pull-down menu to Find Only Listings Added During The Past:

  - 3 Years (the default)
  - 1 Day
  - 1 Week
  - 1 Month

TIP

For more information about search options and the Yahoo site, click on the Yahoo Info link.

In the third option line, you can choose to Find Listings That Contain:

- At Least One Of The Keys (Boolean OR)
- All Keys (Boolean AND) (the default)

In the fourth option line, you can choose to Consider Keys To Be:

- Substrings (the default)
- Complete Words

In the fifth option line, you can choose from a pull-down menu to:

- Display 10 Listings Per Page
- Display 25 Listings Per Page (the default)
- Display 50 Listings Per Page
- Display 100 Listings Per Page

Yahoo Search Strings

- You should use descriptive key words in your search string. The more descriptive words you use, the better the results of the search.
- Unlike other search sites, Yahoo does *not* support the use of operators in the search text string.

In this exercise you will perform searches at the Yahoo search site using multiple key words.

EXERCISE DIRECTIONS

1. If you are already connected to your service provider and your browser is open, continue to step 2.

   OR

   Connect to your service provider and open your browser.

   ✓ *The examples here use Netscape Navigator.*
2. On the Location line, type the following and press Enter.

   http://www.ddcpub.com/learn
3. Click the link to **Lesson 3: Search Engines, Exercise 8, "Yahoo"**.

   The Yahoo advanced search site home page appears.
4. In the Search text box, type:

   personal computer clone
5. Use the default search and display options. Click the Search button.

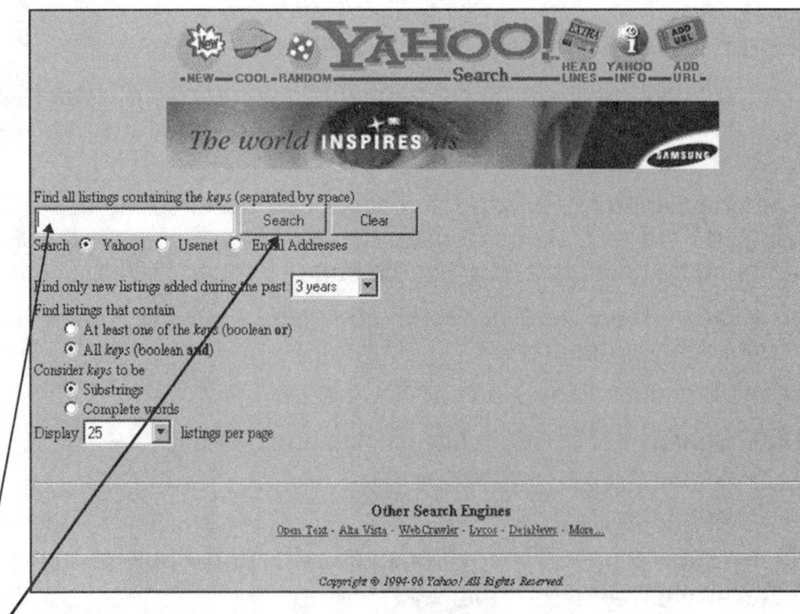

This finds sites whose descriptions contain the words personal, computer, and clones.

6. Read through a few of the matches to see what they say.
7. Click the browser's Back button until you return to the advanced search page.
8. In the search text box, type:

   trade agreement

9. Select the option Consider Keys to Be Complete Words.
10. Click the Search button.

    This finds sites whose descriptions contain the words trade and agreement.

11. Read through a few of the matches to see what they say.

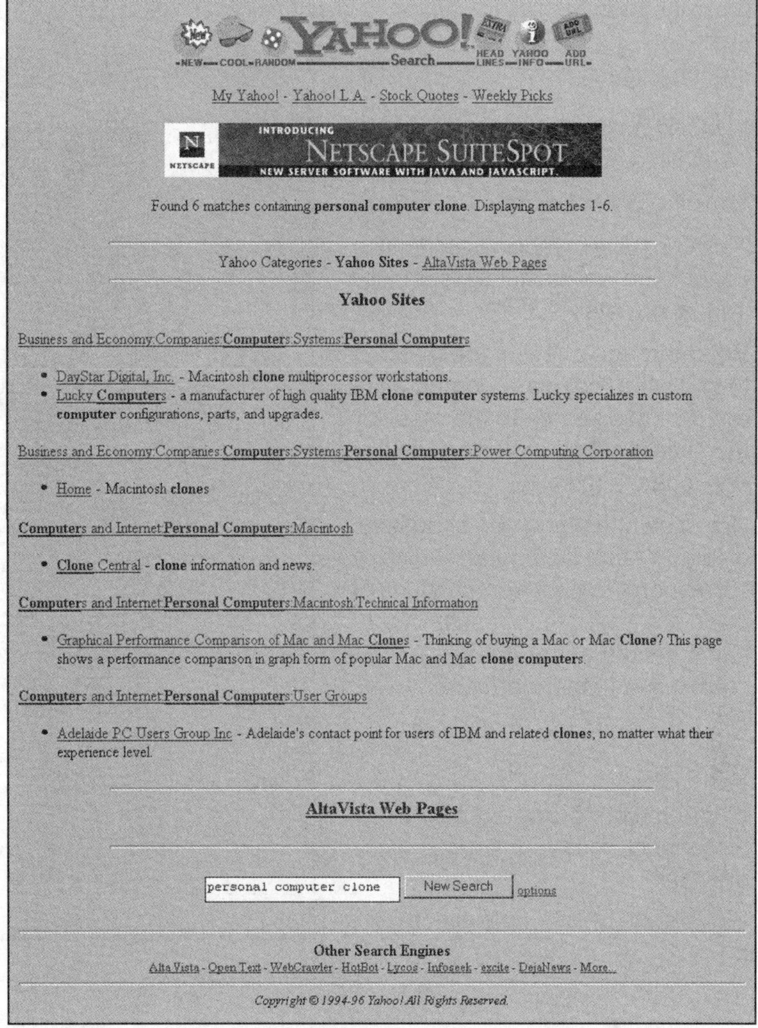

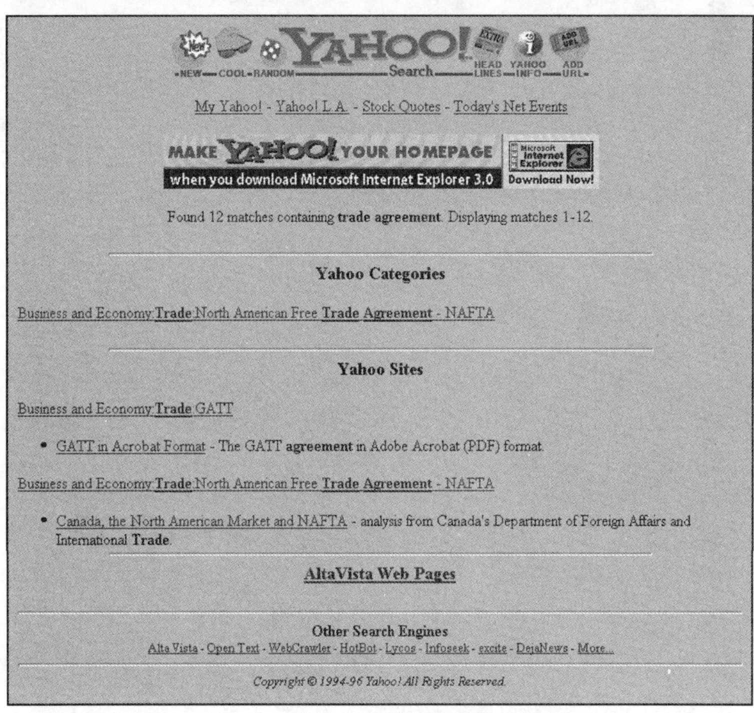

12. Click the browser's Back button until you return to the advanced search page.
13. In the search text box, type:

    stainless steel iron metal
14. Click the Search button.

    This finds sites whose descriptions contain the words stainless, steel, iron, and metal.
15. Read through a few of the matches to see what they say. Compare the result of this search to the result of the similar search you made in the previous exercise.

    Note again that you can choose to display Yahoo Categories which correspond to your search string (if there are any) or the results of the same search at the AltaVista search site (if there are any).
16. Continue on to the next exercise.

    OR

    Exit from your browser and disconnect from your service provider.

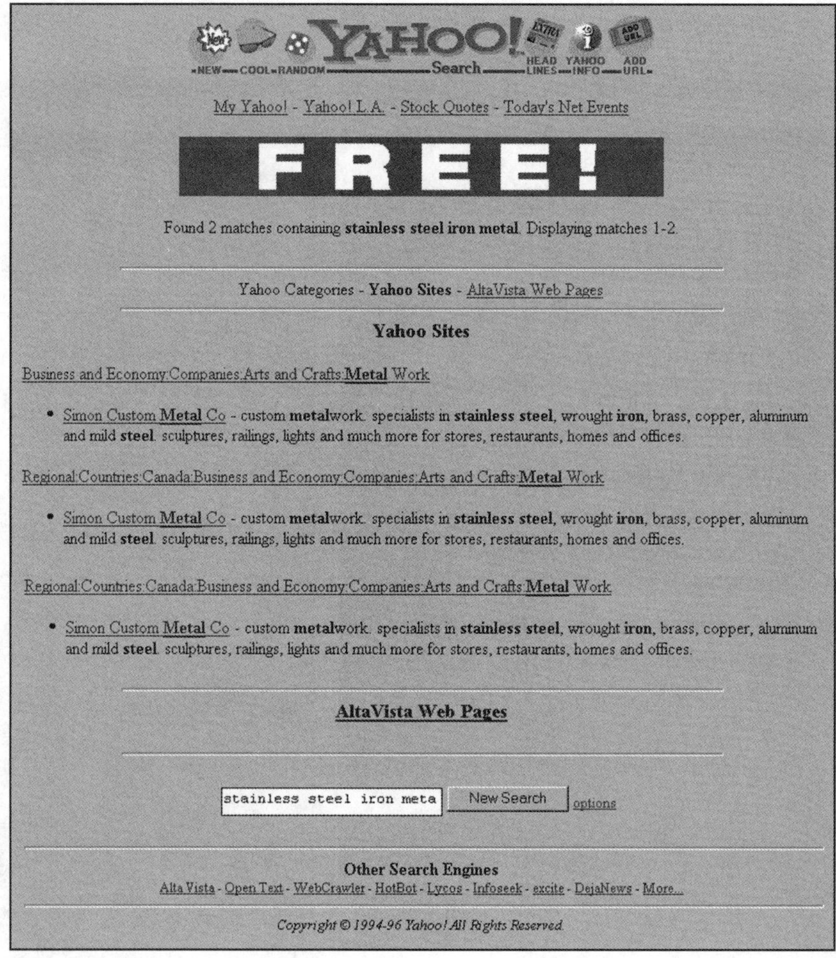

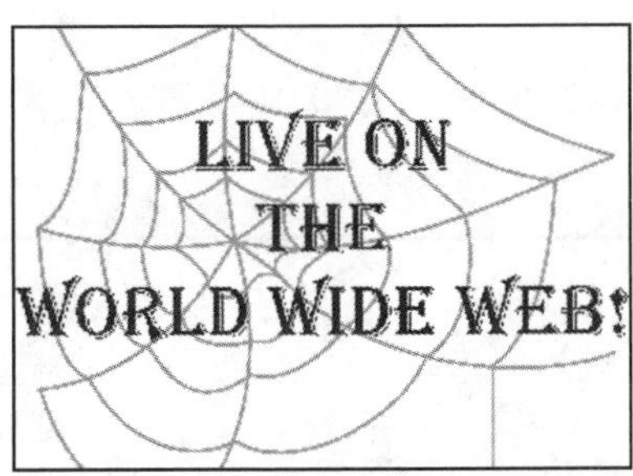

The Yahoo Home Page
http://www.yahoo.com

USA Today Online
http://www.usatoday.com

Time Magazine Online
http://pathfinder.com/@@LmyMXAUAtChDqHGi/time/

National Public Radio
http://www.wrn.org/stations/npr.html

Exercise 9

- ◆ **Common Errors When Searching Catalogs**
- ◆ **Common Errors When Following Links**
- ◆ **When to Stop an Attempt to Connect to a Site**

NOTES

Common Errors When Searching Catalogs

- Error messages let you know that the operation you have attempted to perform could not be completed. Some error messages are straightforward and easy to understand. Others have meanings that are not immediately obvious.
- Fortunately, when doing a catalog search, not much can go wrong. Either the search finds catalog entries that match your text string, or it doesn't.
- When a search of a catalog fails to yield a match, an error message appears which, depending on the site, looks like this:
  - Yahoo: Sorry, No Matches Were Found.
  - Lycos: Search Failed.
  - Excite: No Query Terms Found In Index
  - Alta Vista: No Documents Match The Query. The Term Does Not Appear In The Index. You Might Want To Check Spelling.
- If you do get an error message in response to your search:
  - Check for typographical mistakes in the search text. Look for things like no space between key words or a symbol in the string that isn't an operator.
  - Check for proper capitalization of proper nouns and certain acronyms. Common nouns should not be capitalized. Many search sites are case-sensitive.
  - Check the spelling of the key words. Make sure that they are real words and that they are spelled correctly.
  - Try spelling variations of the key words. Though search sites contain large catalogs, they do not contain everything. The site you're searching may not have indexed anything on the subject you want to find.
  - Try a different search site. As you saw from previous exercises, search results can vary greatly from site to site.

Common Errors When Following Links

- You may also get an error message when you attempt to follow a link on the search results page. This may occur for a number of reasons:
  - The site you are trying to reach may be busy or temporarily down. The site may be denying people access because it is overloaded. (Popular sites are frequently overloaded.)

  - Either the server or the site may no longer exist. Things change rapidly on the Web, and links become outdated quickly. What worked last week, or even yesterday, may not work today. One of the Web's greatest features—its fluidity—can also be a drawback.
  - The server and site may exist, but the link may be incorrect in some way.

Server Unavailable Error Messages

- When your browser is unable to connect to a site from a search link, you will get an error message that looks like this:
  - Permission Denied
  - Too Many Users
- Messages like these indicate that the server is busy or overloaded, or that access is protected in some way.
- When you do get an error message, try the link again later. Pick a time outside normal business hours, like late at night or early in the morning.

Server Not Found Error Messages

- When your browser is unable to find a server, you will get an error message that looks like this:
  - Unable To Locate Server (Netscape Navigator)
  - The Program Could Not Find The Address For... (Microsoft Internet Explorer)

  This message appears when the server you are trying to contact isn't listed in the Web site database used by your own Web server. Perhaps the server doesn't exist, or perhaps it just isn't included in your local database of servers.
- Check the spelling of the URL on the Locator line of your browser. This is frequently the problem. If it is correct, contact the search site, and explain the problem you are having with the link. (All search sites have a way to send them comments.)

Site Not Found Error Messages

- When your browser finds a server but is unable to find a file, you will get an error messages that looks like this:
  - *Not Found* (Netscape Navigator)
  - *The Server Could Not Find...* (Microsoft Internet Explorer)
  - *File Not Found*

  A message like this indicates that the .html file specified in the link could not be found in the specified directory. Sometimes the spelling in the link is wrong, sometimes the file has been deleted from the server, and sometimes (fairly often, in fact) the site has been reorganized. The file you are looking for may still exist, but spelled differently or in a different directory or both.
- To correct this type of error, check the spelling of the file name.

- You can also, in some cases, remove the filename portion of the URL and try connecting to the directory (folder) where the file is supposed to be located. In some cases, you are given a list of the contents of this directory, with links that allow you to click on files to execute them, and ways to move into other directories.
- If you can do this, look for a file that is similar to the one you are looking for. If that fails, look for other directories that might contain similar files.
- If you still can't find the file, contact the search site and explain the problem you are having with the link.

When to Stop an Attempt to Connect to a Site

- Sometimes an attempt to connect to a link location causes the browser to go into "hourglass" mode. When a connection is not made, the browser shows you an hourglass while it continues the attempt, perhaps indefinitely.
- You will have to determine for yourself how long is too long to wait for a connection. Remember, some service providers charge for the time you are connected to the Web.
- To stop the browser's connection attempt:
  - Click the Stop button on the browser. If the browser returns to normal operation, this is all you need to do.
  - If you cannot click the Stop button, press Ctrl+Alt+Del, select Task List (on a Win 95 PC), and quit the browser application.
  - If none of this has worked, turn off your modem. (If you are connected directly to a network, this may not work.)
  - Finally, if all else fails, reboot (restart) your system.

NOTE

Try the link one more time after stopping a "hung" connection. Another attempt may make the connection succeed. A second attempt is always worth trying.

In this exercise you will perform searches that return errors. Then you will correct the source of the error.

EXERCISE DIRECTIONS

1. If you are already connected to your service provider and your browser is open, go to step 2.

   OR

   Connect to your service provider and open your browser.
2. On the Location line, type the following and press Enter:

   http://www.ddcpub.com/learn
3. Click the link to **Lesson 3: Search Engines, Exercise 9 "AltaVista"**.

The AltaVista search page (shown at the right) appears.

4. In the search text box, type:

   FCC +Internet +Site Space

5. Click the Submit button.

   This finds sites which contain the words FCC, Internet, and Site.

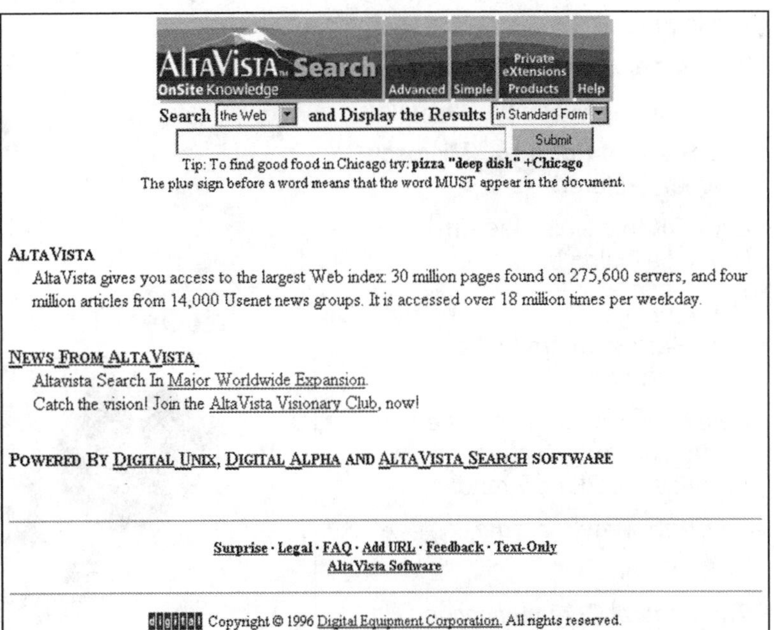

At or near the top of the results page is a listing titled "Finding Information at the FCC Internet Site." Notice the URL for the site:

http://www.fcc.gov/getinfo.html

6. Click the title.
   This is a link to the site.

   The Finding Information at the FCC Internet Site page (shown at the lower right) appears.

7. Edit the URL on the Locator line of your browser. Change the second "c" in "fcc" to a "b," so it reads:

   http://www.fcb.gov/getinfo.htm

8. Press Enter.

   An error message will appear.

   Unable To Locate Server
   (Netscape Navigator)

   Internet Explore cannot open...
   (Microsoft Internet Explorer)

9. Click OK to dismiss the Error Message.

10. Edit the URL on the Location (address) to its original form (***http://www.fcc.gov/getinfo.html***).

11. Edit the URL. Change the filename "getinfo.html" to "gotinfo.html," (change the "e" to an "o"), so it reads:

    http://www.fcc.gov/gotinfo.html

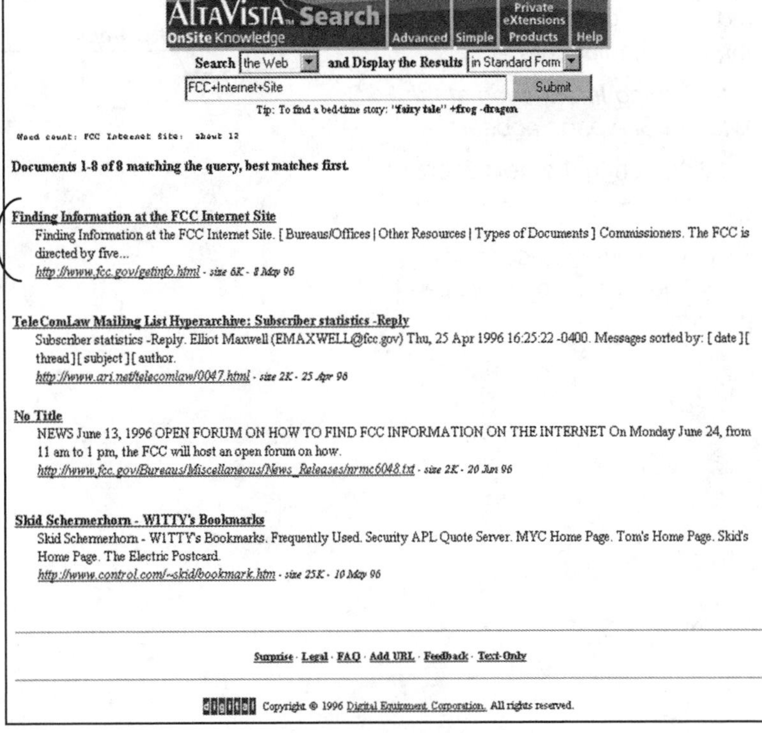

12. Press Enter.

    An error message will appear.

    Error 404... (Netscape Navigator)

    The Site Not Found... (Microsoft Internet Explorer)

13. Click OK to dismiss the Error Message dialog box.

    OR

    Click Back to return to the previous page.

14. Delete the filename from the URL on the Locator line of your browser, so that the URL now reads:

    http://www.fcc.gov/

15. Press Enter.

    The Federal Communication Commission home page appears.

16. To access the Finding Information at the FCC Internet Site, click on the link "Finding Info."

    The Finding Information at the FCC Internet Site page appears.

17. Continue on to the next exercise.

    OR

    Exit from your browser and disconnect from your service provider.

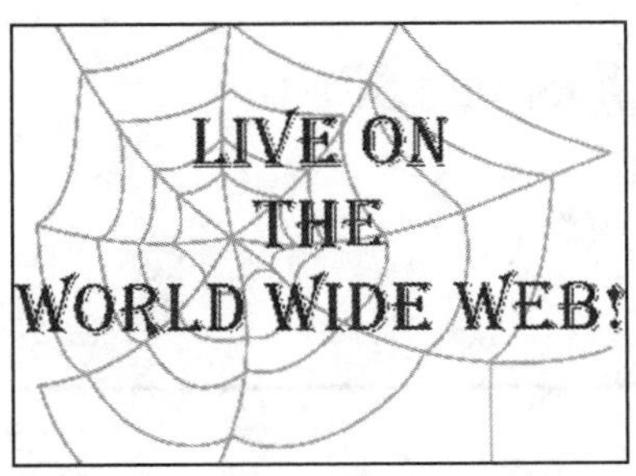

AltaVista HomePage
http://www.altavista.digital.com

WebCrawler Search site
http://webcrawler.com/

US - Agencies (Government Agencies)
http://lmc.einet.net/galaxy/Government/Government-Agencies/US--Agencies.html

Federal Agencies – White House. U.S. Congress. U.S. Senate.
U.S. House of Representatives. Federal Courts. Central Intelligence Agency.
Federal Bureau of Investigation
http://www.ucansee.com/ncpa/htextlinks/government.html

The Home Maintenance and Repair Page – Database of information
about general upkeep and care for homes and appliances.
http://www.homemaintenance.com/

Exercise 10

◆ **Determine the Text String** ◆ **Access the Search Engine Sites**
◆ **Key the Search** ◆ **Examine the Search Results**
◆ **Use Different Search Engines**

NOTES

- As you learned in Exercise 2 of this lesson, there are different types of searches. A subject search by keyword(s) is a practical search that is frequently used. As you have discovered in previous exercises, there are several good search engines. Although additional search sites could have been used, you will work with Yahoo, Excite, AltaVista, and Lycos in this exercise.

Determine the Text String

- The Web has vast amounts of available data; finding the specific data is the task. The text string you use to describe the information you want to find makes a major difference in the results of a search. Narrowing the focus of the search string is important to achieve reliable results. The more narrow the focus for the text string, the more likely you are to get the desired results.
- For example, if you have a virus on your system sector or master boot record (MBR - that special area on your disk that contains programs to be executed when you boot your PC), you will want to research an anti-virus program that will help with that specific type of virus.
- You can use the text string "Viruses" and get some good information; probably even some information on viruses that attack your master boot record. However, you may also get other information such as articles on blackberry disease or a typical tobacco mosaic virus. You won't get information on these human virus areas if you use the search string "computer virus," which is more closely related to the subject. However, if you use "MBR virus" for the text string, you will get the most closely-related information of all.

Access the Search Engine Sites

- As you have seen in the previous exercises, you will access the search engines by keying the URL of the home page of the search engine. Each search engine has different capabilities and search strengths. Taking a look at more than one may prove extremely beneficial in locating the desired data.
- The URLs for search engine sites all follow the standard format of *http://www.name.type of organization*. For example, you will use the following:
  - ***http://www.yahoo.com***
  - ***http://www.excite.com***
  - ***http://www.altavista.digital.com***
  - ***http://www.lycos.com***

- In this example, the Yahoo search engine will be used. The URL for Yahoo is:

  http://www.yahoo.com.

- In the search text box, the text string typed is:

  viruses

  and the Search button is pressed.

- Note the results of 43 matches containing viruses.

- Narrow the focus of the text string with "computer viruses" and 27 matches are found for computer viruses.

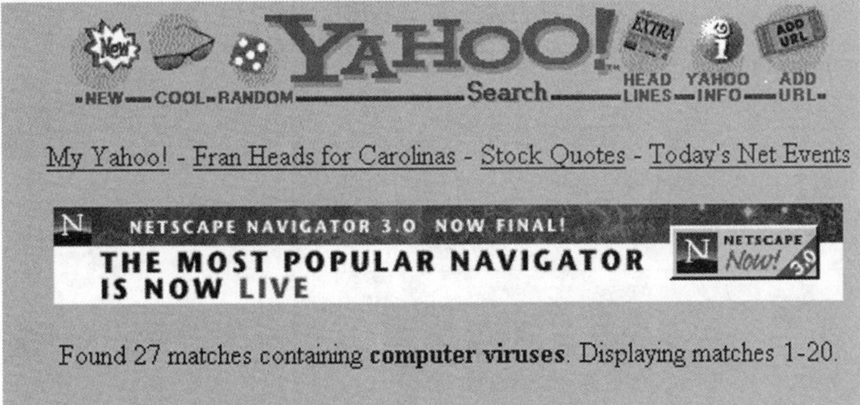

- Narrow the focus of the text string even further to "MBR virus." Note the result of one match.

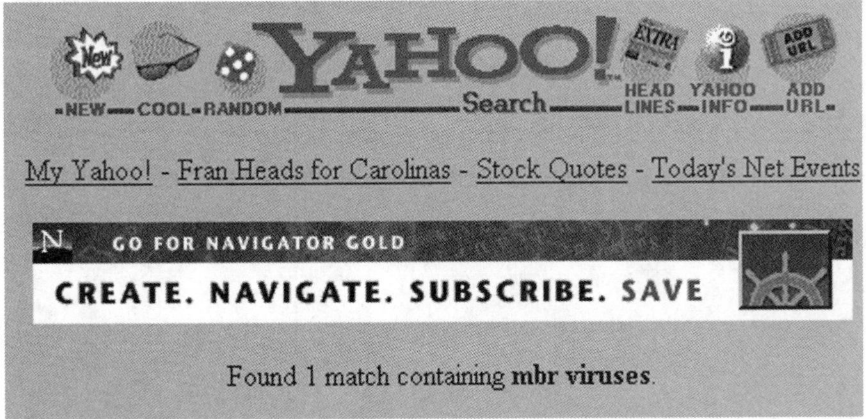

Use Different Search Engines

- The various search engines have more or less search capability. For example, you read claims in Exercise 5 that Lycos has mapped 90% of the Web and that Excite has 50 million Web pages in its catalog, while AltaVista and Yahoo are more conservative sites.
- Running identical text string searches on different search engines net very different results.
- For example, AltaVista is accessed with the following URL:

  http://www.altavista.ditigal.com

- The text string "virus" netted about 50,000 documents that matched the text string. Compare that with Yahoo's 43 matches using the same search string.

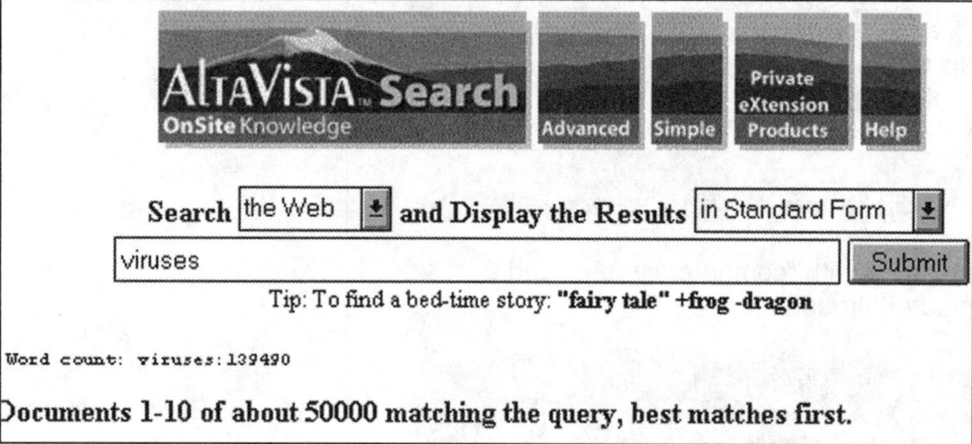

- Jump to the narrowly-focused text string "MBR viruses."
- The results are approximately 10,000 compared with Yahoo's one match.

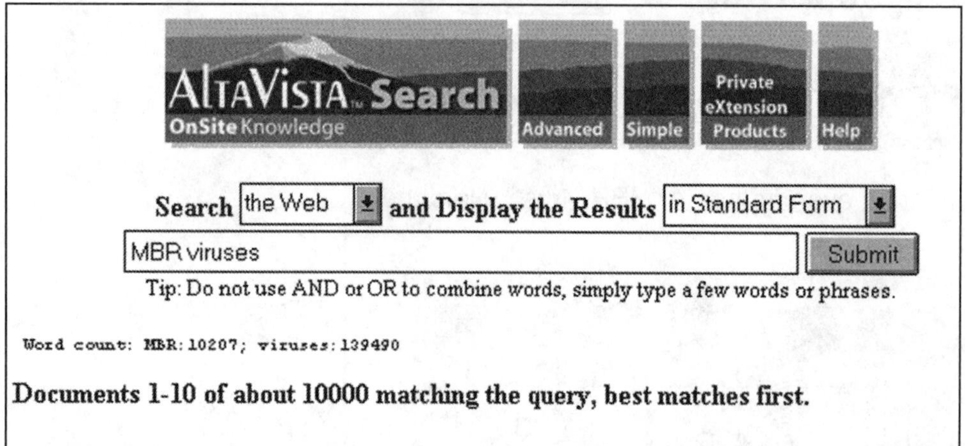

In this exercise you will use various search engines to narrow a search.

EXERCISE DIRECTIONS:

1. If you are already connected to your service provider and your browser is open, continue to step 2.

   OR

   Connect to your service provider and open your browser.

   ✓ *The examples here use Netscape Navigator.*

2. Key the URL for Excite:

   http://www.excite.com

3. Key the text string: viruses.
4. Check your results against those shown on the right.

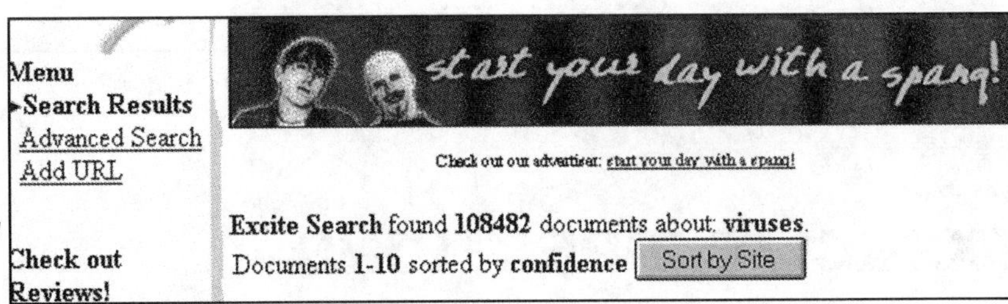

5. Scroll to the bottom of the page and key a more narrow text string as follows:

   computer viruses.

   Then click Search.

Excite Search found **4487033** documents about: **computer viruses**.
Documents **1-10** sorted by **confidence** Sort by Site

6. Check your results against those shown on the right.

Excite Search found **116012** documents about: **MBR viruses**.
Documents **1-10** sorted by **confidence** Sort by Site

7. Key the following narrow text string:

   MBR viruses.

   Then click Search.

8. Check your results against those shown on the right.

9. Access Lycos as follows:

   http://www.lycos.com

10. In the search text box, key the text string: viruses, then click Go Get It.
11. Check for results like those shown on the right.
12. Search for both text strings: computer viruses and MBR viruses. Then click Go Get It.
13. Compare your results with those of Yahoo, AltaVista, and Excite.
14. Continue on to the next exercise.

    OR

    Exit from your browser and disconnect from your service provider.

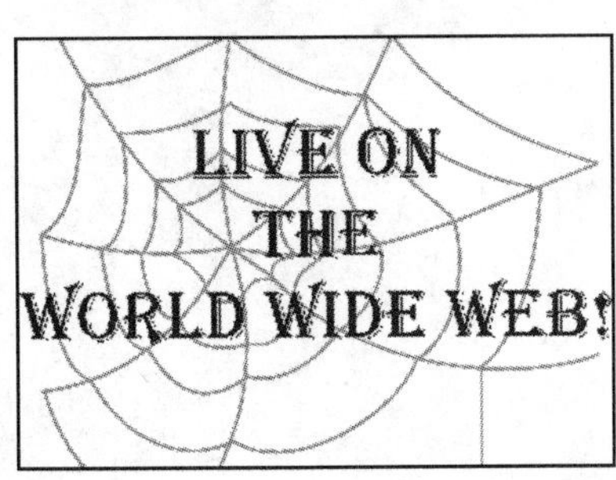

American Red Cross
http://www.crossnet.org/

Internet Classics Archive – Includes masterpieces such as Plato's "Republic," Virgil's "Aeneid," and Homer's "Odyssey,"
http://the-tech.mit.edu/Classics/

Exercise 11

◆ Search Engines – Summary Exercise

In this exercise you will explore sites using Yahoo. You will also narrow a search using the search options in Yahoo.

EXERCISE DIRECTIONS

1. If you are already connected to your service provider and your browser is open, continue to step 2.

   OR

   Connect to your service provider and open your browser.
2. Type the ***http://www.yahoo.com*** URL on the Location line and press Enter.
3. Click the **Reference** link.

   The screen on right should appear.

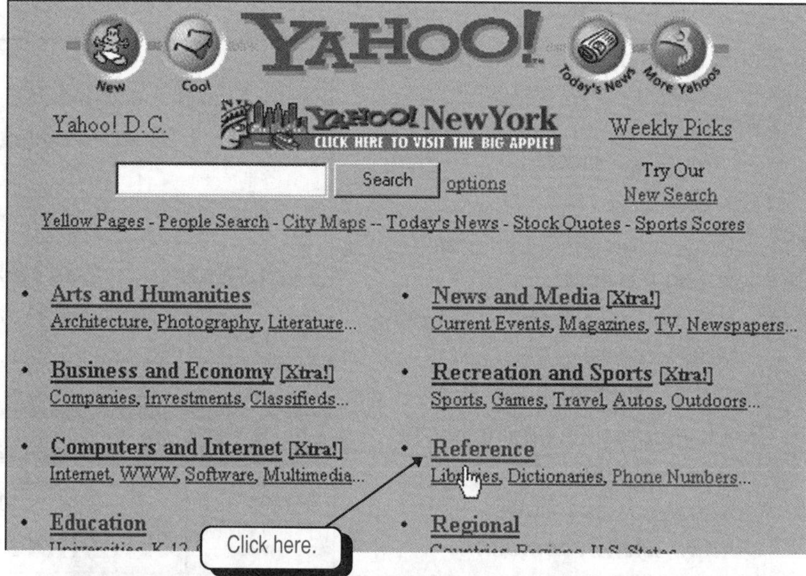

4. Locate the **Maps@** link and click once.

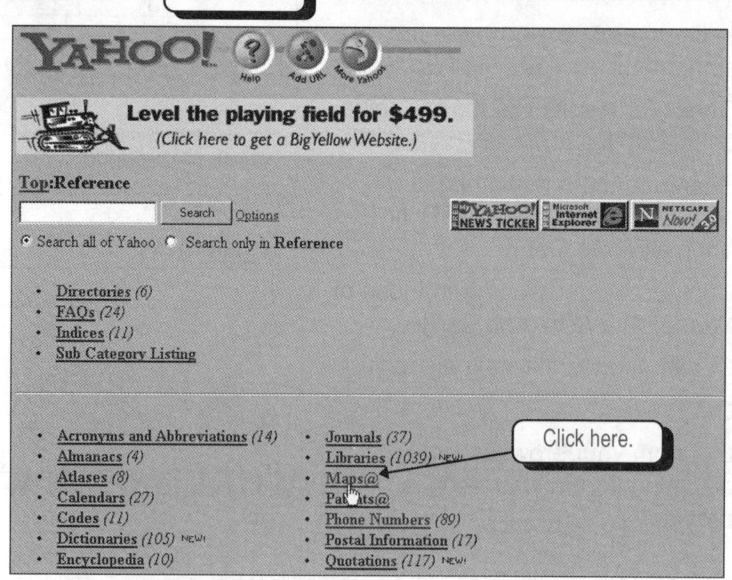

5. Click the link for **Yahoo! Maps** and do the following:
   - Enter the following address: *275 Madison Ave., New York, NY 10016*
   - Click MapIt to see if you can locate a map for the address you entered.

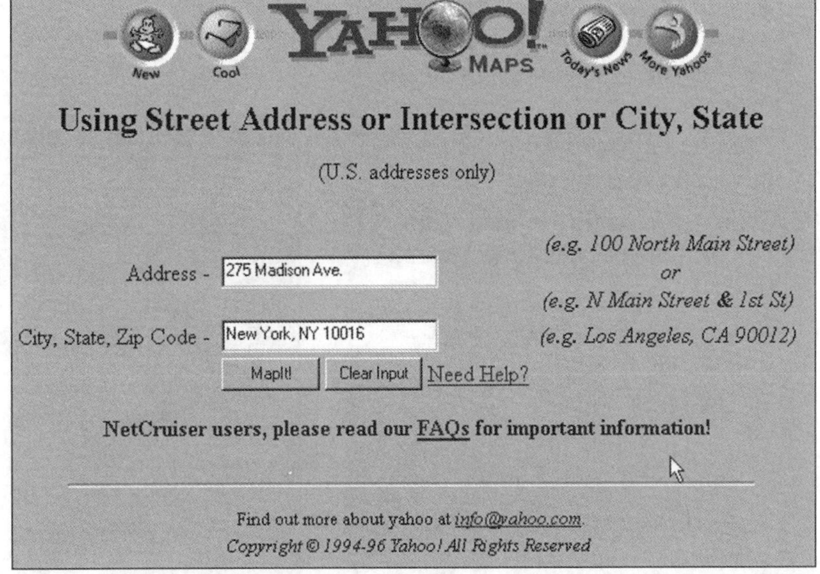

   - Send the map to the printer.
   - Note the example illustrated on the right.

✓ *If you are using the Internet Simulation, skip step 6 and proceed to step 7.*

6. See if you can locate and print a map for another address.
7. Click the Back button to return to the Yahoo opening screen.

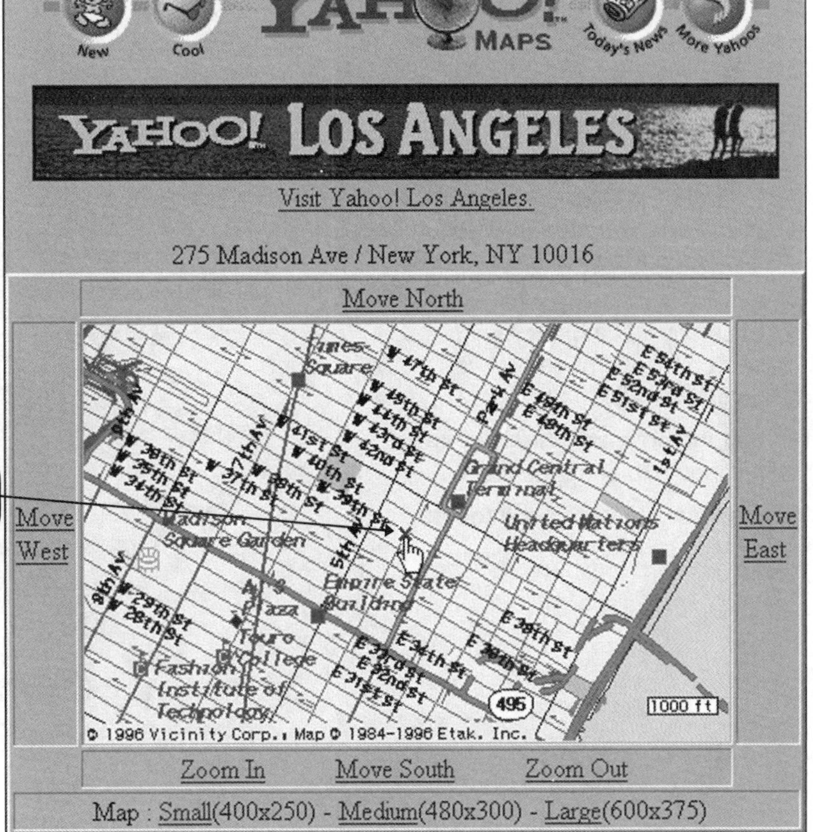

8. Click in the Search text box and type *tea*.
9. Click the Search button.
10. Click any link in the ***tea*** search results page that you would be interested in following.
11. Return to the *tea* search results page.

12. Scroll down and click on the ***options*** link next to the New Search button at the bottom of the page.

    The page that allows you to specify advanced search options displays.

13. Type *green tea* in the Search text box, **but do *not* click the Search button**.
14. Select these options below the Search text box:
    - Search: Yahoo
    - Find only new listings added during the past: 3 years
    - Find listings that contain: All Keys
    - Consider keys to be: Complete words
    - Display 10 listings per page
15. Now click the Search button.

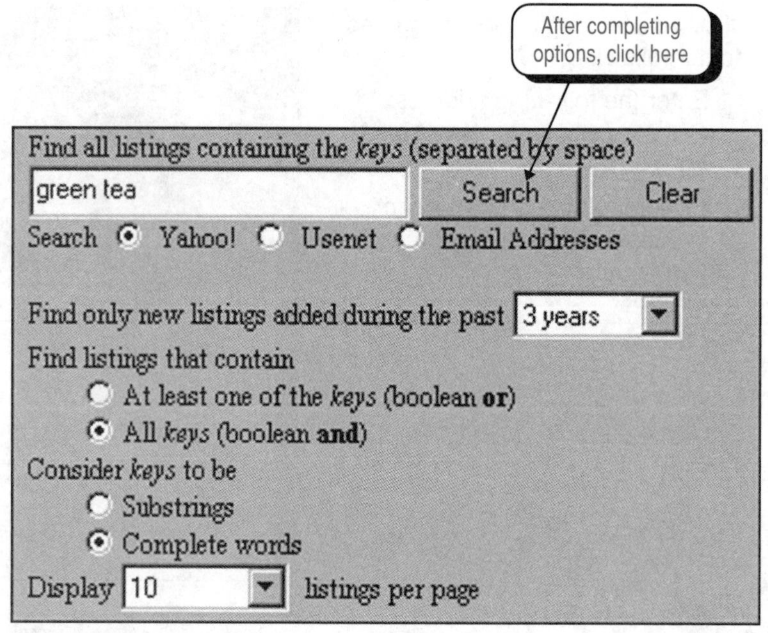

16. Compare this search results page (shown at the right) with that of the previous search.

✓ *If you are using the Internet Simulation, skip to the end of the exercise.*

17. Click any link in the *green tea* search results page that you would be interested in following.
18. Exit the browser when you are finished exploring the links.
19. Disconnect from your Internet service provider.

Yahoo Sites

Business and Economy:Companies:Drinks:Coffee and **Tea**

- Cafe San Juan - Arabica high altitude gourmet estate coffee from Puerto Rico. Available **green** and micro-roasted, wholesale and retail.
- Comexim - Brazilian **green** coffee exporters.
- Donut Lady Cafe, Co - Ithaca, NY - We have a complete coffee price list and accept on-line orders, and we proudly feature **Green** Mountain Coffee Roasters from Vermont.
- Great Eastern **Tea** Company - competition grade **teas** from Taiwan. specialties include Oolong, Iron Goddes, **Green**, Jasmine.
- Kona Coffee Store - estate and commercial, roasted and **green** available.
- Sanwa Chaen - with information about Japanese **Green Tea** and how to order it.

Business and Economy:Companies:Drinks:Coffee and **Tea**:Equipment

- Majestic Coffee - commercial roasters, brewers, books, custom fresh roasted or **green** beans. complete test facility with degree of roast, packaging, moisture, sieve, & vacuum analysis.

Entertainment:Drinks and Drinking:Caffeinated:**Tea**

- Kyoto-Yanoen (Japanese **Tea**, **Green Tea**)

Entertainment:Food and Eating:Countries and Cultures:Japanese:Recipes

- Recipes by Keiko - Recipes by chef extraordinaire Keiko Shiba. Food market for all your culinary needs including the finest **green tea**.

Regional:Countries:Japan:Business

- Sanwa Chaen - with information about Japanese **Green Tea** and how to order it.

Lesson 4: File Transfer Protocol (FTP)

Exercise 1

- File Transfer Protocol (FTP)
- Connect to an FTP Site
- Navigate a Site and Download Files

Exercise 2

- File Types
- Compressed Files
- Encoded Files
- Freeware, Shareware, and Public Domain Software
- Avoid Viruses

Exercise 3

- Search for File Locations
- Download Large Files
- Netiquette for FTP Users

Exercise 4

- File Transfer Protocol – Summary Exercise

Exercise 1

◆ File Transfer Protocol (FTP) ◆ Connect to an FTP Site
◆ Navigate a Site and Download Files

NOTES

File Transfer Protocol (FTP)

- Some sites on the World Wide Web are storehouses of data files and software programs. The files on these sites can be transferred to and from your own computer using a service called **FTP**, the **File Transfer Protocol** service.
- Sites that offer the FTP service are called **FTP sites**.

The FTP Service

- FTP is a **service**, just like the HTTP service you have already seen.
- On the Internet, a service is available when a program, called a **server program**, is running on a remote computer somewhere on the Internet. The server program offers the service to other computer programs, called **client programs**, that ask for it.
- In this case, an FTP site exists because there is an FTP server program running in one of its machines. When you connect to an FTP site, you use an FTP client program in your computer to talk to the FTP server in the remote machine.

The FTP service allows files to be exchanged between computers.

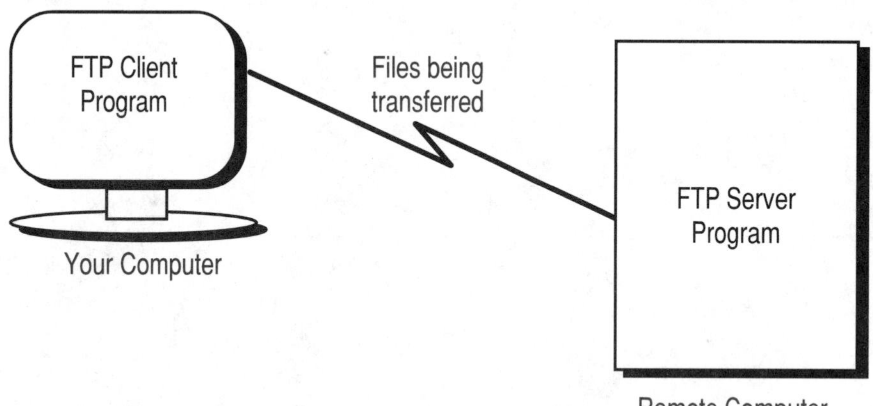

- Because the FTP service allows powerful access to remote computers, it has certain built-in protections.
- Some files and directories on the remote computer will not be accessible via FTP because the system administrator has restricted access to them.
  - In addition, all FTP access requires a **login**. Only people with permission to use FTP at that computer will gain access.

NOTE
When you use FTP to log in to a computer, you are required to type a username and a password. If the username does not match one of those already set up on that computer, or if the password is incorrect, access to the FTP service will be denied.

Anonymous FTP

- To allow general users to access FTP at sites where they don't have a personal login, a general login called **anonymous FTP** has been created.
- Anonymous FTP sites are sites that allow users to login with the username *anonymous*. With the *anonymous* username, any password will work, though network courtesy requires that the user's e-mail address be used as the password. (For more on e-mail addresses, see Lesson 5.)

NOTE

Some online services provide an FTP button on their browser. Clicking this button will also allow you to connect to FTP sites. One popular FTP client program is WinFTP, a program based on WS_FTP. Stand-alone FTP programs like WinFTP support both personal login and anonymous login.

Connect to an FTP Site

- You can connect to an FTP site several different ways. The two most common are:
  - with a stand-alone FTP client program, or
  - with a Web browser
- Both Netscape Navigator and Microsoft Internet Explorer have FTP client software built into them. This means they can act as FTP clients, just as they can act as HTTP clients.
- When you use a browser to connect to an FTP site, you are automatically using anonymous FTP. If anonymous FTP is not supported at a given site, login with a browser may not be possible.

Connect Using a Web Browser

- To connect to an FTP site using a browser, type the correct URL in the Location line.
- As you have seen, when you use a Web browser to view a Web page (that is, to access the site's HTTP service), you type a URL that begins with:

  http://

- To use your browser as an FTP client, you type a URL that starts with:

  ftp://

  ✓ *The "ftp://" at the start of this URL indicates that you want to use the FTP service instead of the HTTP service.*

  For example, the following is the URL for the United States Senate's public FTP site:

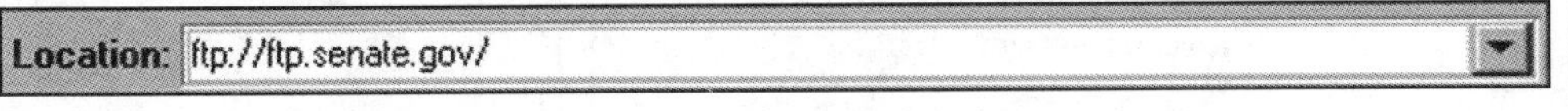

- The following screen shows what this site looks like when accessed with Netscape Navigator.
- Notice that the message at the top of the first screen says "Welcome to the United States Senate's Anonymous FTP Server."

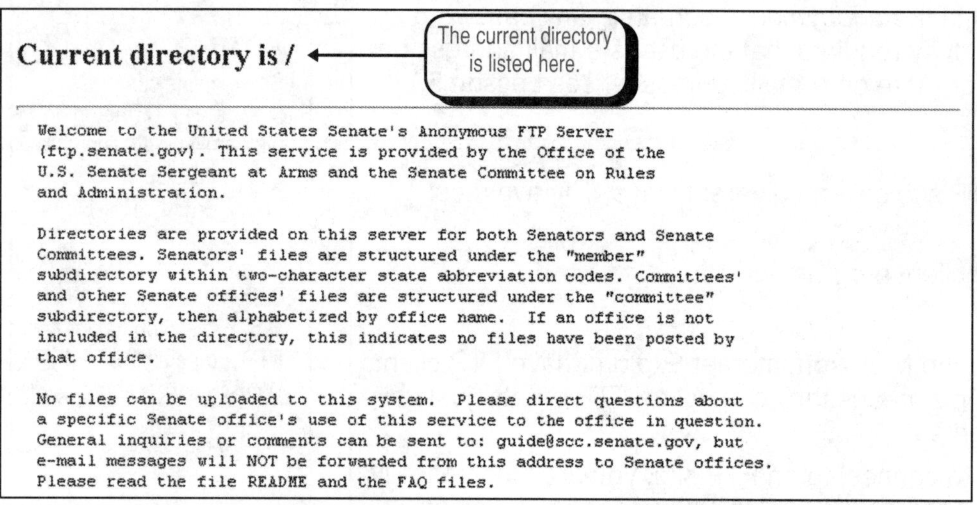

Current directory is /

Welcome to the United States Senate's Anonymous FTP Server (ftp.senate.gov). This service is provided by the Office of the U.S. Senate Sergeant at Arms and the Senate Committee on Rules and Administration.

Directories are provided on this server for both Senators and Senate Committees. Senators' files are structured under the "member" subdirectory within two-character state abbreviation codes. Committees' and other Senate offices' files are structured under the "committee" subdirectory, then alphabetized by office name. If an office is not included in the directory, this indicates no files have been posted by that office.

No files can be uploaded to this system. Please direct questions about a specific Senate office's use of this service to the office in question. General inquiries or comments can be sent to: guide@scc.senate.gov, but e-mail messages will NOT be forwarded from this address to Senate offices. Please read the file README and the FAQ files.

- Lower on the page is a list of files and directories at this site. When you scroll down, you will see something like this:

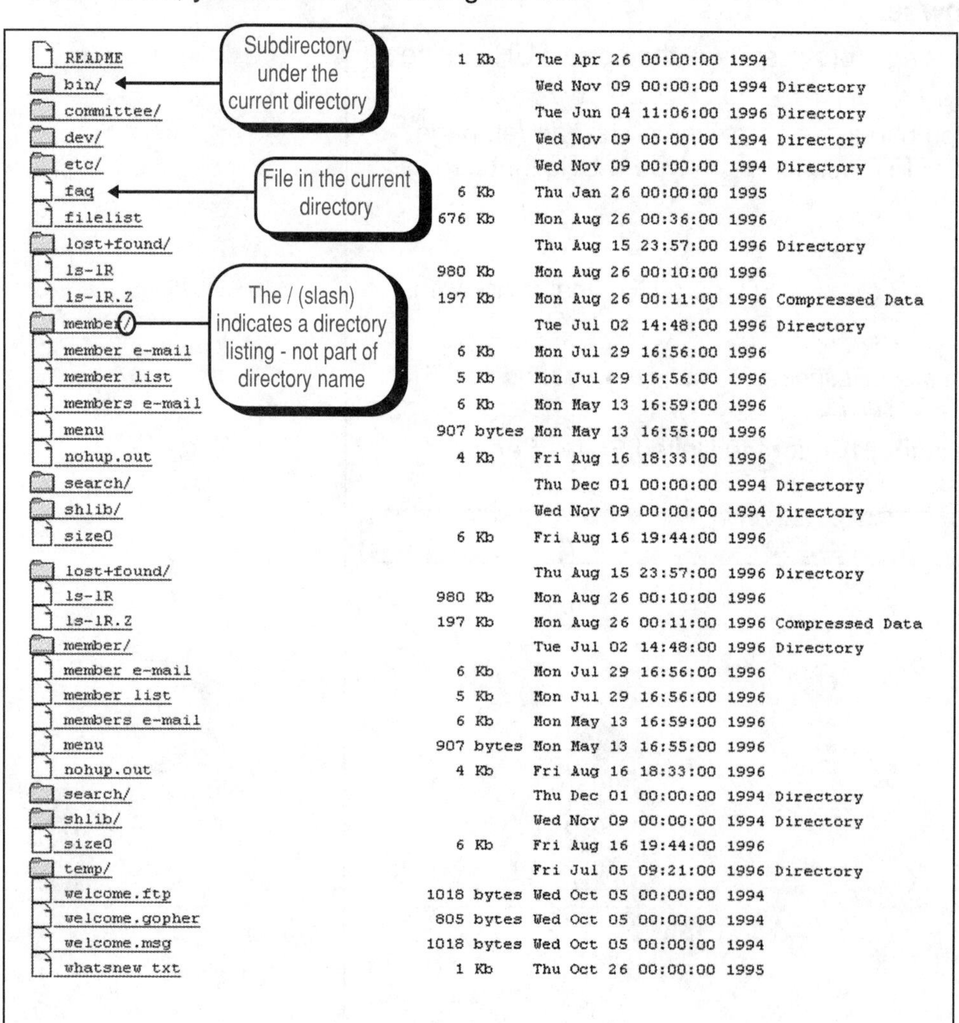

Name	Size	Date	Type
README	1 Kb	Tue Apr 26 00:00:00 1994	
bin/		Wed Nov 09 00:00:00 1994	Directory
committee/		Tue Jun 04 11:06:00 1996	Directory
dev/		Wed Nov 09 00:00:00 1994	Directory
etc/		Wed Nov 09 00:00:00 1994	Directory
faq	6 Kb	Thu Jan 26 00:00:00 1995	
filelist	676 Kb	Mon Aug 26 00:36:00 1996	
lost+found/		Thu Aug 15 23:57:00 1996	Directory
ls-lR	980 Kb	Mon Aug 26 00:10:00 1996	
ls-lR.Z	197 Kb	Mon Aug 26 00:11:00 1996	Compressed Data
member/		Tue Jul 02 14:48:00 1996	Directory
member e-mail	6 Kb	Mon Jul 29 16:56:00 1996	
member list	5 Kb	Mon Jul 29 16:56:00 1996	
members e-mail	6 Kb	Mon May 13 16:59:00 1996	
menu	907 bytes	Mon May 13 16:55:00 1996	
nohup.out	4 Kb	Fri Aug 16 18:33:00 1996	
search/		Thu Dec 01 00:00:00 1994	Directory
shlib/		Wed Nov 09 00:00:00 1994	Directory
size0	6 Kb	Fri Aug 16 19:44:00 1996	
lost+found/		Thu Aug 15 23:57:00 1996	Directory
ls-lR	980 Kb	Mon Aug 26 00:10:00 1996	
ls-lR.Z	197 Kb	Mon Aug 26 00:11:00 1996	Compressed Data
member/		Tue Jul 02 14:48:00 1996	Directory
member e-mail	6 Kb	Mon Jul 29 16:56:00 1996	
member list	5 Kb	Mon Jul 29 16:56:00 1996	
members e-mail	6 Kb	Mon May 13 16:59:00 1996	
menu	907 bytes	Mon May 13 16:55:00 1996	
nohup.out	4 Kb	Fri Aug 16 18:33:00 1996	
search/		Thu Dec 01 00:00:00 1994	Directory
shlib/		Wed Nov 09 00:00:00 1994	Directory
size0	6 Kb	Fri Aug 16 19:44:00 1996	
temp/		Fri Jul 05 09:21:00 1996	Directory
welcome.ftp	1018 bytes	Wed Oct 05 00:00:00 1994	
welcome.gopher	805 bytes	Wed Oct 05 00:00:00 1994	
welcome.msg	1018 bytes	Wed Oct 05 00:00:00 1994	
whatsnew txt	1 Kb	Thu Oct 26 00:00:00 1995	

NOTE

As you can see, FTP sites are generally a lot less interesting visually than HTTP sites!

HINT

UNIX directories are shown with a forward-slash (/), not a backward-slash (\). Thus, the directory named "/" is the root directory on the computer. Many FTP sites are maintained on UNIX computers, so you will often see UNIX conventions.

Navigating to a Site and Downloading Files

Finding the Current Directory

- The current directory is generally shown at the top of the page.

Current directory is /member

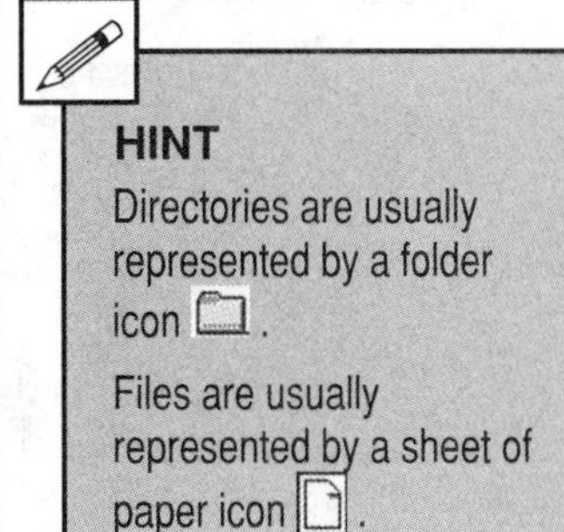

Move from One Directory to Another

- To move to a higher-level directory, click on the "Up to higher level directory" link. If you are already at the top-level directory, of course, this option will not be available.
- To move into a subdirectory, click on a directory name in the list (often with an icon of a folder next to the name).
- To move from a subdirectory back to the parent directory, click on the link that says "Up to higher-level directory."

Up to higher-level directory

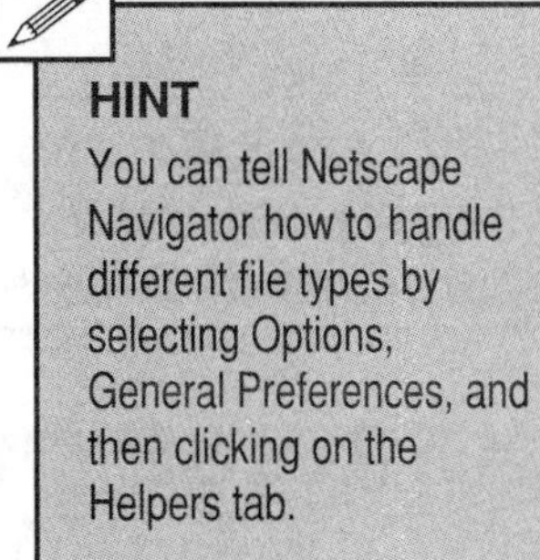

HINT
You can tell Netscape Navigator how to handle different file types by selecting Options, General Preferences, and then clicking on the Helpers tab.

Download Files

- You can download a file to your computer in either of the following two ways:
  - Click on the file name with the left mouse button (the button used to select things). Notice that files are represented by a sheet of paper icon.

    If the file is an ASCII text file, it will be automatically displayed in your browser and stored temporarily on your disk. To save this file in a more permanent location, select File, Save As, specify a file location, and click OK or the Save button.

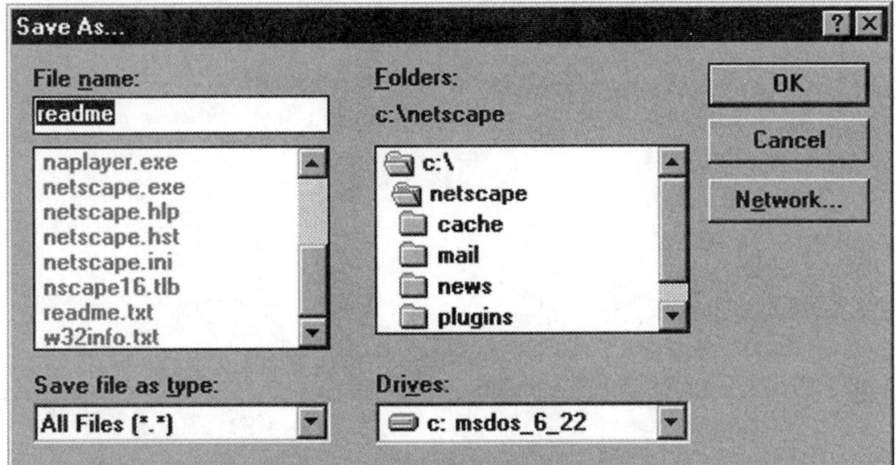

If the file is a not text file, it will be handled by your browser according to the type of file it is.

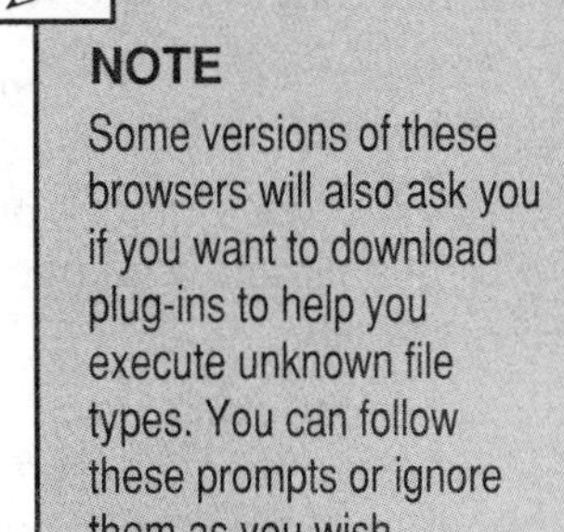

NOTE
Some versions of these browsers will also ask you if you want to download plug-ins to help you execute unknown file types. You can follow these prompts or ignore them as you wish.

- Or, click on the filename with the *right* mouse button to download a file. This brings up a menu such as the following:

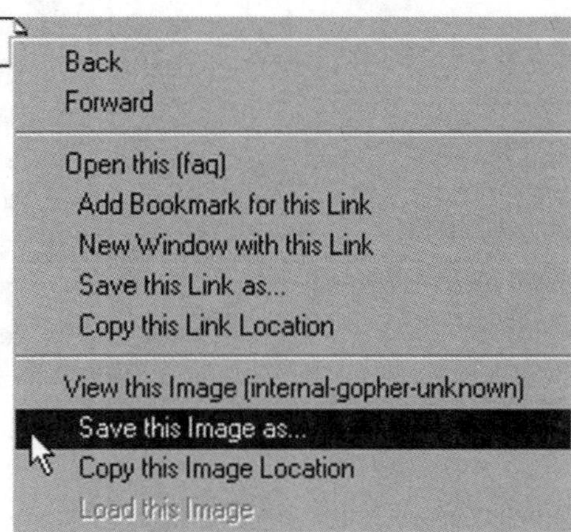

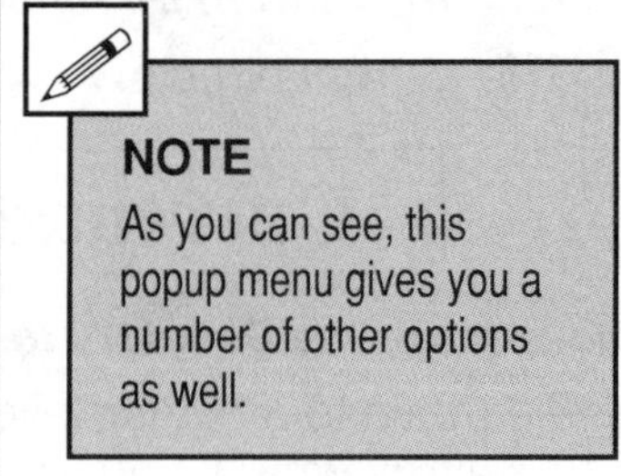

NOTE
As you can see, this popup menu gives you a number of other options as well.

- Select Save from the menu. The Save As dialog box appears, and you can rename the file if you like and save it wherever you wish.
- If the file is big, you will see another dialog box that shows the download progress.

In this exercise, you will use your browser to connect to the U.S. Senate FTP site, navigate around the site, and download files containing the names and e-mail addresses of Senate members.

EXERCISE DIRECTIONS

1. If you are already connected to your service provider and your browser is open, go to step 2.

   OR

   Connect to your service provider and start your browser.

   ✓ *The examples here use Netscape Navigator.*
2. Type the following URL on the Location line:

   ftp://ftp.senate.gov/
3. Press Enter.

   Notice the line at the top that shows the current directory.
4. Scroll down and click on the entry for the directory named "committee."
5. Notice the contents of this new directory. You now see a list of subdirectories, each named for a Senate committee.

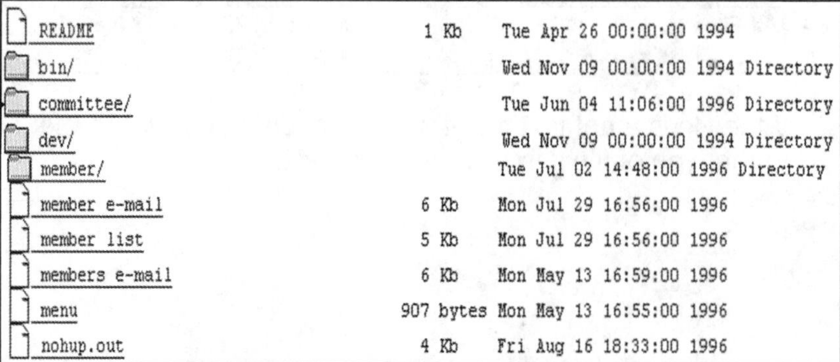

README	1 Kb	Tue Apr 26 00:00:00 1994	
bin/		Wed Nov 09 00:00:00 1994	Directory
committee/		Tue Jun 04 11:06:00 1996	Directory
dev/		Wed Nov 09 00:00:00 1994	Directory
member/		Tue Jul 02 14:48:00 1996	Directory
member e-mail	6 Kb	Mon Jul 29 16:56:00 1996	
member list	5 Kb	Mon Jul 29 16:56:00 1996	
members e-mail	6 Kb	Mon May 13 16:59:00 1996	
menu	907 bytes	Mon May 13 16:55:00 1996	
nohup.out	4 Kb	Fri Aug 16 18:33:00 1996	

6. Click on the highlighted link that says: ***Up to higher-level directory***.

   Notice that you are now back in the directory labeled "/", the root directory of this computer.

7. Scroll down and click with the *left* mouse button on the file named "members e–mail."

8. Select File, Save As from the menu.

9. Select a location on your computer to save the file, name it, and click Save or OK.

   Notice the progress indicator that appears. (If your computer is fast, it appears very briefly.)

10. Click Back to return to the "/" (root) directory display.

11. Scroll down and move the mouse pointer over the entry for the file "members e-mail."

12. Click with the *right* mouse button.

13. Select Save Link As from the menu that appears.

    The Save As dialog box opens again, showing the location you specified in step 9 above.

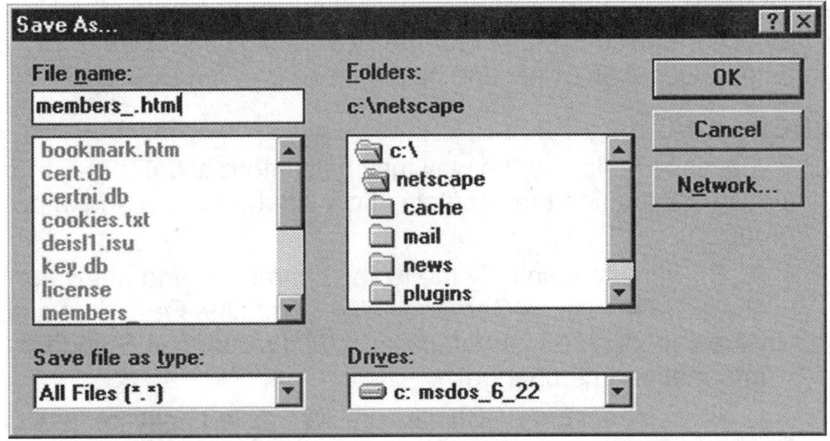

14. Delete the .html extension from the file name and click Save or OK.

    You now have a list of all of the members of the Senate.

    ✓ *Netscape added the .html extension because the file itself didn't have its own extension.*

✓ *If you are using the Internet Simulation, skip step 15 and proceed to step 16.*

15. Browse through this and note any files that may interest you.

    The information made available at this site is always open to the public.

    Some of these files may not be simple ASCII text files. We'll consider other types of files in Exercise 2.

16. Continue on to the next exercise.

    OR

    Exit from your browser and disconnect from your service provider.

Exercise 2

◆ File Types ◆ Compressed Files ◆ Encoded Files ◆ Freeware, Shareware, and Public Domain Software ◆ Avoid Viruses

NOTES

File Types

- There are many types of files available at an FTP site. Among the most common are:
  - document files
  - executable files
  - image files
  - multimedia files
- The above files are grouped by the kind of information they contain. But before we discuss these groups, let's distinguish between two broad file categories: ASCII files and binary files.

ASCII and Binary Files

- If you classify files by the way they hold information, rather than by the kind of information they contain, there are two broad and important groups:
  - **ASCII files** contain only the typing characters and a few control characters, such as Carriage Return and Line Feed, in a standard and widely recognized format, called ASCII (American Standard Code for Information Interchange).
    - For this reason, ASCII files are also called "text" or "plain text" files. Almost every computer in the world can read, display, and print ASCII files.
    - ASCII files have one quirk, however. The ASCII computer "word" (a string of 0s and 1s that contains the code for each character) is only seven bits long (that is, a list of seven 0s and 1s), and programs like e-mail that are geared toward exchanging text files know how to exchange files with seven-bit.
  - **Binary files**—all other computer files—use all eight bits of the computer word. In fact, it's the eight-bit-word aspect that makes a binary file "binary" and not "ASCII."
    - When a program like e-mail tries to exchange a binary file, it treats it like an ASCII file, and ignores the last bit in each word.
    - Keep this distinction in mind when you read this section. It's often important to know which files are ASCII and which are binary. The usual length of a computer "word" is eight bits (i.e., eight 1s and 0s). But ASCII characters use only seven of those bits for their definition.

DEFINITIONS

ASCII – American Standard Code for Information Interchange

ASCII file – File containing ASCII-formatted text only; can be read by almost any computer or program in the world. Only ASCII files can be sent through the e-mail system.

binary file – File containing machine language, i.e., ones and zeros. Binary files must be encoded (converted to ASCII format) before they can be sent through the e-mail system.

- **Document files** include simple ASCII text files and binary files associated with word processors and other programs. These files usually have the following extensions:

(no extension)	Often an ASCII (or "plain text") file, including: • ReadMe files • FAQ (Frequently Asked Questions) files • mailing lists
.txt	ASCII (or "plain text") file
.doc	A generic "document" file, which can refer to: • ASCII text file • Microsoft Word binary document file • FrameMaker binary document file

- **Executable files** include all program files, usually with the following extensions:

.exe	Executable DOS file or self-extracting zip file
.com	Executable DOS file

✓ *Self-extracting zip files have .exe extensions also. See the section called Compressed and Encoded Files later in this exercise for more information.*

HINT

You can download LViewPro, ACDSee95, and the latest version of your favorite Web browser from HTTP and FTP sites. Find them by searching for program names and program types.

Image Files

- **Image files** are binary files that contain pictures. These can be displayed by Web browsers and image programs like LViewPro and ACDSee95.

  Image files have these extensions:

.gif	Graphics Interchange Format file; a common Internet file format.
.jpg, .jpeg	Joint Photographic Experts Group file, a compressed image file format; perhaps the most common format for the Internet, because of its smaller file size.
.tif	Tagged Image Format (TIFF) file; a file type developed originally for scanned images. These days, scanned images are converted to GIF or JPG format before being distributed via the Internet.
.bmp	Bitmap file; Windows makes extensive use of bitmap files, but these are less common on the Internet because of their relatively large file sizes.
.pict	Picture file; a file format associated with Macintosh images; not frequently found on the Web.
.eps	Encapsulated PostScript file; a file format for Adobe PostScript images that are not associated with a page. Not frequently found on the Web.

Multimedia Files

- **Multimedia files** are a large category of files associated with video, sound, and music. These include:

.mpg, .mpeg	MPG file, a video format; requires special software and a special driver to be viewable under Windows.
.avi	Windows video format; can be immediately viewed in Windows 95.
.mov	QuickTime video format; a Macintosh format often found on the Web.
.wav	Sound format. Wave files often contain speech and other sounds.
.mid, .midi	MIDI format music files; requires a MIDI driver for Windows.

HINT
The Web site http://www.tucows.com is a great place to get Internet and applications software.

Compressed Files

- Small files can be transferred easily and quickly using FTP. Large files, many megabytes in size, take a long time to transfer. To make large files smaller and easier to download, FTP sites often contain **compressed files**—files that have been made smaller with a file compression program.
- On PCs, files are frequently compressed with a program called PKZIP. Files compressed with PKZIP are called **zip files**. To unzip these files, you need the companion program PKUNZIP. (A Mac version of PKZIP, called ZipIt, is also available.)
- Some zip files are **self-extracting**. You don't need any program to extract their contents, since they extract themselves when executed. Self-extracting zip files are created with the program ZIP2EXE.

  ✓ *You can find and download PKZIP by doing a Web search on the program name.*
- On Macs, compressed files are frequently created by a program called StuffIt. These files are called **stuffed files** or **sit files** (because they have the extension .sit). You need StuffIt to unstuff them.
- Some Mac compressed files are **self-extracting archives**. Like self-extracting zip files, these files extract themselves when executed. Self-extracting archives are produced by a number of programs, including CompactPro.
- Compressed files have these extensions:

.zip	Files compressed with PKZIP. These files must be uncompressed with PKUNZIP (common on PCs).
.exe	Self-extracting zip file. These files uncompress themselves when executed (common on PCs).
.sit	Files compressed with StuffIt. These files must be uncompressed with StuffIt (common on Macs).
.sea	Self-extracting archive file. These files uncompress themselves when executed (common on Macs).

WARNING
Downloading and executing .exe files from the net can be dangerous to your machine, since they can contain viruses. FTP sites, especially the big ones, are often, but not always, free of virus-bearing files. For more on this important subject, see Avoid Viruses in this exercise.

Encoded Files

- Some binary files are **encoded**—changed from binary format to ASCII format. Encoding is necessary for files that must pass through e-mail and files that are posted to newsgroups.
- Even though encoded files are meant to be e-mailed, you can download or upload an encoded file using FTP.
- Two common encoding schemes for binary files are **UUencoding** and **MIME** (or **Base64)** encoding.
- Encoded files always are ASCII when viewed, though the two encoding schemes each produce files with a different "look."
- File extensions vary for encoded files, since decoders usually recognize encoded files by their contents, not by their extension.
- If you download an encoded file, you must decode it (change it back to binary format) before it can be used.
- Programs for decoding files can be found on many FTP sites. Most Web browsers and e-mail programs can decode files for you.

Freeware, Shareware, and Public Domain Software

- **Freeware** is software that you can download and use for free. Freeware programs have an owner, but you do not have to buy a license or purchase a disk before you can use them. Freeware can be copied and distributed legally.
- One type of freeware is called **public domain software**. Public domain software can be copied and distributed for free. Public domain software has no owner—the "public" owns it.
- **Shareware** is also software that you can download for free. But unlike freeware, shareware is made available by its owners only for a limited time so that you can evaluate its usefulness. After the evaluation period, you are expected to purchase the shareware, which is usually inexpensive, or stop using it.
- Sometimes shareware works on the honor system, and sometimes it stops working after the evaluation period is over.
- Shareware often comes with online documentation that tells you how you can register your copy of the software. Usually, registering the shareware entitles you to get support and updates as they come out.

NOTE

If you do copy and distribute freeware, be sure to include copyright information and any manuals that come with it. Freeware was written by someone generous enough to share it. If you liked the software enough to pass it along, it's good etiquette to give credit to the author.

Avoid Viruses

- Among the hazards of sharing files—either by exchanging disks or passing them back and forth across the Internet—are small computer programs called **viruses**.
- Viruses are computer programs that attach themselves secretly to other programs and are activated when the host program is executed.
- Viruses usually perform some unwanted action, ranging from nuisance to destruction. Some viruses, for example, simply display a message at predetermined times. Other viruses attempt to reformat your hard disk and destroy all your data.
- Because the first act of a virus is to find a host program, viruses must be executable programs. Once executed, the virus attaches itself to another program that is sure to be executed (often a command module of the operating system, like command.com).
- Once a destructive virus enters your system, it can be difficult to remove.
- Viruses are often distributed, knowingly or not, in executable programs people are likely to use. Examples include games, image viewers, movie and sound players—though any executable file could be home to a virus.
- Keep in mind the following information regarding viruses:
  - It is good practice **never** to download and execute an executable program from an unknown or dubious source.
  - Except for macro viruses (see below), no virus can be passed via document files or e-mail messages.

Macro Viruses

- A special class of virus is written in the macro language of a program, like Word, and is passed along in document files. These viruses add themselves to the macro list of other, similar documents and are executed when document macros are executed— it sometimes when the document is first brought up.
- A macro virus is relatively safe—it can only perform actions allowed by the macro language it executes. **Macro viruses are the only kind of virus that can be passed in a non-executable, document file.**

In this exercise, you will log into the Federal Government FTP site, view some text files, and download some image files. Then you will go to an anitvirus FTP site and download virus protection files.

EXERCISE DIRECTIONS

1. If you are already connected to your service provider and your browser is open, go to step 2.

   OR

   Connect to your service provider and start your browser.

   ✓ *The examples here use Netscape Navigator.*

2. Type the following URL on the Location line:

   ftp://ftp.fedworld.gov/pub

3. Press Enter.

   You are now in the Federal Government's anonymous FTP site.

   ✓ *Notice the line at the top that shows the current directory (/pub).*

4. Scan the list. You should see a file named *00-index.txt* at or near the top. In the Fedworld FTP site, this text file contains a description of the files in the directory. Most Fedworld directories have indexes named *00-index.txt.*

5. Click on the entry for *00-index.txt.* After the file is downloaded, your browser will look something like the result shown at the right.

   ✓ *Like other Web sites, FTP sites change frequently.*

6. Scroll through this document. You'll see that it describes the contents of the subdirectories located in ***/pub***. When you are done, click Back on your browser.

Current directory is /pub

Up to higher level directory

00-index.txt	5 Kb	Tue Aug 13 09:14:00 1996 Plain Text
auto/		Thu Sep 05 07:27:00 1996 Directory
bxa/		Thu Aug 22 07:30:00 1996 Directory
cals-std/		Wed Nov 15 00:00:00 1995 Directory
cals/		Thu Jun 06 10:14:00 1996 Directory
commerce/		Wed Nov 15 00:00:00 1995 Directory
doe/		Thu Sep 05 07:51:00 1996 Directory
faa-asi/		Wed Sep 04 07:53:00 1996 Directory
faa-att/		Fri Aug 16 07:58:00 1996 Directory
faa-cai/		Wed Sep 04 08:10:00 1996 Directory
faa-main/		Thu Aug 29 08:09:00 1996 Directory
faa-oai/		Wed Sep 04 13:21:00 1996 Directory
faa-ri/		Sat Aug 31 08:19:00 1996 Directory
fcs/		Sat Aug 24 08:24:00 1996 Directory
gsa-its/		Thu Mar 14 11:52:00 1996 Directory
import/		Sat Feb 17 00:00:00 1996 Directory
irs-92/		Thu Jun 06 10:27:00 1996 Directory
irs-93/		Thu Jun 06 10:27:00 1996 Directory
irs-94/		Thu Jun 06 10:35:00 1996 Directory
irs-95/		Mon Aug 05 09:37:00 1996 Directory
irs-irbs/		Wed Sep 04 19:36:00 1996 Directory

```
The FedWorld FTP site contains more than 10,000 data files of various
sorts that have been produced by U.S. Government agencies. Often, FedWorld
is the original source for these files on the net. The directory index
listings on this site are updated daily. Some of our most popular files
include the Federal Job Announcements in the jobs directory, White House
press releases, IRS tax forms and instructions and Cancer information.


PUB Libraries

File Name    Description
============ ===================================================
AUTO         Vehicle Manufacturers Indexes

BXA          Bureau of Export Administration

CALS         CALS products and documents

CALS-STD     CALS Waiver-Free Specifications and Standards

COMMERCE     Misc. U.S. Department of Commerce Files

DAV-BACN     Davis-Bacon Database --FEE BASED--

DOE          Department-wide Business Information

FAA-ASI      FAA Aircraft Service Information

FAA-ATT      FAA Airman Training and Testing

FAA-CAI      FAA Continued Airworthiness Information

FAA-MAIN     FAA Main File Library - All Files
```

Current directory is /pub/irs-95

Up to higher level directory

00-index.txt	49 Kb	Thu Sep 05 05:01:00 1996 Plain Text
f1040.pdf	51 Kb	Wed Sep 04 22:11:00 1996
f1040a.pdf	43 Kb	Wed Sep 04 22:11:00 1996
f1040as1.pdf	13 Kb	Wed Sep 04 22:11:00 1996
f1040as2.pdf	35 Kb	Wed Sep 04 22:11:00 1996
f1040as3.pdf	32 Kb	Wed Sep 04 22:11:00 1996
f1040c.pdf	107 Kb	Wed Sep 04 22:12:00 1996
f1040e95.pdf	115 Kb	Wed Sep 04 22:12:00 1996
f1040ez.pdf	64 Kb	Wed Sep 04 22:12:00 1996
f1040nr.pdf	67 Kb	Wed Sep 04 22:12:00 1996
f1040nre.pdf	30 Kb	Wed Sep 04 22:12:00 1996
f1040pr.pdf	73 Kb	Wed Sep 04 22:12:00 1996
f1040prh.pdf	30 Kb	Wed Sep 04 22:12:00 1996
f1040sab.pdf	41 Kb	Wed Sep 04 22:12:00 1996
f1040sc.pdf	40 Kb	Wed Sep 04 22:13:00 1996
f1040sce.pdf	29 Kb	Wed Sep 04 22:13:00 1996
f1040sd.pdf	28 Kb	Wed Sep 04 22:13:00 1996
f1040se.pdf	34 Kb	Wed Sep 04 22:13:00 1996
f1040sei.pdf	34 Kb	Wed Sep 04 22:13:00 1996

7. Click on the directory entry for ***irs-95***.
8. Click on the index file for this directory, ***00-index.txt***.

   You'll see that it lists the contents of the directory, in this case a large group of IRS forms, like F1040.PDF, the 1040 form, in PDF (Portable Document Format) format, a format used by Adobe Acrobat. When you are finished scanning the file, click Back on your browser.
9. The IRS-95 directory also contains a file called ***irs-95.htm***. If you click on this file, you will get an HTML document that lists various forms and contains clickable links for downloading those you want.
10. When you are finished scanning the file, click Back on your browser until you are back in /pub.
11. Click on the directory entry for ***sat-imgs***.
12. Click on the index file for this directory, ***00-index.txt*** to get additional information on the files in this directory. *Note that this directory contains image files, mainly GIFs, taken by various satellites.* Click Back on your browser to return to the ***sat-imgs*** directory.
13. Click on the file named ***ear-moon.gif***.
14. If you want to save this file, click Save As on the File menu and specify a directory.
15. Click Back on your Toolbar to return to the ***sat.imgs*** directory. *Note that this directory also contains a few zipped program files (for example, lview31.zip, which contains the LView image viewing program).*
16. Click Back on your Toolbar to return to /pub.

17. Create a bookmark for this page, if you like, by selecting Bookmarks, Add Bookmark in Netscape, or Add to Favorites in Internet Explorer.
18. Browse through this site some more.
19. Next you will download an anti-virus program. Type the following URL:

    ftp://ftp.mcafee.com/pub/antivirus
20. Press Enter.

    This is the anti-virus part of McAfee Associates software's FTP site.
21. Click the file ***00-index.txt*** and scan its contents.

    ✓ *Note that some of the documentation it describes can be read only with Adobe Acrobat Reader, which is also available at this site.*
22. Make note of any anti-virus and documentation files that interest you.
23. The program VirusScan is a good program to note for future download. For more on viruses, see *Appendix B. Viruses*, page 225.
24. Click Back to return to the directory page.

✓ *If you are using the Internet Simulation, skip step 6 and proceed to step 7.*

25. If you want to visit McAfee's Web site and get more information about their products, go to: ***http://www.mcafee.com.***
26. Continue on to the next exercise.

    OR

    Exit from your browser and disconnect from your service provider.

FTP directory /pub/antivirus at ftp.mcafee.com

Up to higher level directory

Date	Time	Size	File
10/02/96	02:00AM	6,369	00-index.txt
03/19/96	12:00AM	2,609,653	acrodos.zip
05/02/96	04:45PM	3,863,257	acroread.hqx
03/19/96	12:00AM	1,452,740	acrowin.zip
04/05/96	05:08AM	530,528	bsh-101e.zip
04/10/96	12:32AM	273,729	bsh10man.zip
09/16/96	07:27PM	346,312	dat-9609.zip
07/31/96	01:19AM	Directory	**french**
10/01/96	03:06AM	1,290,041	nnt252e1.zip
10/01/96	03:06AM	911,672	nnt252e2.zip
10/01/96	03:06AM	2,199,859	nnti252e.zip
07/18/96	04:46PM	14,377	notvirus.zip
09/13/96	03:34PM	1,042,345	nsh232e1.zip
09/13/96	03:35PM	1,413,342	nsh232e2.zip
09/13/96	03:35PM	1,431,031	nsh232e3.zip
09/13/96	03:35PM	1,292,981	nsh232e4.zip
03/18/96	12:00AM	258,669	nsnt2doc.zip
08/20/96	01:49PM	555,541	nts-251e.zip
08/21/96	08:05PM	504,476	osc-251e.zip
08/21/96	08:05PM	746,755	osci251e.zip
04/17/96	04:09AM	4,337	register.txt
09/16/96	07:27PM	473,002	scn-252e.zip
09/16/96	07:27PM	714,000	scni252e.zip
04/18/96	04:06AM	4,058,463	solarisr.taz
08/23/96	04:47PM	1,317,782	v95205e1.zip
08/23/96	04:47PM	486,143	v95205e2.zip

Exercise 3

◆ Search for File Locations ◆ Download Large Files
◆ Netiquette for FTP Users

NOTES

Search for File Locations

- One important reason to use FTP sites is to update your computer programs. Netscape and Microsoft, for example, regularly release updated and beta versions of their Web browsers. To stay current with these programs, you need to download the most recent version. In the case of these two programs, anyone who meets certain, criteria has permission to download copies without charge.
- Many companies release updates to purchased programs via Web and FTP sites. Registered users can download newer versions. This gives customers immediate access to updated versions and saves money for the company.
- Both large and small programs are distributed in this way. Large programs are usually distributed through a network of sites associated with the company. For example:

To get updates to:	Access this location:
Netscape Navigator	***http://home.netscape.com/comprod/mirror/client_download.html***
Internet Explorer	***http://www.microsoft.com/ie/download/***

- In the exercise below, you will have the opportunity to download the latest version of Netscape or Internet Explorer.
- Small programs are often distributed through sites that offer a number of programs for downloading, or links to sites where programs can be downloaded.
- One such site is http://www.tucows.com. When you enter this site, you are asked to pick a location geographically close to you. The following illustration shows the California site.

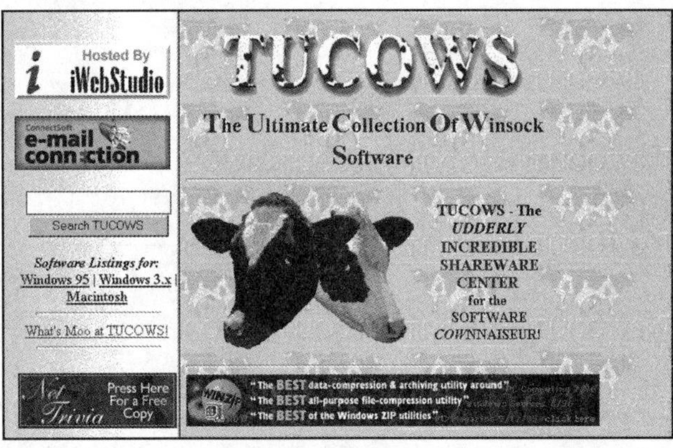

Tucows is a great site for all kinds of software, including viewers, readers, anti-virus scanners, and many Internet utilities. In the exercise steps that follow, you will use the Tucows site to download Eudora Lite, a good stand-alone e-mail program.

- Any time you find a site that contains programs you may want to download, add that site to your bookmarks. Then you can return to that site easily, without having to remember where you found it.
- You can also find the Internet locations of programs you want to download by searching the Web from a search site. (*See Lesson 3 for information on using search sites.*)

Download Large Files

- Many programs, like Web browsers, are large and take a long time to download. Any interruption in the downloading process means you have to start over.
- Many Web sites that offer large files for downloading will provide a choice of FTP sites to download from. To ensure the fastest, smoothest download of a large file (or any file for that matter), use the site geographically closest to you. For example, if you are in California, choose a North American site over a European or an Australian one.

  If the site you are downloading from is far away, the chances of interruption are increased (since the file packets have to travel through more routers to get to you).
- The following illustration shows the Netscape Web page that allows you to pick a download site for Netscape Navigator:

DOWNLOAD SITES

Click on the location nearest to you, and then a server will download the software to your hard disk. Each location carries the same software. We receive the largest number of download requests between 11:30 a.m. and 1:30 p.m. PST. Please try again if you have trouble reaching an available download location.

Download: Daniel Webster College
Download: MIT Lab for Computer Science
Download: Oregon State University
Download: Rutgers University
Download: University of North Carolina
Download: University of Oregon
Download: University of Texas at Austin
Download: University of Texas at Dallas
Download: Washington University in St. Louis
Download: McGill University, Montreal, Canada
Download: Facultad de Ciencias, UNAM, Mexico
Download: Monterrey Institute of Technology and Advanced Studies, Mexico
Download: Universidad Autonoma de Nuevo Leon, Mexico

Download: Netscape Communications, Mountain View, California, U.S.A.
Download: Netscape Communications, Mountain View, California, U.S.A.
Download: Netscape Communications, Mountain View, California, U.S.A.
Download: Netscape Communications, Mountain View, California, U.S.A.

Netiquette for FTP Users

- FTP sites are often large computers at companies or universities. These sites service many kinds of requests, including requests from people working at those organizations or doing business with them.

- For this reason, it is good net etiquette (**netiquette**) to do your downloading in off-hours, like evenings or late at night. This allows the FTP server to do its regular work during business hours.

  ✓ *Remember to allow for time differences. The east coast of the United States is three hours ahead of the west coast.*

- The exception, of course, is an FTP site (like Netscape's) that wants you to download their software as the major part of their regular business. But it is still a good idea to download during off-hours. Your chances of being allowed in are greater (because traffic is less), and your download times will likely be shorter.

In this exercise, you will download the recent version(s) of Netscape Navigator and/or Internet Explorer from the companies' home sites. Then you will access the Tucows site and download Eudora Lite, a mail program used in Lesson 5.

EXERCISE DIRECTIONS

To download Netscape Navigator:

1. If you are already connected to your service provider and your browser is open, go to step 2.

   OR

   Connect to your service provider and start your browser.

2. Type the following URL on the Location line and then press Enter.

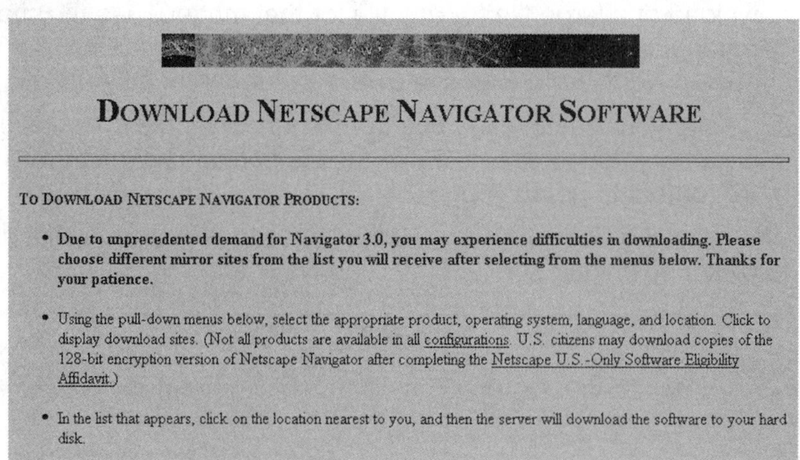

http://home.netscape.com/comprod/mirror/client_download.html

3. Scroll down to the middle of the page, until the download selection area appears (see illustration at right).

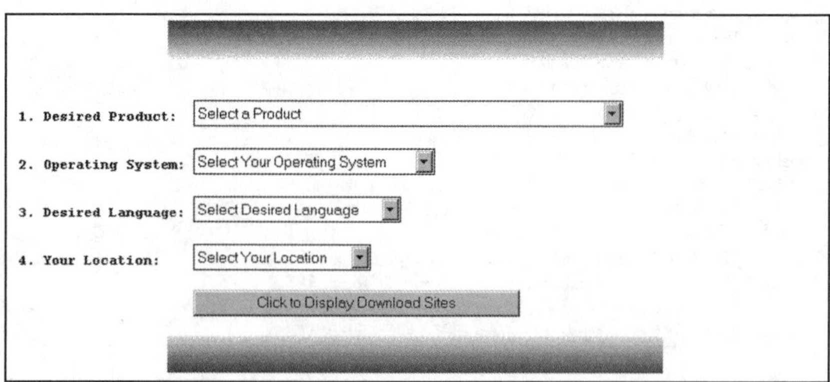

4. Use the pull-down menus to select a product (the latest version of Netscape Navigator), an operating system (such as Windows 95), a language (such as U.S. English), and your location (the list contains continents).
5. Click the button that says "Click to Display Download Sites."
6. If a Security Information dialog box appears, read it, and then click Continue.
7. In the page that appears, scroll down until you see the list of download sites.

DOWNLOAD SITES

Click on the location nearest to you, and then a server will download the software to your hard disk. Each location carries the same software. We receive the largest number of download requests between 11:30 a.m. and 1:30 p.m. PST. Please try again if you have trouble reaching an available download location.

Download: Daniel Webster College
Download: MIT Lab for Computer Science
Download: Oregon State University
Download: Rutgers University
Download: University of North Carolina
Download: University of Oregon
Download: University of Texas at Austin
Download: University of Texas at Dallas
Download: Washington University in St. Louis
Download: McGill University, Montreal, Canada
Download: Facultad de Ciencias, UNAM, Mexico
Download: Monterrey Institute of Technology and Advanced Studies, Mexico
Download: Universidad Autonoma de Nuevo Leon, Mexico

Download: Netscape Communications, Mountain View, California, U.S.A.
Download: Netscape Communications, Mountain View, California, U.S.A.
Download: Netscape Communications, Mountain View, California, U.S.A.
Download: Netscape Communications, Mountain View, California, U.S.A.

8. Select a site near you and click on the Download link next to it.
9. If a Save As dialog box appears, select a directory into which the file will be saved.

   *Note that once the download starts, the source location is an FTP site (with a URL that begins "ftp://"). When you click the **Download** link, you are performing an anonymous FTP login to an FTP server and specifying a directory and file, all in one URL.*
10. When the save is compete, continue with this exercise. To abandon the download before it is completed, click the Cancel button in the Save As dialog box.

To download Internet Explorer:

1. Type the following URL on the Location line and then press Enter:

   http://www.microsoft.com/ie/download/

2. Use the Select Desired Product pull-down menu to select IE 3.0 (or the most recent version) for Windows 95 and click Next.

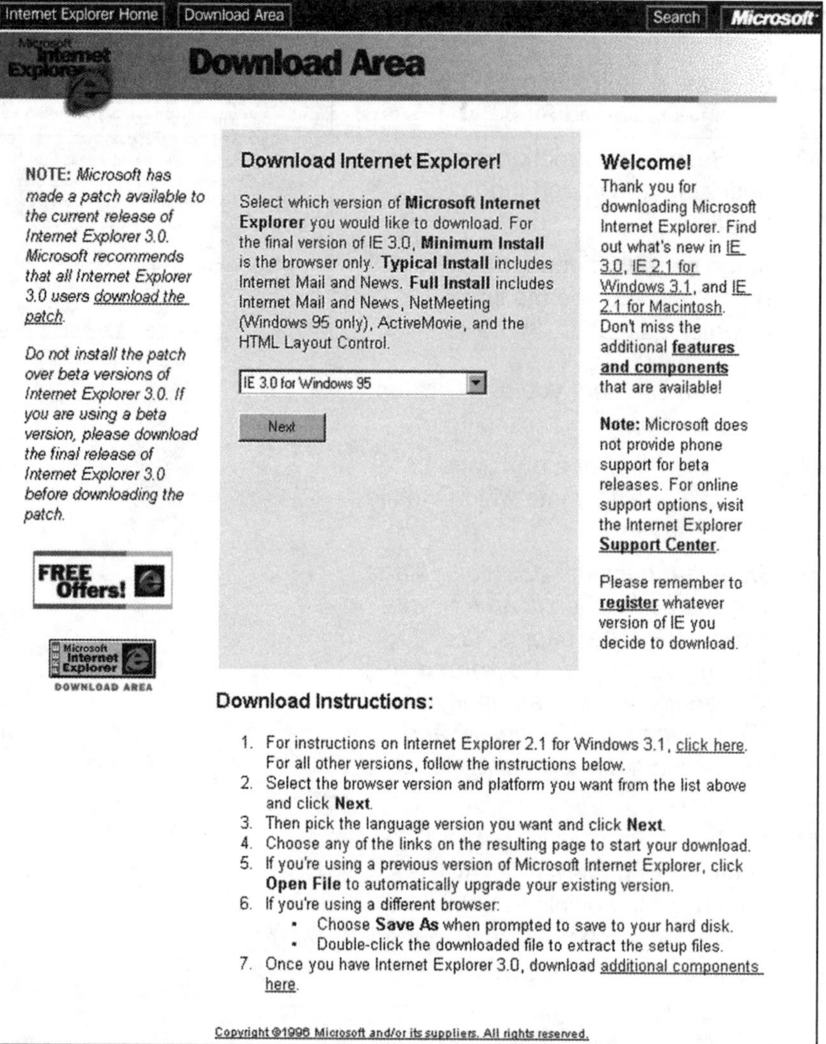

3. Use the Select Desired Language pull-down menu to select:

   US English - IE 3.0 Full Install for Windows 95.

4. Click Next.

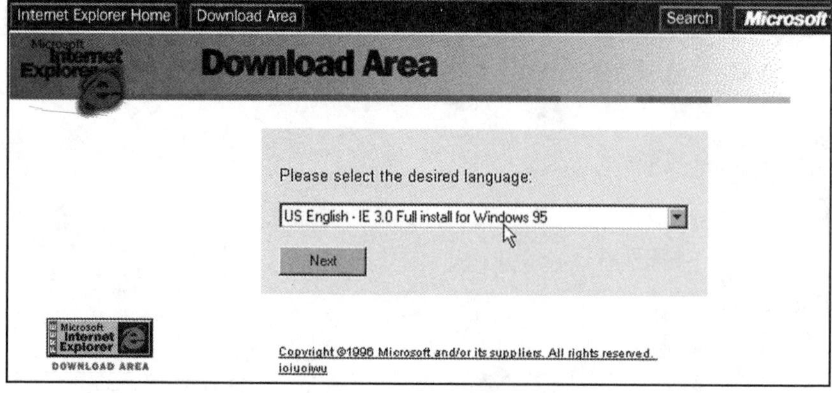

5. In the page that appears, scroll down until you see the list of download sites.
6. Select a site near you and click on the link next to it.
7. If a Save As dialog box appears, select a directory into which the file will be saved.

   Note that once the download starts, the source location is an FTP site (with a URL that begins "ftp://"). When you click the link, you are performing an anonymous FTP login to an FTP server and specifying a directory and file, all in one URL.
8. When the save is compete, continue with this exercise. To abandon the download before it is completed, click the Cancel button in the Save As dialog box.

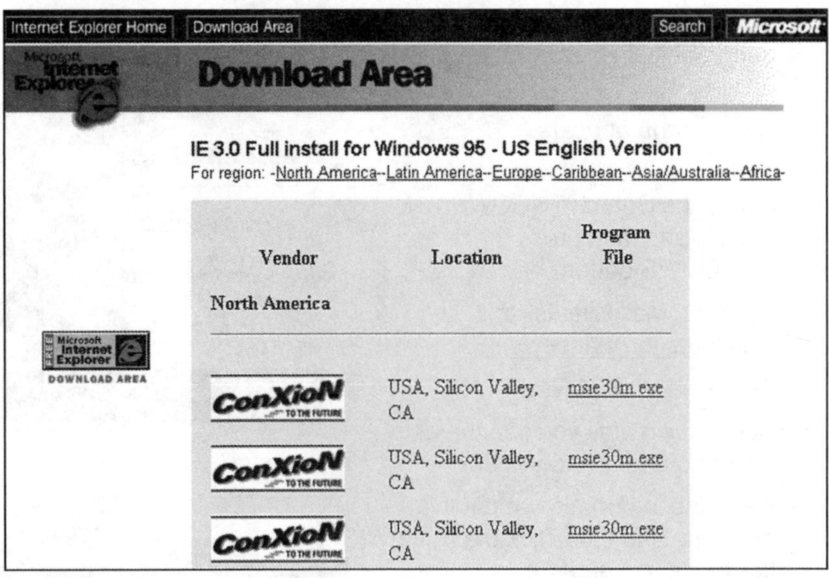

To download Eudora Light mail:

1. Type the URL for the Tucows site and then press Enter:

   http://www.tucows.com

   ✓ *The Tucows site is remodeled from time to time, so the images captured in this lesson may vary slightly from those found on the actual site.*

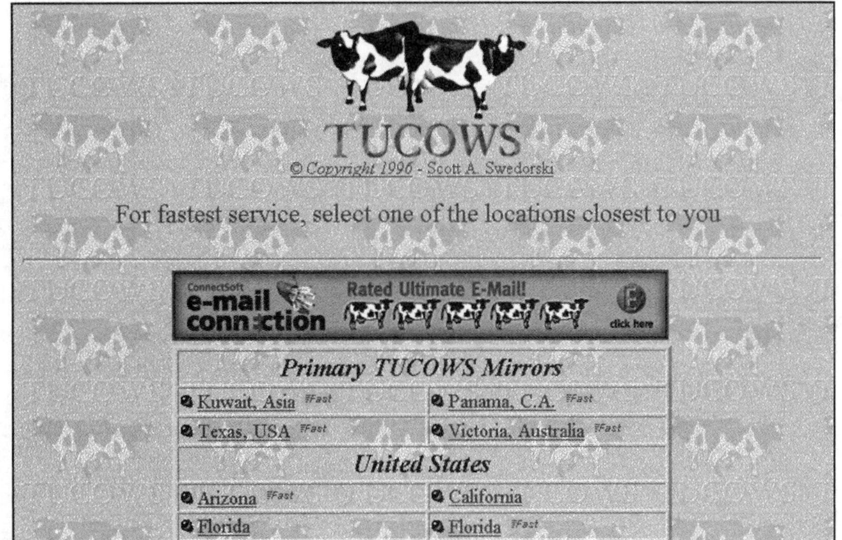

2. Scroll down the page, select a site geographically near you, and click on it.

   A new page appears.

3. Type "Eudora" in the text box above the Search TUCOWS button, and then press the TUOCOWS button.

4. Click on "Mail Clients" and Checkers for Windows 95.

   A new page displays.

5. Scroll down until you see the entry for Eudora for Windows 95.

6. Read the information about this program, and then click the link at the top of this entry.

7. Select a location for the downloaded file.

   ✓ *Note that you can also download a Windows 3.x version, and that a clickable link will take you to the program creator's home page.*

8. When the download is complete, Browse the Tucows site if you like, and download other software. Be sure to create bookmarks (or ad to Favorites) for Web sites you'd like to visit again.

9. Continue on to the next exercise.

   OR

   Exit from your browser and disconnect from your service provider.

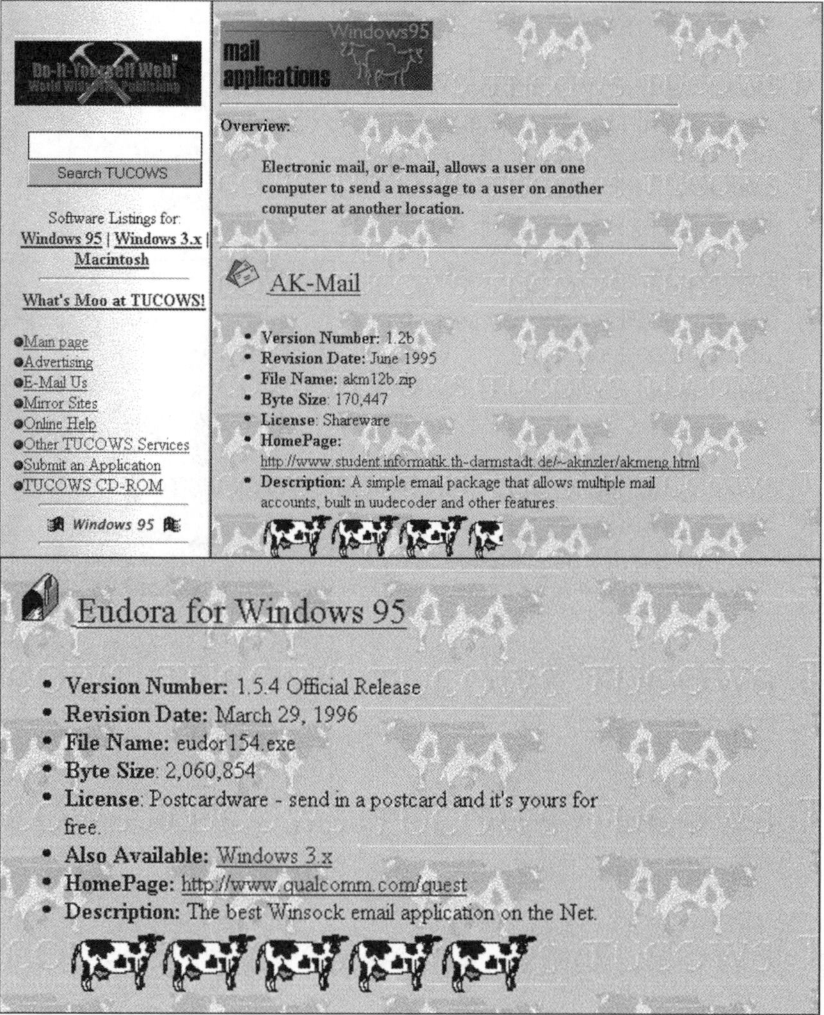

Continue to the next exercise.

Exercise

4

◆ **FTP - Summary Exercise**

In this exercise you will explore the FTP directories at SunSITE at the University of North Carolina and save a picture to your computer.

Note: ***The illustrations in this exercise use Netscape Navigator. If you are using Internet Explorer, your screens and the way directories display may be slightly different. The names of the directories and files should be the same.***

EXERCISE DIRECTIONS

1. If you are already connected to your service provider and your browser is open, go to step 2.

   OR

   Connect to your service provider and start your browser.
2. Type the URL: ***ftp://sunsite.unc.edu*** on the Location line and press Enter.
3. Scroll down, if necessary, and click the entry for the **pub** directory.

   Note: Recall that directory entries are indicated by a forward slash, such as: pub/. With Internet Explorer the slash may not appear.

   The screen on the right displays in Netscape Navigator.

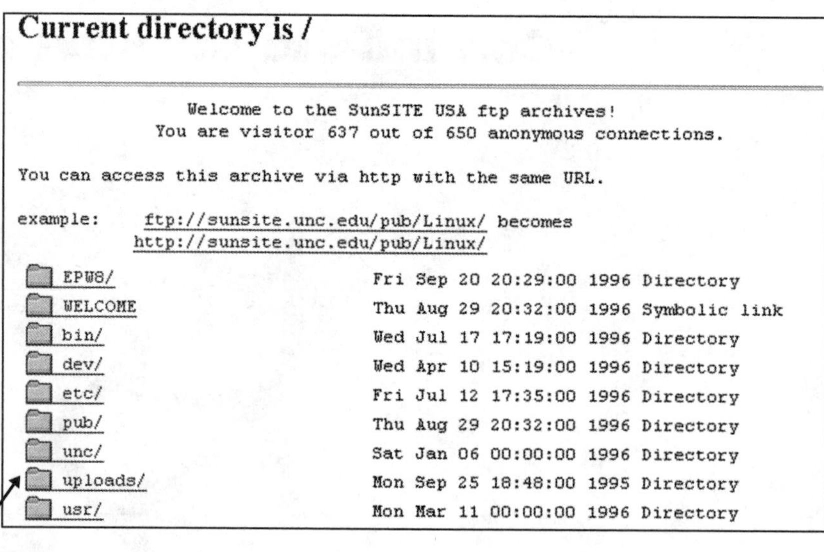

Current directory is /
Welcome to the SunSITE USA ftp archives!
You are visitor 637 out of 650 anonymous connections.
You can access this archive via http with the same URL.
example: ftp://sunsite.unc.edu/pub/Linux/ becomes
http://sunsite.unc.edu/pub/Linux/
EPW8/ Fri Sep 20 20:29:00 1996 Directory
WELCOME Thu Aug 29 20:32:00 1996 Symbolic link
bin/ Wed Jul 17 17:19:00 1996 Directory
dev/ Wed Apr 10 15:19:00 1996 Directory
etc/ Fri Jul 12 17:35:00 1996 Directory
pub/ Thu Aug 29 20:32:00 1996 Directory
unc/ Sat Jan 06 00:00:00 1996 Directory
uploads/ Mon Sep 25 18:48:00 1995 Directory
usr/ Mon Mar 11 00:00:00 1996 Directory
Click here.

4. Scroll down, if necessary, and click the entry for the *academic* directory.
5. Click the entry for the INDEX document to get information about the contents of the subdirectories in this directory.

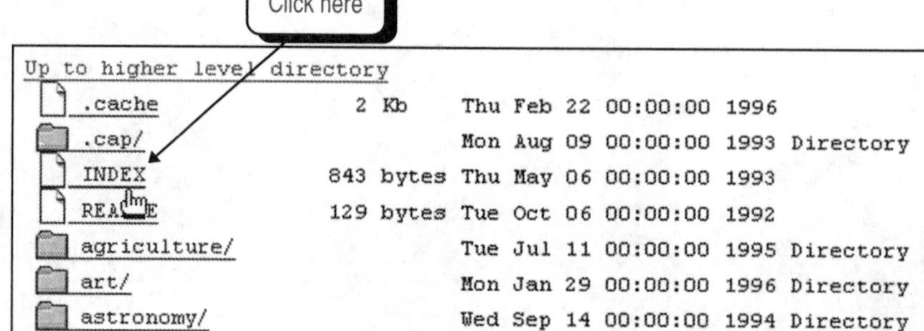

6. Return to the previous level by clicking Back on the Toolbar.
7. Scroll down, if necessary, and click the entry for the **geography** directory.
8. Scroll down, if necessary, and click the entry for the **onward** directory.
9. Scroll down, if necessary, and click on the **onward.html** document.
10. The HTML page shown at the right displays in your browser window.
11. Make a note of links you may wish to access in the future.

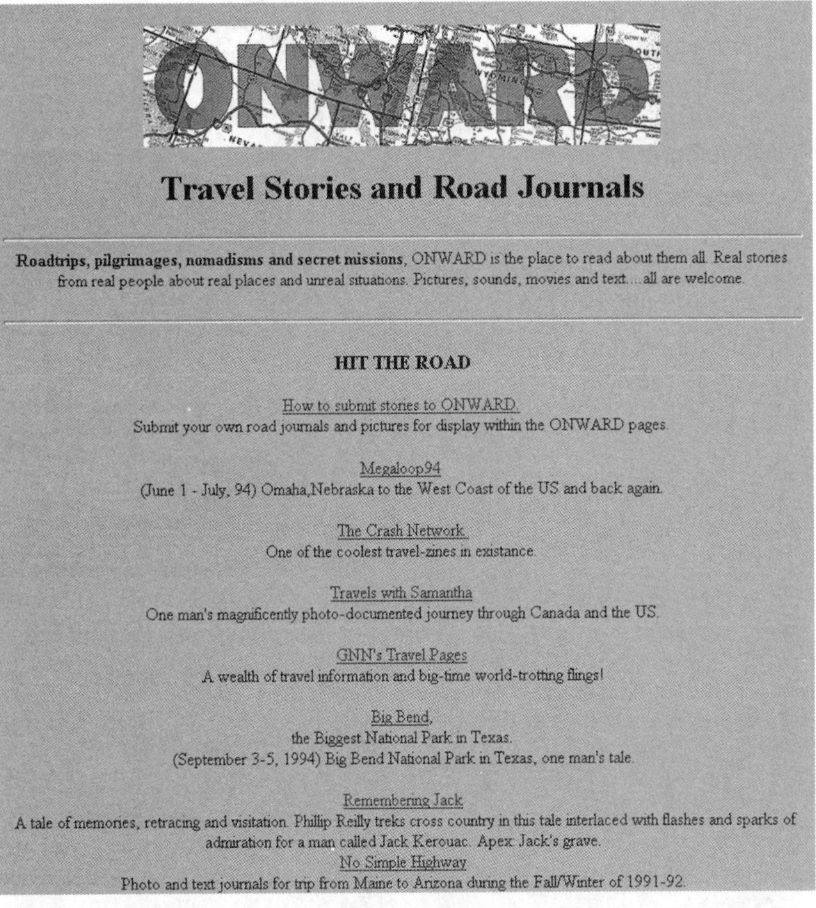

ONWARD
Travel Stories and Road Journals
Roadtrips, pilgrimages, nomadisms and secret missions, ONWARD is the place to read about them all. Real stories from real people about real places and unreal situations. Pictures, sounds, movies and text....all are welcome.
HIT THE ROAD
How to submit stories to ONWARD.
Submit your own road journals and pictures for display within the ONWARD pages.
Megaloop94
(June 1 - July, 94) Omaha,Nebraska to the West Coast of the US and back again.
The Crash Network
One of the coolest travel-zines in existance.
Travels with Samantha
One man's magnificently photo-documented journey through Canada and the US.
GNN's Travel Pages
A wealth of travel information and big-time world-trotting flings!
Big Bend,
the Biggest National Park in Texas.
(September 3-5, 1994) Big Bend National Park in Texas, one man's tale.
Remembering Jack
A tale of memories, retracing and visitation. Phillip Reilly treks cross country in this tale interlaced with flashes and sparks of admiration for a man called Jack Kerouac. Apex: Jack's grave.
No Simple Highway
Photo and text journals for trip from Maine to Arizona during the Fall/Winter of 1991-92.

12. Click Back on your Toolbar to return to the ***onward*** directory.
13. Scroll down, if necessary, and click entry for the **pics** directory.
14. Scroll down, if necessary, and click on ***onward-logo.gif.***

    The image file shown at the right is displayed in your browser.

Current directory is /pub/academic/geography/onward/pics

Up to higher level directory

File	Size	Date	Type
.cache	178 bytes	Fri Feb 23 00:00:00 1996	
.cache+	552 bytes	Fri Feb 02 00:00:00 1996	
onward-logo.gif	47 Kb	Wed Jun 01 00:00:00 1994	Compuserve Image Format
onward-logo2.gif	67 Kb	Sun Jul 31 00:00:00 1994	Compuserve Image Format

15. Click Back on your Toolbar to return to the **pics** directory.
16. Scroll down, if necessary, and click the image file called ***onward-logo2.gif.***

    The image shown on the right displays.
17. When you are finished exploring this FTP site, exit the browser.
18. Disconnect from your Internet service provider.

Lesson 5: Electronic Mail (E-mail)

Exercise 1

- Electronic Mail
- E-Mail Messages
- How E-Mail Works
- Send Messages and Files
- Cautions
- Set Up Your Browser for E-Mail

Exercise 2

- Change Internet Mail Options

Exercise 3

- E-Mail Programs
- Use a Browser for E-Mail
- Receive, Read and Print Mail
- Compose New Messages
- Send Messages

Exercise 4

- Files Attached to E-Mail
- Reply to Mail
- Forward Mail

Exercise 5

- Organize Mail Messages
- Use Address Books

Exercise 6

- Configure Eudora® Light
- Get, Read, And Print Messages
- Compose Messages and Add Attachments
- Send Messages
- Organize Messages

Exercise 1

◆ Electronic Mail ◆ E-mail Messages ◆ How E-mail Works ◆ Send Messages and Files ◆ Cautions ◆ Set up Your Browser for E-mail

NOTES

Electronic Mail (E-mail)

What is E-mail?

- Electronic mail (e-mail) is a method of sending information from one person to another across the Internet.
- E-mail is one of the most frequently used features of the Internet.

What is E-mail Used For?

- E-mail is used for sending messages – business messages and personal messages – to anyone with an e-mail address anywhere in the world.
- E-mail is also used for sending files. These files can be part of the e-mail message itself or they can be **attachments** and "ride" along with the e-mail. Using Internet e-mail, you can send and receive text files, graphic files, program files, application data files – any type of file you wish.
- The only real limitations to sending files by e-mail are these:
  - The size of the disk area (called the **spool**) used to store messages being sent and received. If a file is very large (or the spool area is small), there may not be room in the spool to hold the file.
  - The time it takes to transmit the file. Again, very large files take a long time to send and receive, especially if you are connected to your mail server via a modem. Very large file transfers are easily interrupted, and even when successful, can take several hours to complete.

E-mail Message

Netscape Mail Message Screen

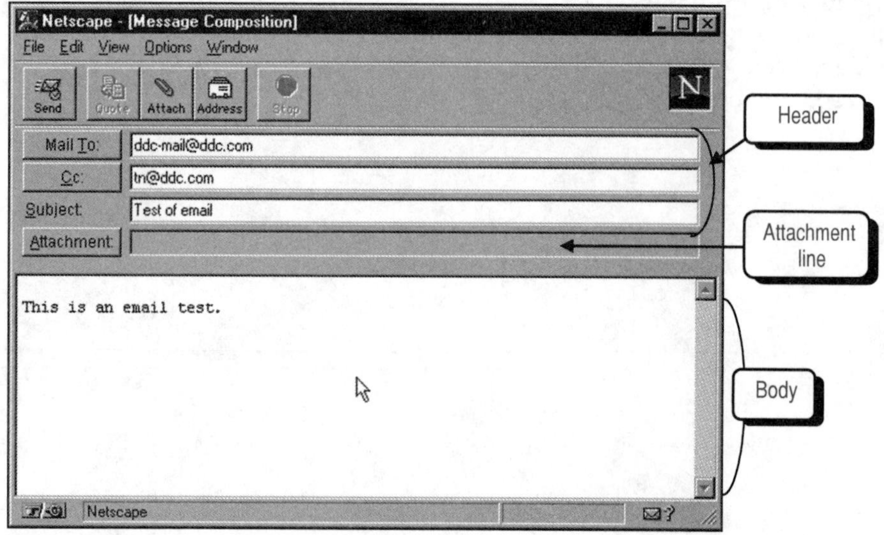

Internet Mail Message Screen

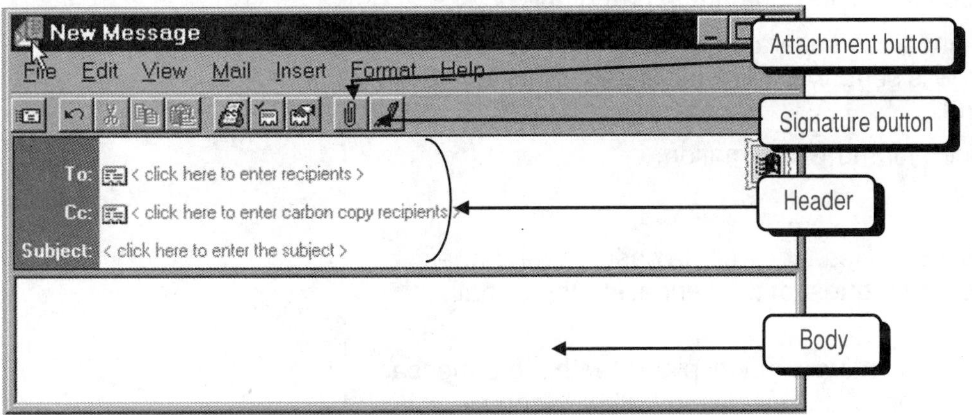

- An e-mail message has four basic parts: the header, the body, the signature (which is actually part of the body), and attachments.

Header

- The top part of an e-mail message is called the header. The header commonly contains the following of fields:
  - The **Date** field – the day, date, and time the message was sent. Some e-mail programs give you the choice of using Universal Time (Greenwich Mean Time), the local time zone, or the sender's time zone.
  - The **To** field – the Internet address of the recipient.
  - The **From** field – the "real name" and e-mail address of the sender. The "real name" is usually the person's name, but it may be the name of a company or any other plain English word(s) or phrase.
  - The **Subject** field – a short description of the contents of the message, as described by the sender.
  - The **Cc** field (Carbon Copy) – the Internet addresses of users who will receive a copy of the message.
  - The **Bcc** field (Blind Carbon Copy) – the Internet addresses of users who will receive a copy of the message, but whose addresses will not be displayed in the message header (same as Cc, but invisible to other recipients).
  - The **Attachments** or **X-attachments** field – shows the name of any attached files or URLs (see Attachments below). The field is called "Attachments" by most e-mail programs, but is listed as "X-attachments" in the text of the header itself.
- Other fields are added by the e-mail program and the mail server. Most of these fields are not important to the message and are typically not displayed (unless "full header" display is selected). E-mail message screen options differ slightly depending on the e-mail program.

Body and Signature

- The **message body** contains the message entered by the sender.
- A **signature** is a few lines of text sometimes added (at the sender's request) by the mail program to the end of the message body. Typically, a signature contains information about how to contact the sender (name,

street address, phone number, FAX number, etc.), but signatures can include any information you wish. The signature is part of the body.

- Signatures are often contained in a separate file and added by the mail program when the message is sent. You will typically not see signature text in a message you send.
- See Exercise 3 of this lesson for more information.

Attachments

- Attachments are binary or ASCII files, or, in some cases, Web pages (URLs), that are "attached" (by request of the sender) to the e-mail message and sent with it.
- In Netscape Navigator, attachments are not displayed within the message text, but the name of the attached file is displayed in the Attachments (X_attachments) field of the header.
- In Internet Mail, the attached file is displayed as an icon at the bottom of the message window.
- See Exercise 4 for more on e-mail attachments.

How E-mail Works

E-mail Addresses

- Each user who wants to send or receive e-mail must have an e-mail account on a mail server. E-mail service is usually supplied by your Internet service provider as part of your regular service. You can assume that anyone with Internet service has an e-mail account.
- Each user with a mail account is uniquely identified by an **E-mail address**.
- E-mail addresses look like this:

  username@domain.suffix

- There are four parts to an e-mail address:
  - The **username** identifies an individual user. (Sometimes the username identifies an automated process like mail response program). The username is always unique within the domain. A username name can consist of any combination of letters and numbers (ASCII characters). Some online services, such as Compuserve, use numbers as usernames.
  - The @ symbol ("at") separates the username from the domain.
  - The **domain** identifies the electronic name of the location of the mail server. The domain name can consist of any combination of letters and numbers (ASCII characters).
  - Sometimes the name of the location may require several **subdomains** to identify the mail server. For example:

    username@domain.subdomain.suffix

  - The **suffix** identifies the type of organization operating the mail server. The most common organizations are:
    - **.com** for companies

  - **.edu** for educational institutions
  - **.net** for networking companies
  - **.mil** for military organizations
  - **.gov** for government departments and groups
  - **.org** for anything not covered in the other groups
- E-mail addresses outside the United States typically have a two-letter suffix designating the country the mail server is in. For example:
  - **.ca** for Canada
  - **.uk** for the United Kingdom
  - **.de** for Germany ("Deutschland")
  - **.au** for Australia
  - **.jp** for Japan

E-mail Protocols

- Mail servers send mail to each other over the Internet using the **Simple Mail Transfer Protocol (SMTP).** SMTP uses the US-ASCII character set.

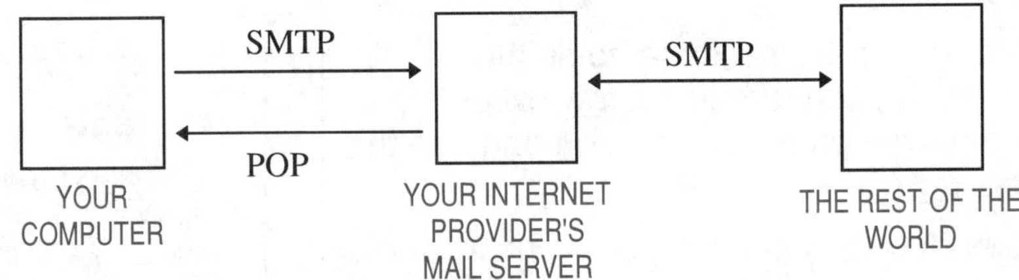

- When you send e-mail to someone, your browser or stand-alone e-mail program uses SMTP to send your e-mail to the mail server, which in turn uses SMTP to send your e-mail on to the recipient's mail server.
- On some networked systems, when e-mail arrives on the mail server, it is immediately available to the user.
- On other networked systems and on systems that use an Internet service provider (including most "home" Internet accounts), e-mail messages are held on the server until it is called for by the user. This transaction is governed by another protocol, called **Post Office Protocol (POP)**.

DEFINITIONS

- **SMTP (Simple Mail Transfer Protocol** – The standard communications protocol for routing e-mail between Internet hosts.
- **POP (Post Office Protocol)** – Indicates availability of a local access number to a public data network.

Send Messages and Files

- E-mail messages can consist only of letters, numbers, and punctuation (i.e., the standard US-ASCII character set). Special characters, like accented characters found in other languages, will be interpreted as ASCII characters and will appear as code when displayed.
- Files sent by e-mail are called **attachments**. Attached files can be in either **ASCII format** or **binary format**.
  - ASCII files can be sent without encoding. Be careful, though – hidden control characters, like the page break "character," can make the file difficult to interpret by the receiving mail program.

- Binary files, such as graphics and application data files, must be encoded as ASCII text before being sent. Types of binary file encoding include:
  - **Multipurpose Internet Mail Extensions (MIME)** or **Base 64 Encoding** – Best for any recipient, regardless of platform, using MIME-compliant e-mail. (Browsers use MIME encoding).
  - **UNIX-to-UNIX Encoding (UUencoding)** – Best for PC and UNIX recipients not using a MIME-compliant e-mail.
  - **BinHex Encoding** – Best for Macintosh recipients not using MIME-compliant e-mail.
- Exercise 4 has more information on attachments and encoded files.

Cautions

- Laws regarding the Internet and electronic transmission of data (including e-mail) are changing and, like the Internet, are changing daily. There are still many gray areas.
- **Copyright** laws, which determine ownership and use of published material, do apply to e-mail messages. Two areas of special concern are these: who holds copyright to (who "owns") e-mail messages and how copyrighted messages may be used.
  - In general, the person who writes the e-mail message holds the copyright (in the broadest sense) to it. There are just a few exceptions, such as messages sent by an employee on behalf of a company. In this case, the company holds the copyright.
  - It is not legal to electronically reproduce any copyrighted work, in whole or in part, and distribute it by e-mail without the copyright holder's permission. For example, copying an article from a local newspaper without that newspaper's permission and sending it by e-mail to a friend is a violation of copyright.
  - Note, however, that most copyrighted material is subject to what is called **fair use**; this means that short quotes and excerpts can be included in reviews, and used for similar purposes .
- E-mail is not a private or secure form of communication. An e-mail message is ASCII text that is sent to the world through numerous routers. At each point, the message may be intercepted and copied. (The legality of copying e-mail in this way is uncertain.)

  Though encryption and certification allow e-mail to be passed securely, these are used only in special circumstances. Most e-mail messages are sent as plain text and can be read by anyone who wishes to do so.
- *Therefore, be especially careful of information you put into an e-mail message.* Things like credit card numbers, driver license numbers, and social security numbers should *never* be sent by unsecured e-mail. The consequences could be disastrous.
- Once you use your e-mail account, your e-mail address becomes known, and you will receive messages from a wide variety of sources. These messages may include junk e-mail, unwanted mail, and inappropriate mail.

  The best way to deal with junk mail, unwanted mail, and inappropriate mail is to delete it. Note that your first reaction may be to reply to the

WARNING

Before including any published work in an e-mail message, obtain permission from the copyright holder.

WARNING

Never send credit card numbers, driver license numbers, and social security numbers, or any other private or sensitive information, through e-mail.

sender or send a complaint to the mail server postmaster. However, doing so may actually prolong the problem as some return addresses are atuo-responders. Auto-responders automatically interpret any response on your part as a request for more information or to be put on their mailing list.

Set Up Your Browser for E-mail

✓ ***Some online services (such as America Online) do not support access to Internet e-mail through browser applications. Check with your Internet service provider to see if you are able to utilize this browser feature.***

Netscape Navigator

- To view e-mail setup preferences, select Mail and News Preferences from the Options pull-down menu. You will use the preference windows to configure Netscape Mail.
- Netscape Mail has five mail and news preference windows. Each preference is marked by a tab, as described below:

Appearance Manages your display. It sets font width, text style, text size, Netscape or Microsoft Exchange for mail and news (Windows only), and pane layout.

Composition Settings related to mail composition. In it you can Allow 8-bit (accommodates the widest range of non-MIME-compliant e-mail programs) or MIME-compliance (accommodates MIME-compliant e-mail programs), send a default carbon copy to recipient, send a default carbon copy to file, and automatically quote the original message in the body of a message reply.

Servers Identifies your Internet provider's e-mail servers. It specifies the SMTP server, POP server, POP server user name, mail directory, maximum file size, whether downloaded messages should be removed from or left on the server, and how frequently to check for e-mail. (For e-mail purposes, you can ignore the settings in the News portion of the display.)

Identity Identifies you to the e-mail world. It specifies your "real" name, your e-mail address, your reply-to address, organization, and signature file, if any.

Organization Tells how you want your mail organized and also whether you want your POP server password remembered between logins.

NOTE

Contact your Internet Service provider or system administrator for this information and how to set up your browser for e-mail.

- Internet Mail offers seven mail and news preference windows. Each preference is marked by a tab, as described below:

Send — Allows you to set-up e-mail message send options, including when to send mail, whether and how to save copies of sent messages, and the mail format in which mail is to be saved and sent. Notice that the default setting Plain Text sends all mail messages in binary or ASCII format. You can change the default setting to HTML to send all files in HTML code. Selecting this option sends mail that contain URL attachments (e.g., Web pages) in HTML code so that the recipient's e-mail program can read the files properly-provided the e-mail program reads HTML code.

Read — You can set options for checking messages, deleting messages from message folders and even to play sound when new messages are received.

Server — The Server window identifies your Internet provider's e-mail servers. It specifies the Outgoing Mail server (SMTP), the Incoming Mail server (POP3) and account, and your server password. If you do not have this information, your Internet Service Provider can give it to you.

Fonts — Lets you choose the font, font color, and the language of the text.

Spelling — This option allows you to choose from several options for checking and correcting spelling errors in the body of your e-mail message.

Signature — Allows you to type in a signature, such as your name or e-mail address, or include a signature file with some or all of your messages. You also have the option not to include a signature.

Connections — Use this window to specify the type of connection you use to send e-mail.

In this exercise, you will change some of your browser's mail preferences.

CAUTION: The exercise directions below presume that you have already set up a mail account with a service provider. If you are not set up with Internet mail, contact your service provider. In this exercise you will set mail options not related to connecting or setting up a mail account.

EXERCISE DIRECTIONS

1. Connect to your Internet service provider.
2. Start Netscape Navigator.

   ✓ *If you are using Internet Explorer, go to Exercise 2.*
3. Select Options, Mail and News Preferences.
4. Click on the Appearance tab.

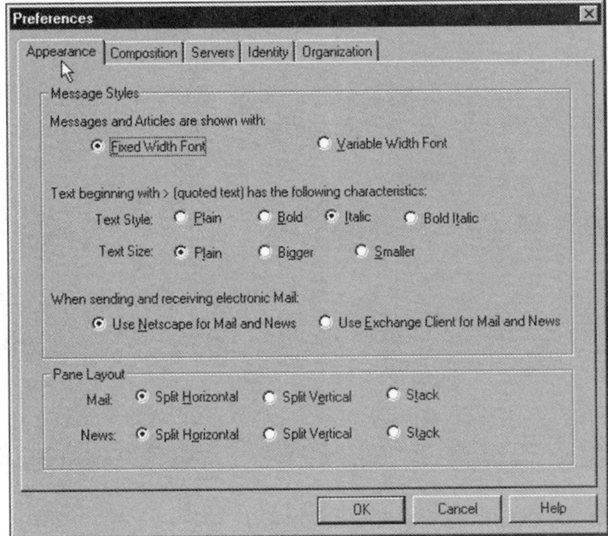

5. Choose among the following:
   - Messages and Articles are shown with:
     - Fixed Width Font—fixed-width characters
     - Variable Width Font—variable-width characters
   - Text beginning with ">" (quoted text) has the following characteristics:
     - Text Style
       Plain, Bold, Italic, Bold Italic
     - Text Size
       Plain, Bigger, Smaller
   - When sending and receiving Electronic Mail (Windows only):
     - Use Netscape for Mail and News
     - Use Exchange Client for Mail and News
6. Click on the Composition tab.

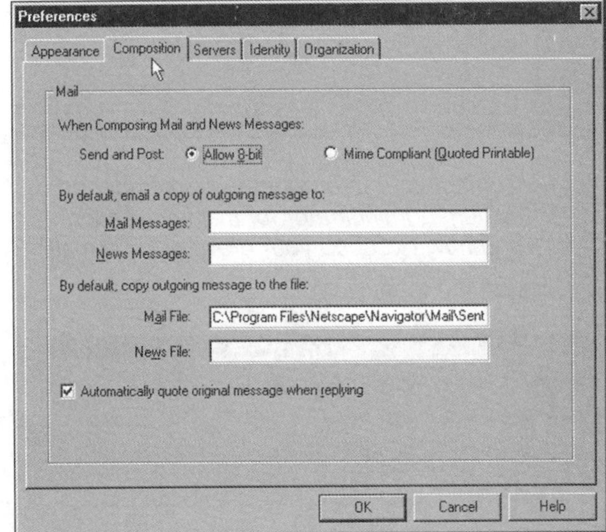

7. Choose among the following:

   When Composing Mail and News Messages:
   - Send and Post
     - Allow 8-bit
     - Mime Compliant (Quoted Printable)

     ✓ *Contact your Internet service provider or system administrator for this information and how to set up your browser for e-mail.*

   By default, e-mail a copy of outgoing messages to:
   - Mail Messages—Enter an e-mail address: your own if you wish to automatically receive a copy of every message you send, or other addresses.

   By default, copy outgoing messages to the file:
   - Mail File—Enter the path for a file: automatically stores a copy of every message you send in a file.
   - Automatically quote original message when replying.
8. Click on the Servers tab.

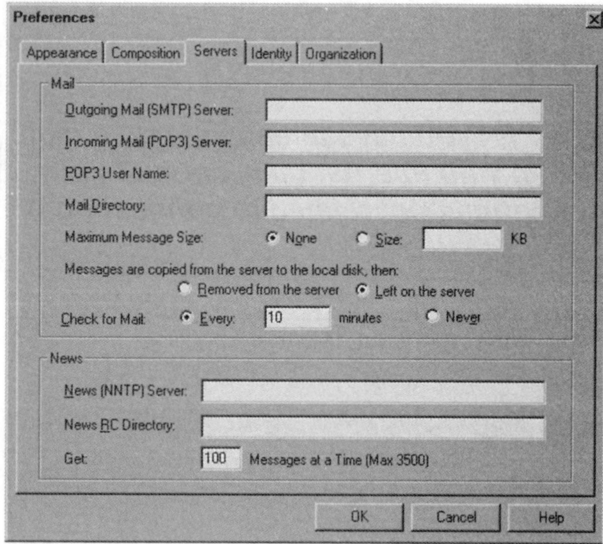

✓ *Contact your Internet service provider or system administrator for this information and how to set up your browser for e-mail.*

9. Click on the Identity tab.

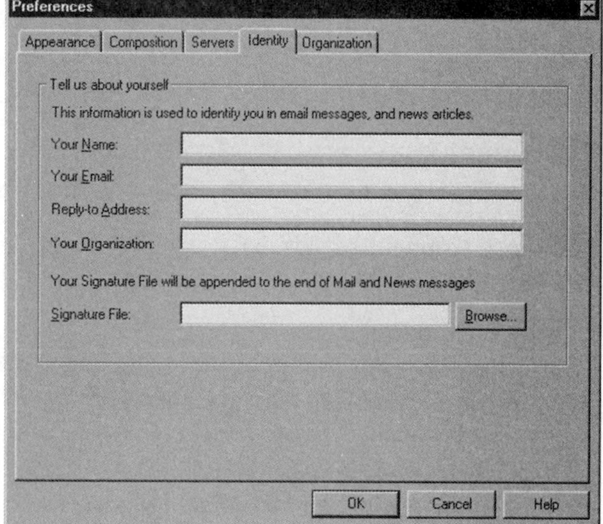

10. Supply the following information:

Your Name	Enter your name, however you want to list it
Your E-mail	Enter your e-mail address.
Reply-to-Address	Enter an alternate e-mail address for receiving your e-mail.
Your Organization	Enter your company name, if applicable.
Signature File	Enter the path of a file containing a signature you want to append to your e-mail messages.

11. Click on the Organization tab.

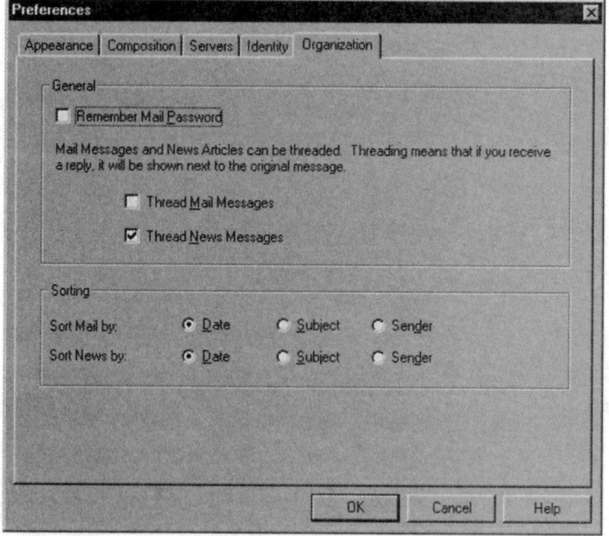

12. Choose among the following:

    Remember Mail Password.
    Thread Mail Messages.
    Sort Mail by Date.

13. Click the OK button to save the settings.
14. Continue on to the next exercise.

    OR

    Exit from Navigator and disconnect from your service provider.

Continue to the next exercise.

Exercise 2

◆ Change Internet Mail Options

NOTES

Change Internet Mail Options

- Internet Mail is the e-mail program that is frequently used with Internet Explorer. When you first set up Internet Mail, the **Internet Mail Configuration Wizard** determines several options for you. You can change these options from the **Mail**, **Options** dialog box. To view e-mail setup preferences, select Options from the Mail menu.

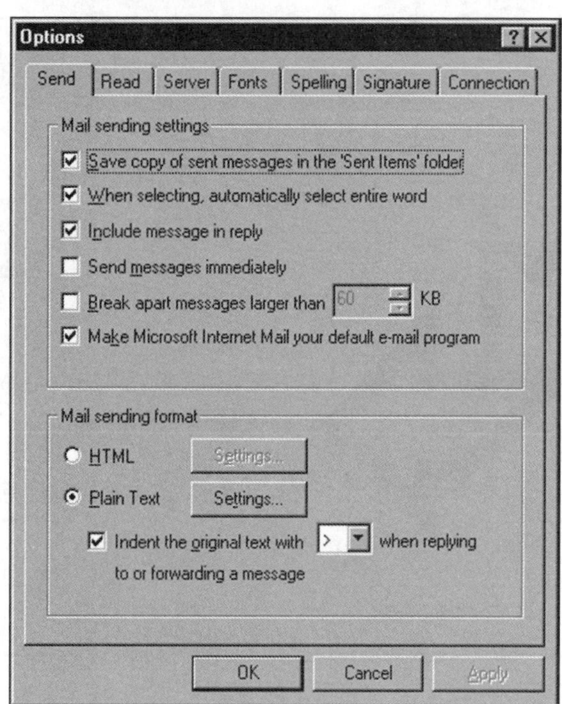

- There are seven mail option windows, each marked by a tab:

Send	Control options for the way messages are sent.
Read	Control options for incoming messages.
Server	Identify your Internet provider's e-mail servers and settings.
Fonts	Change font and color of text for messages.
Spelling	Select spell check features you want to use for composing messages.
Signature	Activate and create a signature to include in your messages.
Connection	Displays how you connect to the Internet.

NOTE

If you use Microsoft Network as your service provider, you will not be able to use Internet Mail at this time.

Internet Mail and News requires an SMTP/POP3 mail server for mail. The Microsoft Network currently does not offer SMTP/POP3 mail.

If you want to use Internet Mail, contact a service provider that has an SMTP/POP3 mail server.

Microsoft Network lets you send mail to other Internet users through its Microsoft Exchange application.

In this exercise you will change some of your browser's mail preferences.

CAUTION: ***The exercise directions below presume that you have already setup a mail account with a service provider. If you are not setup with Internet Mail, contact your service provider. In this exercise you will change mail options that are not related to connecting or setting up a mail account.***

EXERCISE DIRECTIONS

1. If you are already connected to your service provider and your browser is open, go to step 2.

   OR

   Connect to your service provider and open your browser.

   ✓ *If you are using Netscape Navigator, go to Exercise 3.*

2. Start Internet Mail.
3. In the Internet Mail main window, select Mail, Options.
4. Click the Send tab.

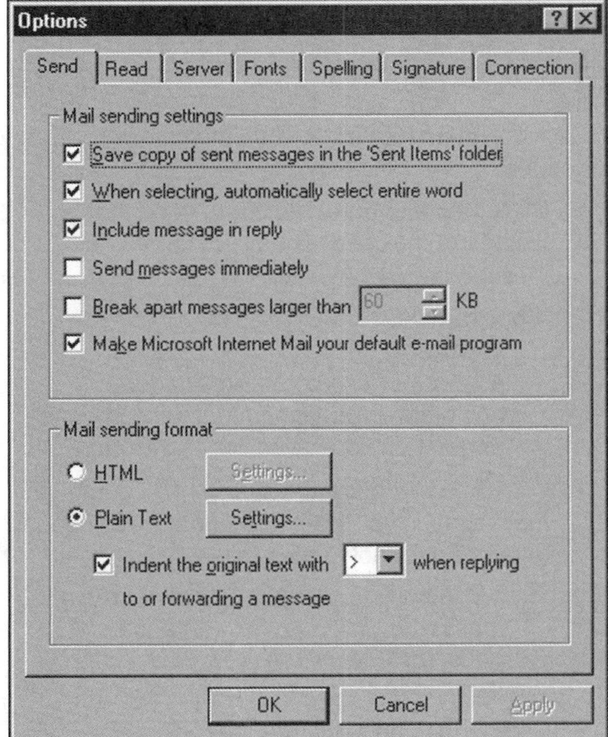

5. If <u>Save copy of sent messages in the 'Sent Items' folder</u> is not checked, click to select it. Do not change any other settings.
6. Click the Read tab and do the following:

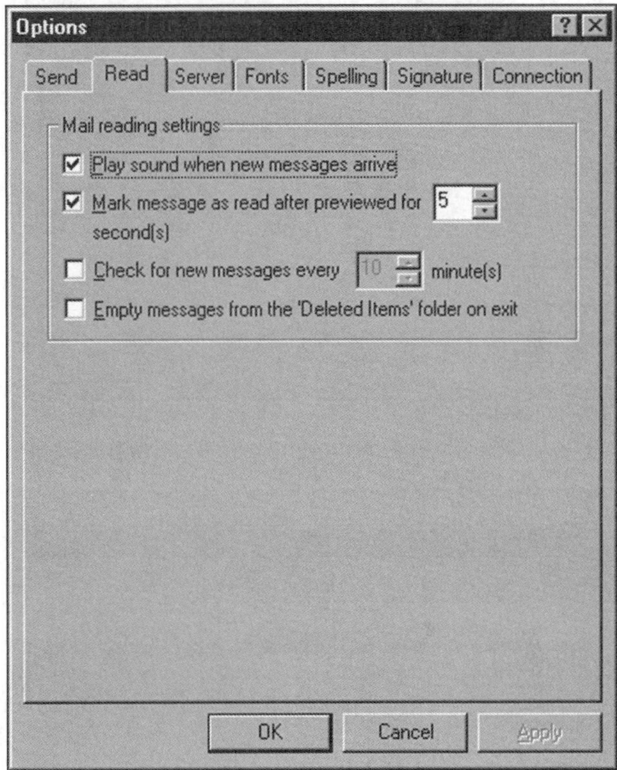

- Click <u>Play sound when new messages arrive</u>, if not already selected.
- Click <u>Mark messages as read after previewed for (5) second(s)</u>.

7. Click the Fonts tab and do the following:

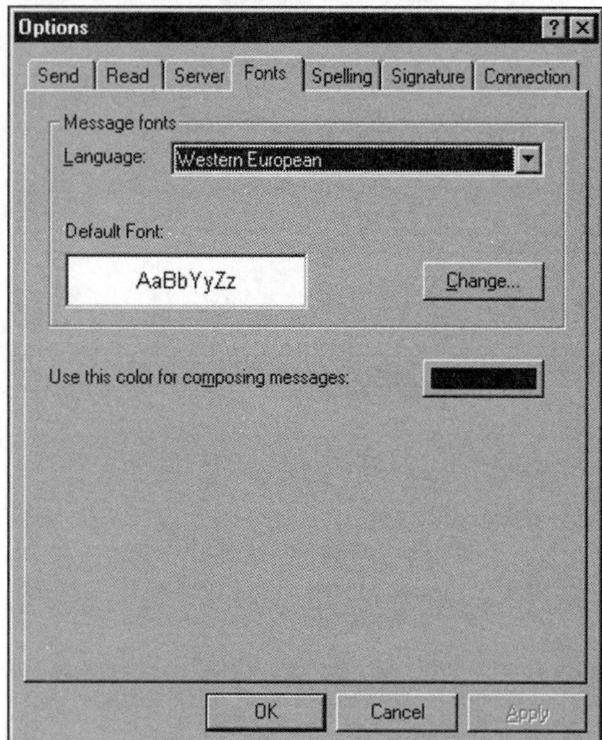

- Click Change button next to the Default Font display box.

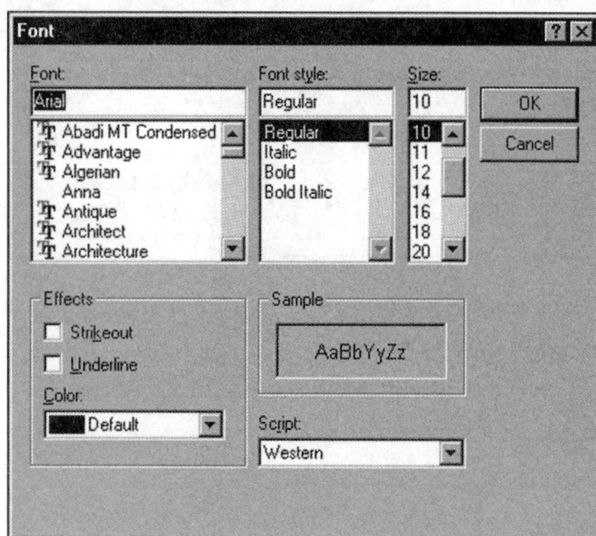

- If desired, select a different font and size and click OK.

8. Click the Spelling tab and note the options that are selected. Change any that you would like.

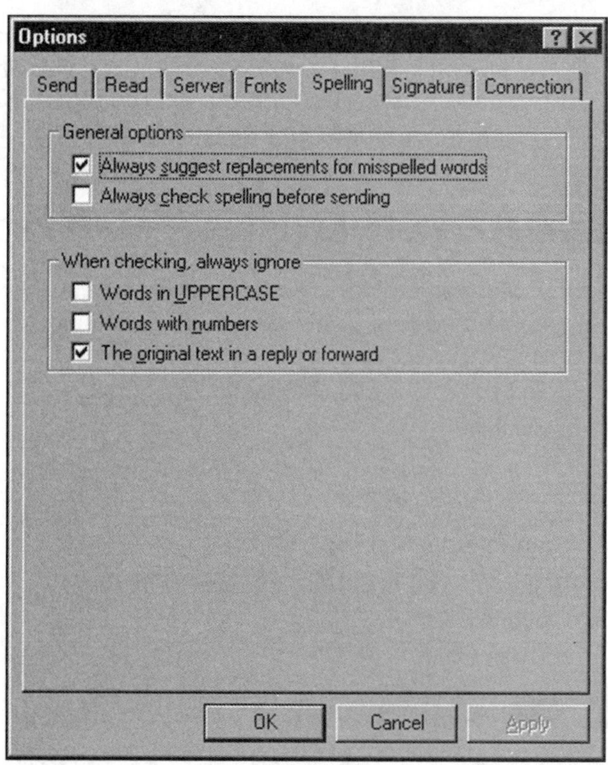

9. Click the Signature tab and do the following, if desired:

   - Click Text and enter the information that you would like included with all of your e-mail messages.

     For example:
     your name
     yourname@isp.com (e-mail address)
     any other information (such as company name) that you would like to include.

   - Click Add signature to the end of all outgoing messages, if you want this signature to appear on all your outgoing messages.

     ✓ *If you want to add a File to every e-mail message, click File, Browse and select desired file to include with your messages.*

   - Click Don't add signature to Replies and Forwards if you do not want your signature to appear on mail that you answer or forward.

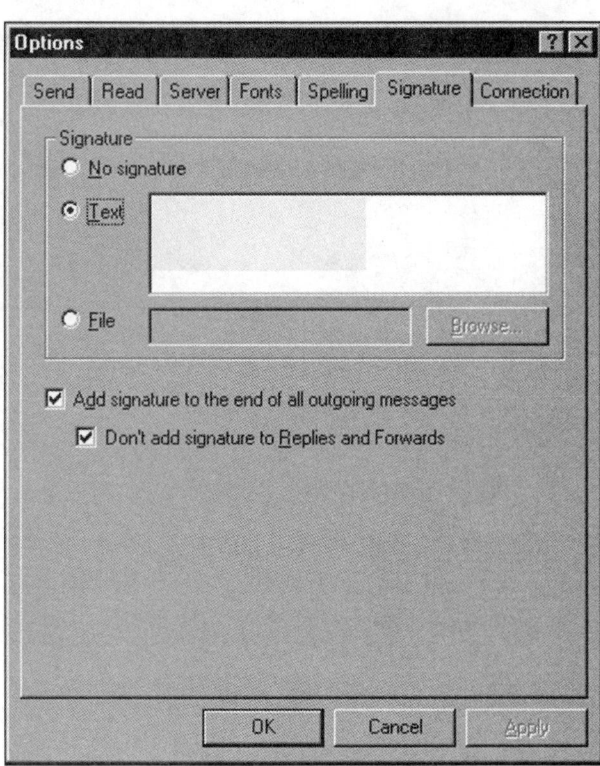

10. You can return to Mail, Options at any time and change any of the settings.
11. Continue on to the next exercise.

    OR

    Exit from your browser and disconnect from your service provider.

Exercise 3

◆ E-mail Programs ◆ Use a Browser for E-mail ◆ Receive, Read and Print Mail ◆ Compose New Messages ◆ Send Messages

NOTES

E-mail Programs

- There are a number of useful Internet e-mail applications. In one of the FTP exercises (Lesson 4, Exercise 3), you downloaded Eudora Light, one of the best freeware e-mail programs currently available. In Exercise 6 of this lesson, you will use Eudora Light for e-mail.
- For most people, though, a good Web browser (like Netscape Navigator or Internet Explorer) will do everything an e-mail program needs to do.

Use a Browser for E-mail

- With a Web browser's e-mail capabilities, you can do all of the following:
  - Send and receive e-mail and attachments (files and Web pages)
  - Read, print, compose, forward, and respond to messages
  - Sort e-mail messages into folders
  - Maintain address books of frequently used e-mail addresses
- In this exercise, you will read e-mail, compose a new message, and print your mail. In later exercises, you will compose replies, add attachments, forward messages to other users, and work with folders and address books.

Netscape Navigator's E-mail Window

- To access e-mail in Netscape Navigator, do one of the following:
  - Click on the mail icon in the lower-right corner of the browser,

    OR
  - Click Window, Netscape Mail.

  The Netscape Mail window appears.

Netscape Main Mail Window

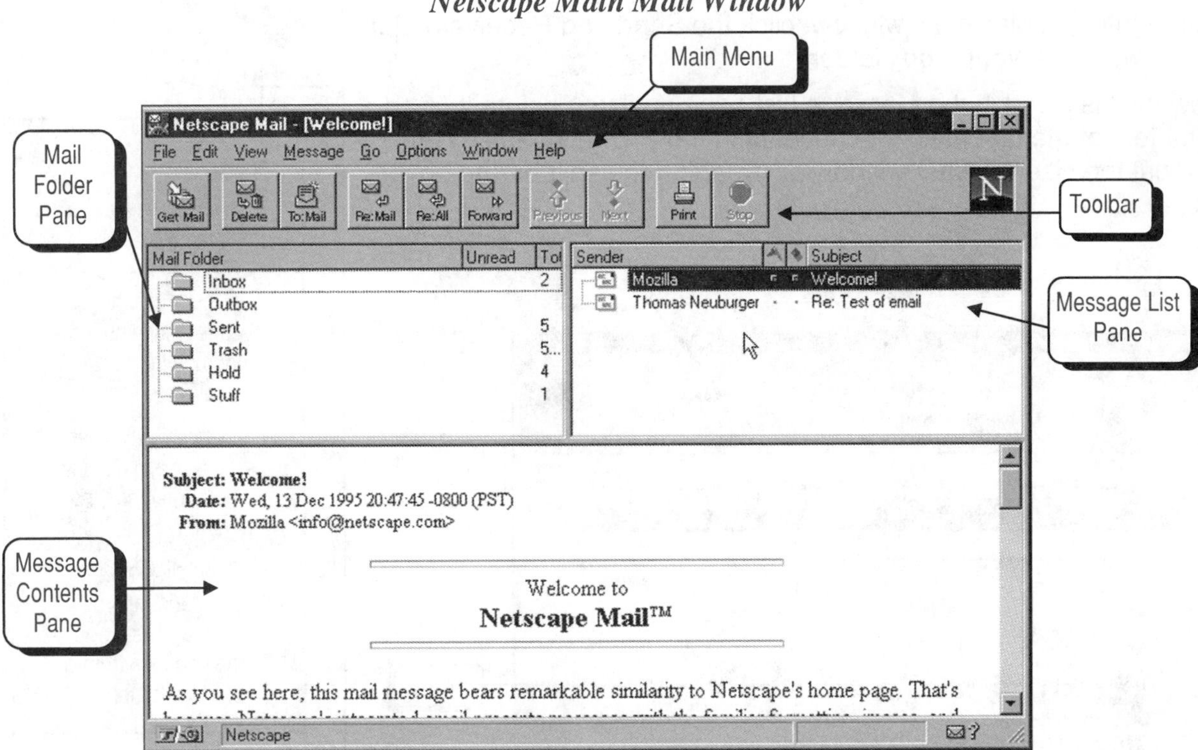

- All mail functions can be started from this window.

Internet Explorer's E-mail Window

- There are several ways to access Internet Mail features.
  - Click on the Internet Mail icon on the Toolbar and select desired option.

OR

Click Read Mail on the Go menu.

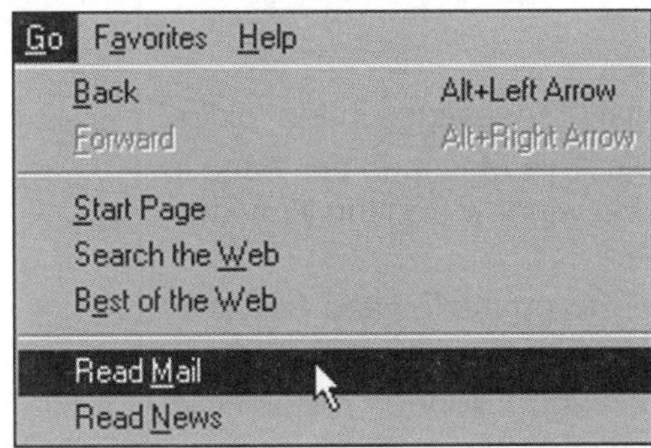

- If you go to the Read Mail window, choose the Inbox Folder from the Folders pull-down list.
- From the Internet Mail main window, click the Send and Receive button to add new mail to your Inbox folder.

  All new mail is listed in the Message List pane until you delete it (read it). The text of the first message appears in the Preview pane. You can adjust the size of either window by dragging the split bar up or down.

TIPS

- If you are sure you have new messages and they are not listed in the Message List pane, make sure the Inbox folder is displayed.
- Highlight any listed message to display the contents in the Preview pane.
- Right-click on a message in the Message list to access mail options from a pull-down menu.

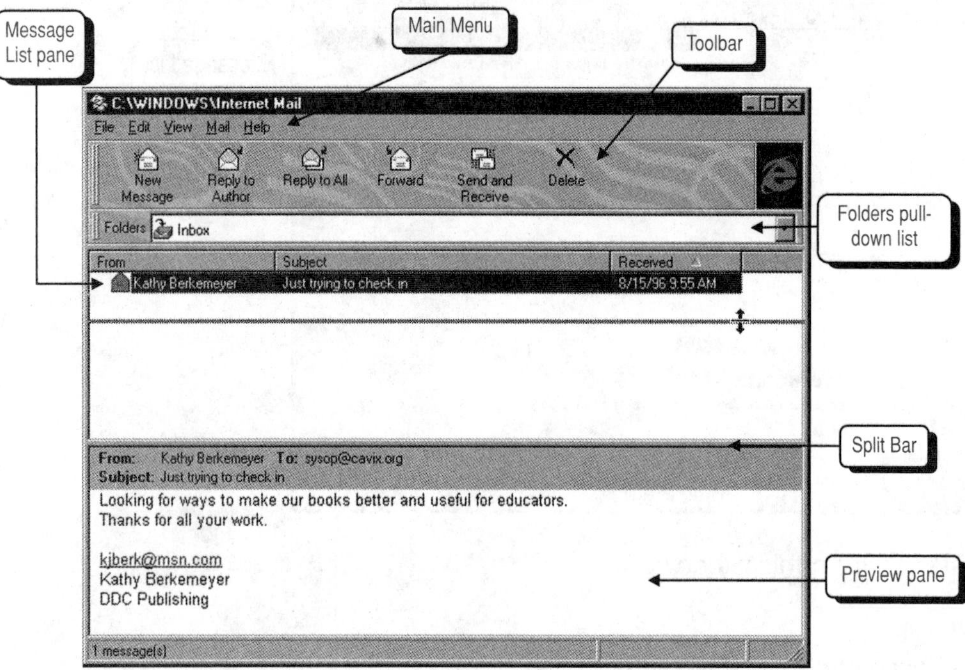

- You can also customize the way this window appears by clicking Preview Pane on the View menu and selecting the desired options:

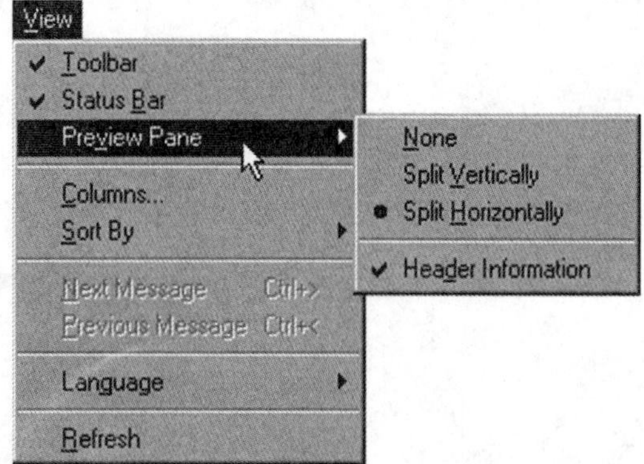

None	Displays only the list of messages in the folder.
Split Horizontally	(Default setting) Displays Message List pane in the top portion of the window and the Preview pane in the bottom.
Split Vertically	Displays Message List on the left and Preview pane on the right.
Header Information	Displays information about sender, recipient, and subject of the message.

- All mail functions can be started from this window.

Receive, Read, and Print Mail

Netscape Navigator

- Using the Netscape browser, you can receive your incoming e-mail by clicking the mail icon in the bottom right corner of the screen and then doing any of the following:
  - Click the Get Mail button on the Netscape Mail toolbar,

    OR
  - Click File, Get New Mail from the Netscape Mail menu,

    OR
  - Use the keyboard shortcut Ctrl+T.
- To read e-mail messages, select a folder in the Mail Folders pane. Then select a message in the Message List pane. The text of the message appears in the Preview pane.
- To print a message, highlight the message in the Mail window and click the Print button on the Toolbar. You can also select File, Print from the main menu.

Internet Mail

- Using Internet Explorer, you can receive incoming e-mail in the following ways:
  - Click the Mail icon on the toolbar and select Read Mail.

    OR
  - Click Read Mail on the Go menu.
- To print a message:
  - Select the message you want to print in the message list.
  - Select Print from the File menu and click OK to send message to printer.

Compose New Messages

- To compose a new message in Netscape Mail click the To Mail  button.
- To compose mail in Internet Explorer, click the Mail button and then click New Message.
- In both cases, a message composition window appears.

Netscape Message Composition Window

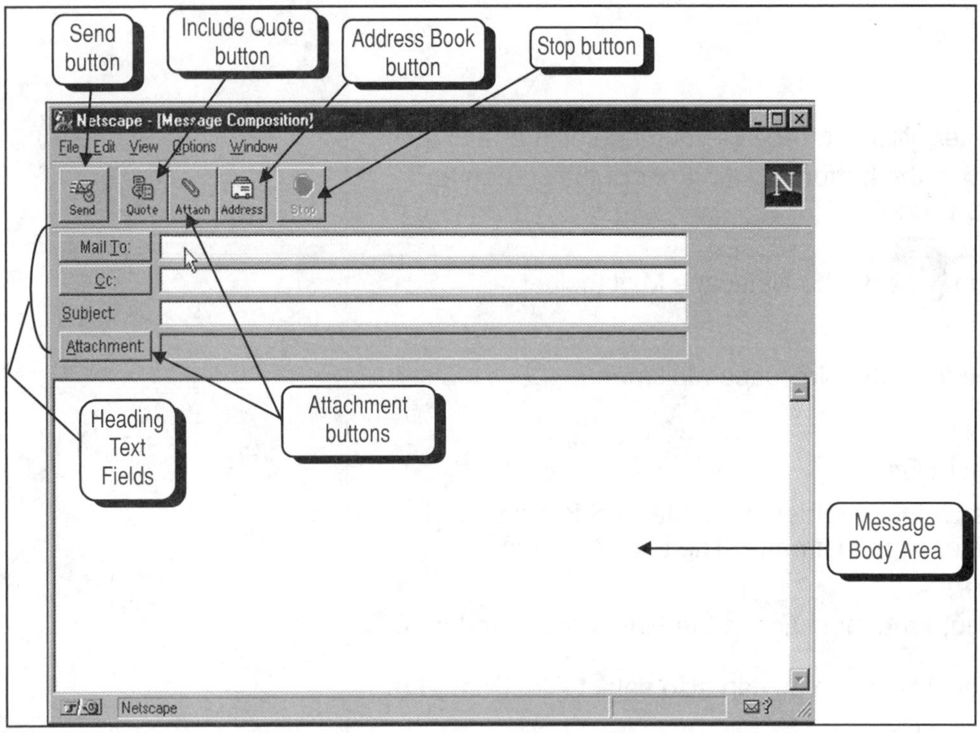

Internet Mail Message Composition Window

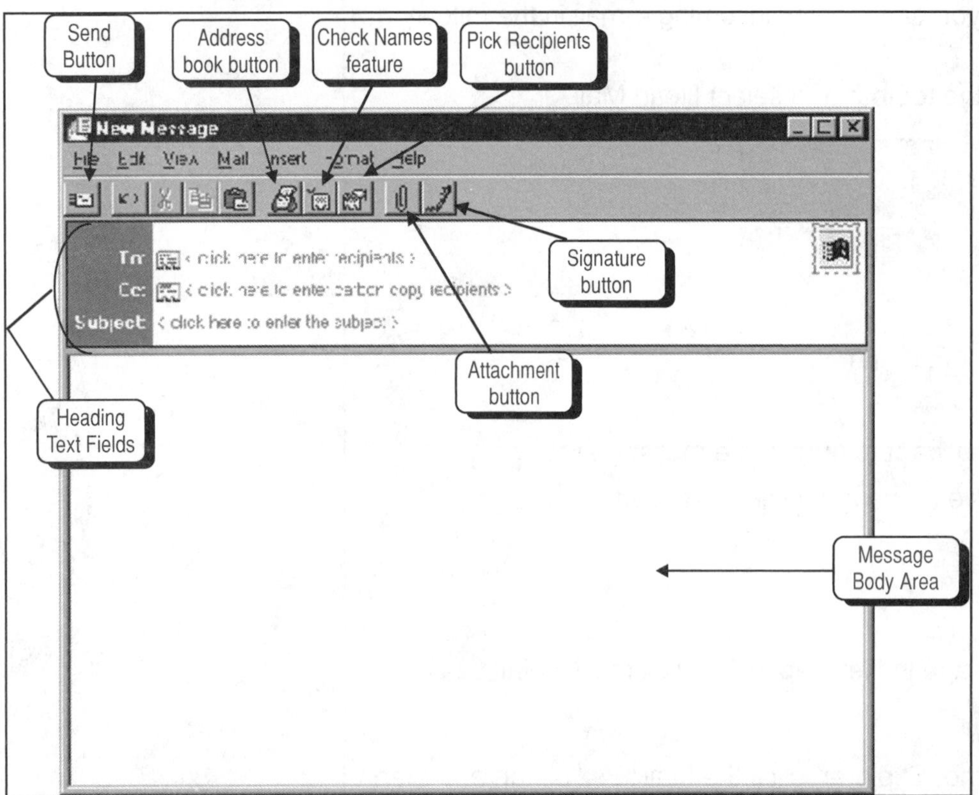

- See Exercise 4 for information on sending replies and forwarding e-mail.

Fill in the Headings

- The **message header** comes before the body of the message and is used by your e-mail program to route your message. It consists of a number of **headings** or **heading fields**. Headings and heading options differ slightly depending on the e-mail program.
- Most e-mail programs offer these message headings:

From	The person sending the mail (you). This field is usually filled in for you, based on information in your Mail preferences.
Mail To	The e-mail address of the person to whom the message is sent.
Reply To	The e-mail address to which replies will be sent.
CC (Carbon Copy)	The e-mail addresses of people who will receive copies.
BCC (Blind CC)	Same as CC, except these names will not appear anywhere in the message.
Subject	A short text description of the contents of the message.
Newsgroups	Names of newsgroups that will receive this message (similar to Mail To).
Followup To	Another newsgroup heading; used to identify newsgroups to which comments should be posted (similar to Reply To).
Attachment	The names of files (text or binary) or URL locations to be sent with the message.

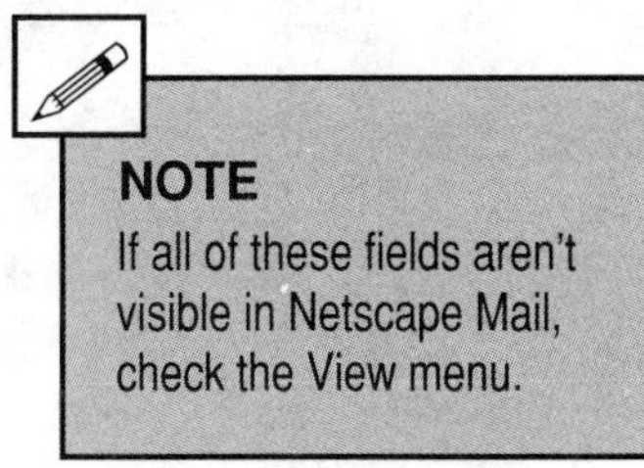

NOTE
If all of these fields aren't visible in Netscape Mail, check the View menu.

Netscape Mail Header

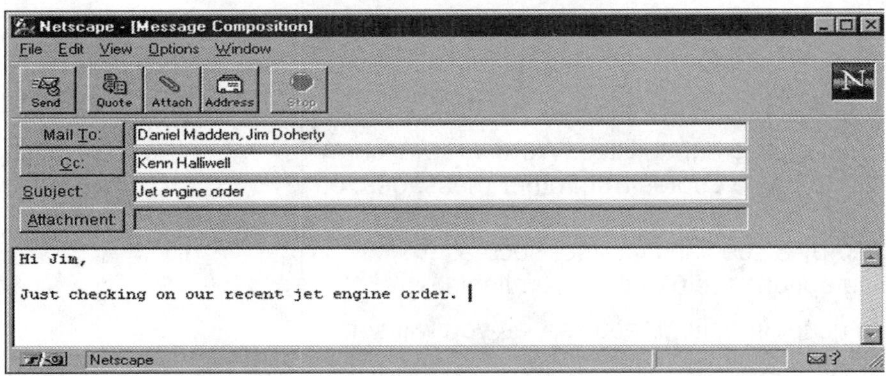

- You can type into the text fields, or click the appropriate buttons to bring up the address book (in the case of addresses) or a file finder (in the case of attachments).

Internet Mail Header

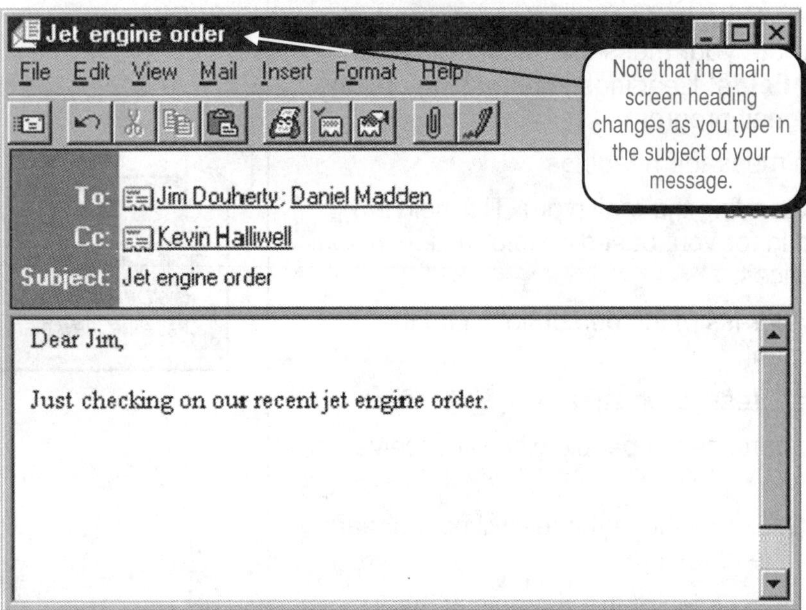

- Internet Mail automatically underlines an address to confirm that it is in correct e-mail format. This does not mean, however, that the address is correct, only that it is in the correct format.
- If the address is not in the correct format, Internet Mail searches your address book for possible matches. If no matches are found, you have the option to Show More Names from the book to locate the correct address.
- Once you are sure an e-mail address is correct, you can right-click the name to display the Add To Address Book dialog box and add the recipient to your address book.

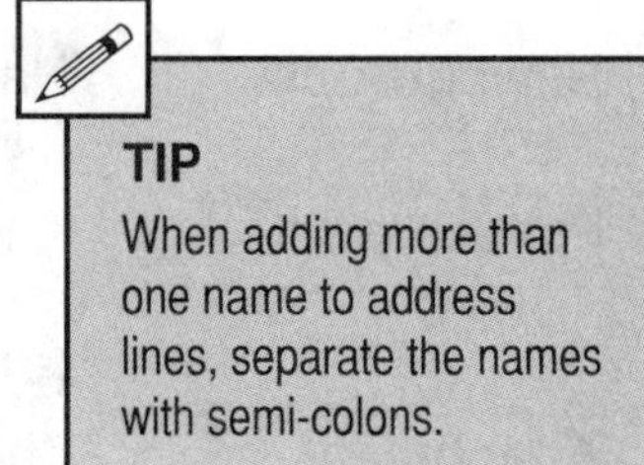

TIP

When adding more than one name to address lines, separate the names with semi-colons.

Compose the Message Body

- Compose the message by typing into the Message Body window.
- Most Web browsers have minimal editing capabilities. Word-wrap occurs automatically, and you can cut and paste quotes from other messages, or text from other programs. Text can be pasted as plain text or in quote format (with each line introduced by a special character such as ">"). Spell-checking and other editing options are usually unavailable.
- Dedicated e-mail programs are richer in editing features, as you will see in Exercise 6, later in this lesson.

Add a Signature

- Many people like to add an e-mail **signature**, a few lines of text with their e-mail address and/or a quotation, to the end of their messages.
- Browsers and e-mail programs can be set to add a pre-designed signature automatically.
- To specify a signature, Click Options, Mail and News Preferences and click the Identity tab.

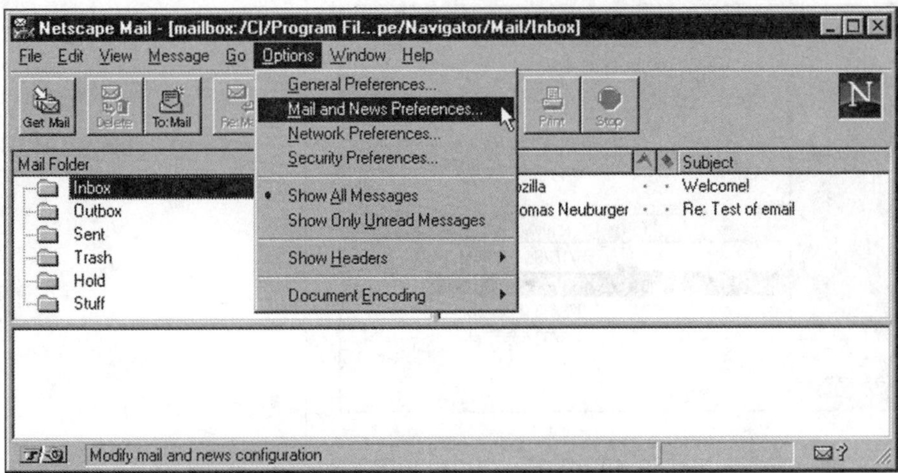

- One of the preferences allows you to select a text file for use as a signature.

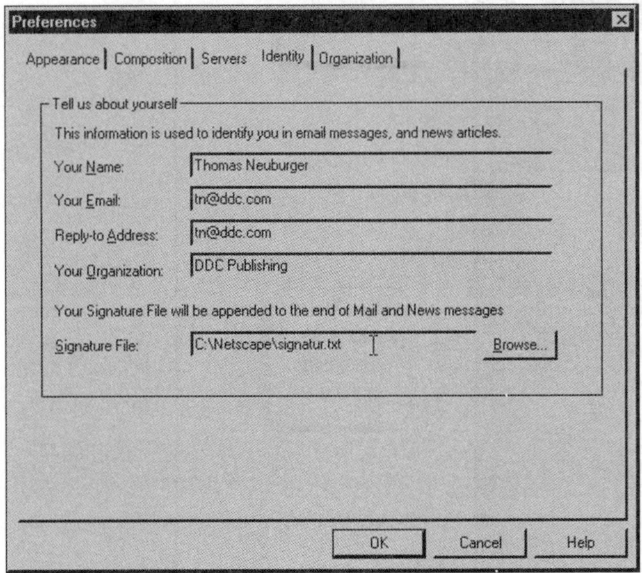

- This file can be created with any text editor.

  ✓ *Signature files must be ASCII text-only and should be short, preferably fewer than five or six lines.*

- To specify a signature in Internet Mail, go to the main Internet Mail window, click Mail, Options, Signature tab.

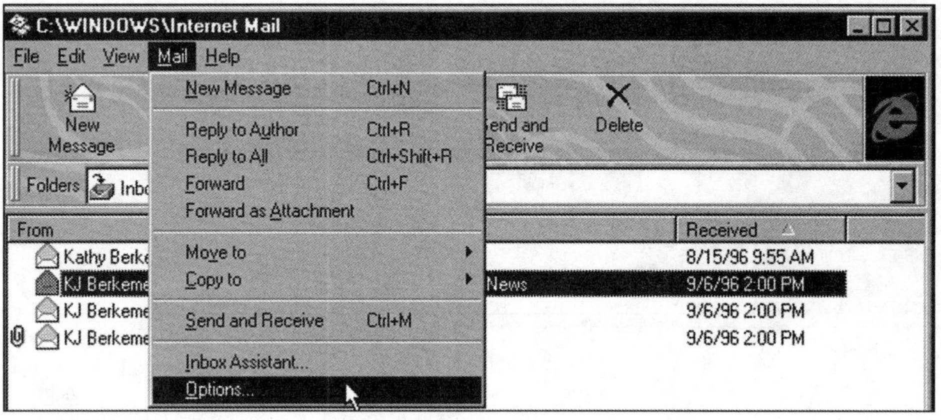

- Click the Signature tab. You can create text to insert as your signature, or you can select a file to insert as a signature.

Internet Mail Options screen

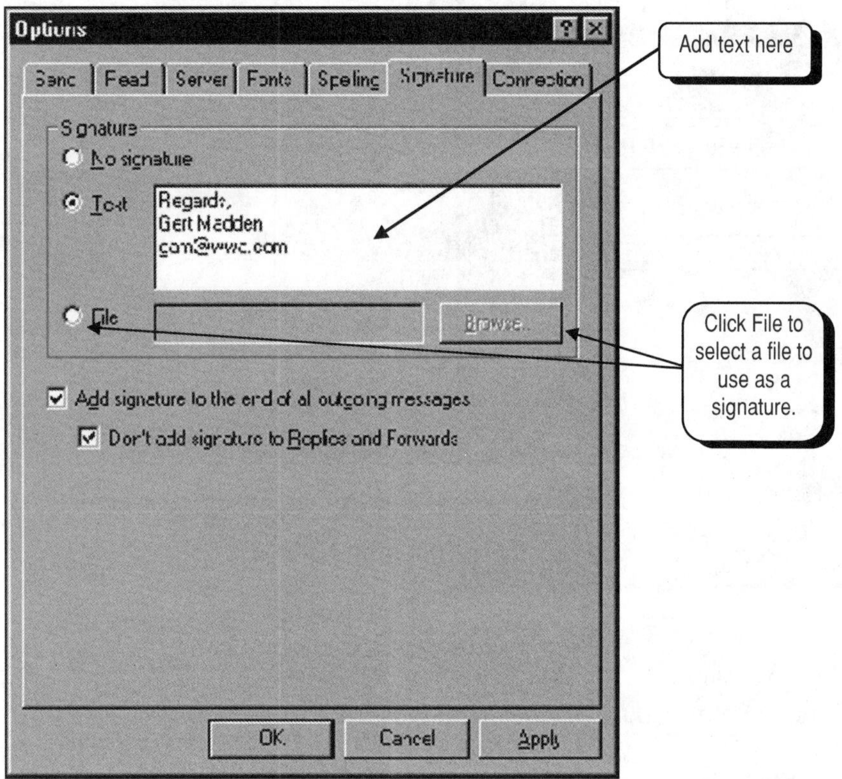

- Select desired signature options:

No signature	Does not add anything to message (default).
Text	Type your signature text in this text box.
File	Select a file you want to add as a signature message.

Send Messages

Netscape Navigator

- Messages can be sent immediately or stored in your Outbox for later delivery.

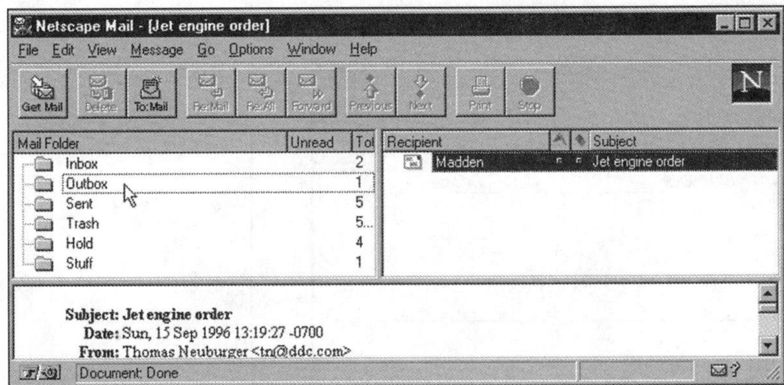

- To send the message immediately:
  - Click Options, Immediate Delivery in the Message Composition window.

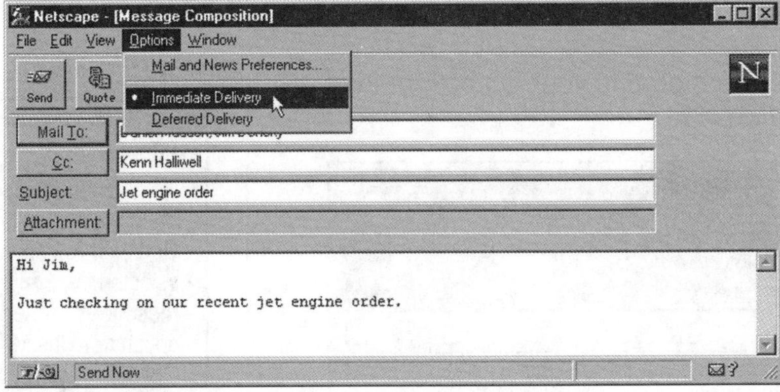

  - Click Send Send or Click File, Send Now.
- To store the message in your Outbox for later delivery:
  - Select Options, Deferred Delivery in the Message Composition window.

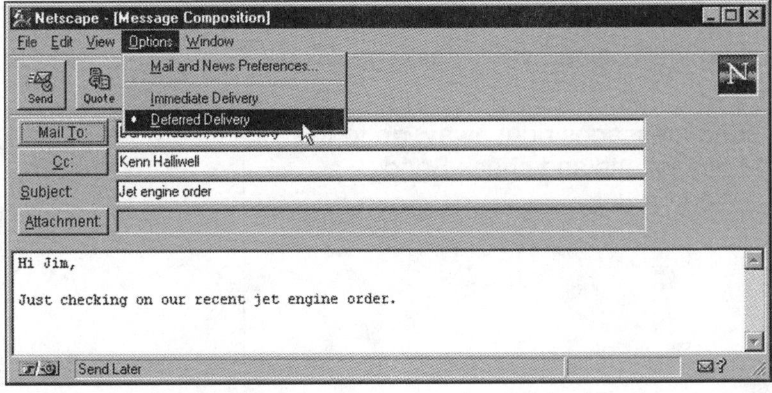

- Click Send [Send] or select File, Send Later.

- To send all messages in your Outbox:
  - Select File, Send Messages in Outbox in the Main Mail window.

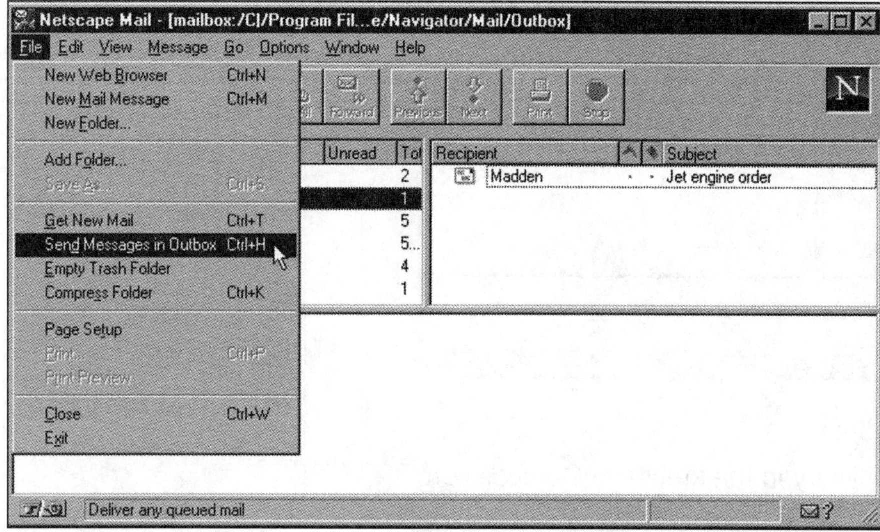

Internet Explorer

- Messages can be sent immediately, or stored in your Outbox for later delivery.

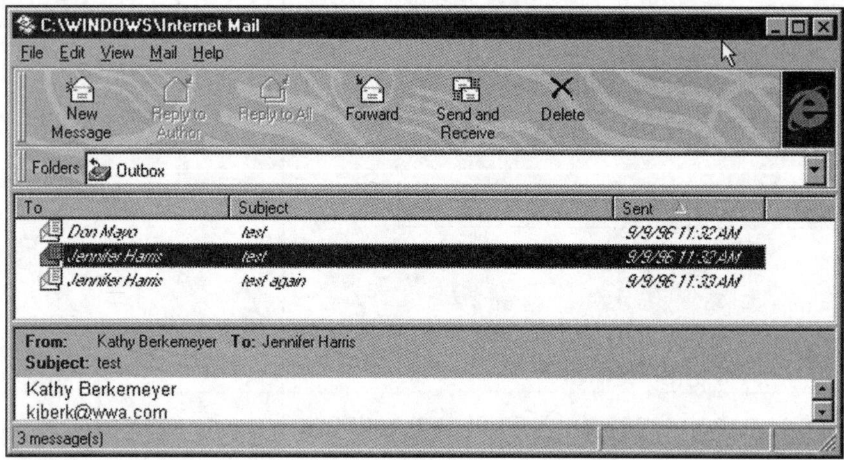

- When you click the Send button on the Toolbar, your message will be sent to your Outbox for later delivery.
- To change this default option and send messages right away, go to the main Internet Mail window, select Mail, Options and check Send messages immediately.

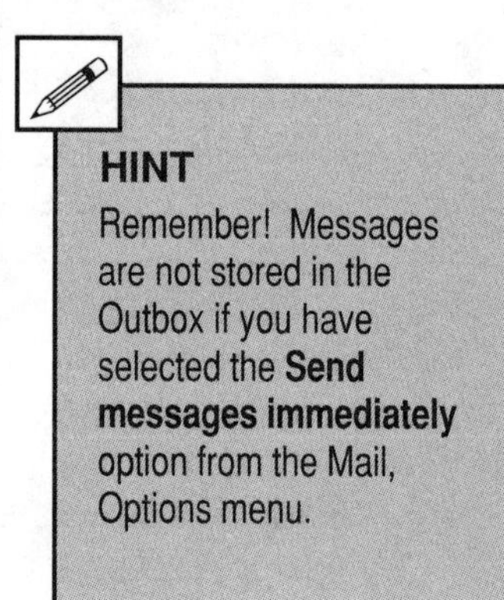

HINT

Remember! Messages are not stored in the Outbox if you have selected the **Send messages immediately** option from the Mail, Options menu.

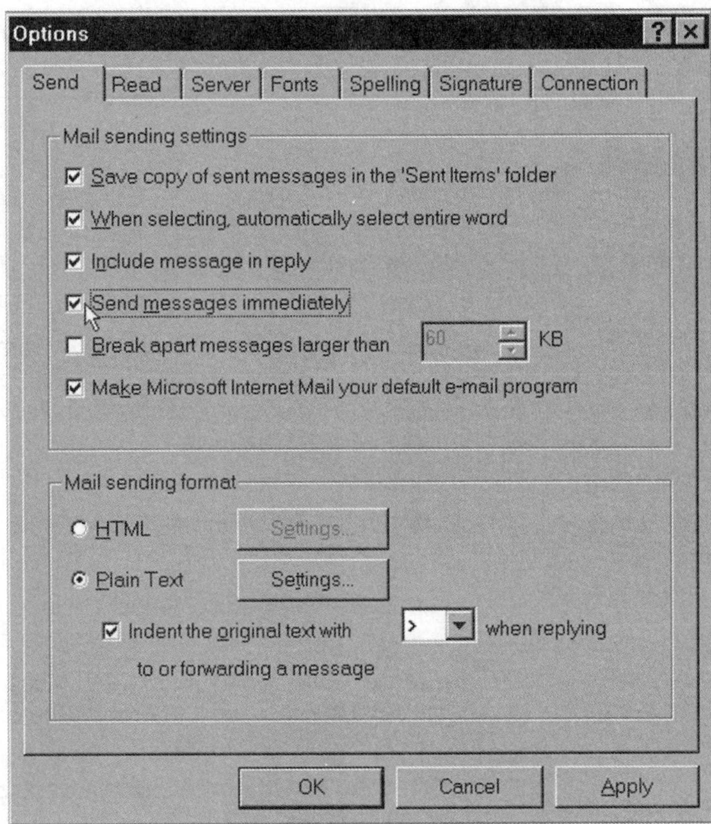

- Click Apply, and then OK to activate settings.
- To send all messages in your Outbox, click Send and Receive in the main Internet Mail Window. You can do this even if you are not in the Outbox. The following message appears:

  ✓ *Clicking the Send and Receive button sends all messages in the Outbox and receives all new messages into the Inbox.*

In this exercise, you will compose, send, read, and print an e-mail message using your browser.

EXERCISE DIRECTIONS

1. If you are already connected to your service provider and your browser is open, go to step 2.

   OR

   Connect to your service provider and open your browser.

   ✓ *Only the Netscape Navigator browser is used in the stimulation.*

2. **Netscape Navigator:** Select Window, Netscape Mail from the main menu.

   Internet Mail: Select the Mail button from the Internet Explorer Toolbar.

3. **Netscape Navigator**: In the Mail window, click the To:Mail button.

   Internet Mail: Click the New Message button.

4. **Netscape Navigator:** In the message compose window, fill in these headers as follows:

Mail To:	***tabellarius@ddcpub.com***
CC:	Add the e-mail address of a friend here, if you like, or your own address. Otherwise, leave this field blank.
Subject:	"Test of e-mail"
Body:	"This is an e-mail test."

   Internet Mail: In the new message window fill in these headers as follows:

Mail To:	***tabellarius@ddcpub.com***
CC:	Add the e-mail address of a friend here, if you like, or your own address. Otherwise, leave this field blank.
Subject:	"Test of e-mail"
Body:	"This is an e-mail test."

5. **Netscape Navigator:** Select Options, Immediate Delivery. (This option may already be selected.)

   Internet Mail: Select File, Send Message. This will send the message as well as the contents of the Outbox immediately.

6. **Netscape Navigator:** Click the Send button.

   Internet Mail: Go to the Internet Mail main window and select the Sent Items folder from the Folders pull-down list.

7. **Netscape Navigator:** Select the Sent folder.

   Internet Mail: In the Message List pane, select the message you just sent. Read the text of the message in the Preview pane.

8. **Netscape Navigator:** Click on the message to view the message. Print the message by clicking the Print button.

   Internet Mail: Print the message (if a printer is connected to your computer) by clicking the Print button.

9. Continue on to the next exercise.

   OR

   Exit from your browser and disconnect from your service provider.

Continue to the next exercise.

Exercise 4

◆ **Files Attached to E-mail** ◆ **Reply to Mail** ◆ **Forward Mail**

NOTES

Files Attached to E-mail

- Many e-mail messages contain added attachments, usually files. (Some attachments can be URLs—Web pages in HTML form.)
- You can attach either ASCII files or binary files, or both.
  - ✓ *See Exercise 1 in this lesson, or Lesson 4 on FTP, for more information on ASCII and binary files.*
- If binary files (such as data files from programs like Microsoft Word) are attached, the e-mail program will automatically encode them into one of the two major ASCII encoding schemes—MIME (Base64) encoding or UUencoding. Encoded files are often automatically decoded by the receiving e-mail program, though sometimes they are not.
  - ✓ *Sometimes encoding and decoding doesn't work as it should. The most common problem is an encoding scheme that isn't understood by the receiving program. Keep in mind that browsers typically use MIME encoding for binary attachments.*

Add Attachments to Your Netscape Mail

- To add an attachment to an e-mail message:
  - Click either the Attach button on the Toolbar or the Attachment button in the message header of the Message Composition window.

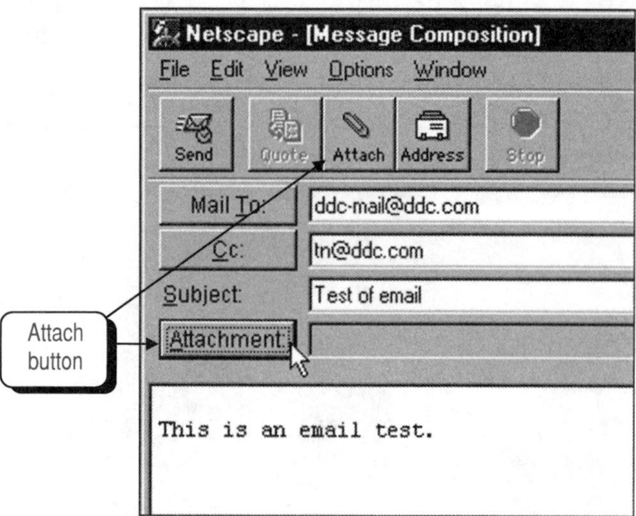

  - In the Attachments window, click either Attach URL Location or Attach File. A dialog box will allow you to choose which URL or file to attach.

DEFINITIONS

ASCII – American Standard Code for Information Interchange

ASCII file – File containing ASCII-formatted text only; can be read by almost any computer or program in the world. Only ASCII files can be sent through the email system.

binary file – File containing machine language, i.e., ones and zeros. Binary files must be encoded (converted to ASCII format) before they can be sent through the email system.

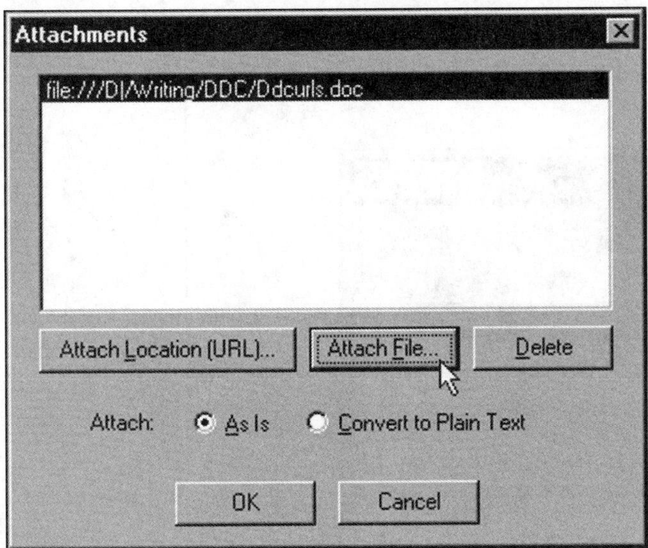

- Choose to attach the file or URL either As Is or as Plain Text.
  - *Select As Is* to send binary files in ASCII-encoded form and URLs as full HTML source code.

    Encoded binary files will be decoded back into binary form by the receiving e-mail program, if the encoding format is understood and if the e-mail program automatically decodes attachments.

    HTML source code (ASCII text that contains HTML code) can be interpreted by a Web browser and displayed as a Web page.
  - *Select Plain Text* to extract the viewable text from the HTML coding in attached URLs. This turns a Web page into a plain text document for easy reading.
- Click OK to confirm the attachment.

Attachments will be sent in the form specified.

IMPORTANT

If you are sending an attached binary file to someone for the first time, confirm with them that they are able to decode it. If they cannot, some other method of transmitting the file will be needed.

Add Attachments to Your Internet Mail

- To add an attachment to an e-mail message:
  - Click the Attach button on the toolbar of the Message Composition window. Select the file, click Attach.

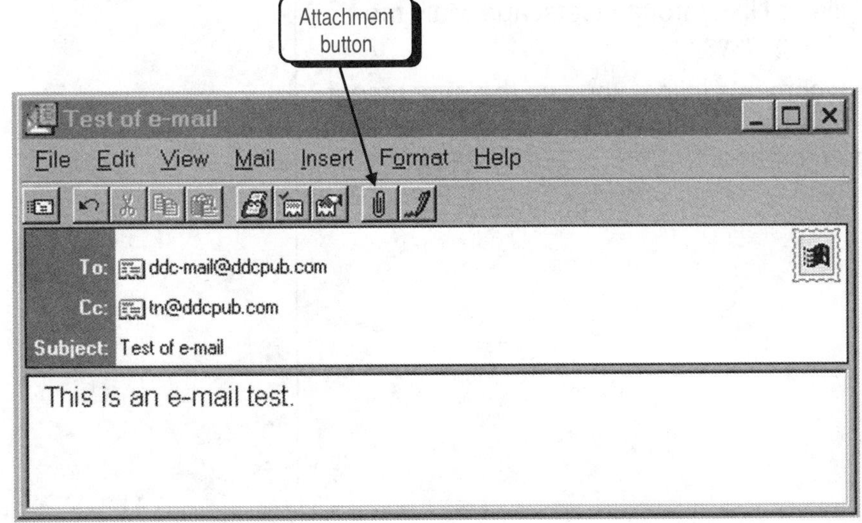

OR

Click, File Attachment on the Insert menu, select the file you wish to attach and click the Attach button.

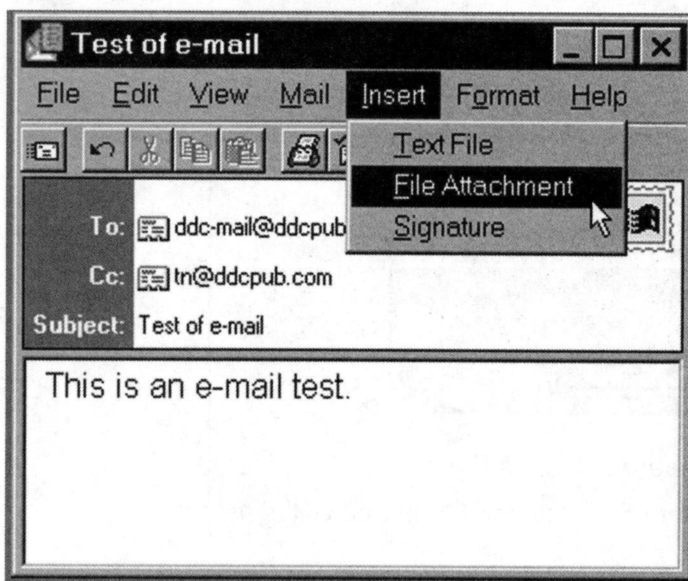

- In Internet Mail all files and file attachments are automatically sent in plain text format or MIME format unless otherwise specified.
- To attach HTML formatted files such as Web pages:
  - Click the Attach button, select the file, click Attach, click Format, select HTML. This option formats the current outgoing message in HTML code.
  - The HTML option is not a default setting. Only the currently-selected outgoing message will be formatted in HTML code. All subsequent attachments will be saved and sent in plain text format unless you reactivate the HTML code feature.
  - If the recipient's e-mail program cannot interpret HTML code, the file will be shown as an attached text file. The recipient can open the file attachment in any Web browser.

View and Save Attachments You Receive in Netscape Navigator

- When you receive an attached file or URL through Netscape Mail, the information is displayed in one of two ways.
  - If you have selected View, Attachments Inline, you see the attachment appended to the body of the message. If the attachment is HTML code, you will see a fully formatted Web page.

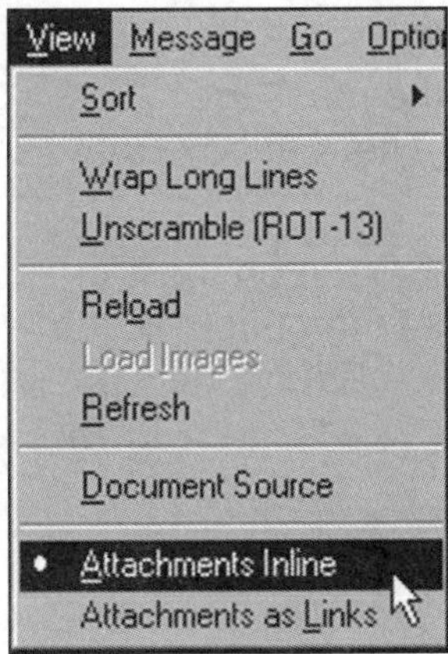

- If you have selected View, Attachments as Links, you will see a link in the body of the message to the attachment. Clicking on this link allows you to specify a Save As location for the attachment.

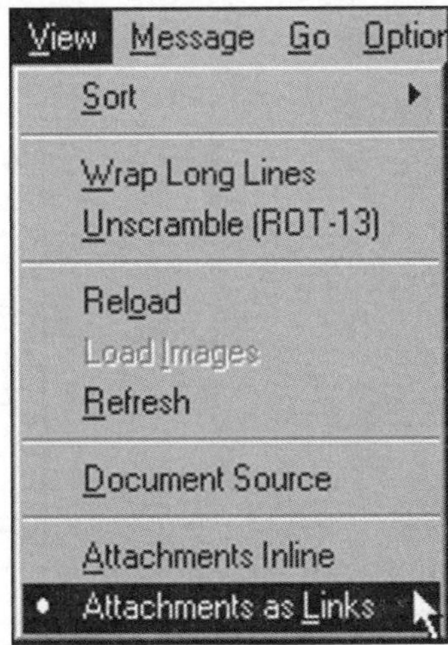

- Most browsers can decode both MIME encoded (Base64) and UUencoded messages.

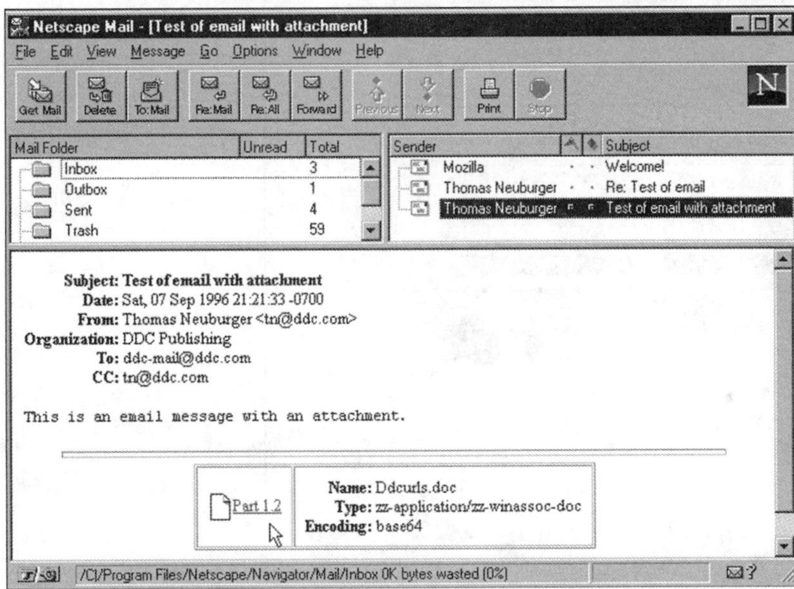

View and Save Attachments You Receive with Internet Mail

- When you receive a message with a file attachment, the message appears in your Inbox folder with an attachment icon. There are two ways to view the attachment:
  - Select the message from the message list, and click Open on the File menu (or double-click on the message) to open it. At the bottom of the window you will see the attachment file icon. Double-click on the icon to open the attachment file.

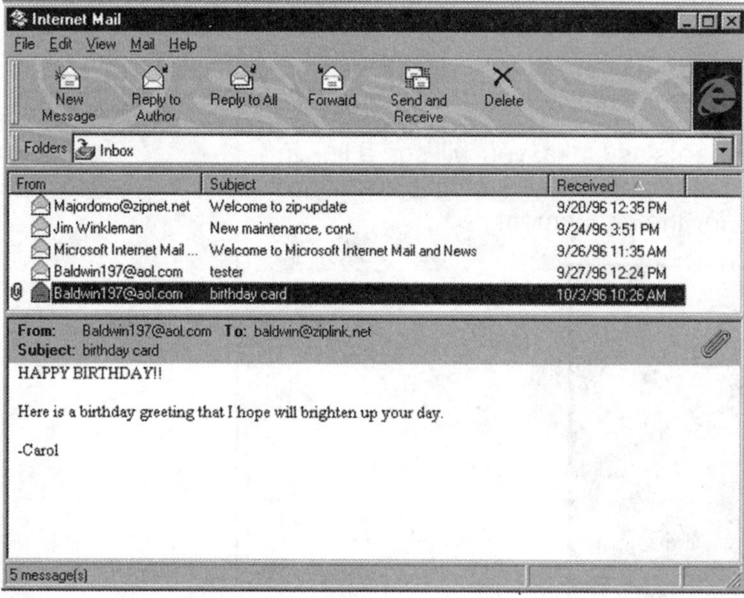

OR

From the message list, highlight the message with the attachment. In the Preview pane, you will notice the Attachment icon in the upper right-hand corner. Click on the icon to see the file name, and then click on the file name to open the attached file.

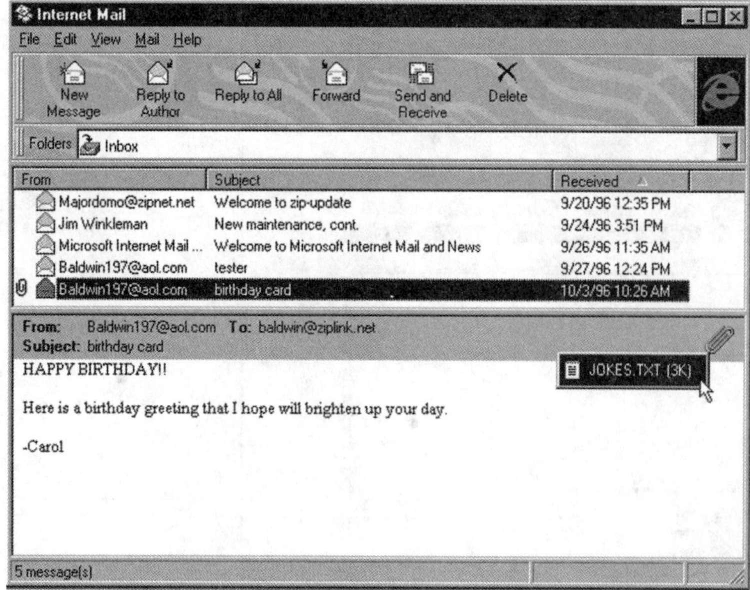

- You can save an attachment by opening the message, clicking File and selecting Save As Attachment.

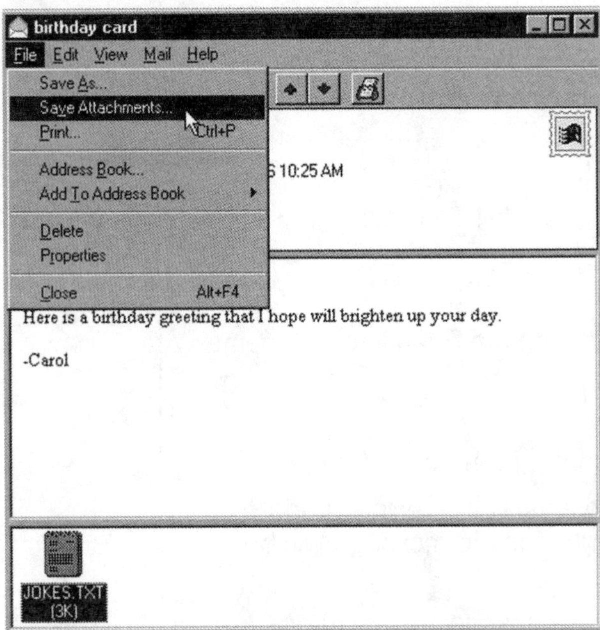

Reply to Messages in Netscape Navigator

- To reply to a message sent to you:
  - Select a message in the message list.
  - Click either of these buttons:

(to reply to everyone on the From line)

Re:All (to reply to everyone on the From and CC lines)

A message composition window appears, with the original message in quote format (that is, with each line preceded by a special character like “>.”)

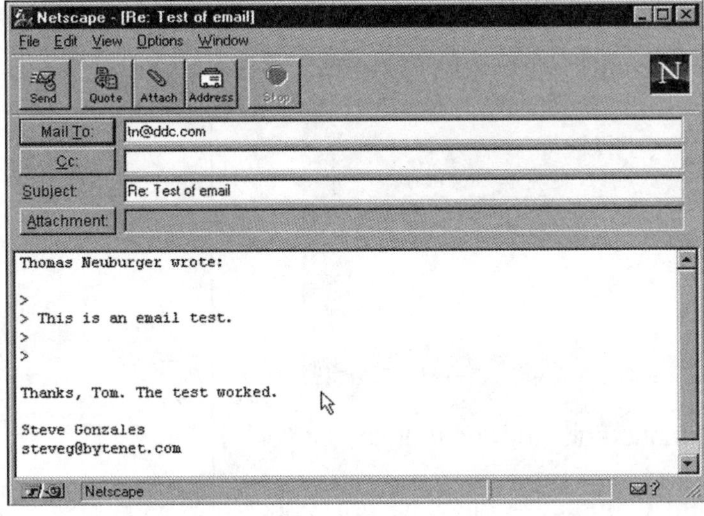

- Compose your reply just as you would a new message. You can edit header lines and type whatever body text you wish.
- When you are done, click Send.

Reply to Messages in Internet Mail

To Reply to a message sent to you:

- Select the message in the message list.
- Click either of these buttons on the Internet Mail Toolbar:

Reply to Author (to everyone on the From line)

Reply to All (to everyone on the From and CC lines)

The Message Composition window contains all the recipient address information as well as a subject heading. The old message will be included with your response.

- Type your message as you would a new message. You can edit header lines and add addresses. Remember: Each addressee must be separated with a semi-colon.
- When you are done, click the Send button.

Forward Mail in Netscape Navigator

■ To forward a message you have received to another address:

- Select a message in the message list.
- Click the Forward button.

A message composition window appears, with the original message included as an attachment.

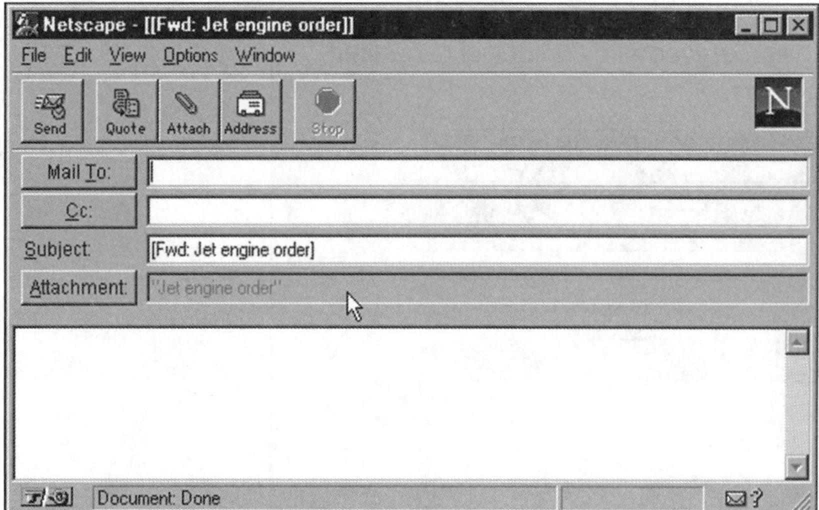

- Add an e-mail address to the To line and edit other header lines if you wish.
- Add text to the message body, or leave the body empty, as you wish.
- When you are done, click Send.

Forward Mail in Internet Mail

- Select the message from the message list and click the Forward button.
- Fill in the e-mail address information by either typing each name or selecting the recipients from your address book.
- Type your message as you normally would and click the Send button.

OR

- If the message file is open, click the forward icon and follow the directions above.

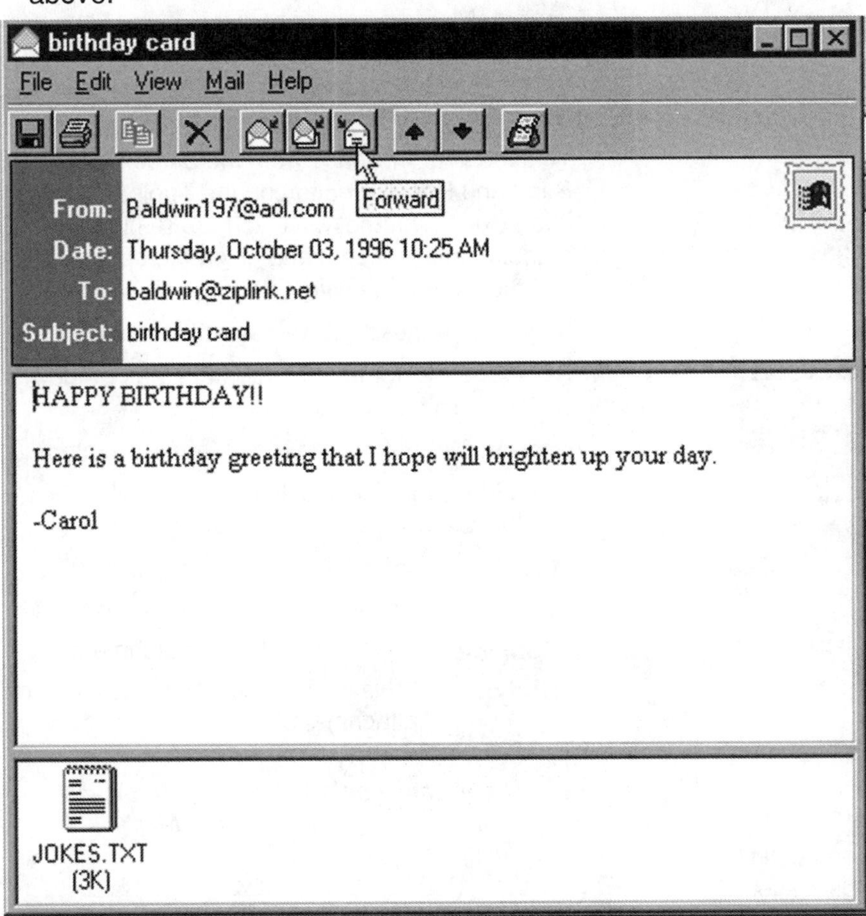

> **HINT**
> You can access all of the mail send commands by right-clicking on the message in the Message list.

Work Offline

- If your Internet service provider charges for time spent online, or if you are using one phone line for voice and data, you may wish to do all message composition offline. To make the most efficient use of your online time, do this:
  - Go online to get your mail.
  - Go offline to read mail and compose messages and replies. Make sure Deferred Delivery is selected. Click Send to place each outgoing message in your Outbox.
  - Go online to send all Outbox messages.

> ***In this exercise, you will reply to messages, send a message with an attached file, and receive an attachment in an e-mail message.***

EXERCISE DIRECTIONS

1. If you are already connected to your service provider and your browser is open, go to step 2.

   OR

   Connect to your service provider and open your browser.

   ✓ *Only the Netscape Navigator browser is used in the stimulation.*
2. Bring up the browser's main Mail window by selecting Netscape Mail from Window Menu.
3. Check for incoming mail.
4. If your Internet service provider charges for time spent online, go offline now by disconnecting from the provider. You can read and write responses to e-mail messages offline.

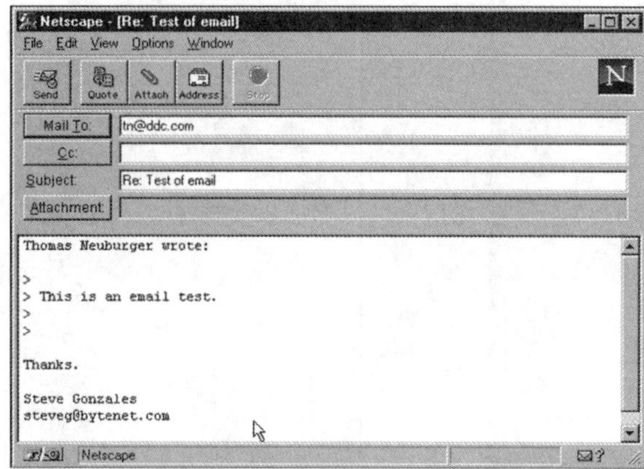

5. Now let's reply to the message you received.

   Netscape Navigator: In the Message Folder pane, select Inbox; in the Message List pane, select the message you received from the DDC e-mail program; then click the "Re:Mail" button.

   Internet Mail: In the Message List pane, select the message you received from the DDC e-mail program and click the Reply to Author button.
6. **Netscape Navigator:** In the Message Composition window, type "Thanks" on a new line below the quoted message. Then press Return and type your name and e-mail address.

   Internet Mail: Type "Thanks" at the prompt (just above the old message) in the Message Composition window. Notice that all the return address information is inserted for you. Click the Send button.
7. **Netscape Navigator:** Select Options, Deferred Delivery and click the Send button. The message is now in your Outbox.

   Internet Mail: If you have selected Send messages immediately on the Mail Options menu, your reply will be sent right away. If you have not selected this option, Internet Mail stores your message in the outbox folder until you are ready to send it.

   To send your message from the outbox, click the Send and Receive button on the Toolbar. Also, upon exiting Internet Mail, you are reminded of outgoing mail not sent and given the opportunity to send it before leaving the program.
8. Now send a message with an attachment.

   Netscape Navigator: In the main Mail window, click the "To:Mail" button.

   Internet Mail: Click the New Message button.
9. In the Message Composition window, fill in these headers as follows:

Mail To:	***tabellarius@ddcpub.com***
CC:	Add your own e-mail address.
Subject:	Test of e-mail with attachment
Body:	"This is an e-mail message with an attachment."

   ✓ *The example below shows the Netscape Navigator dialog box. Internet Mail's is similar.*

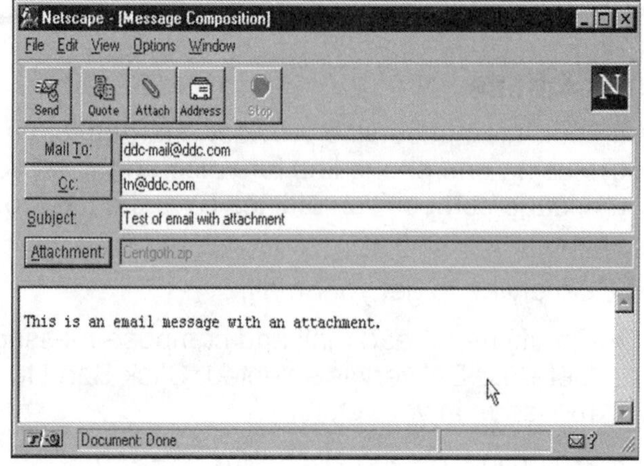

10. **Netscape Navigator:** Click the Attachment button and in the Attachments dialog box, click Attach file. Then select a short data file or zip file to add as an attachment. Click Open and then OK. Click Send. The file is now in your outbox.

    Internet Mail: Click the Attachment button (paper clip) on the Toolbar or choose Insert from the menu and select a file by type. From the Insert Attachment dialog box, choose a short file from a program you use regularly to add as an attachment to your message. Single-click on the file and click Attach or simply double-click the file to attach it to your message.

    ✓ *Web transmission is not secure. Choose a file without proprietary or important personal information.*

    Click Send. The file is now in your Outbox.

    ✓ *If you are using the Internet Simulation, skip step 11 and proceed to 12.*

11. Go online by reconnecting to your Internet service provider.

12. **Netscape Navigator:** In the main Mail window, select File, Send Messages in Outbox. Then select File, Get New Mail.

    Internet Mail: Click the Send and Receive button on the Toolbar to send the mail in your outbox and to any receive mail that might be coming to you. If you are not connected to your Internet service provider, you are prompted to connect when you click the button.

    ✓ *If you are using the Internet Stimulation, skip 13 and 14 and proceed to step 15.*

13. Disconnect from your Internet service provider.

14. In a short time, a copy of the message you sent will be delivered to you, with attachment. (Recall that your address was on the CC line.) To download this file, reconnect to your service provider.

15. **Netscape Navigator:** Click Get Mail.

    Internet Mail: Click the Send and Receive button on the Toolbar.

    The file with the attachment will appear in your Inbox.

16. **Netscape Navigator:** Select Inbox in the Message Folder pane, and then select the file with the attachment in the Message List pane. Note how the Message Contents pane displays the link to the attached file.

    Internet Mail: Click on the message in the Message List pane. Notice that in the upper right-hand corner of the Preview pane there is a paper clip. Single-click the paper clip to see a brief description of the attached file.

17. **Netscape Navigator:** Click on the link to the attached file, and click Save to save it to a new location. (At the moment, it is in a temporary holding area).

    Internet Mail: Double-click the file with the attachment. Highlight the attachment icon at the bottom of the screen to save it to a new location. (At the moment it is in a temporary holding area.)

    ✓ *If you are using the Internet Simulation, skip step 18 and proceed to 19.*

18. Click the Get Mail button (Netscape) or Send and Receive button (Internet Mail) and do any other mailing you like, including mailing to yourself.

19. Continue on to the next exercise.

    OR

    Exit from your browser and disconnect from your service provider.

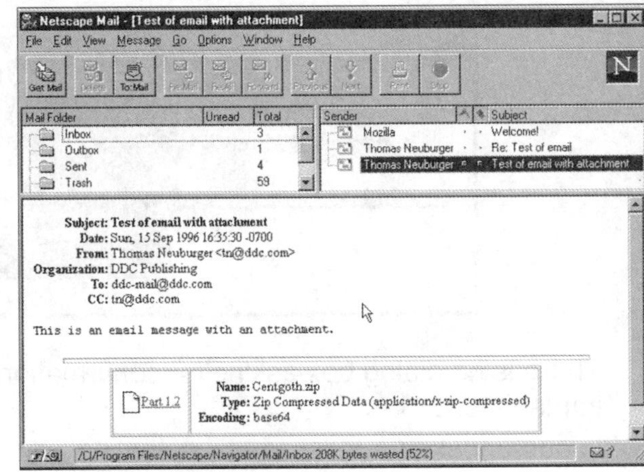

Exercise 5

◆ **Organize Mail Messages** ◆ **Use Address Books**

NOTES

Organize Mail Messages

Delete Mail Messages in Netscape Navigator

- You can delete an e-mail message using Netscape in any one of four ways. First, highlight the message in the Message List, then:
  - Press the Del key.

    OR

    Click the Delete button.

    OR

    Click Edit, Delete Message.

    OR

    Click the *right* mouse button on the message and select Delete Message.

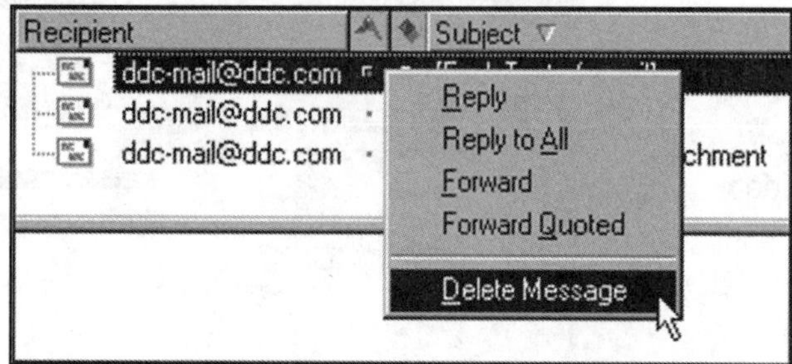

There is no dialog box asking for confirmation. The message is deleted immediately.

- You can undelete a message by selecting Edit, Undo or pressing Ctrl-Z.

Delete Mail Messages in Internet Mail

- You can delete an e-mail message using Internet Mail in any one of the following ways. First, highlight the message in the Message List, then:
  - Press the Del key.

    OR

    Click the Delete button .

    OR

    Click File, Delete.

WARNING

Be careful when deleting messages. A deleted message can be undeleted only if the deletion was the last action performed.

OR

Click the *right* mouse button on the message and select Delete.

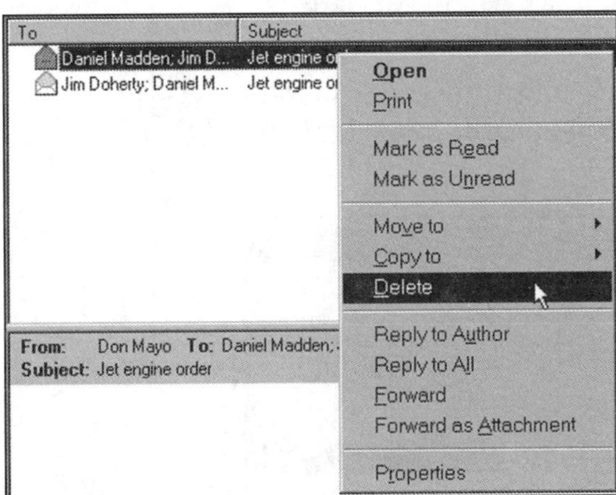

- There is no dialog box asking for confirmation of intent to delete. The message is deleted and sent to the Deleted Items folder.
  - You can undelete a message by choosing the Deleted Items folder from the Folders pull-down list. Highlight the deleted message, select Mail, either Move To or Copy To, and click the Inbox.

File Messages into Mail Folders in Netscape Navigator

- E-mail messages are filed into **message folders**. For Netscape, a message folder is really a file, not a folder or subdirectory, that contains e-mail messages. (For some other programs, like Eudora Light, message folders are directories.)

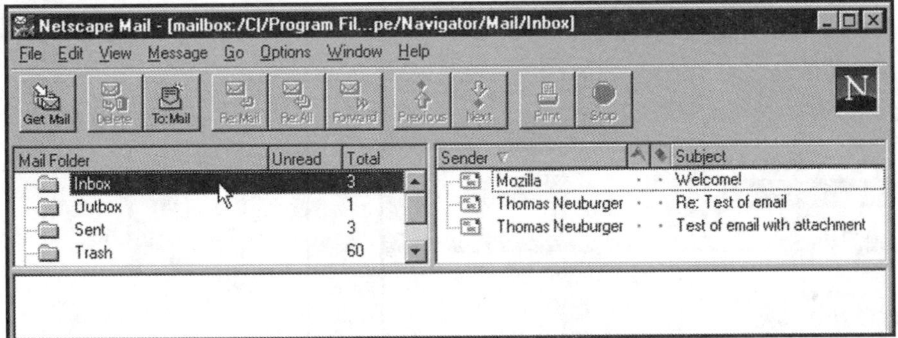

- All Netscape message folders are at the same level of hierarchy. There are no folders within folders.
- The Inbox, Outbox, Sent, and Trash folders are created as necessary by Netscape Mail. You can create and delete folders as you wish.
- To create a new folder, select File, New Folder, fill in the folder name, and click OK.
- To add an existing mail file (for example, a Eudora mailbox file) to the folder list, select Add Folder, browse to the name of the mail file, and click Open.

  The file is added to the folder list, and Netscape will attempt to interpret its contents as mail messages.

WARNING

Be careful when deleting folders in Netscape Mail. At this point, the file is in the folder list until you delete it from disk. There is no other way for Netscape to remove the new folder. To both delete the file from the folder list and preserve it, use Windows Explorer to copy the file to a new name, delete the folder from Netscape Mail, then restore the file to its original name in Windows Explorer.

- To delete a mail folder, select Edit, Delete Folder. You can also click on the folder with the *right* mouse button and select Delete Folder. (Only empty folders can be deleted.)
- You can move and copy messages to a different folder.
- To move messages to a different folder, select the messages in the Message List pane, drag them to the Message Folder pane, and drop them over the folder name.

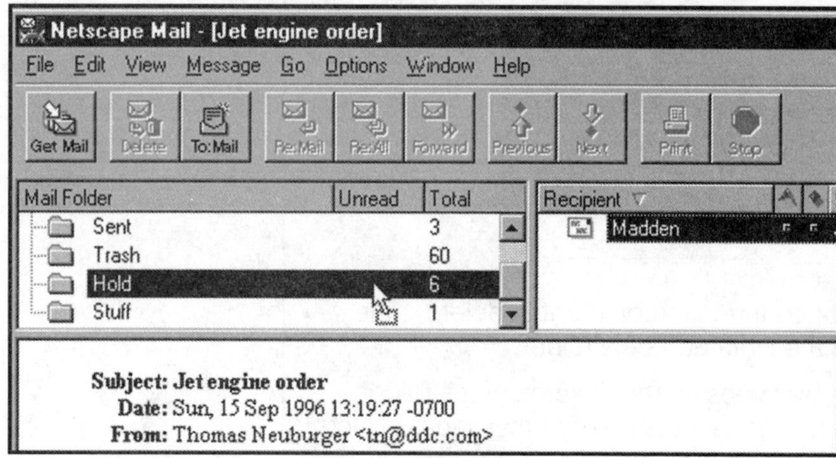

- To copy messages to a different folder, select the messages in the Message List pane, drag them to the Message Folder pane, *hold down the Ctrl key,* and drop them over the folder name.

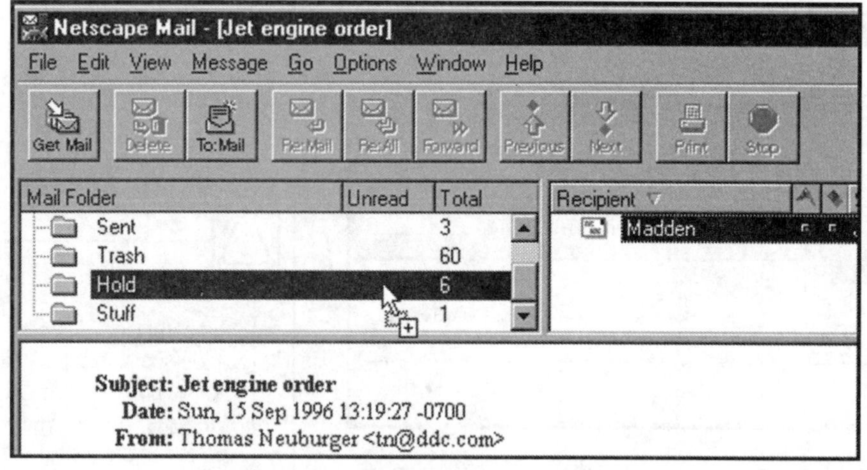

✓ *Be sure the mouse cursor is over the name of the folder when you drop the message. Otherwise, the message will not be moved or copied.*

File Messages in Mail Folders in Internet Mail

- E-mail messages are files in message folders. A message folder is really a file, not a folder or subdirectory, and contains e-mail messages. (For some other programs, like Eudora Light, message folders are directories.)

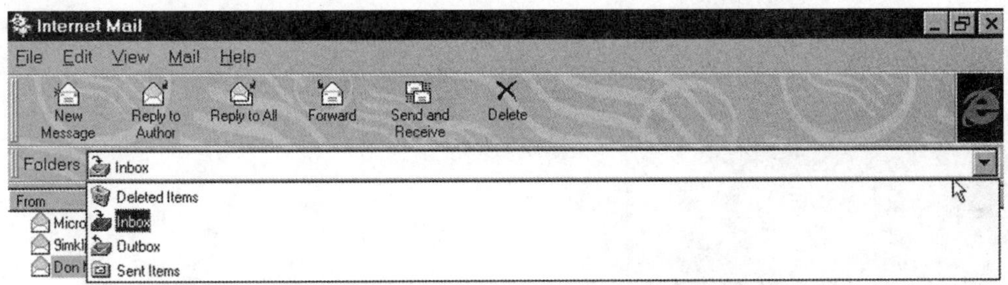

- All Internet Mail message folders are at the same level of hierarchy. There are no folders within folders.
- The Deleted Items, Inbox, Outbox, Sent Items are constant folders that store messages per your instruction.
- To create a new folder, select File, Folder, Create and fill in the folder name. Click OK.
- You can only delete a folder that you have created. To delete a folder that you have created select File, Folder, Delete. Click Yes.
- You can move and copy messages from one folder to another by highlighting a message from the message list, choosing Mail, and Move To and selecting the destination folder.

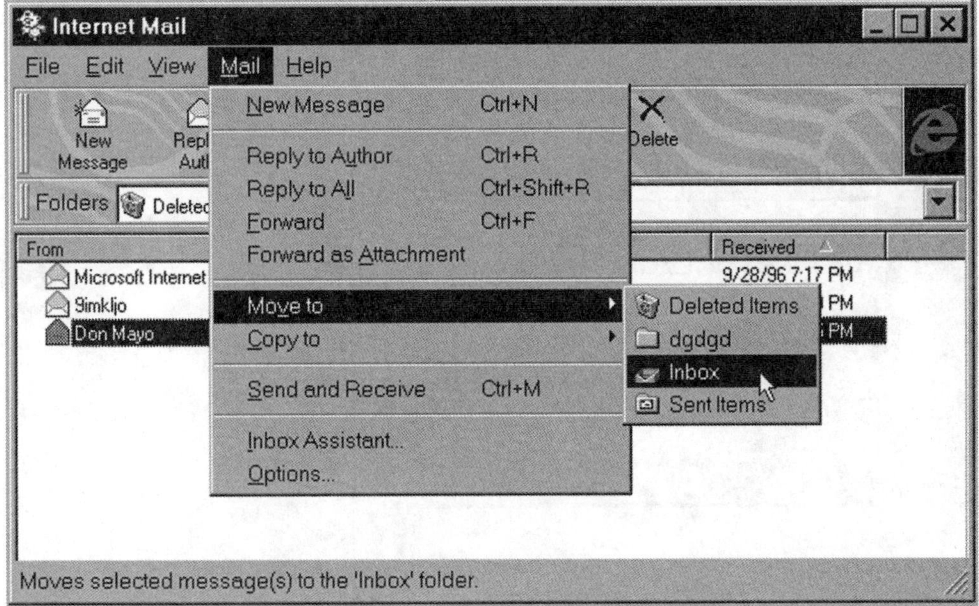

Sort Messages in Netscape Navigator

- Your e-mail messages can be sorted in a number of ways, including by date, subject, sender, and message number.
- Messages can also be **threaded**. This means that they are grouped so that replies to a message are listed with the original message. When threaded messages are sorted, the threads are kept together.
- Threading messages is useful if you have a great deal of mail, especially from mailing lists.

To sort mail messages, select View, Sort, and select sort option. Options on the Sort menu are self-explanatory.

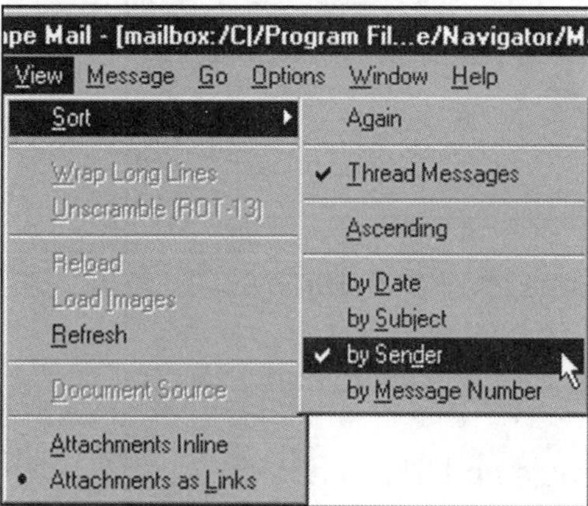

Sort Messages in Internet Mail

- Your mail messages can be sorted in a number of ways: From, Subject, Received, and Ascending order.
- To sort mail messages, select View, Sort by and choose the desired option.

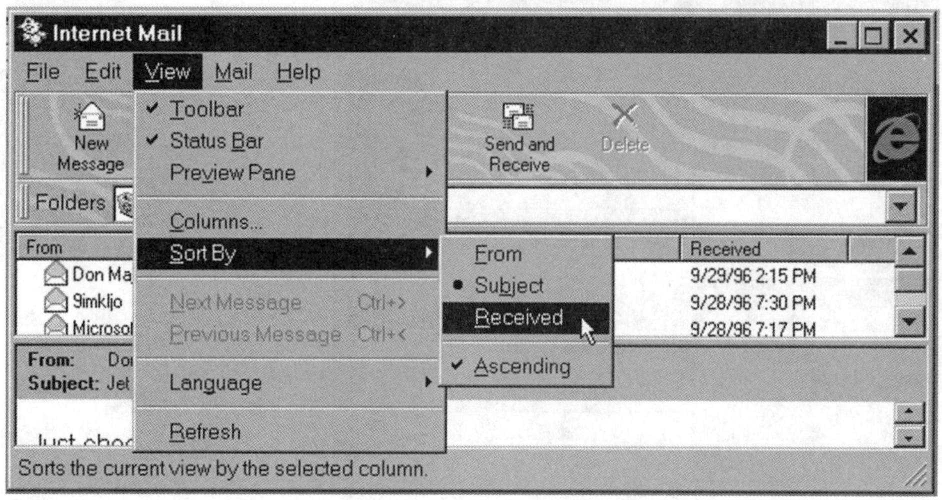

Save Messages as Files in Netscape Navigator

- E-mail messages can be saved as ASCII files. To do this, select File, Save As and use the Save As dialog box to select a filename and location.
- If the message is *not* in HTML form, you may have to change the extension of the file name to .txt before saving it.

Save Messages as Files in Internet Mail

- E-mail messages can be saved as files. To do this, click File, Save As and use the Save As dialog box to select a filename and location.

Use Address Books in Netscape Navigator

- Netscape Mail uses **address books** to store frequently used e-mail addresses.
- Address books can be used to insert addresses into header fields.

- To work with Netscape's address book, select Window, Address Book. The address book window appears.

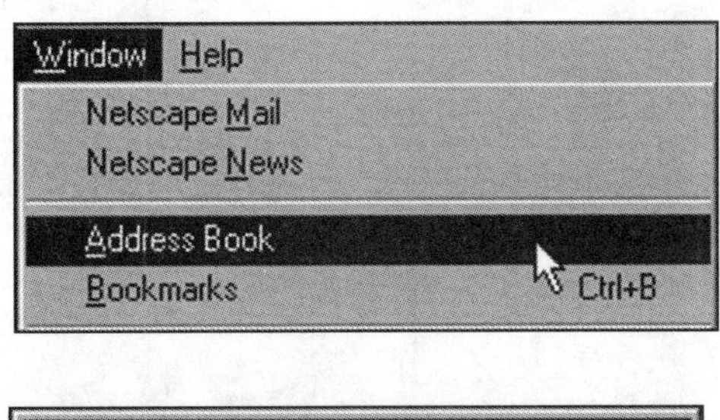

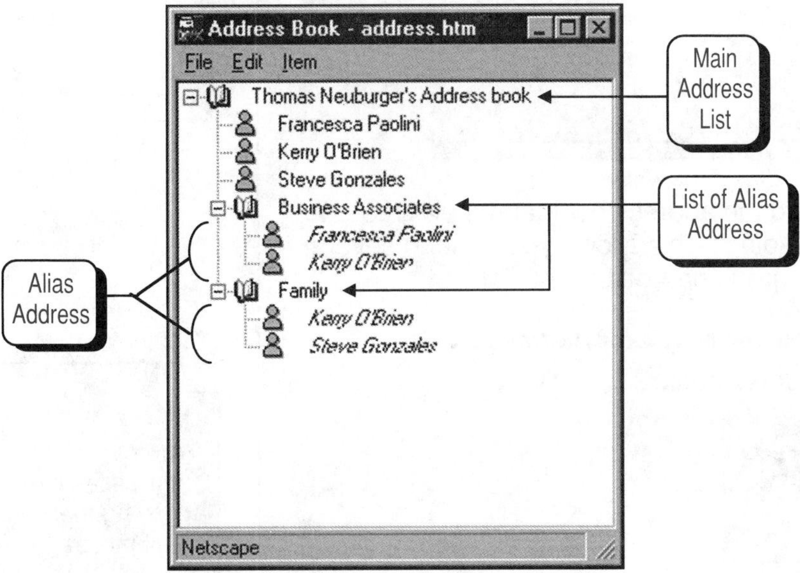

- Note that the address book is hierarchical, with three kinds of items – users, lists, and aliases.
  - A *user* is a single e-mail address, such as sjones@somehost.com. All user addresses are listed in the first part of the address book.
  - A *list* is a "book" of *aliases* that access different users addresses. An alias is a shortcut. It represents a connection to the actual address. If any changes are made to a user address, the alias will also be changed. Lists of alias addresses appear after the main list of user addresses.
  - You can add and delete names, create address lists, and import address books from other mail programs.

Use Address Books in Internet Mail

- In Internet Mail, you can use the **address book** to store frequently used e-mail addresses.
- From the address book you can insert addresses into the header fields.
- To access the address book, click on the Address Book icon on the New Message window Toolbar, or Click File, Address Book.

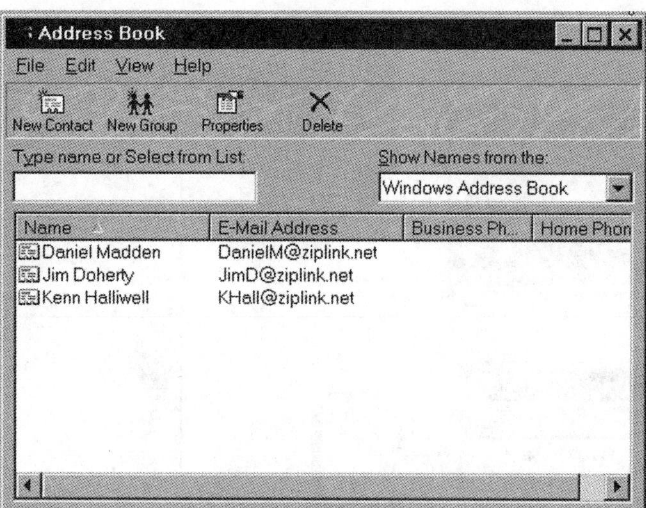

- You can add individual entries into the address book and then create a group listing under one group heading. This allows you to send several recipients mail by clicking on the group name from the list.

Create and Modify Entries in the Netscape Navigator Address Book

- To add a user address to the address book:
  - Click Item, Add User 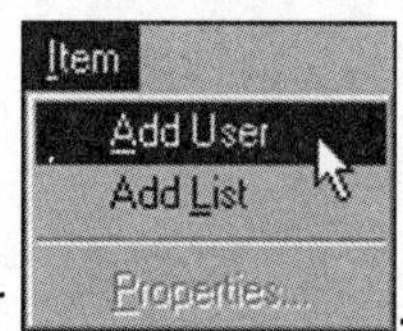.

  - The Address Book Properties dialog box appears.

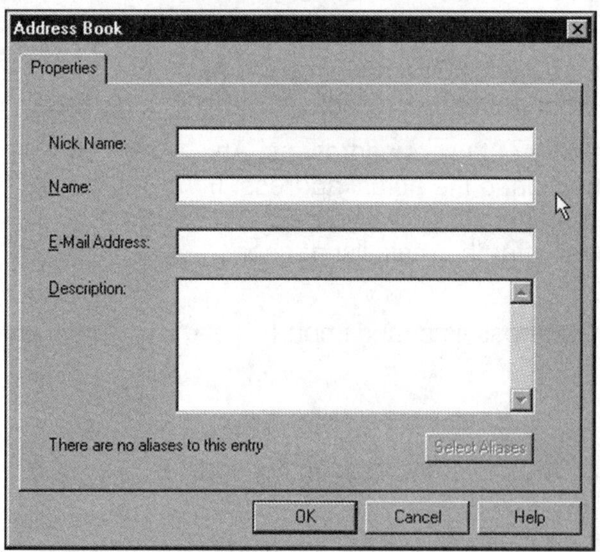

  - Fill in the Name and E-mail Address fields. (The other fields are optional.) The Name field will appear in the Address Book. The E-mail Address will be used when messages are sent.
  - Click OK.

  Note that this user address is added to the top level of the address book, and that the name in the label is *not* italicized.

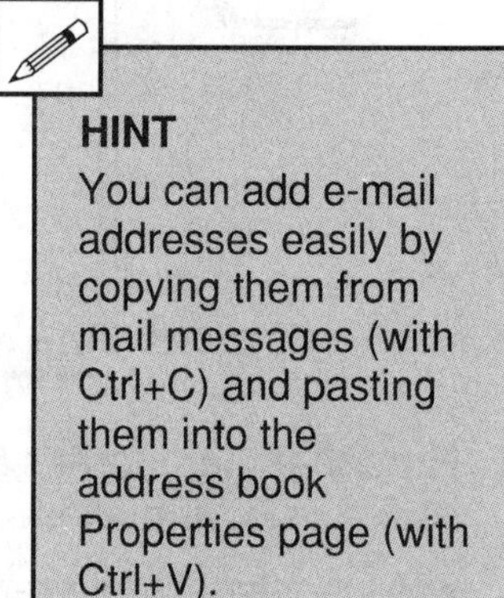

HINT
You can add e-mail addresses easily by copying them from mail messages (with Ctrl+C) and pasting them into the address book Properties page (with Ctrl+V).

- To delete a user address, highlight the address and press the Del key or select Edit, Delete.
- To create an address list:
  - Select Item, Add List 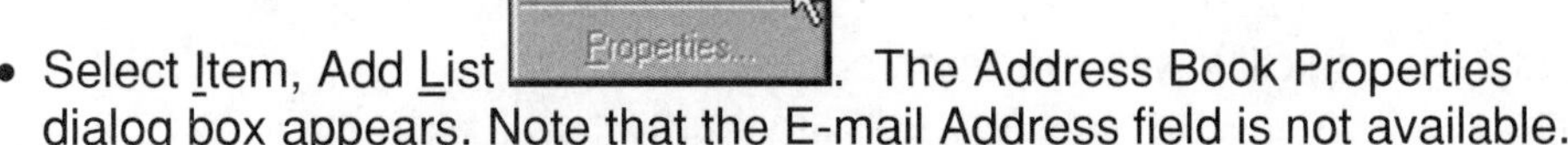

. The Address Book Properties dialog box appears. Note that the E-mail Address field is not available.

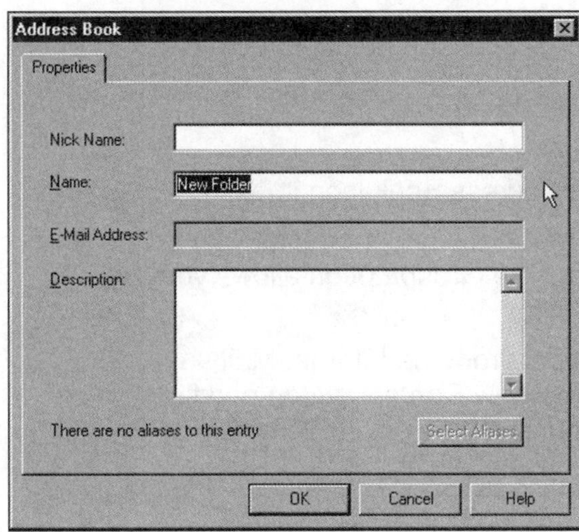

  - Fill in the Name field. (The other fields are optional.) The Name field will appear in the Address Book as the name of the address list.
  - Click OK.
- To add alias user addresses to an address list:
  - Select a user name from the main part of the Address Book.
  - Drag the user name to the address list.

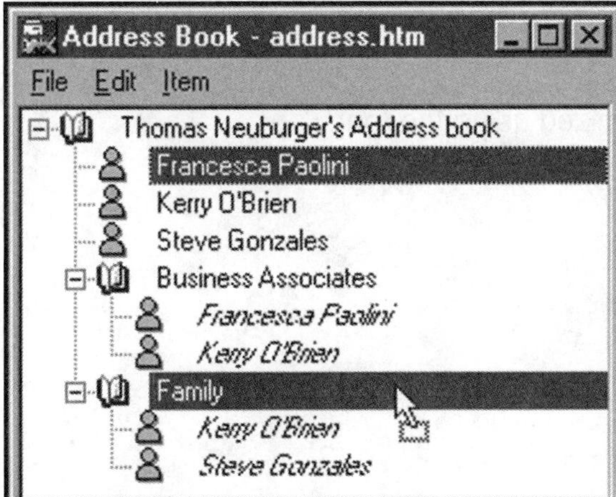

An alias to the user address is added to the address list, and the name in the label is italicized. (Italicized names are aliases, or pointers to names in the main part of the list.)

- To add alias address lists to an address list:
  - Select an address list from any part of the address book.
  - Drag this list to another address list.

    An alias to the address list is added to the address list (it looks like a user alias), and the name of the added address list is italicized, indicating that it is an alias.
- To modify any entry in the address list, click with the *right* mouse button on the entry and select Properties from the menu. Then edit any item you wish and click OK.
- To open and close address lists, click on the + or – sign next to the name.

Create and Modify Entries in the Internet Mail Address Book

- To access the address book, click on the Address Book icon .
- You can add separate entries to the address book and then later combine addresses into separate groups. The Group option allows you to send mail to several recipients at one time.
- To add a single address to the Address book from the Internet Mail screen, select File, Address Book, click the New Contact button and fill in the necessary information in the Properties dialog box. Click OK.

  OR
- To add a single address to the Address book from the New Message screen, click the Address book icon, click the New Contact button, and fill in the necessary information in the Properties dialog box. Click OK.

  OR
- From the New Message screen click File, Address Book, click the New Contact button, and fill in the necessary information in the Properties dialog box. Click OK.
- When communicating via an e-mail program, the most important contact information is obviously the e-mail address. Internet Mail gives you several other address options so that you can customize each entry as you wish.
- Address Book information can be customized using the four Tab options in the Properties dialog box:

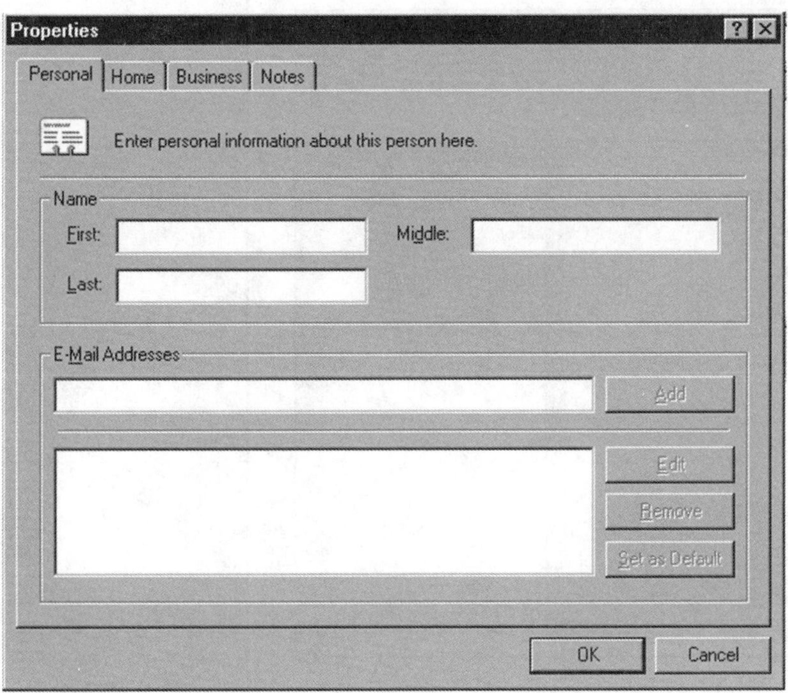

Personal	Name and E-mail address information.
Home	Home address, phone, fax, cellular phone, and Personal Web page information
Business	Company address, Business Web page, and Job title information.
Notes	Anything you want to remember about this person.

Insert Addresses from the Address Book into E-mail Messages in Netscape Navigator

- You can insert addresses from the address book into an e-mail message as follows:
  - Open the Mail Composition window in any way you wish.
  - Click the button next to any address item, like the Mail To: field. The Select Address dialog box appears.

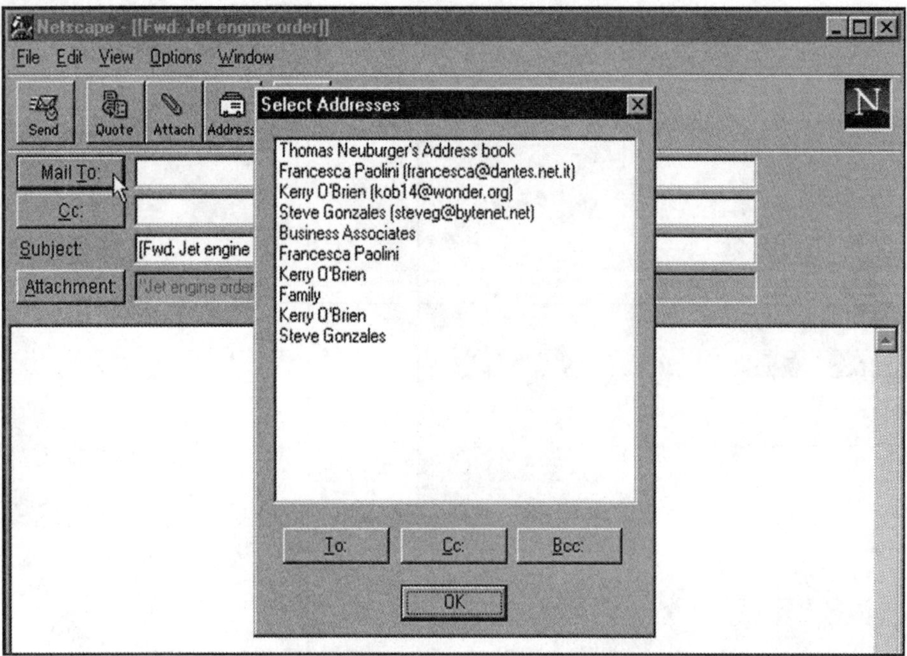

- In the Select Address dialog box, double-click each address that you would like to appear in that field.
- When you are done, click OK.

■ You can also create new mail messages as follows:

- Open the Address book with Window, Address Book.
- Select an address with the right mouse button and click New Message.

  The Mail Composition window appears, with the selected address in the Mail To field.

Insert Addresses from the Address Book into E-Mail Messages in Internet Mail

■ You can insert addresses from the address book into an e-mail message as follows:

- Open the New Message window or any message window where inserting an e-mail address is required.
- Click the card icon on the To: or Cc: recipient address line to access the Address book.

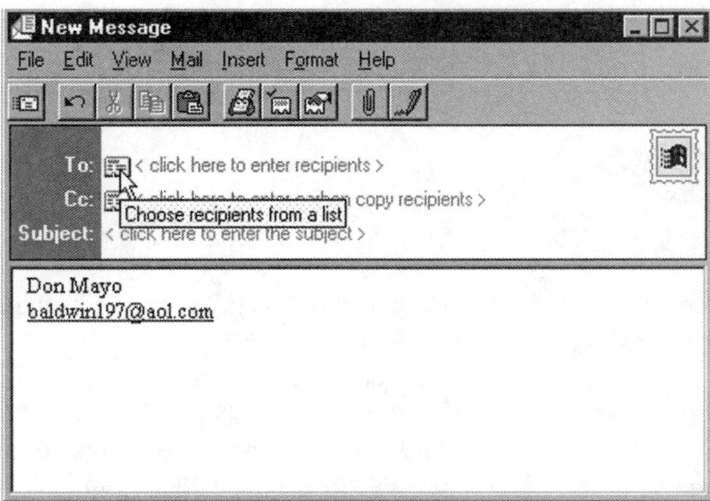

- You can now choose the name of the recipient from the list of names in your address book.
  - After highlighting the name from the list, click the appropriate recipient line box: To or Cc.
  - If you simply click, for example, the To button, the highlighted name will appear in the Message Recipients box. Click OK.

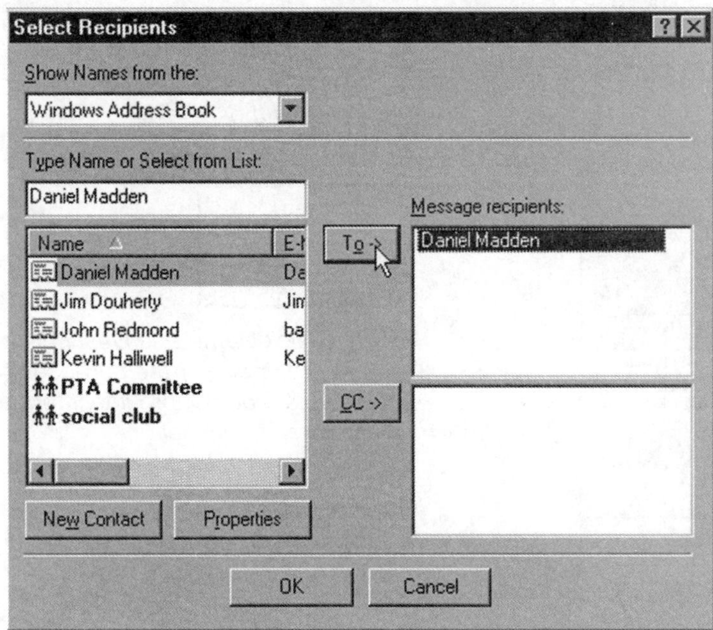

- Notice that the name is now on the To recipient line, underlined to verify that the full address (which you will not see) is in correct e-mail format.

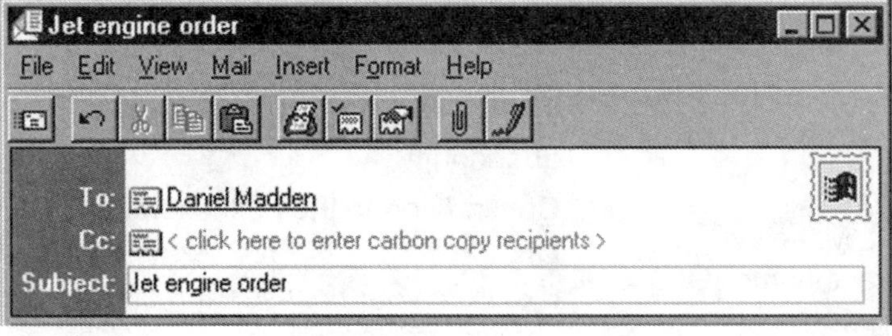

In this exercise, you will create and use mail folders and an address book.

EXERCISE DIRECTIONS

FOR NETSCAPE NAVIGATOR

1. If you are already connected to your service provider and your browser is open, go to step 2.

   OR

   Connect to your service provider and open your browser.

   ✓ *This exercise uses Netscape Navigator. For Internet Explorer and Internet Mail, see next page.*

2. Click Window, Netscape Mail.
3. Select File, New Fol 'er.
4. Enter the name St ˙ for the new folder name, and click OK.
5. Select the Sent folder in the Mail Folders pane, and then select one of the messages you have mailed in previous exercises.
6. Hold down the Ctrl key, drag the message to the Stuff folder, and drop it. Make sure the mouse pointer is over the folder's *name* when you drop the message.

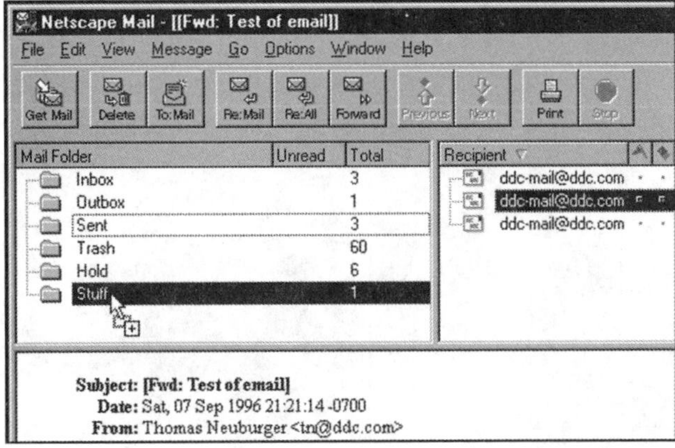

Note the + sign next to the message icon you are dragging, indicating that you are copying the message, not moving it

7. Click on the Stuff folder and verify the presence of the new message.
8. Select the Sent folder again.
9. Select a different message.
10. *Without holding down the Ctrl key*, drag the message to the Stuff folder, and drop it. Make sure the mouse pointer is over the folder's *name* when you drop the message.
11. Click on the Stuff folder and verify the presence of the new message.
12. Click on the Sent folder and verify the absence of the moved message.
13. Click Window, Address Book and, using the procedures listed on pages 206-208, complete the following tasks:
    - Add the following three usernames and e-mail addresses to the address book:

Names	E-Mail Addresses
Bill Brady	Bill@ddcpub.com
Michael Frew	Michael@ddcpub.com
Diana Wray	Diana@ddcpub.com

    ✓ *The Nick Name and Description fields are optional. For the purpose of this exercise, do not provide information in either of these fields.*

    - Create the following two Address lists:

Names
Friends
Associates

    ✓ *The Nick Name and Description fields are optional. For the purpose of this exercise, do not provide information in either of these fields.*

    - Add Bill Brady (as an alias) to the Friends address list.
    - Add the two other usernames (as aliases) to the Associates address list.
14. Now return to the Netscape Mail window and click To:Mail.
15. In the Message Composition window, click the Mail To button and use the Select Addresses dialog box to insert two addresses into the new mail message.
16. Complete the message in the Mail Composition window if you wish, or select File, Close to abandon it.
17. Continue on to the next exercise.

    OR

    Exit from your browser and disconnect from your service provider.

FOR INTERNET MAIL

1. If you are already connected to your service provider and your browser is open, continue to step 2.

   OR

   Connect to your service provider and open your browser.

   ✓ *This exercise uses Internet Explorer.*
2. Click the Mail icon to start Internet Mail.
3. Click File, Folder, and Create.
4. Enter the name Stuff for the new folder name, and click OK.
5. Select the Sent folder in the Folders pull-down list and then select one of the messages you mailed in a previous exercise.
6. Right-click on the message, click Move to, and click on the Stuff folder to move the message.

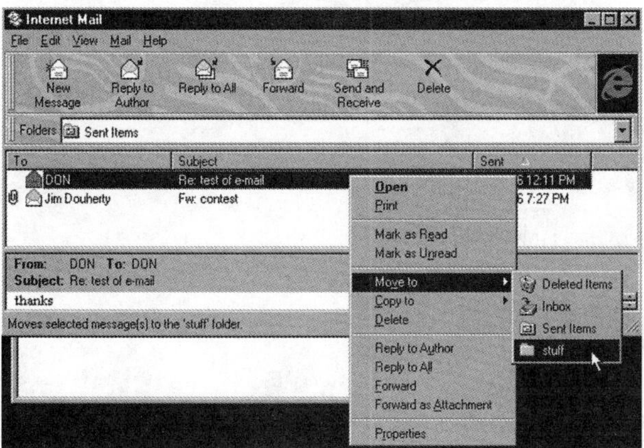

7. Click on the Stuff folder and verify the presence of the new message.
8. Click on the Sent folder and verify that the moved message is no longer in the Sent folder.
9. Click File, Address Book and, using the procedures mentioned on pages 208-210, complete the following tasks:
   - Add at least three e-mail addresses to your address book.
   - Go to your Inbox folder and add the e-mail addresses of the senders of each message to your address book. (up to three).

   HINT: In order to add an e-mail address from an e-mail message to your address book, you must first open the message and then right-click on the name or names in the address lines.

   - From the Address Book, create a group entry with at least three of the addresses in your address book.
10. Return to the main Internet Mail screen.
11. Go to the New Message composition window.
12. Click the To: choose recipients icon.
13. From the Address book, add at least two names on the To: recipient address line.
14. From the Address book, add at least one name to the Cc: Line
15. Complete the message in the Mail Composition window if you wish, or select File, and Close.
16. Experiment as much as you want with mail folders and the address book. Send or abandon messages as you choose.
17. Continue on to the next exercise.

    OR

    Exit from your browser and disconnect from your service provider.

Exercise 6

◆ **Configure Eudora® Light** ◆ **Get, Read, and Print Messages**
◆ **Compose Messages and Add Attachments**
◆ **Send Messages** ◆ **Organize Messages**

NOTES

✓ *Eudora® is a registered trademark of the University of Illinois Board of Trustees, licensed to QUALCOMM Incorporated.*

Configure Eudora Light

- In Lesson 4, Exercise 3, you downloaded a copy of Eudora Light, one of the best freeware stand-alone e-mail programs available. There is also a commercial, full-featured version of Eudora called Eudora Pro (Windows) or Eudora Mail Pro (Macintosh)
- To open the Settings dialog box, start Eudora Light. The main Eudora window appears.

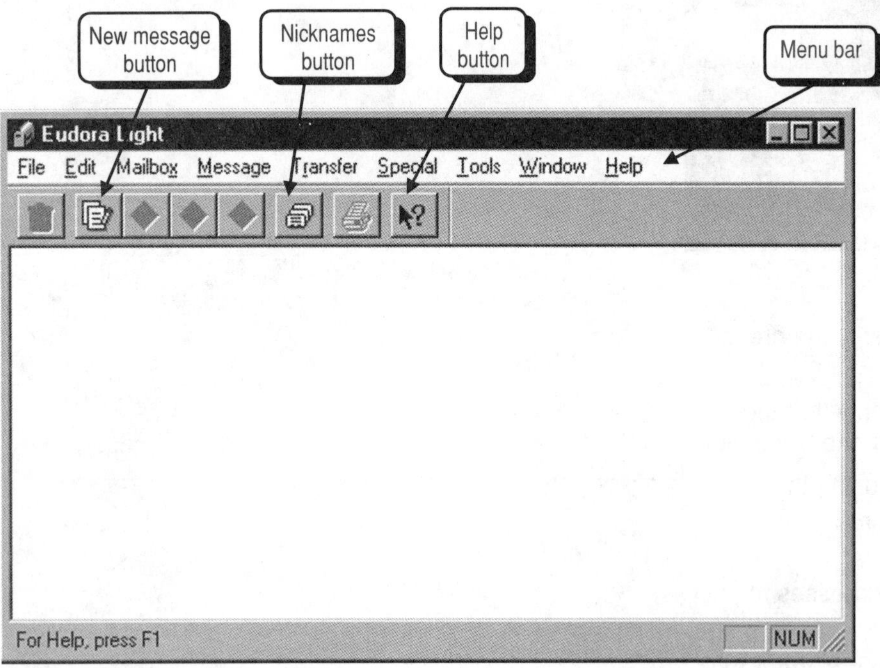

- At the top of the main Eudora window is a menu bar with the following items—File, Edit, Mailbox, Message, Transfer, Special, Tools, Window, and Help.

Eudora Light Toolbar

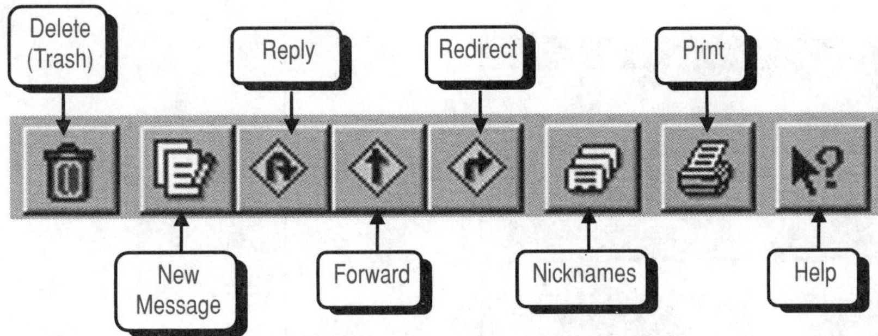

- It contains the following buttons, from left to right.

 Delete or Trash button (inactive if there are no messages in the window)

 New Message button

 Reply button (inactive if no message is selected)

 Forward button (inactive if no message is selected)

 Redirect button (inactive if no message is selected)

 Nicknames button

 Print button (inactive if no message is selected)

 Help button

- Depending on what is selected in the main Eudora window, some buttons may be inactive.
- Before using Eudora to send and receive messages, you must configure it to operate with your mail server.
- Eudora provides several categories of settings you can use to configure the program.
- To open the Settings Dialog window, start Eudora Light, then in the program window, select Tools, Options in the main Eudora window. The Setting dialog box appears.

- On the left side of the Settings dialog box is a scroll list containing the Settings categories.

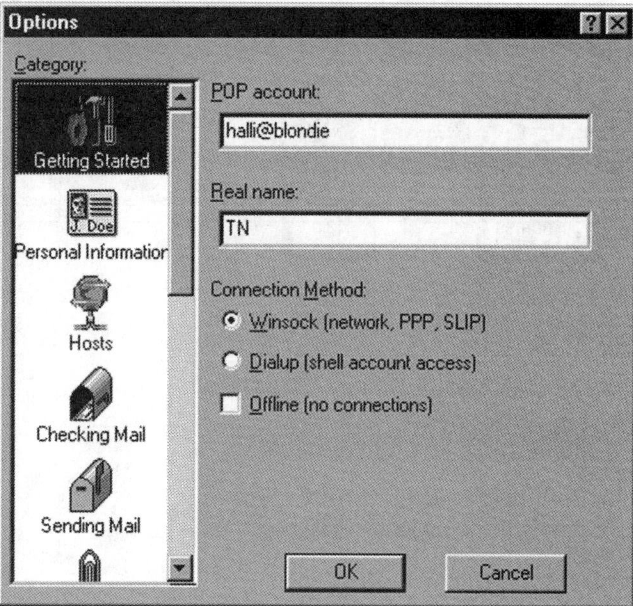

- Configure Eudora as follows:

  ✓ *Contact your Internet service provider for the following information if you don't already have it. (Most service providers provide this information with their welcome letter.)*

  - Click on the **Getting Started** icon at the top of the scroll list. The Getting Started Settings window shows the minimum information Eudora needs to send and receive e-mail.
  - POP Account — The address, in the form *username@hostname*, of your e-mail account on the POP mail server.
  - Real Name — Your "real" name. This is added to the From field of messages you send.
  - Connection Method — The way you connect to the mail server's network. The choices are *Winsock* for direct connection, SLIP, or PPP; or *Dialup* for shell account access. If you have a SLIP or PPP account with your service provider, select Winsock.
  - Offline Connection — Check the Offline check box if you don't want to connect automatically when you first start Eudora.
  - Click on the **Personal Information** icon. It's next in the scroll list. These settings specify who you are.

POP Account	Your e-mail account. If you supplied the POP account information in the Getting Started Setting window, this field will be filled in automatically.
Real Name	Your "real" name. Again, if you already supplied this information, this field will be filled in automatically.
Return Address	Your "reply to" address. For most users, this is the same as your e-mail address (username@domain.suffix).

Dialup Username Your username if you're using Dialup.

- Click on the **Hosts** icon. It's third in the scroll list. These settings contain information about your mail servers.

POP Account Your e-mail account. If you supplied the POP account information in the Getting Started Setting window, this field will be filled in automatically.

SMTP The host name of your SMTP server. If it's the same as your POP server, leave this line blank. Otherwise, your service provider can give you this information.

- For now, leave all other options as is. You can return at any time to change these settings.

Receive, Read, and Print Messages

- To receive mail from your server, select File, Check Mail in the main Eudora window.
- If your mail server requires a password to access your POP account, a password dialog window will appear. Enter your password and click OK.
- To read your incoming messages, select the In folder from the Mailbox menu. Then double-click on the message you want to read. A message window will appear displaying the message.

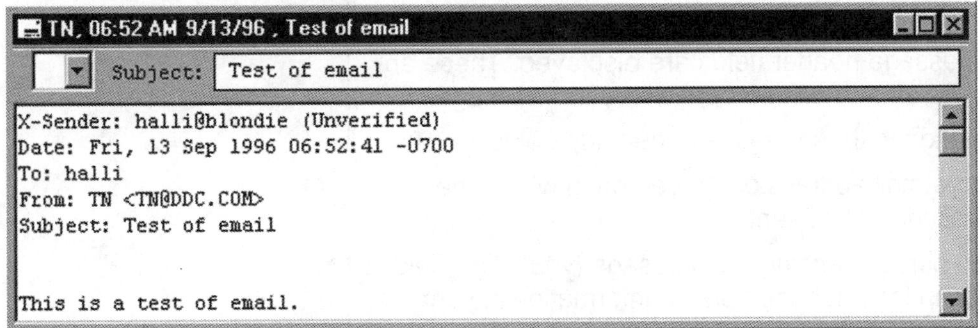

- When a message window is open and selected, all buttons on the Eudora Toolbar are active—including the Delete (Trash) button, the New Message button, the Reply button, and the Help button.

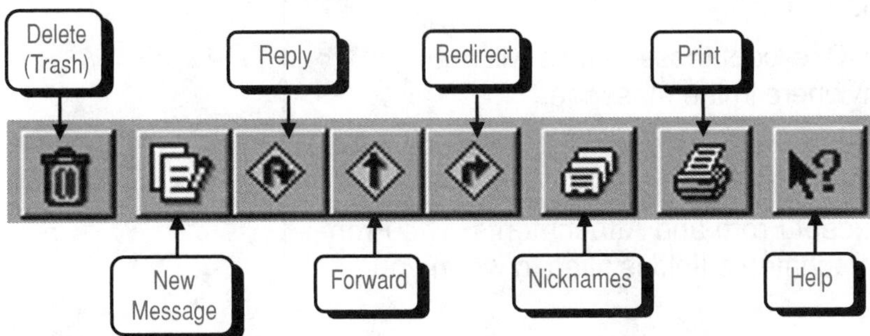

- To print a message, click on the message in the mailbox folder to select it, and select File, Print in the main Eudora window.

Compose Messages and Add Attachments

- To compose a new message, select Message, New Message in the main Eudora window. A message composition window appears.

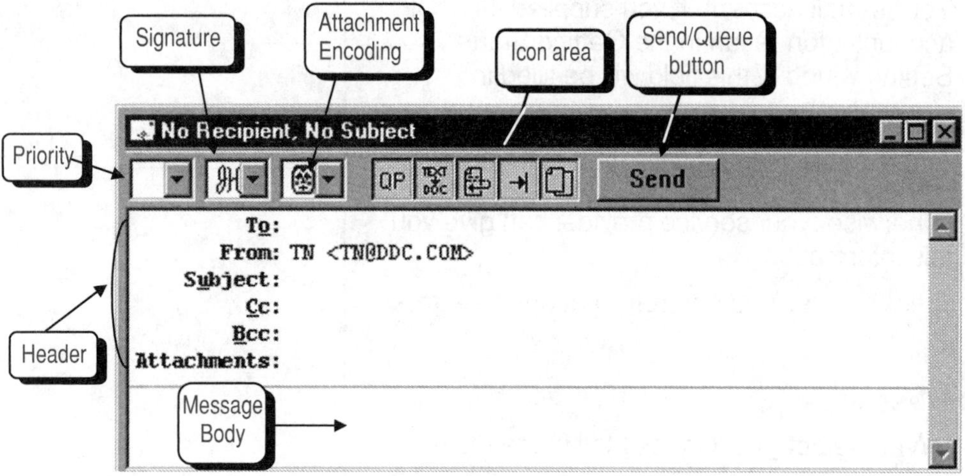

- When a message composition window is open and selected, the following buttons are active on the Eudora Toolbar page – the Delete (trash) button, the New Message button, the Forward button, the Nicknames button, the Print button, and the Help button.

Fill In the Headings

- At the top of the screen, message header fields are displayed. These are used by mail servers to route and otherwise deal with your message.
- Fill in all necessary information in these message heading fields:

To	The e-mail address of the person to whom the message will be sent.
From	The person sending the message (you). This field is filled in for you based on the information in your Settings.
Subject	A short text description provided by you of the contents of the message.
Cc (Carbon Copy)	The e-mail addresses of people who will receive copies of the message.
Bcc (Blind Carbon Copy)	Same as CC, except these names will not appear anywhere in the message.
Attachments	A list of files (text or binary) or URL locations to be sent with the message.

- You can type text into all fields except From and Attachments. The From field is filled in for you, and the Attachments field is filled in when you attach a file to the message.

Compose the Message Body

- Compose the message by typing into the message body area of the composition window.
- Eudora has minimal editing capabilities. Word-wrap occurs automatically, and you can cut and paste quotes from other messages, or text from other programs. Spell-checking and other editing options are not available.

Add a Signature

- Many people like to add an e-mail **signature**, a few lines of text with their e-mail address and/or a quotation, to the end of their messages.
- Eudora can be set to add a pre-designed signature automatically. To create a signature, select Tools, Signature in the main Eudora window. The Signature text window appears. Type in the text you want to appear in messages.
- You can add a signature to messages in two ways:
  - Select Use Signature in the Sending Mail Settings.
  - Use the Signature On/Off pull-down menu in the message composition window icon area. (Note: the JH icon stands for the signature of John Hancock, a famous signer of the Declaration of Independence.)

Add Attachments

- To attach a file to a message:
  - Select the encoding method for attachments by either of these methods:
    - Using the Attachments encoding popup in the message composition icon bar, or
    - Selecting Tools, Options in the main Eudora window and then choosing Attachments from the scroll list.
  - Select Message, Attach File in the main Eudora window. A dialog box allows you to choose which file to attach.

  - Locate the document (file) you want to send, select it, and click the OK button.
  - The name and location of the file appears in the Attachments field in the message header.

Send Messages

- Messages can be sent immediately or stored in your Out mailbox for later delivery.
- To send the message immediately:
  - Select Tools, Options in the main Eudora window. In the Options window scroll bar, select the Sending Mail Settings. Then select Immediate Send. (The checkbox is *checked*.)
  - Click the Send button **Send** in the message composition window.
- To store the message in your Out mailbox office for later delivery:
  - Select Tools, Options in the main Eudora window. In the Options window scroll bar, select the Sending Mail Settings. Then deselect Immediate Send. (The checkbox is *unchecked*.)
  - Click the Queue button **Queue** in the message composition window.
- To send all messages in your Out mailbox:
  - Click File, Send Queued Messages in the main Eudora window.

Organize Messages

Delete Messages

- Two steps are required to delete a message. First, place the message in the Trash mailbox. Then empty the Trash.

  ✓ *Deleting the message will not delete attachments. To delete attachments, use the same method you use to delete other files from your computer.*
- To place a message in the Trash mailbox, select the message and either:
  - Press the Delete key.

    OR
  - Click the Delete (Trash) button on the Toolbar.

    OR
  - Click Edit, Clear in the main Eudora window.
- To empty the Trash, either:
  - Click Special, Empty Trash in the main Eudora window.

    OR
  - Click Tools, Options in the main Eudora window. Select Miscellaneous Settings in the Options window scroll bar. Then select Empty Trash On Exiting.

Transfer Messages to Mailboxes

- For Eudora, a **mailbox** is a file that holds e-mail messages. A **mail folder** is a directory that contains mailboxes. You can create both mail folders and mailboxes to keep your messages organized. (Some other mail programs use these concepts differently.)
  - For example, let's say you are corresponding with the sales offices of the company you work for. You can create a mail folder named Sales Offices to hold all messages to and from the sales offices. In this mail

folder, you can create a mailbox for each office, for example, Los Angeles, Chicago, and New York.

Now when you receive a message from the New York sales office, you can transfer it to the mailbox named New York in the mail folder named Sales Offices.

Later, when you need to find a message from the New York sales office, you can go directly to the New York mailbox inside of the Sales Offices folder. This way you don't have to rummage through large numbers of unrelated messages looking for it.

- To transfer messages to another mailbox:
  - Select a message in an open mailbox (for example, the In mailbox).
  - To transfer the message into a mailbox at the top level of the hierarchy, select Transfer, *mailboxname*.
  - To transfer the message into a mailbox within a folder (directory), select Transfer, *foldername, mailboxname*.
- To create a new mailbox:
  - Select a message in an open mailbox (for example, the In mailbox).
  - Select Transfer, New from the Eudora main menu. The New Mailbox dialog window appears.

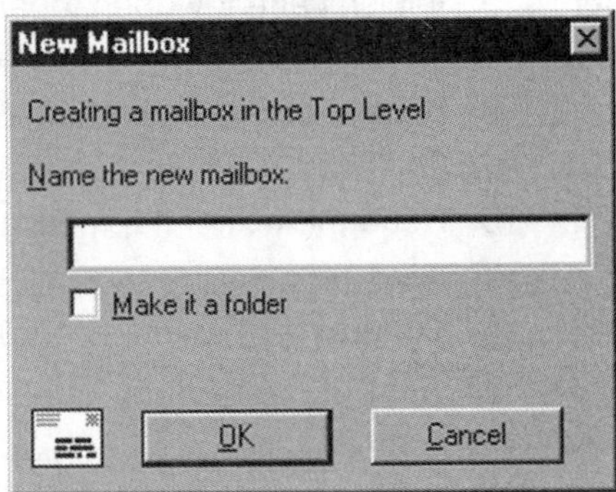

  - Type a name in the text box.
  - If you don't wish to transfer the message, select Don't Transfer, Just Create A Mailbox.
  - Click OK.
- To create a new mail folder (directory):
  - Select a message in an open mailbox (for example, the In mailbox).
  - Select Transfer, New from the Eudora main menu. The New Mailbox dialog window appears.
  - Type a name in the text box.
  - Select Make It A Folder.
  - Click OK.

  Note that the message is not transferred; a mail folder has simply been created.

- To create a new mailbox within a mail folder:
  - Select a message in an open mailbox (for example, the In mailbox).
  - Select Transfer, *foldername,* New. The New Mailbox dialog window appears.
  - Type a name in the text box.
  - If you don't wish to transfer the message, select Don't Transfer, Just Create A Mailbox.
  - Click OK.

In this exercise, you will compose, send, read, and print an e-mail message.

CAUTION: ***The exercise directions below presume that you have already set up an e-mail account with a service provider. If you are not set up with Internet Mail, contact your service provider. In this exercise you will change mail options that are not related to connecting or setting up a mail account.***

EXERCISE DIRECTIONS

1. If you are already connected to your service provider, go to step 2.

   OR

   Connect to your service provider.
2. Start Eudora Light.
3. In the main Eudora window, select Message, New Message. The message composition window appears.
4. In the message composition window, fill in the header and body text as follow:

To:	***tabellarius@ddcpub.com***
Subject:	"Test of e-mail"
CC:	Add your own e-mail address.
Body:	"This is an e-mail test."

5. Select Tools, Options in the main Eudora window. In the Categories window, select the Sending Mail Icon and then select Immediate Send. Click OK.
6. Click the Send button.
7. Check for incoming mail by selecting File, Check Mail in the main Eudora window. You should receive a message indicating that you have new mail. Click OK. A copy of the message you sent, a response to the message you sent, or both should be waiting for you.
8. If it isn't already open, open the In mailbox by selecting Mailbox, In.
9. Double-click on the summary for the copy of the message you just sent. A message window appears.
10. Read the text of the message in the message window.
11. Print the message by selecting File, Print from the Eudora main menu.
12. Exit Eudora Light by selecting File, Exit.
13. Disconnect from your Internet service provider.

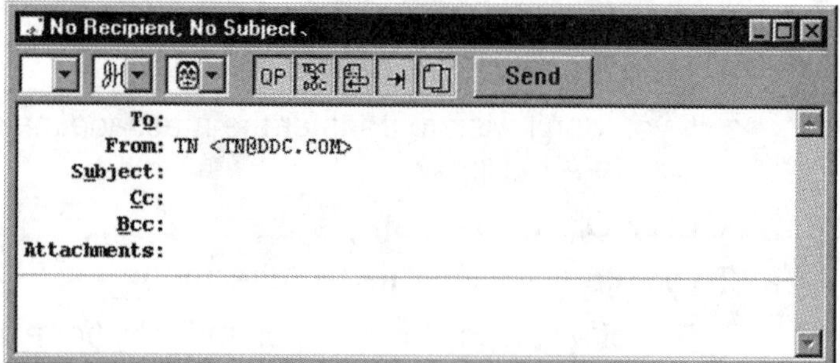

What is Netiquette?

Searching the Net – commonly known as Surfing – is fun and exciting. The Net is a great resource for everything from understanding the do's and don'ts of buying a new car, to paying bills, to researching school term papers. Over the Net you can purchase concert tickets, order steaks for the weekend cookout, and make new friends. The ability to communicate with people and visit places all over the world from the comfort of your home, classroom, or office is amazing.

It is important, however, to use this great communication tool responsibly. Respectful communication with others and a cooperative attitude when taking advantage of the many resources available on the Internet are indispensable. This is why the essential practice of Netiquette (net etiquette) has developed over time.

Netiquette is a set of behaviors that should be adhered to when you travel down the information super-highway. Generally speaking, there are very few actual "Net Laws" (excluding Federal laws for prosecuting Internet hackers, virus terrorists, etc.), and those that exist are generally devised by the Internet community itself. Therefore, the job of policing the Net is up to those who use it.

We have surfed the Web and asked our experts for general Internet behaviors and compiled the list below.

FTP Etiquette

FTP, or File Transfer Protocol, allows you to transfer data files and software programs from FTP sites to your computer over the Internet. If you are using a browser program to access an FTP site, you will use anonymous FTP. This means that you won't need a login name or password to gain access to the FTP site server. (see Lesson 4, Exercise 1, for more information). We are allowed access to these vast storehouses of information through the generosity of the individual FTP host institutions (universities, organizations, etc.), therefore; it is important that we play by their rules.

Some FTP Netiquette Hints and Tips:

- Respect any posted hours at an anonymous FTP host. As a general rule, most sites ask that **you not access their databases between the hours of 8 am and 5 pm**, as these are the hours when they are busiest. Remember to verify time zones: for example, when it is 5 pm on the east coast it is only 2 pm on the west coast.
- If you log on to an anonymous FTP site (without using a browser application) as an anonymous user, it is recommended that you use your full Internet e-mail address as your password.
- Use available site help files before asking for help. Many sites provide README and INDEX files that provide answers to commonly asked questions.
- Many FTP hosts post rules particular to their site. Be aware of these postings and follow the rules strictly.
- Only download files you know you will need. Don't tie up the network downloading information you don't need.

E-Mail Etiquette

The written word is a powerful tool in terms of communication, so caution should be taken in how it is used on the Internet. Remember: an e-mail message will almost always be taken at face value. The reader is not afforded the luxury of nuance. Since your message will not be accompanied by facial expression or vocal inflection, it is imperative that you write with clarity and courtesy. Keep sarcasm to a minimum or delete it altogether.

This does not mean that mail to friends cannot be funny or mildly satiric, but be aware that your message can be misinterpreted. Know your audience and, above all, minimize the risks.

Some E-Mail Netiquette Hints and Tips:

- Using all capital letters gives a word very strong emphasis. It can also have the effect of SHOUTING! In general, it is better to use upper- and lowercase letters as you would when writing a letter.
- Enclosing a word with *asterisks* has a different effect. Asterisks indicate a mild emphasis and serve the same purpose as italics (which normally canot be sent over the Internet).
- Signature "smileys" can help to indicate mood or tone of voice:

  :-) I'm happy. (Made with a colon, dash, and right parenthesis. Tilt head to the left for full effect.)

  ;-) Just joking. (Made with semi-colon, dash, and right parenthesis.)

  :-(I'm unhappy. (Made with colon, dash, and left parenthesis.)
- Be careful when replying to a message. If your reply is to be automatically sent back to the originating address, verify that the address is not connected to a list or group. A personal response intended for a specific person may end up in the hands of many.
- Common Net acronyms include:

  FAQ Frequently asked questions

  FYI For Your Information

  BTW By The Way

  IMHO In My Humble/Honest Opinion

  RTM Read The Manual

  LOL Laughed Out Loud (at what you wrote)

  YMMV Your Mileage May Vary
- Electronic mail is not protected and not private. Your message can be forwarded or copied to anyone, anywhere. Think of it as an electronic postcard – fully exposed and able to be read by anyone who comes in contact with it. Computer and network hackers can easily access anything sent across the Internet. Assume anyone with a computer has the potential to read your message. Be careful what you write.
- Never send chain letters over the Internet. Not only are they annoying but they are forbidden by many Internet service providers and if you participate in sending them, your privileges may be revoked.
- Angry or heated messages are called "flames." Everyone seems to agree that "flames" are childish and never necessary. Take the time to calm down before sending emotional responses.
- Use the subject or RE: line to clearly state the topic of your message. This is the first thing the recipients will see in their e-mail directory.
- Keep messages concise. When replying to a message, be sure to include enough information from the original message so that your reply is understood. Delete anything from the original message that is irrelevant.
- Messages should have lines that are no more than 65-70 characters in length and generally no more than 12 lines. Do not assume that the person has the same size screen or that the wrap feature will automatically make the message "fit."
- If you send a long message, it is a good idea to tell the recipient at the beginning of the message so that they have the option of downloading it to read later.
- There are many other rules and procedures that you will learn as you become an experienced Net user. School labs and office environments will have their own procedures which are strictly enforced. Check with your teacher or Network administrator for more information.

Appendix B: Viruses

Introduction

Viruses are malicious software written to deliberately attempt some form of destruction to someone's computer. They are instructions or code that have been written to reproduce as they attach themselves to other programs without the user's knowledge. Viruses can be programmed to do anything a computer can do. Viruses are a nuisance, but if you know how they work and take the necessary precautions to deal with them, they are manageable. It is essential that we all understand the natures of these programs, how they work, how they can be disinfected, etc. No one is exempt from viruses; strict precautions and anti-virus programs are the answer.

Viruses are potentially destructive to one file or to an entire hard disk, whether the file or hard disk is one used in a standalone computer or in a multi-user network. Like biological viruses, computer viruses need a host, or a program, to infect. Once infection has been transferred, the viruses can spread like wildfire through the entire library of files. Like human sickness, viruses come in many different forms; some are more debilitating than others.

Origins of Viruses

How do you get a virus? They can come from a couple of places:

- An infected diskette
- Downloading an infected file from a bulletin board, the Internet, or an online service.

Knowing where viruses are likely to be introduced will make you sensitive to the possibility of getting one.

Categories of Viruses

Viruses come in two categories:

- Boot Sector Viruses
- File Viruses

Boot Sector Viruses may also be called System Sector viruses because they attack the system sector. System or boot sectors contain programs that are executed when the PC is booted. System or boot sectors do not have files. The hardware reads information in the area in the sections on bootup of the computer. Because these sectors are vital for PC operation, they are prime areas for a target by viruses.

Two types of system sectors exist: DOS sectors and partition sectors. PCs characteristically have a DOS sector and one or more sectors created by the partitioning command, FDISK, or proprietary partitioning software. Partition sectors are commonly called Master Boot Records (MBR). Viruses that attach to these areas are seriously damaging ones.

File Viruses are more commonly found. Characteristically, a file virus infects by overwriting part or all of a file.

Timing of Viruses

Viruses come in many sizes and with various symptoms. For example, a virus may attach itself to a program immediately and begin to infect an entire hard disk. On the other hand, the virus can be written to attack at a specific time. For example, the Michaelangelo virus strikes on his birthday each May.

Some viruses are written so that they delay letting you know of their existence until they have done major damage.

Virus Symptoms

How can you tell if you have a virus? Hopefully, you will install anti-virus software in your PC that will identify viruses and make you aware immediately upon entry to your system. Otherwise, you may experience different symptoms such as:

- Slow processing
- Animation or sound appears out of nowhere
- Unusually heavy disk activity
- Odd changes in files
- Unusual printer activity

Precautions

Most viruses spread when you have booted the computer from an infected diskette. A healthy precaution here would be only to boot from the hard drive.

- Backup all files. At least two complete backups are recommended.
- Even new software can come with a virus; scan every diskette before use.
- Mark all software program attributes as read only.
- Research and update anti-virus products on an ongoing basis to have the latest protection.
- Since there are many types of viruses, one type of anti-virus protection won't disinfect all viruses. A multiple anti-virus program library is the recommended approach.

Appendix C: Internet History

How it all Began

The grandfather of the global Internet was actually called ARPANET, short for Advanced Research Projects Agency Network. It was a network developed by scientists and military experts which allowed them to share information and research data. The unique feature of ARPANET was its ability to route information around sections of the network that might be knocked out by a natural disaster or nuclear attack.

A more recent relative to today's Internet was a project funded by the National Science Foundation in the 1980s. NSF had built six supercomputers for scientific research, but then needed a means whereby researchers in remote areas of the country could have access to them. The NSFNET accomplished this by creating a communications backbone- (a system of high-speed phone lines)- to which everyone with the right kind of equipment could connect. The ARPANET, which used the same communications technology, was eventually absorbed into the NSFNET.

Before long, every major university and government agency was connected to the NSFNET backbone, making their collective networks part of the growing whole. Regional networks from other countries adopted the same communications standards and connected to the backbone, as did commercial online services and networks from the private sector.

Today's Internet has outgrown its cold war roots and become an international cooperative of networks, all willing to work together to share information and resources, collaborate, and communicate. In that respect it's the most promising technological and cultural advance the world has seen in a long time.

Today's Internet Network

The Internet is not a single network but a collection of connected networks that all use the same communications protocol. It is composed of hosts (servers) and millions of clients worldwide.

Information on the Internet moves like this:

- A client requests a resource—the current weather report, for example—from a remote host. The request is sent as a packet of numbers which include the remote host's location and the name of the requested file.
- The request goes first to the local host (maintained by an Internet service). The local host reads the location of the remote host and routes the request in that direction. This takes only a few microseconds.
- The request is sent through a number of large routers and across high-speed telephone lines until it reaches the remote host.
- The remote host processes the request and routes the information back to the local server to the client. The information is sent in a series of data packets that get assembled—in order—by the client's Internet software.

Part of the wonder—and some of the frustration—of the Internet is that the information packets may be sent along completely different paths. Eventually it all gets put back together again when it reaches its destination.

A good familiar comparison is the street and highway system. Commuters may leave home, and drive on slow neighborhood streets, then move onto faster through streets, thoroughfares, and freeways on their way to a specific destination. On the way back home they may take a completely different route (especially if there is an accident or traffic tie-up) but still end up back home again.

How it All Works

The Domain Name System

Because the Internet is not a single network, a **domain** name system is used to identify the exact location of Internet hosts and the primary Internet activity of that host. It's not unlike the telephone numbering system that includes country codes, area codes, and individual phone numbers.

An Internet address (IP address) is made up of a four-part series of numbers. The domain name system translates the numbers into a user-friendly system of text-based names. So instead of typing in 128.337.392.449 to order a pizza over the Internet, you can type in "www.pizzahut.com." It's easier for people to remember.

Domain

A domain is a distinct category or partition of Internet use.

Reading from left to right, a domain name describes the following:

- the client name (user name)
- the local server name (the name of the local network the client belongs to)
- the Internet sub-domain (initials of a university, for example)
- the Internet domain

Internet domains include the following:

Domain:	Used By:
.com	commercial/business
.gov	government
.edu	educational
.org	various organizations
.mil	military
.net	network resources

TCP/IP

The communications protocol used for Internet connections is **TCP/IP** (short for Transmission Control Protocol/Internet Protocol). It is actually a suite of protocols that work together to make the Internet work.

TCP/IP does several things:

- enables remote login
- routes data between Internet hosts
- makes sure data packets are error-free and assembled in the right sequence
- converts text-based domain names into numerical IP addresses

SLIP/PPP

Part of the TCP/IP protocol includes SLIP or PPP, which enables your computer modem to connect to a local server via the phone lines.

SLIP

SLIP (short for Serial Line Internet Protocol) is used to transmit data over serial lines (the communications port on most PCs) and dial-up telephone lines. SLIP lets your PC act like an Internet machine; however, SLIP is somewhat unreliable since it has no error-checking capability.

PPP

PPP (short for Point to Point Protocol) is the improved successor to SLIP. Basically, it connects your computer to the Internet the same way a SLIP connection does, but it is slightly faster and more reliable. To use PPP, both the host and your computer must have PPP installed. Otherwise you must use SLIP.

If you are using Microsoft Windows 95, the Windows dial-up adapter is PPP compatible.

Glossary

address book A place where frequently used e-mail addresses are stored.

anonymous FTP A special kind of FTP service that allows any user to log on. Anonymous FTP sites have a predefined user named "anonymous" that accepts any password.

Archie A database system of FTP resources. It helps you find files that exist anywhere on the Internet.

ARPAnet (Advanced Research Projects Administration Network) Ancestor to the Internet: ARPAnet began in 1969 as a project developed by the US Department of Defense. Its initial purpose was to enable researchers and military personnel to communicate in the event of an emergency.

ASCII file (American Standard Code for Information Interchange) File containing ASCII-formatted text only; can be read by almost any computer or program in the world.

attachment File(s) or web pages(s) enclosed with an e-mail message.

Base64 (MIME) encoding One of the encoding schemes, used in the MIME (Multipurpose Internet Mail Extensions) protocol.

binary file A file containing machine language (that is, ones and zeros) to indicate that the file is more than plain text. A binary file must be encoded (converted to ASCII format) before it can be passed through the e-mail system.

BinHex An encoding scheme for the Macintosh platform that allows a file to be read as text when passed through the e-mail system.

bookmark A browser feature that memorizes and stores the path to a certain web site. Creating bookmarks enables a quick return to favorite sites.

browser A graphic interface program that helps manage the process of locating information on the World Wide Web. Browser programs such as Netscape Navigator and Microsoft Internet Explorer provide simple searching techniques and create paths that can return you to sites you visited previously.

chat (Internet Relay Chat) A live "talk" session with other Internet or network users in which a conversation is exchanged back and forth.

client program A computer program designed to talk to a specific server program. The FTP client program is designed to ask for and use the FTP service offered by an FTP server program. Client programs usually run in your own computer, and talk to server programs in the computers it connects to.

client A computer that is signing onto another computer. The computer that is logging on acts as the client; the other computer acts as the server.

complex search Uses two or more words in a text string (and may also use operators that modify the search string) to search for matches in a search engine's catalog.

compressed file A file that has been made smaller (without lost data) by using a file compression program such as pkzip or StuffIt. Compressed files are easier to send across the Internet, as they take less time to upload and download.

copyright The legal right of ownership of published material. E-mail messages are covered by copyright laws. In most cases, the copyright owner is the writer of the message.

crawlers Another name for search engines.

directories Also referred to as folders. Directories are lists of files and other directories. They are used for organizing and storing computer files.

domain The portion of an Internet address that follows the @ symbol and identifies the computer you are logging onto.

downloading Copying files (e-mail, software, documents, etc.) from a remote computer to your own computer.

e-mail (electronic mail) A communication system for exchanging messages and attached files. E-mail can be sent to anyone in the world as long as both parties have access to the Internet and an Internet address to identify themselves.

encoding A method of converting a binary file to ASCII format for e-mail purposes. Common encoding schemes include Uuencoding and MIME (Base64) encoding.

fair use The right to use short quotes and excerpts from copyrighted material such as e-mail messages.

FAQ (Frequently Asked Questions document) A text document that contains a collection of frequently asked questions about a particular subject. FAQs on many subjects are commonly available on the Web.

file "File" is a general term usually used to describe a computer document. It may also be used to refer to more than one file, however, such as groups of documents, software, games, etc.

folders/ directories Folders, also referred to as directories, are organized storage areas for maintaining computer files. Like filing cabinets, they help you manage your documents and files.

font A typeface that contains particular style and size specifications.

freeware Software that can be used for free forever. No license is required and the software may be copied and distributed legally.

FTP (File Transfer Protocol) The method of remotely transferring files from one computer to another over a network (or across the Internet). It requires that both the client and server computers use special communication software to talk to one another.

FTP site An Internet site that uses File Transfer Protocol and enables files to be downloaded and/or uploaded. When you access an FTP site through a browser application, however, your log-in is considered “anonymous” and will not allow uploading.

FTP (File Transfer Protocol) A computer program used to move files from one computer to another. The FTP program usually comes in two parts: a server program that runs in the computers offering the FTP service, and a client program running in computers, like yours, that wish to use the service.

Gopher A menu system that allows you to search various sources available on the Internet. It is a browsing system that works much like a directory or folder. Each entry may contain files and/or more directories to dig through.

heading fields (headings) Individual fields, like To and From, in the header of an e-mail message.

hierarchically structured catalog A catalog of web sites that is organized into a few major categories that have sub-categories under them. Each sub-category has additional sub-categories under it. The level of detail in this structure depends on the particular web site.

home page A web site’s starting point. A home page is like a table of contents. It outlines what a particular site has to offer, and usually contains connecting links to other related areas of the Internet as well.

host A central computer that other computers log onto for the purpose of sharing and exchanging information.

hot lists Lists of web sites that you have visited or “ear-marked” and wish to return to later. Your browser program will store the paths to those sites and generate a short-cut list for future reference.

HTML (HyperText Mark Up Language) The programming language used to create web pages so that they can be viewed, read, and accessed from any computer running on any type of operating system.

HTTP (HyperText Transfer Protocol) The communication protocol that allows for web pages to connect to one another, regardless of what type of operating system is used to display or access the files.

hypertext or hypermedia The system of developing clickable text and objects (pictures, sound, video, etc.) to create links to related documents or different sites on the Internet.

inbox Where incoming e-mail messages are stored and retrieved.

Information Superhighway Nickname for the Internet: a vast highway by which countless pieces of information are made available and exchanged back and forth among its many users.

Internet A world-wide computer network that connects several thousand businesses, schools, research foundations, individuals, and other networks. Anyone with access can log on, communicate via e-mail, and search for various types of information.

Internet address The user ID utilized by an individual or host computer on the Internet. An Internet address is usually associated with the ID used to send and receive e-mail. It consists of the user's ID followed by the domain.

Internet Protocol The method of communication which allows information to be exchanged across the Internet and across varying platforms that may be accessing or sending information.

ISP (Internet Service Providers) Private or public organizations that offer access to the Internet. Most charge a monthly or annual fee and generally offer such features as e-mail accounts, a pre-determined number of hours for Internet access time (or unlimited access for a higher rate), special interest groups, etc.

links Hypertext or hypermedia objects that, once selected, will connect you to related documents or other areas of interest.

login A process by which you gain access to a computer by giving it your username and password. If the computer doesn't recognize your login, access will be denied.

macro virus A virus written in the macro language of a particular program (such as Word) and contained in a program document. When the document is opened, the macro is executed, and the virus usually adds itself to other, similar documents. Macro virus can be only as destructive as the macro language allows.

message header The group of heading fields at the start of every e-mail program, used by the e-mail system to route and otherwise deal with your mail.

meta-tree structured catalog Another term for hierarchically structured catalog.

modem A piece of equipment (either internal or external) that allows a computer to connect to a phone line for the purpose of dialing into the Internet, another network, or an individual computer.

modem speed (baud rate) Indicates at what speed your computer will be able to communicate with a computer on the other end. The higher the rate, the quicker the response time for accessing files and web pages, processing images, downloading software, etc.

multimedia The process of using various computer formats: pictures, text, sound, movies, etc.

multithread search engines Software that searches the web sites of other search engines and gathers the results of these searches for your use.

netiquette (Network etiquette) The network equivalent of respectfulness and civility in dealing with people and organizations.

network A group of computers (two or more) that are connected to one another through various means, usually cable or dial-in connections.

newsgroup A bulletin board of news information. Users specify which news topic they are interested in, and subscribe to receive information on that topic.

newsreader A program that allows you to read and respond to Usenet newsgroups.

offline The process of performing certain tasks, such as preparing e-mail messages, prior to logging onto the Internet.

online The process of performing certain tasks, such as searching the Web or responding to e-mail, while actually logged onto the Internet.

online services Organizations that usually offer Internet access as well as other services, such as shareware, technical support, group discussions, and more. Most online services charge a monthly or annual fee.

operators Words or symbols that modify the search string instead of being part of it.

outbox Where offline e-mail messages are stored. The contents of an outbox are uploaded to the Internet once you log on and prompt your e-mail program to send them.

packet A body of information that is passed through the Internet. It contains the sender's and receiver's addresses and the item that is being sent. Internet Protocol is used to route and process the packet.

platform Refers to the type of computer and its corresponding operating system, such as PC, Macintosh, UNIX. The Internet is a multi-platform entity, meaning that all types of computers can access it.

POP (Post Office Protocol) The method used to transfer e-mail messages from your mail server to your system.

public domain freeware Software that can be used for free; usually the author is anonymous.

quote format A way of displaying text quoted from other e-mail messages, most frequently used in replies. Quoted text usually has a character like ">" at the start of each line. Some e-mail programs let you set the style of quoted material.

search engine A software program that goes out on the Web, seeks web sites, and catalogs them – usually by downloading their home pages.

search sites Web sites that contain catalogs of web resources that can be searched by headings, URLs, and key words.

self-extracting archive Macintosh-platform compressed file that does not require external software for decompression. These files usually end with an .sea extension.

self-extracting file PC-platform compressed file that does not require external software for decompression. These files usually end with an .exe extension.

server program A computer program that offers a service to other computer programs called client programs. The FTP server program offers the FTP service to FTP client programs. Server programs usually run in computers you will be connecting to.

server A computer that is accessed by other computers on a network. It usually shares files with or provides other services to the client computers that log onto it.

shareware Computer programs, utilities and other items (fonts, games, etc.) that can be downloaded or distributed free of charge, but with the understanding that if you wish to continue using it, you will send the suggested fee to the developer.

signature A few lines of text automatically appended to the body of an e-mail message. Signatures usually include the sender's address plus other information.

simple search Uses a text string, usually a single word, to search for matches in a search engine's catalog.

.sit file A Macintosh file compressed by using a compression application called StuffIt.

SLIP (Serial Line Internet Protocol) Software that allows for a direct serial connection to the Internet. SLIP allows your computer to become part of the Internet – not just a terminal accessing the Internet. If your computer is set up with SLIP, you can Telnet or FTP other computers directly without having to go through an Internet provider.

SMTP (Simple Mail Transfer Protocol) The method used to transfer e-mail messages between servers and from your system to your mail server.

spiders Another name for search engines.

standalone FTP client program A standalone computer program designed to talk to an FTP server program running at a remote computer site that offers FTP services. The FTP client program can ask for the files you want and send files you wish to deliver. The client program runs in your computer; the server program runs at the site.

start page The opening page within a browser application. This is the page from which all other web site links are built. A browser's start page is its home page by default, but you can customize your browser to begin with any web site as your start page.

subject-structured catalog A catalog organized under a few broad subject headings. The number and names of these headings depend on the web site.

surfing the Internet Exploring various World Wide Web sites and links to search for information on the Internet. Using FTP, WAIS, and Gopher servers can further assist in the surfing/searching process – as can a good Internet browser.

TCP/IP (Transmission Control Protocol/ Internet Protocol) The communication system that is used between networks on the Internet. It checks to make sure that information is being correctly sent and received from one computer to another.

Telnet A program that allows one computer to log on to another host computer. This process allows you to use any of the features available on the host computer, including sharing data and software, participating in interactive discussions, etc.

text format file Same as the ASCII format file: a document that has been formatted to be read by almost any computer or program in the world.

text string A string of ASCII characters. The text string may or may not contain operators.

threaded messages Messages grouped so that replies to a message are grouped with the original message. When threaded messages are sorted, threads are kept together.

uploading The process of copying computer files (e-mail, software, documents, etc.) from one's own computer to a remote computer.

URL (Uniform Resource Locator) A locator command used only within the World Wide Web system to create or hunt for linked sites. It operates and looks much like an Internet Address.

Usenet A world-wide discussion system, operating on linked Usenet servers, consisting of a set of newsgroups where articles or messages are posted covering a variety of subjects and interests. You can use your browser or a newsreader program to access the newsgroups available from your Internet provider's Usenet server.

UUencoding One of the encoding schemes, short for UNIX-to-UNIX encoding. UUencoding is common on all platforms, not just UNIX.

virus A small, usually destructive computer program that hides inside innocent-looking programs. Once the virus is executed, it attaches itself to other programs. When triggered, often by the occurrence of a date or time on the computer's internal clock/calendar, it executes a nuisance or damaging function, such as printing a message or reformatting your hard disk.

WAIS (Wide Area Information Servers) A system that allows for searches for information based on actual contents of files, not just file titles.

Web robots Software which automatically searches the Web for new sites.

Web Site A location on the Internet that represents a particular company, organization, topic, etc. It normally contains links to more information within a site, as well as suggested links to related sites on the Internet.

World Wide Web (WWW) An easy-to-use system for finding information on the Internet through the use of hypertext or hypermedia linking. Hypertext and hypermedia consist of text and graphic objects that, when you click on them, automatically link you to different areas of a site or to related Internet sites.

zip file PC file compressed with pkzip. Zipped files usually need to be unzipped with pkunzip before they can be used.

Index

F

H

I

T

U

V

W

Y

Network Compatible Site License for DDC Internet Simulation CD-ROM

With the DDC Site License, all networked computers in your classroom or office can access the simulated Web sites and hyperlinks used in the exercises in *Learning the Internet*. Install the CD once and access the Internet Simulation on all connected computers—even the computers that don't have CD-ROM drives.

Internet simulated on CD

- No Modem Needed
- No Waiting to Download
- No Internet Connection Needed

Order Form

275 Madison Avenue,
New York, NY 10016

Phone: (800) 528-3897
Fax: (800) 528-3862
URL: http://www.ddcpub.com

Accept my order for:

Qty.
___ Cat. No. NZ-15CD Internet Simulation Site License......$200.

☐ Check enclosed. ☐ Please bill me.

Add $2.50 for postage & handling.
NY State residents add local sales tax.

☐ Visa ☐ Mastercard

____
Card No.

____
Exp. Date

____
Name

____
School/Firm

____
Address

____
City, State, Zip

____
Phone

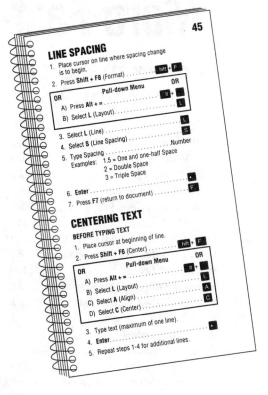

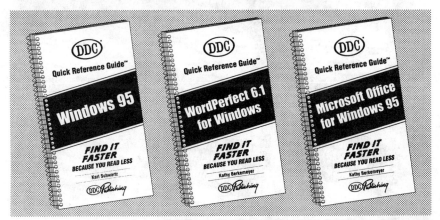

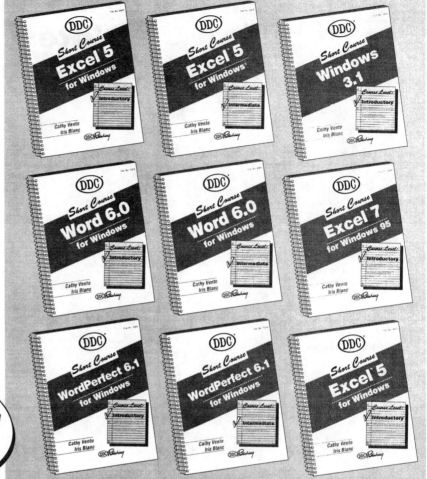

Notes